CROSS-CULTURAL PERSPECTIVES
ON LEARNING

CROSS-CULTURAL PERSPECTIVES ON LEARNING

Edited by

Richard W. Brislin
University of Hawaii

Stephen Bochner
University of New South Wales

Walter J. Lonner
Western Washington State College

SAGE Publications

Halsted Press Division
JOHN WILEY & SONS
New York–London–Sydney–Toronto

Distributed by Halsted Press, a Division of
John Wiley & Sons, Inc., New York

Printed in the United States of America

Library of Congress Cataloging in Publication Data
Main entry under title:

Cross-cultural perspectives on learning.

   Papers from a conference sponsored by and held at the Culture Learning Institute of the East-West Center, Jan. 28-Feb. 3, 1973.
   Bibliography: p.
   Includes index.
   1. Ethnopsychology—Addresses, essays, lectures.
I. Brislin, Richard W., 1945-   ed. II. Bochner, Stephen,
ed. III. Lonner, Walter J.,   ed. IV. East-West Center. Culture Learning.
Institute.
GN270.C74   301.2′01′9   73-91353
ISBN 0-470-10471-6

FIRST PRINTING

CONTENTS

Series Preface   *viii*

Editors' Preface   1

Introduction   3

Part I. Learning Another Culture

Chapter 1: Culture Training, Cognitive Complexity and
             Interpersonal Attitudes
             HARRY C. TRIANDIS   39

Chapter 2: Cognitive Differentiation and Culture Training
             ANDREW R. DAVIDSON   79

Chapter 3: A Behavioral Analysis of Culture Learning
             GEORGE M. GUTHRIE   95

Chapter 4: Adjustment Problems of Foreign Muslim Students in
             Pakistan
             S. M. HAFEEZ ZAIDI   117

Chapter 5: Unofficial Intervention in Destructive Social Conflicts
             LEONARD W. DOOB   131

Part II. Empirical Studies of Perception and Cognition

Chapter 6: An Ethnographic Psychology of Cognition
             MICHAEL COLE   157

Chapter 7: Universals and Cultural Specifics in Human Categorization
             ELEANOR ROSCH   177

Chapter 8: Ecology, Cultural Adaptation, and Psychological
             Differentiation: Traditional Patterning and
             Acculturative Stress
             JOHN W. BERRY   207

Part III. Contributions from Hologeistic Studies

Chapter 9: Initiation Ceremonies and Secret Societies as Educational
   Institutions
   WALTER E. PRECOURT   231

Chapter 10: Parental Acceptance-Rejection and Personality Development:
   A Universalist Approach to Behavioral Science
   RONALD P. ROHNER   251

Part IV. Approaches from Different Perspectives

Chapter 11: Resocialization into Culture: The Complexities of Taking
   a Worldwide View of Psychotherapy
   JURIS G. DRAGUNS   273

Chapter 12: Primitive Mentality—Civilized Style
   DOUGLASS PRICE-WILLIAMS   291

Chapter 13: An Analysis of the Prepublication Evaluation of
   Cross-Cultural Manuscripts: Implications for Future Research
   WALTER J. LONNER   305

About the Contributors   321

Author Index   325

Subject Index   333

CROSS-CULTURAL PERSPECTIVES ON LEARNING

SERIES PREFACE

With this volume, this series inaugurates a pioneering effort to present collections of comparative studies in cross-cultural topics and interdisciplinary research. The series is designed to satisfy a growing need to integrate research, method and theory and to dissect issues in comparative analyses across cultures. The recent ascent of the cross-cultural method in social and behavioral science has largely been due to a recognition of methodological power inherent in the comparative perspective; an international approach to the study of behavioral, social and cultural variables can only be done within such a methodological framework.

Each volume in the series will present substantive cross-cultural studies and considerations of the strengths and weaknesses of its various methodologies. The various disciplines which will be embraced are anthropology, political science, psychology and sociology. Either individual researchers have become knowledge-able in more than one discipline or a partnership has developed between and among specialists. This series will cross these interdisciplinary boundaries and will attempt to interrelate methods that have been developed within the various disciplines. While one individual volume may represent integration of only a few disciplines, *the cumulative totality of the series will reflect an effort to bridge gaps of methodology and conceptualizations across all disciplines and many cultures.*

The co-editors of the series, as well as its sixteen-member Editorial Advisory Board, are dedicated to the tasks and scope described above. We are pleased that this inaugural volume, *Cross-Cultural Perspectives on Learning,* includes the work of both anthropologists and psychologists. We are indebted to the chapter authors for their contributions, and we are especially appreciative of the work done by the Culture Learning Institute of the East-West Center in hosting the Symposium, "The Interface Between Culture and Learning," that originally made this volume possible.

— Walter J. Lonner
Western Washington State College
Bellingham, Washington

—John W. Berry
Queen's University
Kingston, Ontario

EDITORS' PREFACE

This book emanated from a conference entitled "The Interface Between Culture and Learning" sponsored by and held at the Culture Learning Institute of the East-West Center from January 28 to February 3, 1973. The Director of the Institute, Dr. Verner Bickley, was continually supportive of the project from its inception to its culmination in this book. Stephen Bochner developed the idea during his tenure as a visiting senior fellow at the Institute in late 1971 and early 1972. Shortly after his own tenure as a visiting fellow, Richard Brislin was given administrative responsibility for the project upon becoming a permanent staff member at the Institute. He immediately asked Bochner, who by then had returned to the University of New South Wales, to start a process of collaboration-at-a-distance. Brislin had the main responsibility for choosing the participants, whose product constitutes the major portion of this book. (The space limitations and focus of this volume preclude publishing all papers delivered by the 25 invited participants, and all are once again thanked for their participation.)

Bochner came to Hawaii in early January, 1973, and helped with the burden of running the conference just as Brislin was ready to be committed to the care of Juris Draguns, the conference's therapist. After the conference's last lei had wilted, Brislin and Bochner invited Walter Lonner, a conference participant, to join in the editing process. This invitation was stimulated largely by his editorial roles in cross-cultural psychology, including his being co-editor of the series inaugurated by this volume.

The editorial work was done while the editors, respectively, were in Honolulu, Hawaii; Sydney, New South Wales; and Bellingham, Washington. Among the amusements that encouraged high output were air, postal, and rail strikes in Sydney, power failures which meant Bochner could not use his electric typewriter, and a tendency for mail from the United States to remain in Manila, Philippines, for long periods of time. (Did you say that you wanted to collaborate, Mr. Cross-Cultural Researcher?) The three-way correspondence among the editors is replete with communication difficulties due to Australian versus American (correct) English (example: a cosmopolitan is defined as anyone who has heard of Alf Garnett); diatribes about the nature of editorial deadlines (an Aussie deadline = the agreed upon date ± 2 years, while the U.S. definition is supportive of Freud's anal retentive character); invocations serving the primary function of catharsis; and the uncanny way in which answers from one person preceded the questions of the other two.

Letters often contained unsolicited advice on such topics as marital bliss. An example: "Have wives do the indexing, as index time promotes domestic harmony by reducing the level of after-dinner conversation to nil." Freudian slips prompted long-range 25¢ psychoanalysis, as in a draft of some comments on hologeistic studies which referred to the Hymen Relations Area Files.

The splitting of editorial chores found Brislin and Lonner editing the manuscripts, corresponding with authors, keeping Bochner advised of developments, and searching for the miracle that would allow us to publish everything we ultimately could not publish. Meanwhile, Bochner was "down under" finding himself with the major responsibility for drafting the introductory chapter.

We are indebted to many people for the many forms of encouragement they gave. Mrs. Louise Kahabka, Hazel Tatsuno, Karen Shiroma, and Patricia Kim provided first-rate secretarial support. Members of the Sage Publications staff were very helpful with their good advice at various stages of the book's preparation. Finally, we must thank the contributors who were so cooperative in meeting the first deadline we set, breaking the norm for academia in so doing. They have probably spoiled us for future work of this kind.

R.B.
S.B.
W.L.

INTRODUCTION

STEPHEN BOCHNER
RICHARD W. BRISLIN
WALTER J. LONNER

An introductory chapter to a collected volume such as this one should be rather like a carefully chosen hors d'oeuvre: it must not overwhelm the main course, satiate the reader, or put him off, but should stimulate and whet the appetite for what is to follow. There is, in fact, a need to strike a balance between saying too much and not saying enough, and the organization of this chapter reflects this aim. A correct mixture of the bland with the spicy is also desirable in a good appetizer. The readiness of the editors to spar a little with their contributors has, we hope, achieved the right degree of liveliness in the mixture.

THE IDENTITY CRISIS IN CROSS-CULTURAL PSYCHOLOGY

Cross-cultural psychology, like many other adolescents, is suffering from an identity crisis. "Outsiders" have trouble integrating the heterogeneous aims, methods, conceptual frameworks, levels of sophistication, substantive areas, and theoretical leanings of those who call themselves cross-cultural psychologists. "Insiders," also, are a little puzzled about the precise nature of cross-cultural psychology, and in private conversation with their peers will often voice serious doubts about the very existence of such a discipline as a separate and identifiable enterprise. Publicly however, these very same uncertainties tend to make cross-cultural psychologists academically aggressive and/or defensive; behold the mandatory inclusion, in the introductory passages of most books and review articles in the field, of a favorably slanted definition of cross-cultural research, an out-of-context quotation from Kluckhohn on culture, and a quick commercial regarding the advantages of "going cross-cultural."

The insecurity of the discipline is also reflected in the tight tribal structure of its practitioners. There has emerged a highly visible "inner sanctum" or "inner circle" of cross-cultural psychologists (most of them Westerners), who attend and dominate all the important meetings, conferences, and symposia. The sheer brilliance of these heavyweights, and their prolific output, has significantly influenced the shape of cross-cultural research.

We feel that the time has now come for the adolescent to be guided through his next rite of passage. The diffidence and the resulting tendency to oversell the advantages of cross-cultural psychology are no longer necessary. We have also gone past the stage in the development of a discipline where a highly unified approach is essential to sustain the fledgling. Cross-cultural psychology is now strong enough to withstand the infusion of some new blood. Indeed, there is a positive need to widen the circle of cognoscenti as a way of avoiding the incestuous situation that arrested the development of Freud and Hull. We hope that the present book will make a contribution to the emergence of a more integrated and at the same time more representative persona for cross-cultural psychology.

CROSS-CULTURAL PSYCHOLOGY AS META-METHOD

Earlier we referred to the confusion, shared by both players and onlookers, regarding the nature of cross-cultural psychology. The problem is not just a question of semantics, because, as in all scientific endeavor, the selection of topics and strategies is greatly influenced by how a researcher defines his field. In cross-cultural psychology this can sometimes lead to quite absurd results. As one exasperated *Journal of Cross-Cultural Psychology* consultant recently put it: "An investigation done in Africa by a French psychologist on an American grant, using a Swiss theory and a test developed in England, does not necessarily make that study cross-cultural."

There is no doubt in our minds that the full flowering of cross-cultural research will depend on firmly and securely laying to rest the myth that cross-cultural psychology is a separate academic discipline. This statement might seem like a paradox, particularly coming from the mouths of the authors who regard themselves as militant cross-cultural psychologists. There may also be screams of anguish from those who would see such a view as heretical, and leading to the abdication of the territorial imperative. We now propose to defend our view, and in the process allay the anxieties of those who feel that we may be cutting away the ground from under their very feet. Although some of the ideas expressed are not new (e.g., Strodtbeck, 1964), the need to reaffirm these principles does not seem to have diminished (see Chapter 13 in this volume).

Before an examination of the logical status of cross-cultural psychology can proceed, its location on the family tree must be determined. Figure 1 presents a (rough) schematic picture of scientific psychology. The game is to locate cross-cultural psychology on one of the rows on the chart, that is if general admittance is allowed in the first place. In short, is cross-cultural psychology a

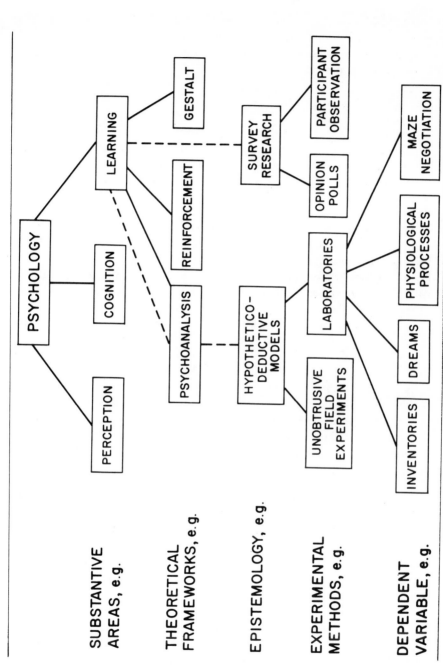

SUBSTANTIVE AREAS, e.g.

THEORETICAL FRAMEWORKS, e.g.

EPISTEMOLOGY, e.g.

EXPERIMENTAL METHODS, e.g.

DEPENDENT VARIABLE, e.g.

Figure 1. The Psychic Unity of Psychology

[5]

bastard, as some unkind people allege, or does it have a legitimate place in psychology, and if so, where?

Exclusion is no longer an issue for cross-cultural psychology. If we take the contents of the present volume as indicative of the sort of research now being done, the essential psychological nature of the work is undisputable, including the material presented by the two nonpsychologist authors. Some of the words may ring a little odd, some of the methods sound a little bizarre, but all are within the latitude of acceptance of the mainstream of psychological thought. At least that was the unanimous opinion of the psychologists at the conference where these papers were first read. Fortunately, the "dog-in-the-manger" attitude is becoming less prevalent in the social sciences, and it would be gratifying if this book could contribute to a further breaking down of the barriers between the various specialties.

An unresolved problem for cross-cultural psychology is its logical status within the wider field of scientific psychology. A major source of confusion has been to conceive of cross-cultural psychology as a substantive area. A glance at Figure 1 indicates the error of this view. Cross-cultural psychology does not deal with some particular set of conceptually or empirically related phenomena, such as for instance the psychology of learning with its central theme of behavior modification as a result of experience. A further perusal of Figure 1 may arouse initial consternation, because cross-cultural psychology does not seem to fit into *any* of the classifications. Cross-cultural psychology is not a set of theoretical principles, such as the reinforcement model with its laws of effect and contiguity, Gestalt theory with its notions of good form and closure, or psychoanalysis with its hydraulic energy model. Nor does cross-cultural psychology provide an alternate epistemology or a new strategy of inference. At the same time, cross-cultural psychology is not *just* another experimental method, it is not *just* the conceptual equal of the unobtrusive experiment or the stratified opinion poll.

The inability to locate cross-cultural psychology in Figure 1 or its equivalent has generated a good deal of muddled thinking. The identity crisis of the "insiders," and the allegations of doubtful paternity by the "outsiders," both have their source in there being no obvious row in which to deposit cross-cultural psychology. The solution is to regard cross-cultural psychology as a meta-method. That is to say, cross-cultural psychologists explore the various substantive areas of psychology, from various theoretical standpoints, using both experimental and survey methods, in the laboratory or in the field, with a variety of measuring instruments and devices. In fact, they go about their business just like anyone else in psychology. But, as the term "meta-method" implies, there is a special logic or strategy behind the utilization of general research techniques that additionally and explicitly characterizes cross-cultural research.

This additional ingredient is the conviction that psychological data "improve" as a function of the degree of cross-cultural input that enters into designing and carrying out a psychological investigation. Such a belief has a major influence on the selection of topics, subjects, instruments, and explanatory principles employed, and on the methodological problems that have to be solved. For instance, a psychologist who values the insights that a cross-cultural perspective affords will almost certainly be led to use a design in which the treatment is replicated transculturally, and consequently will also be confronted with the equivalence problem that is the natural concomitant of such a design.

In sum, cross-cultural psychology is not a theoretical framework, not one of Cronbach's (1957) "two disciplines," not an experimental method, nor a class of dependent variables. Cross-cultural psychology is a meta-method with all of the areas of psychology grist to its mill. But there are pitfalls for the unwary, as many psychologists quite eminent in their own fields have learned to their cost and astonishment. There is more to "doing" cross-cultural research than hopping on a plane with a briefcase full of psychological tests. The material in this volume gives a good indication of the skills and personal attributes required for successfully "going cross-cultural."

ETHICAL ISSUES IN CROSS-CULTURAL RESEARCH

A number of ethical problems are raised in every psychological investigation employing human subjects. A major issue is the use of deception and its impact on subjects, experimenters, and the professional image of psychology (Argyris, 1968; Kelman, 1968). A related problem concerns the possible lowering of the self-esteem of subjects exposed to stressful, degrading, or humiliating experiences, particularly in the light of recent evidence that debriefing does not always have the "undoing" effects claimed for it (Walster, Berscheid, Abrahams, and Aronson, 1967). These issues have all received extensive airing in the literature (e.g., American Psychological Association, 1973), and are introduced here merely to provide a springboard for raising a set of ethical problems that are more subtle, less frequently debated, and directly relevant to cross-cultural research.

A general question that may profitably be asked by all psychologists, but which takes on a special significance in the context of cross-cultural work, relates to the choice of topic for study. One facet of the question is this: How does a person judge when the degree of harm that an experiment may do to its participants is outweighed by the wider benefits that society might gain from the results? And to put a further twist on this question, at what point is it unethical to do nothing at all (McGuire, 1972)? When do gaps in our knowledge become so pressing that ignoring them constitutes an act of professionally delinquent behavior? For instance, considering the issue of conflict reduction (see the chapters by Doob and Triandis in this volume) *does* it matter that more people are not working in this area?

After having decided on a topic, a research worker has to design the study, recruit his subjects, and collect the required data. In the beginning of this section we noted that the main ethical problem in intra-cultural manipulated research has been in the indiscriminate and insensitive overuse of deception. In cross-cultural research the ethical issue is not as clearly focused, although insensitivity on the part of the investigator is clearly a "g" factor underlying all of the specific manifestations of morally indefensible research behavior being perpe-trated in the name of science on people from other cultures across the globe.

At the conference which gave rise to this book, a recurrent theme related to the ethics of how to conduct oneself, as well as how to conduct one's research, while in the field. In particular, it was felt that researchers have a responsibility to a greater segment of the culture in which they are guests, rather than just to the participants in their own studies. There was a general consensus that when this larger commitment is not carried through, the researcher can be validly accused of having "ripped off the culture," even if his data are collected according to the most acceptable ethical guidelines. If nothing of value is left behind, the culture does not benefit from cross-cultural research. One partici-pant likened safari-style research to the activities of mining companies in the Third World, who extract the riches of these regions primarily for the benefit of their Western shareholders. Whether this analogy is fair or not, it is true that the activities of some cross-cultural researchers have attracted a "bad press," and left behind a bitter taste in the mouths of the local people, who felt rather shabbily treated. Thus a recent article in *Parade* had the following to say about Harry Klein, a resident of Tubai, an island 450 miles south of Tahiti:

> Klein doesn't think much of the other Americans he occasionally sees pass through Tubai and the other islands. Missionaries irritate him; he thinks the code they preach is essentially alien to the Polynesians. College professors don't impress him either. An American came here some time ago to study the economy of Tubai for a Ph.D. thesis. Comments Klein sourly: "Now he'll go home and write a bloody lot of junk. What for? Maybe it's good for him. Might even make him a big man, a professor. Then he can teach the same junk to other students. Here no one will ever read it or care about it." [Harrington, 1973, p. 22]

The point that we make is that *Parade,* a weekly "Sunday Supplement" to thousands of United States newspapers, has an estimated readership of 30 million people, which is probably more readers than all the professional social science journals combined. Thus whether Klein's experiences are representative or not, the publicity given to his views does not cast the profession in a favorable light. Unfortunately Klein is not alone in his attitude. According to participants at the conference, the feelings expressed in the *Parade* article are fairly common among the lay public. The anthropologists admitted that their biggest problem in graduate education is to find suitable field sites for Ph.D. candidates, as fewer and fewer cultures are now willing to let outsiders come in to "study" them (see also Keesing and Keesing, 1971, p. 405). The story was told of a North American Indian Chief who sent a form letter to chairmen of anthropology departments across the United States, in which he asked that no further requests be made for permission to allow students to live on his reservation. Other participants agreed that they had found not only indifference but downright hostility in doing cross-cultural work. But despite the fundamental importance of this issue to the conduct of cross-cultural investigations, previous writings on the subject of gaining entry into a research setting are very disappointing. The issue was apparently debated at the Ibadan conference (DeLamater, Hefner, and Clignet, 1968), but the published report makes only a veiled reference to the discussion, and so is not very helpful in this regard. The only extended presentation of this issue, as far as we are aware, is a little known essay by Tagumpay-Castillo (1968).[1] The author is a Filipino social scientist who has apparently met many visiting researchers in her day, and her classification of these scholars into a number of categories is not always flattering. Here are some types that a person on the *receiving* end of a cross-cultural research project is likely to encounter:

The "data-exporter." He is, in the words of Professor Alex Inkeles, the fellow who does research "safari style." He takes everything he can by way of data and leaves nothing of value to the country of study. Sometimes he is called the "hit and run" researcher, with more "runs" than "hits." If research were a movie with a plot, he would easily be the villain.

The "hypothesis-tester" and "theory-builder." He has some theory as to how development proceeds, and his aim in overseas research is to add as many cultures or societies to his sample as he can in order to arrive at a universal generalization.

The "greenhorn." We can usually tell the newcomer from the "old-timer." The former has THE explanation, the latter has only a hunch.

The "idea-stimulator" and "research-facilitator." He is a real gem. Professionally secure, very competent, he has no great compulsion to see his byline. He asks the right questions so that we may figure out for ourselves what the right answers might be; he assists in obtaining research support so that these answers might be forthcoming. Most of all, the research project is ours, not his. The only flaw of this precious gem is that he is such a rare specimen.

The "penny-collaborator." He happens to have access to some money, not too much, but some. "How about a cooperative project?" he says. "I'll provide the money and you do the study."

The "professional overseas researcher." To him, overseas research is a way of life. He lives from research grant to research grant. "Tough life," he says, "I can't stand the winters in New York anymore."

The "CIA scholar." Everyone says he exists and is reputedly doing an excellent piece of basic strategic research, but it is impossible to describe him because like the "Invisible Man," we cannot see him. [Tagumpay-Castillo, 1968, pp. 30-32]

Ethical Guidelines for Cross-Cultural Research

It is not our intention to adopt the mantle of moral guardian to the profession. Our aim in this section is to conclude the discussion on ethics by drawing attention to some emerging norms regarding the conduct of cross-cultural research and researchers.

The overriding principle in the conduct of cross-cultural research should be to achieve equal-status cooperative collaboration at every step in the research process. How many studies in the literature can truly be said to have been jointly planned, designed, and carried out by equal partners from more than one culture? Very few, which is a pity, not just on ethical grounds, but also on practical and methodological grounds, because a joint effort from the very beginning right through to the bitter end is much more likely to produce "real" data (see Glaser and Taylor, 1973), rather than just another set of artifactual ornaments to someone's *curriculum vitae*.

Thus it is highly desirable that collaboration should begin at the point where the research problem is isolated, the concepts clarified, and the utility of the findings for each culture assessed. An actual attempt to achieve such an aim was the 1968 workshop at the East-West Center, under the leadership of the late F. K. Berrien (Bochner, 1969; Meredith, 1969). Prior to the workshop, Berrien toured Southeast Asia and interviewed a large number of the psychologists in the region, in order to survey their research interests, assess their competence, and sound out their willingness to participate in joint research with colleagues in other countries. Berrien later carefully teamed each of a dozen American psychologists with an Asian counterpart, the matching being done with such variables as age, experience, and eminence in mind. It was altogether a masterly exercise in applied sociometry, and probably the first time that the marriage broker concept had been used as a framework for an international gathering of scholars. Once the pairs were selected, each team was encouraged to enter into mutual correspondence before the workshop. The workshop itself lasted for two weeks, and consisted of teams having individual meetings, at which a research project was planned. Later in the workshop these teams presented their design to the group as a whole for comment and criticism.

Notwithstanding these unprecedented efforts, Berrien's dream was not realized, since practically no research has emerged directly from the activities of the workshop. True, many individual Asian psychologists greatly benefitted from their entry into the international scientific community, and many Americans made useful international contacts, but the basic purpose of generating a dozen truly cross-cultural research projects was not achieved. It may be instructive to dwell briefly on the possible reasons for this; two stand out.

(1) Despite Berrien's respect for and knowledge of "foreign" cultures, the meta-framework of the workshop was American, particularly in the assumption that psychological research requires large quantities of money. Even in a semi-advanced country like Australia the majority of psychological research is still being done only with the aid of a good idea, unpaid student help, bits of homemade equipment, and materials requisitioned under the false pretense of being needed for teaching purposes. In countries like Pakistan or Indonesia, actual paper to write on is scarce, books and journals practically nonexistent, and scientific communication is hampered by the prohibitive cost of international postage. Most academics, including very senior people, have second jobs in order to survive, and the normal teaching load in their "first" job can be 20 hours a week. Thus very few Asian institutions are geared, at the present time, to accommodate an American-style research "industry." What Asia does need, and could cope with, are books, journals,[2] some basic equipment, and a few qualified people to act as "idea-stimulators" and "research-facilitators."

(2) Despite Berrien's painstaking search for competent and talented Asian participants, the level of experience, up-to-dateness, empiricism, and general research skill was plainly lower in the non-Western contingent[3] than among the Americans at the workshop. This should not be taken as an indication of cultural superiority on the part of the authors of this chapter, and indeed we take no pleasure in making this statement. But up to the present time the *published* literature has maintained a massive silence on this issue. Are we not collectively mature enough now to bring it out into the open? We think so, and hope that this problem will be looked at as a legitimate area for research and action by the profession.

The imbalance in the regional affiliations of the chapter authors in this volume indicates that the situation has not changed substantially since 1968. Nor can one expect very much improvement until the academic infrastructure in Asia and elsewhere achieves closer parity with the great research centers of the Western world. Western psychologists can contribute to a worldwide raising of standards by adopting the following guidelines in their cross-cultural field work. Many of the guidelines are implicit in Berrien's (1970) description of a "super-ego" for cross-cultural research.

(1) A research problem should be defined in collaboration with a member of

the "other" culture. Ideally, the discussions should be conducted in both locations. Topics should be of theoretical or practical interest in both cultures. Not only will this win a Western psychologist the genuine friendship of his collaborator, but also he will be less likely to be hoist by the petard of non-equivalence implicit in safari-style research.

(2) When "on site," the visitor should work with a local research colleague on an equal-status basis. If there is no such person available, then he should train promising people, giving special attention to teaching skills (e.g., survey methods) that could lead to the permanent employment of the assistant after the project is completed and the researcher has returned home.

(3) Joint publication should be the norm rather than the exception. Senior authorship should rotate between the team. However, as H. Van Buren (personal communication) reminded us, the researcher should make sure that co-authorship is a desired commodity. In some cultures joint participation at a scholarly meeting might be more valued. The researcher must be sensitive to the preferred method of information dissemination, and be prepared to adapt to the local system.

(4) In some cultures, the "pure science" approach, in which the primary and only aim is to test some theoretical model, is seen as being too "precious." For instance, one of our contributors (Rosch) expressed the view that individuals from other cultures should be selected for study if, and only if, the "other" culture provides an important link, either as variable or as treatment, in testing some superordinate psychological theory. One wonders if the New Guineans, where Rosch did her work, would agree with her (culturally influenced) priorities, in view of the many practical problems that the Pacific Islanders are facing. With educational research, health education, conflict resolution, cargo cultism, population control, and other similar bread-and-butter issues crying out to be attended to, some outsider's preoccupation with theory construction may not be appreciated. The wise theoretician will achieve a compromise solution to his problem by designing studies that have both a theoretical and practical yield. Not only is there then something for everyone, but, according to Lewin, such studies are the best kind, anyway.

(5) If possible, itinerant social scientists should adopt a variant of the Peace Corps model, and try to become members of the community in which they are working. In particular, they should be sensitive to some of the less obvious effects of their behavior. For instance, on his recent research visit to Indonesia, Bochner noticed that, on the one occasion when he arrived at an informant's home by hired Mercedes, his reception was subtly different from the treatment he received when travelling by betchak or on the back of a local friend's motorcycle.

(6) Sometimes researchers can use their findings to help or become an advocate for another culture. For example, Berry (see Chapter 8) recently

testified in a major court case involving Cree Indians, basing his case on the data referred to in the chapter. Some cultures will welcome researchers if it is considered that the visitors will "speak to the world" through their research. Similarly, the leaders of some cultures have come to appreciate the older ethnographies, because in many instances such documents are the *only* existing materials available for use in teaching the culture's history to the current generation. Recently, several anthropologists have volunteered their services to record and collect exactly those materials which the members of a given culture want collected (e.g., Sept., 1974 issue of *Current Anthropology*).

In the final analysis, the ethical conduct of cross-cultural research is not just a moral imperative, but a practical one as well, because cross-cultural researchers, more than any other brand of psychologist, are dependent on the good will and cooperation of their subjects.

CROSS-CULTURAL PERSPECTIVES ON LEARNING

As the title of this book indicates, the substantive theme of the volume revolves around the relationship between culture and learning. Although the definition of learning implicit in the material is quite broad, it is still well within the limits set by the usage of the term in orthodox circles. As in general psychology, learning from a cross-cultural perspective refers to the modification of behavior due to experience; however, the cross-cultural approach does differ in emphasis from traditional learning psychology, particularly in the classes of independent or antecedent variables considered to be important, the classes of dependent or consequent variables that are measured and quantified, and the degree of ambiguity and looseness that is tolerated in the functional relationships recorded. The main features, strengths, and problems inherent in taking a cross-cultural view of learning will now be presented.

Culture as Independent Variable

Regardless of what a cross-cultural investigator actually manipulates or selects for study, the independent variable in his mind's eye is the culture or subculture to which the specific experimental subjects or treatments belong. That, of course, is one of the main points of "going cross-cultural"—to exploit large differences in developmental experiences, family structure, ecological features, and the like. But there are problems, too, when broad and complex classes of cultural variables are being manipulated. In particular, rigor and precision suffer, variables tend to become confounded, and alternate explanations appear like a lot of jack-in-the-boxes every time an interpretation is offered. The situation is further complicated in that a cross-cultural perspective shows up the limitations of the simpler models of behavior, and thus pushes the committed investigator into a complex conceptual framework containing many theoretical and methodological booby traps.

What Is the Dependent Variable?

Although dependent variable measures in cross-cultural studies do not differ greatly from responses that are recorded in general psychology, a cross-cultural framework makes it much more difficult to assume that behavior consists of static and molecular responses. In some areas of general psychology it may be possible to ignore that behavior is an on-going and reactive process, conceptualize the dependent variable as a fixed outcome, and thereby vastly simplify (and trivialize) the researcher's approach to the problem in hand. In cross-cultural psychology, however, the denial of "behavior as process" cannot be sustained for long, because even a partially blind person realizes sooner or later that the responses of individuals (the traditional dependent variable category of general psychology) are also an ingredient in the cultural environment (or independent variable) that contributes to the determination of those very same responses.

What Is an Acceptable Level of Rigor?

Departments of psychology across the world air condition their animal laboratories, while the humans tending these creatures are left to swelter and/or freeze in their unprotected offices. The equitable laboratory climate also houses banks of computers capable of delivering an astonishing variety of sensations, and intricate recording systems that measure, graph, correlate, and analyze the eagerly awaited responses. But despite all the help that modern science can provide, even the reinforcement schedules of individual laboratory rats are not that easy to regulate, nor are their responses a cinch to record. One of Bochner's rat-runner colleagues discovered this when he realized after a semester's work that the "interesting" results he was getting were highly correlated with systematic fluctuations in the city power supply into which his equipment was hooked.

So it is not surprising that field studies of cultural effects on, say, behavior modification will almost certainly contain features unlikely to endear the report to the editor of the *Journal of Experimental Psychology*. This raises the very important issue of double standards, an issue that, to our knowledge, has not been discussed in the published literature, although it is frequently a topic of heated debate when cross-cultural psychologists meet. The problem can be stated in terms of the following question: Should cross-cultural research be judged by the same criteria as experimental laboratory work? The question is not new, since it has been asked generally in connection with research on human subjects, particularly when the inquiry is conducted in natural settings, but the problem reaches extreme proportions in designs that employ cultural differences as a treatment variable.

In principle, there are two alternatives to the problem of experimental rigor in cross-cultural research, and these echo the distinction sometimes made between the clinical and experimental approaches in general psychology (Meehl, 1954). One "solution" is to argue that the traditional concepts and methods of rat and knee-jerk psychology are not appropriate to inquiries that consider the effects of whole cultures on their inhabitants, and that attempts to extend and adapt traditional methods for such a purpose are misguided. Cross-cultural research should go its own way, and not be hampered by the dead hand of experimental psychology.

The opposing view states that what distinguishes cross-cultural psychology from the earlier anthropological approaches is precisely a concern with method. Indeed, the whole raison d'etre of cross-cultural psychology lies in the application of the methodological armament of experimental psychology to areas studied in the past through the largely idiographic eyes of the explorer, novelist, or anthropologist.

Our own position on this issue is unequivocally on the side of an experimentally oriented cross-cultural psychology. It is our belief that the special contribution of cross-cultural psychology lies in the application of experimental techniques to areas previously studied by other means, not to supplant past findings, but as a way of complementing and extending the work being done from nonexperimental perspectives. At the same time, we are very much aware of the immense difficulties associated with achieving an acceptable level of methodological rigor in cross-cultural research (see e.g., Chapter 4 in Brislin, Lonner, and Thorndike, 1973), and would have to acknowledge that it is unrealistic to expect the same degree of control as is achieved in other types of research. And yet we are loath to apply a double standard to our work, because to do so would be to defeat the whole purpose of cross-cultural research.

We seem to have created a massive double bind for ourselves and for those who sympathize with this position, since we are also sensitive to the possibility that if cross-cultural studies were rigidly evaluated on the usual criteria, the discouragement generated by such a policy would result in very little non-trivial research being done, and even less published. Walter Lonner, as editor of the *Journal of Cross-Cultural Psychology,* as well as others associated with it, have been concerned about the temptation to publish only eloquent cross-cultural research reports written up by fecund Yank psychologists, sacrificing at the same time important but less well-written manuscripts prepared by less well-practiced psychologists from other parts of the world. From the point of view of building up a viable school of cross-cultural psychology, the methodological purist can be as destructive as the low standards he is tilting against.

Clearly some compromise is called for, and in reconciling the requirements of method with the realities of cross-cultural research, we have been guided by the following consideration. A double standard in the sense of changing the rules of research is an unacceptable and self-defeating solution to the problem. But a double standard in the sense of turning a *temporary* blind eye to some currently unavoidable problems has much to commend it, provided the basis for the relaxation in stringency is explicitly stated. This style of criticism will have the effect of reminding the research worker of the standards he should be aiming at, without at the same time crippling him in his efforts to achieve the necessary expertise. The underlying principle is well understood in sporting circles, where a system of handicapping places graded obstacles in the paths of the participants, with the size of the handicap a variable positive function of relative success against the field. Thus if the handicapper is good at his job, and the handicaps are adjusted after each contest, every entrant has a chance of winning, and yet no one is in any doubt about what constitutes an expertly sailed boat or a well ridden horse.

What we are proposing as a general principle for evaluating research studies is a kind of negative handicap system with allowances for the complexity, novelty, or intransigence of the research area, with the allowances gradually being withdrawn as the area develops. One further condition must also be satisfied: to qualify for an allowance in the methodological stakes, a particular study should make a contribution that could not have been achieved by a more orthodox approach.

In applying these principles to cross-cultural research, it can be seen that the issue of rigor is not a simple matter of applying the standard criteria of scientific method to a study's design, implementation, and data analysis. At least three other major considerations must be taken into account: (1) What are the potential benefits to theory and practice of adding a transcultural dimension to the design? (2) How complex is the problem being investigated? (3) Is the research area fairly well developed, or is it still at the exploratory stage where a lot of single-culture pioneering work is necessary? The answers to these questions will, in combination, influence the evaluation of the methods and procedures employed. Although the actual weighting of the various elements in the evaluative matrix is not amenable to a precise definition, some general guidelines are available. Potentially, "going cross-cultural" can act as a stimulus to theory building, exercise the ingenuity of research workers in extending or developing appropriate procedures, and provide a wider backdrop for the psychological phenomena under scrutiny. If these conditions are satisfied, we at any rate are prepared to live with a modicum of looseness in the system for the time being.

Learning Another Culture

"Subjective culture." Research in the area of "subjective culture" provides a good illustration of a moderately tight theoretical system in which broad cultural factors are regarded as independent variables for specific, measurable, and socially significant outcomes. The chapter by Triandis gives a general overview of the theory and research in this area, and is complemented by the chapter following it, in which Davidson describes an experiment typical of the genre. A central issue for both authors is the extent to which intergroup conflict arises out of differences in the way cultural groups perceive their social environments.

Although there is nothing very new in the proposition that members of different cultures construe reality in idiosyncratic ways, Triandis's formulation of these differences in terms of a variation in "subjective culture" is a novel and potentially useful adjunct to an understanding of intergroup conflict. In particular, the formulation draws attention to the problems of communicating across cultural boundaries, points to some of the attitudinal correlates of cross-cultural "misunderstandings," and is capable of making explicit predictions regarding the conditions under which trans-cultural communication is likely to be enhanced.

Triandis and his associates use the theoretical interplay between culture and learning to good effect in their research. Many of the elegantly designed studies have the threefold function of testing the central hypotheses of the model, contributing to a general theory of communication, and devising curricula for conflict-reducing programs. These three theoretical birds are often dispatched with one missile, particularly in experiments where individuals are trained to understand the subjective culture of other groups. Some of the features of these studies are worth noting in more detail, because they illustrate many of the special strengths of the cross-cultural method referred to earlier in this chapter.

By selecting subjects from different cultures, it is possible to manipulate a greater than usual variation in implicit cognitive structure, leading to special opportunities for "pure" research. The larger contrasts in initial cognitions also provide a fairly stringent test for the prediction of reduced conflict after the subjective cultures have converged. And in using ordinary people with real problems as experimental subjects, with the accent on improving cross-cultural communication (Davidson's chapter is particularly helpful here), the research program can be seen as making a desirable contribution to the respective cultures of the participants. Finally, to structure the study of cross-cultural encounters, Triandis shows good judgment in the selection of the concepts he borrows from general psychology. Role, attribution, and reinforcement theory are all used to advantage.

In many ways, the work of Triandis and his associates can be held up as an exemplar of cross-cultural research. However, to Bochner especially, the mathematically based "paradigm" of behavioral intentions featured in the chapter seems an unnecessary and distracting element. The paradigm is too complex, much too abstract and general, and it is difficult to see how it could be falsified (although in fairness to Triandis the chapter does contain some quite specific proposals for translating the various elements of the model into empirical operations). Even so, the real world is unlikely to resemble the clean, aseptic, and sterile set of simultaneous equations provided.

A too rigidly preconceived mold, no matter how elegant, tends to stultify rather than expand the horizons of research. Those with an investment in a model often spend time criticizing methodologically and conceptually adequate but disconfirming studies on the basis of picayune detail, when they might be better employed revising the theory in line with the data. The dissonance area provides a prime example of how a research program degenerated because of a misguided rearguard action against the theory's critics (e.g., Chapanis and Chapanis, 1964; Fishbein and Ajzen, 1972).

The question has to be asked whether cross-cultural psychology, at the present stage in its development, can afford the luxury of high level systems building. We think not, mainly because, as we have already indicated, an overemphasis on theory can become a real straitjacket on research. Unless the "owner" of a model has an open attitude to his "property," little development is likely to occur beyond the first published version. Unfortunately, so much of a developer's ego is usually involved that revisions in models are even scarcer than hen's teeth. Furthermore, these petrified fossils are far from harmless, since precious research resources tend to be diverted into devising ingenious means of counter-disconfirming the disconfirmations, leading in extreme cases to what Ring (1967) deplored as a "fun and games" mentality in the protagonists. It would be disastrous if cross-cultural psychology fell into that particular mire.

We should make it clear that we are not here talking specifically about the subjective culture model, but are voicing our opposition to a general style of research, and hope that both Triandis and Davidson will forgive us for using their chapters as a springboard from which to leap into the fray. In case we are misunderstood, we should also make it clear that we are not arguing against the use of the hypothetico-deductive method in cross-cultural research. Our misgivings relate only to the use of highly abstract, internally consistent (and hence rigidly inflexible), and mathematically based sets of interlocking propositions as the main source of experimental hypotheses.

As a postscript to the theoretical issue of culture training, one of the editors (Bochner, a one-time resident of Hawaii during his student days), took some of the contributors to the present volume for a beach picnic to beautiful Hanauma Bay, renowned for its easily accessible coral formations. After providing his distinguished guests with snorkels and masks, he warned the bathers not to touch the coral, because it is extremely sharp and even a small cut can cause a painful and slow-healing wound. He reinforced his lecture by exhibiting some old scars he carried from a snorkeling accident some months prior to the day of the picnic. Notwithstanding all this, three of the visitors soon emerged from the water with bleeding hands, protesting that the coral did not *look* sharp under water. Fortunately, the heated discussion of the relative merits of cognitive versus behavioral learning[4] that ensued soon distracted the victims from their self-inflicted wounds. The same issue is touched on by Guthrie in his chapter, although not at the depths that the importance of this topic merits.

A Behavioral Perspective. Guthrie's chapter provides a counterpoint to the cognitive orientation of the "subjective culture" framework. Like Triandis, he conceptualizes culture as the independent variable in his system, but for Guthrie culture consists of an all-pervasive matrix of reinforcement contingencies. This also is not a particularly novel view, but the analysis becomes more interesting when Guthrie applies it to an examination of the problems an adult encounters as he moves from one culture to another for a sojourn involving some degree of participation in the "alien" society.

The complex ramifications of sojourn research are well understood by Guthrie, and his chapter contains allusions to many of the "pure" and practical aspects of inquiring into overseas adjustment. In particular, he considers three factors that in combination account for most of the variance in the performance of persons sojourning in an "alien" culture. These are (1) the pre-departure cognitive and informational training a prospective sojourner undergoes; (2) his character and personality; and (3) his experiences in the second culture, particularly those early in the sojourn. Guthrie views the transfer of a person to an alien society as a naturally occurring experiment in which a massive manipulation of important social psychological variables has taken place, and draws attention to opportunities for research in the fields of social learning, culture-personality relationships, and culture training. The framework is unashamedly behavioral, with the sojourn regarded as a major shift in reinforcement schedules. Numerous examples from the Peace Corps literature, all reinterpreted from the perspective of classical and instrumental conditioning, "reinforce" the theoretical points being made.

A useful contribution to the area of sojourn research would be a comparison of the predictions arising from different theoretical standpoints. Such an exercise was carried out by LeVine and Campbell (1972) for ethnocentrism. They looked at the implications of reinforcement, cognitive congruity, reference group, and social structure theories, noting where the theories made similar as well as conflicting predictions. Analyses of this sort are very helpful, although the final test, of course, is an empirical one; only first-rate data can decide which of any set of predictions from different theories is the most adequate.

Sojourn Research in Pakistan. One major variable in culture learning is the target population whose behavior is being modified, leading some authors to approach the topic through a consideration of the fate of specific subgroups under specifiable cultural conditions. In this regard, Guthrie was primarily concerned with Peace Corps volunteers, and Precourt (Chapter 9), with initiates and members of secret societies. A further group that has been the focus of research is the foreign student population, and the psychological impact of studying abroad (on both the student and the host country) is understood reasonably well. (Two recent reviews of the field are Eide, 1970, and National Liaison Committee, 1971.)

The bulk of the sojourn literature is about the interaction of students from the so-called underdeveloped countries with Western nationals and institutions, or the aftermaths of such interactions. There are also a few studies that have looked at the other side of this coin, with Western students and professors on sojourn in underdeveloped countries under scrutiny. Practically nothing, though, is known about the effect of educational exchange between two "under-developed" nations. In fact, most people would probably be surprised to discover that such countries exchange students at all. Thus Chapter 4 by Hafeez Zaidi, which is about the social and psychological adjustment of foreign Asian and African students in Pakistan, is of interest if only because of its rarity.

The design of Zaidi's study itself, however, is quite unremarkable, as are the findings, except in the sense that Muslim foreign students in Pakistan appear to be facing the same sorts of problems as foreign students everywhere. Language barriers, insufficient financial support, shallow social relationships with host nationals, homesickness, and the "mote-beam" mechanism (Morris, 1960) all appear in predictable array, reminding us of the many differences that exist among the various non-Western cultures of the world. The reminder may not be as necessary today as it was a decade ago, but there are still a great many people, including some within the profession, who lump all Asians (or "Asiatics," as the press in Australia used to call them in the 1950s) into one big undifferentiated mass.

In this connection, those of our readers who have access to BBC Television will be reminded of the appalling Alf Garnett (brilliantly played by Warren Mitchell). Alf's social world is very simple, consisting merely of "us" and "them." In particular, Alf makes no distinction whatsoever between the various groups in the Indian subcontinent, and in this probably reflects the perceptions of a sizable proportion of the British public. Zaidi's article does show that the world is more complex than that, and in so doing provides a new perspective on the process of culture learning.

The attempt by Zaidi to invoke dissonance principles to account for the findings is not altogether convincing. On the other hand, the descriptive, down-to-earth material that makes up the bulk of Hafeez Zaidi's report provides welcome relief from the more abstruse writings of some of our other contributors. More generally, Zaidi's contribution illustrates some of the difficulties, alluded to earlier in this chapter, that face researchers in the less developed countries. The more current, fashionable work that Western social scientists can cite is simply not available. Consequently, there is an overdependence on the older, "classical" studies, which are inevitably dated. For instance, in the argument that Zaidi was developing, he would have found the current literature on attribution just as helpful as Triandis did, but there is no point in chiding Zaidi for not using something that he does not have access to. There is no simple solution to the problem, but at least its existence should be acknowledged, so that (in the language of Triandis's chapter) the subjective cultures of researchers in different parts of the world can begin to converge. Zaidi realizes the problem, and was kind enough to give the editors permission to discuss his chapter in these terms.

Conflict Reduction. Doob's chapter is an account of a highly idiosyncratic approach to conflict reduction. Doob's personal and professional interests lie in staging and evaluating unofficial volunteer interventions in other people's "troubles." He shows good sense in beginning his chapter with an analysis of the characteristics and motives of the interveners, since the first reaction to such persons is to regard them as either cranks, busybodies, or saints. The only consideration preventing us from having the same reaction on second and all subsequent occasions is that Leonard Doob himself does not fit any of these categories. Perhaps our profession makes us overly cynical, but the issue is important insofar as the motivations attributed to the intervener by his "clients" will determine his effectiveness as a conflict reducer. This issue is not satisfactorily resolved in the chapter, probably because there is little empirical evidence to draw on in this regard.

Doob discusses the immense difficulties in obtaining the "right" people to participate in his groups, that is, those who are willing, able, receptive, and sufficiently influential to carry the message into the hinterland of the workshop. Although the odds are clearly stacked against all these conditions being satisfied, this does not invalidate the program unless there is empirical evidence that such people cannot be assembled. Reading between the lines of the chapter suggests that the standard of the participants in actual workshops has varied a great deal, from the utterly hopeless to the acceptable.

One conflict reduction technique that we were surprised not to see in Doob's treatment is the use of superordinate goals as studied by the Sherifs (Sherif, 1967; Sherif and Sherif, 1969). Superordinate goals refer to outcomes desired by all people involved, even though the people may have strong affiliations with groups in conflict. The attainment of the goals demands participation from members of all groups. In their well-known Robber's Cave study and elsewhere, the Sherifs have provided ample and vivid evidence that the quest for superordinate goals reduces intergroup tension.

Empirical Studies of Perception and Cognition

Assessing Cognitive Ability. In many ways, the work of Cole and his associates can be regarded as a model for cross-cultural research. Their inquiry is concerned with the relationship between culture and cognition, and raises a number of fundamental issues, including the ultimate question about the existence of racial differences in intelligence. At the same time, their field work has impinged on such practical problems as curriculum development for the school system of the country in which they were working. The methodology employed is impeccably experimental, and involves a sensitive extension and adaptation of traditional instruments and procedures, all within the context of a thorough understanding of the culture in which the work is being carried out. Finally, it is unlikely that the conclusions that Cole and his associates arrived at could have emerged from research done in a purely mono-cultural setting.

The central issue raised by Cole is how to interpret "poor performance" in cross-cultural cognitive testing. Simply stated, the problem is as follows: What does it mean when a group of subjects perform less adequately (to some criterion) than another group on a test that has been specifically designed to tap a universal ability? Empirically, there are many groups in addition to Cole's subjects (the Kpelle) whose relative performance on a variety of cognitive and intellectual tests is inferior. Thus Australian aborigines do not do as well on the Porteus Maze as American subjects (Porteus, 1965). New Guineans are less adept at the Queensland Test than White Australians (McElwain and Kearney, 1970), and the performance of Black children in the United States on a wide variety of laboratory tasks is inferior relative to that of their White counterparts (Jensen, 1969). Any light, therefore, that Cole might be able to throw on this problem would have consequences reaching far beyond the boundaries of his particular studies.

Cole observed that the poor performance of the Kpelle on some of the experimental tasks that he placed before them was not matched by a successful solution of analogous real life problems. Cole felt that there was something odd about a laboratory task which produced results so very discrepant from the everyday problem solving behavior of the Kpelle. (Note that Cole could not have made this observation had he not had an intimate knowledge of the Kpelle culture.) To reduce the discrepancy, Cole set out to alter systematically the nature of the experimental task until a satisfactory performance was achieved by his subjects.

To some observers this might seem like progressively lowering the bar on a set of high jump posts until an athlete cleared the barrier, and then pronouncing him the champion. Cole would vehemently disagree. He would argue that he was merely ensuring that the experimental situation contained features that were structurally analogous to real life situations, and that any judgments about relative levels of ability simply reflect an ethnocentric bias.

The issue of deficit performance will not be resolved until the construct undergoes further clarification. In practical terms, there are at least three explanations why the Kpelle (or the New Guineans, or the Australian aborigines) perform poorly at experimental tasks that they carry out with great skill in natural settings:

(1) Because the subjects were faking, frightened, bored, did not understand the questions, were hostile, ingratiating, deceitful, or under orders not to cooperate. (All of these problems were encountered by Bochner [Porteus, Bochner, Russell, and David, 1967] in his work in Central Australia.) If indeed these are the reasons for a low test score, then the psychologist is not earning his pay, or rather his grant money, and the deficit in subject performance is really an unobtrusive index of the experimenter's incompetence. The question of race and intelligence has become a lively issue, and hence the subject of discussion whenever social scientists meet. Brislin believes that much of the problem in minority group "other culture" test performance can be explained exactly by the empirical findings associated with the points made in the first sentence of this paragraph. However, his remarks to that effect at professional meetings have usually been greeted by yawns. Either (a) he is not a good public debater, or (b) social scientists prefer to believe that test performance *does* measure competence and hence conclude that issues of subject understanding, boredom, and in-gratiation are trivial. Defense mechanisms mitigate against accepting (a), whereas recent articles by McClelland (1973) and Jorgenson (1973) suggest that (b) is a likely answer. The article by McClelland is particularly valuable, since it rep-resents the views of a high-status social scientist who, after carefully examining exactly what tests measure, concludes that many problems have been over-looked, especially the nature of external criteria. The article by Jorgenson is a sensitive effort by a Black psychologist to show, as clearly as he can, why the content and administrative procedure of different tests inevitably lead to low performance by Black test takers, relative to Whites.

(2) Because the experimental task was in fact a poor analogue of the daily activity it was supposed to capture. For instance, tracing a maze printed on a piece of paper may be too remote from the real-life tracking task it is supposed to represent. More research is urgently needed to establish greater congruence between experimental tasks and cultural "structures," and Cole's work with the Kpelle may well provide a lead in this regard.

(3) Because the subjects could not make a connection between the laboratory task and the "cultural" structure, despite the existence of a reasonable congruence between the two, as established by some independent procedure. If this were the case, then further research would need to address itself to answering the question why, and not avoid the issue by making the experimental task "easier" through the provision of more structure.

Although we share Cole's belief in the psychic unity of mankind, we feel there is a better chance of establishing that proposition if we allow for the possibility of its being falsified. Until much more is known in this field, a two-tailed rather than a one-tailed research strategy is indicated.

Human Categorization. The chapter by Rosch illustrates how a cross-cultural setting can sometimes provide experimental conditions that could not be reproduced readily in a laboratory. Indeed, the studies that she describes could probably not have been done other than cross-culturally.

Rosch's research interests are "pure" as the driven snow, and therefore of no immediate interest to the culture in which the inquiry was conducted. Although Rosch's work is highly regarded by her professional peers, to be consistent we must record our disapproval of studies in which cultures are treated simply as a convenience. At the same time, it would be churlish of us not to acknowledge the sophistication and elegance of Rosch's work, which is concerned with how humans categorize their world. In particular, she attacks the prevailing digital model of categorization, which consists of a logical conjunction of discrete criterial attributes. In its stead, she has proposed an analog model, where categories are composed of a core meaning (the prototype, the clearest case, or the best example of a category) which is surrounded by other members of decreasing similarity or "prototypeness." To test her model, she employs learning paradigms in experiments where subjects are taught a set of chromatic terms in the color domain, or a set of form names in the geometric domain, predicting that the names for focal (or prototypic) colors and shapes will be learned more easily than the names of nonfocal ones. Such hypotheses can only be tested with subjects who lack the relevant codes, and the Dani people of New Guinea provided exactly the right conditions under which Rosch could test her hypothesis.

The bulk of Rosch's chapter consists of a review of the relevant literature, and a description of her own (single-culture) previous work on categorization. Clearly, Rosch becomes a cross-cultural psychologist only when it suits her, but we don't mean this comment to sound nasty. In the best tradition of scientific inquiry, she has committed herself to an unfolding research program, and she will incorporate a cross-cultural dimension into the design of a study only if a question emerges that calls for such a development. While we respect her dedication, it must be pointed out that in research programs of this nature, "other" cultures have the same logical status as bits of laboratory equipment acquired to do a specific job. Unfortunately, such a treatment of culture often leads to the kind of methodological and ethical problems discussed earlier in this chapter. And yet, pure research is quite compatible with an involvement in the affairs of the culture under scrutiny, as Berry's work (discussed below), for instance, has shown. There is really no excuse for an experimenter's remaining totally aloof, and we would like to see all cross-cultural psychologists, particularly those engaged in "pure" research, build at least an element of "cultural payoff" into their studies.

Cultural Ecology. Earlier we alluded to the conceptual evasiveness that many research workers exhibit in the face of complex culture-personality relationships. Someone who is not afraid to grasp this particular nettle is John Berry, who has explicitly recognized that cultures are a uniquely human adaptation to recurrent ecological presses. It should be stressed that Berry is not proposing a simplistic theory of environmental determinism, but a sophisticated model in which ecological variables constrain, pressure, and nurture cultural forms which in turn react back on the physical environment. A good example of this process was the perfect balance of nature that apparently existed for thousands of years in Australia before the days of Captain Cook. Anthropologists have attributed this outstanding example of conservation to the cultural "rules" that determined where the inhabitants could live, what and when they could hunt, and who they could reproduce with (Elkin, 1964).

Ecological-cultural-behavioral models such as Berry's do not look for cause and effect relationships, but for feedback cycles that can best describe a functioning system. Such a theoretical perspective provides almost infinite points of entry for research. Berry's work has been in the domain of perceptual and cognitive differentiation—psychological processes that he sees as being closely linked with ecological and cultural forces. Because the model is given detailed presentation in Berry's chapter, we will here confine ourselves to making some general comments about his research program.

The value of taking a systemic approach has already been emphasized. Another feature worth noting is the use that Berry makes of traditional psychological tests under "exotic" conditions. As a by-product of his empirical work, Berry was forced early on in his career to consider the methodological problem of cross-cultural equivalence, and at least one of his contributions in this area has become a standard reference (Berry, 1969).

Berry has also successfully combined "pure" with action-oriented research. Thus the theory of psychological differentiation has been enriched by having "its limits tested" under unusual conditions (and may indeed require modification as a result). At the same time, the people with whom Berry has worked have benefited from his public stand on a number of issues vital to the preservation of their culture. Finally, the empirical results that Berry reports are undoubtedly "messy," and would leave many journal editors shaking their heads. And yet there is no doubt that denying publication to studies of this kind would be a serious disservice to psychology. In evaluating Berry's work we can see a good case for applying the negative handicap system proposed earlier in this chapter.

The three chapters dealing with empirical studies of perception provide a marked contrast in methodology, research styles, and underlying values. Cole was primarily interested in the "ecological relevance" (Sells, 1969) of his experimental procedures. Rosch was preoccupied with testing a relatively molecular theory, in contrast to Berry who was developing a general systems model encompassing the interrelationship between ecology, culture, and cognition. Once again, a fairly representative overview of the area has been achieved.

The Hologeistic Method

The papers by Precourt and Rohner are based in large part on the use of the Cross-Cultural Survey Method, also called the hologeistic method (Naroll, 1970). In very general terms, the method involves relating two or more variables as reported in ethnographies from all over the world. The number of ethnographies consulted is usually 100 or more. The social scientist using the method consults one of these original sources and records the ethnographer's comments about different variables, for instance, methods of child rearing and type of economy. There is then a coding procedure to put the observations into mathematical terms so that statistical analyses will be possible. The same variables are recorded for all the other ethnographies, and then they are interrelated to determine the degree of association among them. Some social scientists use the Human Relations Area Files (HRAF) which is a facility available at many large university libraries. The developers of HRAF have organized ethnographies into an easily usable filing system either on paper or on microfilm, and they have noted where information about different variables can be found. Other social scientists prefer to search through the original ethnographies themselves to find the information they are seeking. Except for this step, the people using HRAF versus original ethnographies engage in the same set of practices. The most sophisticated of the HRAF users, in fact, also consult original ethnographies since HRAF has not organized materials for all the world's societies on which there are records. The president of HRAF, Raoul Naroll, has often said that the files are only a start for a good cross-cultural study.

The hologeistic method (whether or not that specific term is employed) has been used most often by anthropologists, and Precourt and Rohner are members of this discipline. At the conference, however, they were in a decided minority amid their colleagues in psychology. Perhaps inevitably, these anthropologists were challenged with incisive questions and were pressed hard to defend the hologeistic method. They gave a good accounting of themselves in explaining progress on solving some of the problems with the method, eight of which are listed below. Questions one through four are covered in the available literature (e.g., Naroll and Cohen, 1970; Guthrie, 1971; Brislin, Lonner, and Thorndike, 1973). The last four were brought out more clearly at this conference than in any prior discussion or written treatment.

(1) Do correlations between two variables, such as initiation ceremonies and mother-son relationships, demonstrate a functional relation between the two, or

do they represent the diffusion of the two variables? Ancient societies have migrated and other societies have been established from them, giving societies in the hologeistic sample possible common historical roots. Put in statistical terms, can the societies in a hologeistic sample be considered independent when they have the same historical root? Without independence of observations, statistical tests should not be used. This is the familiar Galton's problem.

(2) Are there not likely to be errors in the available ethnographies since the people writing them have had different types of training, have participated in the society in different ways, have possessed differential command of the local language, and so on? An approach to a solution has been the use of data quality control indexes. Rohner, Dewalt, and Ness (1973) have explored data quality control in great detail, using data from the study discussed in Rohner's chapter.

(3) Will different people who study the original ethnographies be likely to code the material in quite different ways? Critics of coding practices point out that much information is lost in the transformation from an ethnographer's description to a coder's number on a scale.

(4) When large numbers of ethnographic accounts are coded and interrelated, won't some be statistically significant by chance alone? Will correlations that are *not* in line with an hypothesis be given as much attention as those in accordance with an hypothesis? We feel that Guthrie (1971) has written about these problems in a very penetrating manner, but that his insights have been met by a conspiracy of silence from hologeistic practitioners.

(5) What is the basis for ethnographers' decisions on the psychological states of the people they have investigated? In hologeistic studies, some of the variables coded are personality traits such as "dependence," "emotional stability," and "generosity" (see Rohner's chapter). The freedom with which anthropologists record their decisions about such traits, based only on their impressions, and the freedom with which hologeistic practitioners subsequently use them, is disturbing to psychologists. Members of this latter group would be hesitant to make more than tentative conclusions about such traits even after extensive cross-cultural adaptation of personality measurement techniques and assessment of large numbers of people in any one culture. Psychologists have fewer qualms about ethnographers' judgments about such society-wide variables as kinship or economic systems, but are unlikely to accept pronouncements on individual-difference variables like personality traits without seeing extensive documentation for the reasons behind each trait judgment.

(6) Will some conclusions for hologeistic studies be based on ethnographers' own common sense theories which they bring to their field site, and hence inevitably find? For instance, the hypothesis in Rohner's study that parental rejection causes distortion of normal personality development is undoubtedly held by most anthropologists. If they find support for the hypothesis in the

societies they study (especially if the "support" consists only of impressions), it is difficult to determine whether the reason is because the hypothesis is true or because they interpreted an ambiguous set of data to support their predilections.

(7) Are the correlations resulting from hologeistic methods being over-interpreted? The typical correlation coefficients relating two variables are in the vicinity of $r = \pm .30$, and if this is squared to show the percent of true variance accounted for, the resulting figure (called the coefficient of determination) is 9%. Consequently, the unaccountable variance is 91%. We feel that such percent-accounted-for figures should be the basis for arguments in discussion sections, not the significance level of the original correlation (see also Bakan, 1967, for criticisms of using significance levels as a basis for discussion). If they were so used, conclusions would be far more modest. The correlations reported in Chapter 10, Table 1, have a mean absolute value of .43, yielding an average coefficient of determination of 18.5%. The correlations in Precourt's study (the four used in his "results" section to support his hypothesis) have an average absolute value of .44 and thus an average coefficient of determination of 19.4%. The generous conclusion that can be made from such data is that a contribution has been made when even this small amount of variance can be accounted for. If these low figures are taken more seriously, however, then there will inevitably be additional efforts to find reasons for the now unaccountable variance, a figure heretofore completely ignored by hologeistic practitioners.

(8) Is there a lack of concern with the reliability of individual observations in hologeistic studies? Critics concerned with this point charge that, because the basis of every hologeistic study is the observations and reports of individual ethnographers, there should be reliability studies of such observations. Put more simply, do different ethnographers studying the same culture at the same point in time agree when they make observations about average age of weaning, method of payment for bridewealth, and so on? Naroll (1973) reported on one such study, and findings showed little reliability (i.e., consistency) in observations of the same society. The data quality control procedures (Naroll, 1962) can determine if there are gross systematic biases, but not the effects of ethnographers being just plain wrong in their observations in the first place.

We have been more harsh with the hologeistic method than most writings, partly so as to offset the overstated claims of others (Naroll, 1970) and to draw attention to still unsolved problems. We hope that the defense to our listing is not the familiar, "But despite these problems we still get statistical significance and interpretable results." Such a defense focuses attention only on the statistical rather the practical significance of the results, and it does not specify why the observed relations are not higher. The reasons for the unaccountable variance are neglected.

Earlier in this chapter we mentioned that cross-cultural research has more methodological issues to be solved than ordinary research done within one country. A study of the hologeistic method, and perhaps use of it in a small study, is a good way to communicate this point to students. Of course, the method involves the use of materials in a library and so actual travel to another culture is not necessary. Yet, if students learn the method by doing a study, and are still willing to engage in cross-cultural research despite the many methodological problems (like the eight we listed) with which they are inevitably faced, then we have new devotees who should be treasured. They will have entered the cross-cultural specialty only after careful consideration of its advantages and disadvantages.

It is as easy for anthropologists to be critical of the psychologist's parsimony and attempts at precise manipulation of variables as it is for psychologists to renounce the cross-cultural survey method as being too molar and perhaps inherently inaccurate. In defense of the hologeistic method (psychologically), it must be remembered that certain classic "survey-type" studies done by anthropologists served as starting points for many important cross-cultural studies in psychology. For example, part of Berry's model building, as he explains in his chapter, was dependent upon socialization data that Barry, Child, and Bacon (1959) extracted from ethnographies. It must also be remembered that the cross-cultural survey method has only recently benefited from the use of high-speed computers, and a growing number of practitioners are now making impressive gains through the use of the method.

Coming back to the present two papers, Precourt and Rohner have overcome some of the difficulties of hologeistic studies, and they report their efforts in their methodology sections. Precourt's formulation of a hidden curriculum is very useful and has been incorporated into the chapters by Draguns and Price-Williams. The multiple methodology procedure outlined by Rohner, earlier defended by Campbell (1968; Campbell and Fiske, 1959), is very sophisticated. Such studies will continue to provide important hypotheses worthy of further investigation with more robust methods.

Approaches from Different Perspectives

The last three chapters urge that the careful study of heretofore esoteric or unanalyzed areas can clarify our thinking about learning in a cross-cultural perspective. Juris Draguns discusses psychotherapy as practiced in a variety of cultures and chides scholars for considering psychotherapy only as a part of the abnormal or deviant. He supports his view that taking a much broader look at how the myriad forms of psychotherapy "fit" into a culture will yield ample rewards for any researcher interested in the phenomena of learning or social change. Unfortunately, because few "facts" have been established in this diffuse area of inquiry, Draguns is limited to a discussion of the issues that must be faced and the directions in which research could go. This has to be done without the benefit of a discussion of several model studies. He has summed up his position in a very colorful manner in an oral presentation which was later revised and published (Draguns, 1973), and which in many ways is a companion piece to this chapter. In that speech and subsequent article he dealt with psychopathology, but the argument is similar for different forms of psychotherapy:

> My own conviction is that, culturally, psychopathology is a caricature, an exaggeration, a reduction to absurdity of culturally shared mechanisms and trends. It is a twisted mirror through which we may peer at the cultural reality. With the help of suggestions presented here, I hope that we may come closer to learning its angle of refraction.

The central thesis of Price-Williams' contribution is that psychology may have to develop a new set of epistemological categories to describe adequately and to elucidate altered states of consciousness. There is an important question lurking behind the chapter: Is there one basic universal epistemological mode, with cultural variants, but in its essentials one system of mentation that characterizes the cognitive processes of human beings everywhere? Or are there several different epistemologies? This of course, is the very question that exercised Cole in Chapter 6; but the issue does gain a starker definition when considered within the context of altered states of consciousness, and this angle of approach avoids getting tangled up with racist distinctions between "civilized" and "primitive" mentalities.

The bulk of the chapter deals with the psychology of altered states of consciousness, approached through an analysis of the thought processes of non-Western cultures. The argument depends substantially on equating the "logic" of altered states with the cognitive rules of certain non-Western societies. We feel the following points may help place the chapter in proper perspective.

(1) All societies have members and institutions whose modes of "unaltered" thought fall outside the empirical, linear, "scientific" mold. For instance, the African spirit mediumship and spirit possession that Price-Williams refers to has many Western counterparts, of which the Catholic Church is only one example, particularly in practices such as taking the sacrament, appealing for the intercession of the saints, or expiating guilt through the confessional. On the reverse side, many so-called primitive cultures had a perfectly sound empirical understanding of the principles of astronomy, agriculture, navigation (e.g., Gladwin, 1970), architecture, and other pure and applied sciences. Elsewhere, Bochner (1973) has argued[5] that the basic differences between cultures reside in their value systems rather than in their epistemologies, but the exposition of that view here would take us too far afield.

(2) It is questionable whether altered states of consciousness can in fact be equated with the Datura, Zen, and other non-Western systems that Price-Williams reviews so perceptively. In any event, explaining the unknown in terms of a further unknown is unlikely to advance matters, unless of course one accepts the existence of an as yet unexplored epistemological domain. Yet that

is precisely what is at issue, and no one, not even one of our distinguished contributors, should be allowed to beg so big a question unchallenged.

(3) Price-Williams has with consummate skill and erudite scholarship conducted us on a fascinating tour of the highways and byways of non-Western thought and philosophy. However, he has neglected to explore areas that are closer to home both culturally and professionally—topics such as hypnosis, dreams, narco-analysis, and sensory deprivation. Many of these phenomena resemble altered states of consciousness at least to the same degree as do the more exotic experiences that Price-Williams quotes. Perhaps Price-Williams should be cautioned to first extend traditional methods and epistemologies in, say, hypnosis research before making his gigantic leap into the unknown. On the other hand, a breakthrough may be hastened if someone like Price-Williams has the courage to take that particular tiger by the tail, even if it turns out to actually be one in the end. Should it, however, turn out to be a rhinoceros, or better still a unicorn, then all of psychology will benefit from the new perspective afforded it. If the reader is mystified by this array of beastly metaphors, he may enlighten himself on these and other matters by perusing the essay under discussion.

What the Butler Saw

In all fields of endeavor, the goings-on in the corridors of power are regarded with a degree of horrid fascination, particularly by those excluded from these lofty regions. Nowhere is this more so than in the academic's attitude toward his eminence grise, the Journal Editor. We often pray to him, and even more frequently curse him, but seldom do we catch a glimpse into his mysterious domain. Who among us has not wondered about the strange and obscure rituals that our humble offerings are treated to. True, we are tranquilized with rejection rates, or beguiled with useful information on how to set out tables, quote references, or punctuate subheadings, but really useful feedback is rare. Lonner's chapter sets out to fill this gap in the lives of cross-cultural research workers.

Some of the generalizations Lonner is able to draw from his data source (evaluations by *Journal of Cross-Cultural Psychology* consultants) provide a bird's-eye view of cross-cultural psychology. For instance, the "inner sanctum" of the profession seems to be moving away from correlational (survey) studies to experimental (manipulated) designs, a move that can only be applauded. Lonner's tip-toe through his semiprivate correspondence also provides some confirmation for the meta-method status of cross-cultural psychology referred to earlier in this introduction, and there is a clear indication that if purist methodological standards were rigidly enforced, the Journal would become so slim as to disappear altogether if stood upright. Members of the profession as a whole, particularly those with a historical bent, will see this content analysis as a useful cumulative record of the development of a gradually forming professional identity.

Lonner's purpose in tallying the insights and (occasional) insults of those who reviewed so many papers is primarily directed toward graduate students intending to do cross-cultural research. That is, neophytes who find these archival data of interest may learn lessons from them. Newcomers may be able to consult the chapter and then start research programs by weeding out errors of design, or rationale, or sample selection *before* their studies are initiated, and not afterwards with dumbfounded apologies. We feel that Lonner's chapter can be examined profitably in conjunction with the treatment of ethics in cross-cultural research, discussed earlier. One approach to the problem of ethics is to publish such good research that leaders of different cultures will invite researchers back, and Lonner's chapter should help in achieving that goal.

SUMMARY AND CONCLUSION

This chapter began with a discussion of the main features, strengths, and problems of taking a cross-cultural perspective in psychology. The contents of the book were then briefly described and assessed. Several general themes about the nature of cross-cultural research emerged in the course of the discussion, in particular the view that cross-cultural psychology is essentially a meta-method that influences the way in which research questions are selected and subsequently translated into experimental operations. Thus although the studies described in the present volume cover a multitude of theoretical approaches, substantive areas, and data-gathering procedures, they are linked by all having a cultural variable as the experimental treatment or as a comparison point.

The studies that follow illustrate how, in the hands of a sensitive and ingenious researcher, a cross-cultural perspective can lead to a more extensive and a more forceful variation in the independent variable(s) than is usually possible in single-culture designs. Indeed, some problems can probably only be studied cross-culturally.

A decision to collect data in several cultures acts as a stimulus in at least two areas—"instrumentation" and theory building. Tests and procedures have to be extended, translated, made comparable and ecologically relevant, and in the process undergo an evaluation that is probably more stringent than the one that initially introduced these operations to the literature. Theoretical frameworks, likewise, are enriched by the scrutiny that they receive under "unusual" conditions. Finally, the ethical concomitants of psychological research gain a special definition under cross-cultural circumstances, and make it more difficult to ignore that all psychological practice, whether pure or applied, involves moral issues.

In evaluating the rigor of cross-cultural research, we proposed that some allowance be made for the immense complexities associated with working in a variety of cultural settings, but warned that this should not be interpreted as a mandate for sloppy research. More generally, we applauded the hardy few who grasp the nettle of the systemic interplay between ecology, culture, and behavior; and we raised our eyebrows at misguided attempts to discover THE universal key to all behavior everywhere. We criticized the tendency to translate one set of concepts into a different theoretical dialect, on the grounds that unless one or both of the "languages" were enriched, the exercise had little utility. At the same time, we also deplored the tendency of some psychologists to dispose of all that went before, which is closely allied with a desire to give birth to new, unique and world shattering sets of concepts. From time to time we voiced our opposition to what might be called mindless empiricism—the aimless gathering of "facts" in studies that scatter tests and measurements in the air, with data fallout who knows where.

In our comments we criticized, sometimes quite trenchantly, the essays that constitute this book. Our approach should not be interpreted as an unobtrusive index of the personal relationships we enjoy with our contributors, nor is it the manifestation of a death wish for the volume. Rather, it reflects our opinion that an open, critical and informed attitude toward the topics by all concerned, including ourselves, is more likely to achieve the scholarly aims of the contributors than a defensive or pseudo-laudatory approach.

THE FUTURE

In the past, the main source of knowledge about the interrelationship between cultural variables and individual behavior has come from cultural anthropology. Psychologists were, until quite recently, either not interested in this area, or felt that they were not sufficiently equipped to make a useful contribution. During the last 20 years the method of cross-cultural psychology has emerged to fill this gap, and the present book is representative of the kind of research that has been gradually gathering momentum. No doubt the specialty as a whole and we in particular have rushed into many places where angels fear to tread, but we have done so with our eyes wide open. It is an exciting field to be in, since so much remains to be done.

NOTES

1. We are grateful to Everett Kleinjans for bringing this essay to our attention.

2. The *Journal of Cross-Cultural Psychology* is distributed gratis to about 75 key institutions in countries that cannot afford to subscribe to many social science journals. This

includes all issues published to date, in agreement with and through the cooperation of the publisher, Sage Publications.

3. We are making this statement only about psychology, and not about all academic disciplines.

4. A good introduction to the behavioral approach in culture training can be found in Trifonovitch (1973). The volume of which this article is a part, *Topics in Culture Learning,* will never win a prize for being easily available to readers. Copies can be obtained at no charge by writing to the Director, Culture Learning Institute, East-West Center, Honolulu, Hawaii, 96822.

5. See Note 4 for information on obtaining the publication of which this article is a part.

REFERENCES

American Psychological Association (1973) Ethical Principles in the Conduct of Research with Human Participants. Washington, D.C.: American Psychological Association.

ARGYRIS, C. (1968) "Some unintended consequences of rigorous research." Psychological Bulletin 70: 185-197.

BAKAN, D. (1967) On Method. San Francisco: Jossey-Bass.

BARRY, H., I. CHILD, and M. BACON (1959) "Relation of child training to subsistence economy." American Anthropologist 61: 51-63.

BERRIEN, F. (1970) "A super-ego for cross-cultural research." International Journal of Psychology 5: 33-39.

BERRY, J. (1969) "On cross-cultural comparability." International Journal of Psychology 4: 119-128.

BOCHNER, S. (1969) "The Honolulu workshop-conference on psychological problems in changing societies." Australian Psychologist 3: 158-162.

– – – (1973) "The mediating man and cultural diversity," pp. 23-37 in R. Brislin (ed.) Topics in Culture Learning. Honolulu: East-West Center.

BRISLIN, R., W. LONNER, and R. THORNDIKE (1973) Cross-Cultural Research Methods. New York: John Wiley.

CAMPBELL, D. (1968) "A cooperative multinational opinion sample exchange." Journal of Social Issues 24(2): 245-258.

––– and D. FISKE (1959) "Convergent and discriminant validity by the multitrait-multimethod matrix." Psychological Bulletin 56: 81-105.

CHAPANIS, N. and A. CHAPANIS (1964) "Cognitive dissonance: five years later." Psychological Bulletin 61: 1-22.

CRONBACH, L. (1957) "The two disciplines of scientific psychology." American Psychologist 12: 671-684.

DeLAMATER, J., R. HEFNER and R. CLIGNET [eds.] (1968) Social Psychological Research in Developing Countries. Journal of Social Issues 24, 2.

DRAGUNS, J. (1973) "Comparisons of psychopathology across cultures: issues, findings, directions." Journal of Cross-Cultural Psychology 4: 9-47.

EIDE, I. [ed.] (1970) Students as Links Between Cultures. Oslo: UNESCO and the International Peace Research Institute.

ELKIN, A. (1964) The Australian Aborigines. Garden City, N.Y.: Doubleday Anchor.

FISHBEIN, M. and I. AJZEN (1972) "Attitudes and opinions." Annual Review of Psychology 23: 487-544.

GLADWIN, T. (1970) East Is a Big Bird. Cambridge, Mass.: Belknap Press.

GLASER, E. and S. TAYLOR (1973) "Factors influencing the success of applied research." American Psychologist 28: 140-146.

GUTHRIE, G. (1971) "Unexpected correlations and the cross-cultural method." Journal of Cross-Cultural Psychology 2: 315-323.

HARRINGTON, R. (1973) "One man's special island." Parade, January 7: 21-22.

JENSEN, A. (1969) "How much can we boost IQ and scholastic achievement?" Harvard Educational Review 39: 1-123.

JORGENSON, C. (1973) "I.Q. tests and their educational supporters." Journal of Social Issues 29(1): 33-40.

KEESING, R. and F. KEESING (1971) New Perspectives in Cultural Anthropology. New York: Holt, Rinehart & Winston.

KELMAN, H. (1968) A Time to Speak. San Francisco: Jossey-Bass.

LEVINE, R. and D. CAMPBELL (1972) Ethnocentrism. New York: John Wiley.

McCLELLAND, D. (1973) "Testing for competence rather than for 'intelligence.' " American Psychologist 28: 1-14.

McELWAIN, D. and G. KEARNEY (1970) Queensland Test Handbook. Melbourne: Australian Council for Educational Research.

McGUIRE, W. (1972) "Social psychology," pp. 219-242 in P. Dodwell (ed.) New Directions in Psychology 2. Middlesex, England: Penguin.

MEEHL, P. (1954) Clinical Vs. Statistical Prediction. Minneapolis: University of Minnesota Press.

MEREDITH, G. (1969) "The East-West Center conference-workshop on psychological problems in changing societies." International Journal of Psychology 4: 143-145.

MORRIS, R. (1960) The Two-Way Mirror. Minneapolis: University of Minnesota Press.

NAROLL, R. (1962) Data Quality Control. New York: Macmillan.

――― (1970) "What have we learned from cross-cultural surveys?" American Anthropologist 72: 1227-1288.

――― (1973) Remarks made at a session on hologeistic studies, Society for Cross-Cultural Research, Philadelphia (February).

――― and R. COHEN [eds.] (1970) A Handbook of Method in Cultural Anthropology. New York: Natural History Press.

National Liaison Committee [on Foreign Student Admissions] (1971) The Foreign Graduate Student: Priorities for Research and Action. New York: College Entrance Examination Board.

PORTEUS, S. (1965) Porteus Maze Tests: Fifty Years Application. Palo Alto, Calif.: Pacific Books.

――― S. BOCHNER, J. RUSSELL, and K. DAVID (1967) "Age as a factor in Australid mentality." Perceptual and Motor Skills 25: 3-16. (Mongr. Suppl. I-V25).

RING, K. (1967) "Experimental social psychology: some sober questions about some frivolous values." Journal of Experimental Social Psychology 3: 113-123.

ROHNER, R., B. DeWALT, and R. NESS (1973) "Ethnographer bias in cross-cultural research: an empirical study." Behavior Science Notes 8(4): 275-317.

SELLS, S. (1969) "Ecology and the science of psychology," in E. Willems and H. Raush (eds.) Naturalistic Viewpoints in Psychological Research. New York: Holt, Rinehart & Winston.

SHERIF, M. (1967) Group Conflict and Cooperation: Their Social Psychology. London: Routledge & Kegan Paul.

――― and C. SHERIF (1969) Social Psychology. New York: Harper & Row.

STRODTBECK, F. (1964) "Considerations of meta-method in cross-cultural studies." American Anthropologist 66: 223-229.

TAGUMPAY-CASTILLO, G. (1968) "A view from Southeast Asia," pp. 20-49 in S.E.A.D.A.G., American Research on Southeast Asian Development: Asian and American Views. New York: The Asia Society.

TRIFONOVITCH, G. (1973) "On cross-cultural orientation techniques," pp. 38-47 in R. Brislin (ed.) Topics in Culture Learning. Honolulu, Hawaii: East-West Center.

WALSTER, E., E. BERSCHEID, D. ABRAHAMS, and V. ARONSON (1967) "Effectiveness of debriefing following deception experiments." Journal of Personality and Social Psychology 6: 371-380.

PART ONE. LEARNING ANOTHER CULTURE

Chapter 1

CULTURE TRAINING, COGNITIVE COMPLEXITY
AND INTERPERSONAL ATTITUDES

HARRY C. TRIANDIS

University of Illinois at Urbana

THE PROBLEM

A major social problem of our time concerns the poor interpersonal relationships among individuals who belong to different cultures. Aggression is common across racial, ethnic, religious, and linguistic boundaries. The problem can be seen vividly in the tensions of police-citizen relations of the American ghetto, the separation of Belgian universities by language, the communal conflict in Northern Ireland, the language riots of India, and in many other settings. Even in situations where cooperation is highly desirable, such as when a husband-wife pair or a boss-subordinate pair consists of individuals from different cultures, or a clinician interacts with his client, cultural differences lead to major interpersonal difficulties. In numerous other settings—schools, industries, bars, hospitals, neighborhoods, city halls, and religious establishments—intercultural relations are difficult.

The present paper will examine some ideas that may prove helpful in improving intercultural relations. We define a *cultural group* as a group of individuals who speak a mutually understandable dialect. Such groups have unique ways of perceiving their social environment which Triandis et al. (1972b) analyzed under the label "subjective culture." When people belong to different cultures or have different subjective cultures, interpersonal interaction is painfully unpleasant; however, when individuals are trained to understand the subjective culture of other groups, there is some evidence of improved intergroup relationships (Fiedler et al., 1971).

INTRODUCTORY THEORETICAL CONSIDERATIONS

It is convenient to distinguish two classes of factors that can cause poor interpersonal relationships between members of two cultural groups. First there are *external* factors which surround the relationship. These can be real differences in the goals of the two groups or sharp differences in the distribution of resources. For example, when one group is in a position to exploit the other economically, they have actually different goals and the uneven distribution of resources is real. This is what LeVine and Campbell (1972) call realistic conflict. Second, there are *internal* factors, which can be examined as difficulties in the relationship which occur because of different perceptions of the environment, which lead to misunderstandings, disconfirmed expectations, and perceived role conflict.

The external factors usually lead to internal factors causing conflict. For example, when group A exploits group B, it is very likely that group A will develop cognitive supports for its action. Such supports can be in the form of "the Bs are inferior and deserve to be exploited" or "the Bs need my help because they cannot take care of themselves, and if there are any advantages to me from the relationship, they are fair returns for the work I do." The latter form of rationalization is well known in colonial history.

The elimination of the external factors described above requires a rearrangement of economic and institutional factors. The change is more likely to come through the efforts of economists, or through political processes (both gradual and revolutionary). The psychologist is better equipped to deal with the internal factors. Here examination of the multiple goals of groups might result in the discovery of superordinate goals (Sherif et al., 1961), and the focusing on such goals can lead to a more effective relationship and greater cooperation.

In the present essay we are not concerned with psychological reactions to the above mentioned external factors, or the interactions of external and internal factors. Rather, we limit our concern to a problem that is more subtle and occurs even when external factors do not operate to cause conflict. The problem is that members of different cultural groups develop idiosyncratic ways of looking at their social environment. Thus, even when external factors do not operate, difficulties occur because of these differences in the perception of the social environment.

Some Specific Examples

We propose to proceed inductively. Let us consider some examples of intercultural difficulties. These will lead to the development of a set of principles for the analysis of intergroup conflict due to differences in subjective culture.

A common problem in cross-cultural encounters involves the expectations people bring to social situations. For example, in most cultures servants do most of the domestic tasks, including the cleaning of shoes. However, in the United States cleaning ladies typically do not clean shoes. Now if a person from another culture visits the United States and asks an American cleaning lady to clean his shoes, she is likely to perceive his request as inappropriate. The crucial question is, however, what attributions she makes concerning his behavior. If she attributes it to "ignorance of American customs," she may not be upset. On the other hand, if she attributes it to a personality syndrome (i.e., the visitor is domineering, or obnoxious), there will be damage to the interpersonal relationship.

More subtle difficulties arise when a person from another culture expects respect to be given to him because of his age, profession, or other status, and expects this respect to be manifested in "different speech"—soft, polite, hesitant. An exuberant American is likely to be loud, and what is worse, critical, when the visitor deviates from his expectations. In such a case the damage to the relationship can be irreparable when the person comes from a culture where superiors have been trained never to forget the "insubordination" of their subordinates.

Note that both of the above examples can be analyzed in terms of behaviors appropriate for a role. In the first, the visitor assumes that his role (master-servant) allows him to ask the cleaning lady to clean his shoes; the American cleaning-lady/guest-of-the-household role, however, is incompatible with this behavior. In the second example, the old-to-young-man role, or the expert-to-apprentice role, leads the visitor to expect a particular quality in the interaction. When this is violated it produces problems.

Many of these problems are not immediately visible, because relations across cultures are often formal, polite, and remote; nevertheless, the cooperation pattern between individuals does suffer, and the relations are not as effective as they might have been without these "unpleasant incidents." Any one of these incidents does not damage a relationship permanently, but a series of them often does, and one of the most common responses is flight. The disgusted visitor leaves and never returns.

Understanding these human interactions requires closer analysis.

The More Detailed Analysis

A major problem in intercultural behavior is that each interactor is unable to control the behavior of the other. He cannot do so because he does not understand the causes of the other's behavior. He does not know, for example, how the other analyzes his social environment and what constitutes a reward for the other. In short, he makes *wrong attributions* concerning the behavior of the other.

Effective intercultural relations require *isomorphic attributions.* Isomorphic attributions correspond to the idea: "If I had been raised in that culture and had had the kinds of experiences that he has had, I would do exactly what he did."

Since a person sees his own behavior as controlled by external factors (Jones and Nisbett, 1971) and usually reasonable, as well as desirable, isomorphic attributions result in a positive evaluation of the other.

Interpersonal competence means, in part, that a person is able to reinforce the other. If a person is to reinforce another, he needs to control resources. He also needs to know what is reinforcing to the other. In intercultural encounters, part of the difficulty stems from ignorance of what is reinforcing to the other. One knows what is reinforcing the other, in part, if one knows his subjective culture.

In intercultural exchanges we often do not know what is reinforcing, because we do not know the exact persons, situations, and so on which make an exchange rewarding or unrewarding. The ability to make isomorphic attributions means exactly that—the person can correctly infer what is likely to be reinforcing, to what extent, under what conditions, and the like, and hence he is able to reinforce the other.

An example from the files of Greek psychiatrist, George Vassiliou, will illustrate the role of attributions in intercultural behavior. It is well known that Greeks perceive supervisory roles as more "bossy" than do Americans, who tend to favor participatory procedures (Triandis and Vassiliou, 1972a). When an American who favors employee participation interacts with a Greek who expects and wants a "bossy boss," one can get the sequence of behavior described by Vassiliou:

Behavior	Attribution
American: How long will it take you to finish this report?	*American:* I asked him to participate.
	Greek: His behavior makes no sense. He is the boss. Why doesn't he tell me?
Greek: I do not know. How long should it take?	*American:* He refuses to take responsibility.
American: You are in the best position to analyze time requirements.	*Greek:* I asked him for an order.
	American: I press him to take responsibility for own actions.
	Greek: What nonsense! I better give him an answer.
Greek: 10 days.	*American:* He lacks the ability to estimate time; this time estimate is totally inadequate.
American: Take 15. Is it agreed you will do it in 15 days?	*American:* I offer a contract.
	Greek: These are my orders: 15 days.

In fact the report needed 30 days of regular work. So the Greek worked day and night, but at the end of the 15th day, he still needed one more day's work.

Behavior	Attribution
American: Where is the report?	American: I am making sure he fulfills his contract.
	Greek: He is asking for the report.
Greek: It will be ready tomorrow.	(Both attribute that it is not ready.)
American: But we had agreed it would be ready today.	American: I must teach him to fulfill a contract.
	Greek: The stupid, incompetent boss! Not only did he give me the wrong orders, but he does not even appreciate that I did a 30-day job in 16 days.
The Greek hands in his resignation.	The American is surprised.
	Greek: I can't work for such a man.

The above example shows that at almost every point the behavior of one member of the intercultural dyad leads to an attribution that does not match the attribution of the actor. This is an extreme example of nonisomorphic attributions. In such situations the behavior of each is not under the control of reinforcements that the other can provide, because they are working at cross-purposes.

Isomorphic attributions are not an unmixed blessing. When a person "knows that he knows" what makes the other behave, he is likely to be able to control the other's reinforcements, and hence his behavior; but this kind of knowledge, in most human relationships, is still very limited. The other often does not behave as expected. When this happens, among people who are supposed to be able to control each other, the effect on the relationship is devastating. In many families, when people think they have a good understanding of the bases of other people's behavior, such failure of prediction is the cause of irreparable damage to relationships. Thus, we note that in traditional Greek villages there are many more cases of brothers not being on speaking terms with each other, fathers disowning the children, brothers killing their sisters, and the like than occur in the United States. Here behavior that breaks norms leads to devastating interpersonal consequences.

In traditional societies there are often very strong norms for behaving according to ingroup norms. The traditional Greeks even have a special word, philotimos, to describe the person who behaves according to the norms of his ingroup. This is the most valued attribute of any human, and a random sample of Athenians used it to describe themselves more frequently than any other attribute (Vassiliou and Vassiliou, 1966).

It is easy to see why in traditional societies norms and roles are unusually clear and sanctions are certain. In such societies there is much greater interdependence among relatives. There are no insurance companies to take care of the sick and old; their relatives do. Thus, if these relatives were to behave unreliably, life would be characterized by uncertainty and anxiety. By having strong norms and enforcing them with violent certitude, people in such societies ensure that others do in fact behave according to norms.

One great difficulty in intercultural encounters occurs when the member from culture A is used to weak norms, and the member from culture B is used to strong norms, concerning a particular behavior. Here a person is likely to behave in ways which would be "inexcusable" from the other's perspective.

It is, thus, not only when norms are different that intercultural encounters can lead to interpersonal hostility. When the *strength* of the connections between norms and behavior is not the same, the effects can be equally serious. Norm disagreements, furthermore, are only one element that causes problems.

To summarize, then, effective intercultural behavior requires similar differentiations of the significant aspects of the social situation, accurate knowledge of the way one person differs in his attributions from another, accurate expectations, similar role definitions, and similar strengths in the connections between norms or roles on the one hand, and behavior on the other. The effective intercultural individual knows how to analyze the behavior of the other, and he focuses on the rewards and punishments the others will experience for particular behaviors. He attributes such behavior to complex interactions of situational and subjective culture variables rather than merely to the culture of the other.

THE CONTENT AND STRUCTURE OF INTERCULTURAL DIFFICULTIES

It is again convenient to distinguish two kinds of difficulties: in content and in structure. A difference in content is concerned with the way a particular behavior is defined, as for example, when person P defines the behavior as a "request" and person O as "an order." A difference in structure concerns the cognitive structures involved in the interactions, as for example, when a person sees much difference between a stimulus person with a Ph.D. and a person with an M.A., while another person places both stimulus persons in the category "educated people" and sees no difference between them.

The distinction between content and structure is not always easy to make, but it is made here to allow examination of two bodies of social psychological literature: the analysis of subjective culture (Triandis et al., 1972b) and studies of cognitive complexity.

There is considerable evidence that when people use words with different meanings they have trouble communicating. Triandis (1959, 1960a, 1960b) did both field studies and laboratory experiments which showed that similarities in the meaning of words lead to the perception of the achievement of effective communication and also to interpersonal attraction. Back, Bunker, and

Dunnagan (1972) found that, in a discussion group that examined the relationship of "science and society," those who had shared similar meanings of key words, like "model" or "empirical research," were able to communicate with each other and remained together, while those who had different meanings became frustrated and left the group.

While differences in the meaning of words are fundamental, other kinds of differences in subjective culture can also result in interpersonal difficulties. Subjective culture includes norms, roles, attitudes, values, and many other concepts. To explore the relevance of these concepts to interpersonal relationships, we need to understand how they are related to interpersonal behavior. The sections that follow will present a paradigm relating several elements of subjective culture to behavior. It is likely that the elements of this paradigm are the most crucial in interpersonal relationships; that is, when people differ in one of these elements, this leads to much difficulty. In short, the paradigm is presented as a means of examining a more limited set of concepts than is usually used by social scientists. Campbell (1963) pointed out that social scientists use about 80 concepts, such as acquired drive, attitude, norm, role, and value, to describe consistencies in social situations which result in consistencies in human responses. The bewildering number of such acquired behavioral dispositions used by social scientists makes cummulative work difficult. The paradigm has the virtue that it focuses on only some of these concepts, and by implication ignores most of the others. It can be used as a guide in data collection to discover the most important differences in subjective culture. These differences can then be used for intercultural training. However, such training also has the effect of increasing cognitive complexity, because it provides new ways of looking at the world.

Cultures differ in the amount of differentiation that characterizes them. It seems likely that the greater the similarity in the differentiations made by two individuals, the more effectively they will interact. In the sections below, then, we will also examine cultural differences in differentiation and their implications for cross-cultural training. From these reviews we will be able to describe a form of cultural training called a *culture assimilator,* which is a programmed learning approach designed to increase isomorphic attributions between members of two cultures. It accomplishes this by giving information about both content (differences in norms, roles, etc.) and structure, kinds of differentiations that are needed to understand the point of view of the other culture.

PARADIGM FOR RESEARCH ON INTERPERSONAL BEHAVIOR

Kuhn (1962) has argued that science is not a series of discoveries or methodologies, but a series of paradigms—socially determined ways of looking at phenomena. Immature sciences tend to utilize a large number of paradigms. Scientific work done in such cases is typically noncumulative, and results obtained by one scientist have small effects on the scientific community. When a paradigm is finally accepted, the work becomes cummulative; but scientific communication is no longer understandable to those who do not share the paradigm, since such communication tends to be stated in a language idiosyncratic to the paradigm. Scientific revolutions involve the rejection of old paradigms. After a scientific revolution, old findings, experiments, and instruments are seen differently and are used for different purposes. A paradigm cannot be falsified; however, large bodies of data inconsistent with it increase dissatisfaction with it. When a new paradigm is offered that better accounts for a larger number of observations, the old paradigms are abandoned.

From Kuhn's perspective, social psychology is an immature science. There are at least three major paradigms, and some minor variations, which can readily be identified. The paradigms can be seen most sharply by contrasting two recent textbooks, McGuiness (1970) and Stotland and Canon (1972). McGuiness (1970) employs a stimulus-response contiguity and reinforcement paradigm that has been widely used in psychology (Skinner, 1953), sociology (Homans, 1961), and social psychology (Berger and Lambert, 1968). A variation considers social exchange, as proposed by Thibaut and Kelley (1959) and elaborated by Foa (1971). Social learning mechanisms, such as those deriving from imitation (Bandura and Walters, 1963), vicarious experiences (Berger, 1962), and the percentage of the time a person reinforces another (Byrne, 1969) are elaborations within that paradigm.

A second recent text (Stotland and Canon, 1972) uses a paradigm emphasizing cognitive determinants. Greatly influenced by Tolman (1951), Lewin (1951), and Deutsch (1968), it focuses on cognitive determinants of action. At the animal level, Irwin (1971) and Bolles (1972) have provided the most important statements of this paradigm. At the human level, major representative viewpoints include Miller, Galanter, and Pribram (1960), Locke (1968), and Nuttin (1972). Reviews by Scheerer (1954) and Zajonc (1968) document this tradition in social psychology. Major theories of interpersonal behavior (e.g., Heider, 1958) and attitude change (e.g., Festinger, 1957) in social psychology, and an important theory of action by Dulany (1968), modified by Fishbein (1967), as well as the work of Ryan (1970), are in this tradition.

A third paradigm reflects the work of sociologists and anthropologists. The emphasis is on *customs, norms, roles,* and the subject's *self,* which is formed through social interaction. Summaries may be found in Sarbin (1954) and Sarbin and Allan (1968).

What follows is one person's view of a single paradigm combining the strengths of these three paradigms.

Theoretical Concepts

Acts. An act is a socially defined pattern of muscle movements. Specific acts, such as hitting, taking off one's hat, or spitting at somebody's face, are too brief, subject to too many influences, and too numerous to constitute the appropriate primitive terms of good theory. Such acts do not have meaning in themselves. They acquire meaning only from the contexts in which they occur. Furthermore, they are typically organized into patterns that reflect particular goals and intentions.

A *goal* is an outcome of a sequence of specific acts. Individuals can report goals under instructions such as "What are you trying to do?" or "What do you hope to get?"

A *behavioral intention* is a cognitive antecedent of an act. Answers to the above two questions may yield information about either goals or intentions. The first question might be answered, for example, by a subject with the sentences "I am trying to reach my mother on the phone" (goal) or "I am calling my mother" or "I intend to speak to my mother." The second question might result in "I hope to get my mother on the phone" or "I intend to speak to my mother on the phone."

Acts are obviously complex. They differ in a number of ways, such as in duration, intensity, frequency, and probability of occurrence. Each of these attributes of acts can be used as dependent variables for the paradigm, and the expectation is that results will be different for each dependent variable. For example, Farina, Chapnick, Chapnick, and Misiti (1972) showed that radical subjects administered intensive shocks to conservatives, but the correlation of intensity and duration was -.56. On the other hand, conservative subjects administered shocks that were both relatively intense and of long duration (r of .49) to radicals. Berkowitz has also found different patterns of results in laboratory studies of aggression, for the duration and intensity dependent variables.

The frequency of the act is in part a function of how natural it is for the particular organism. Seligman (1970) has discussed the tendency of rats to associate tastes with illness but not with footshock, while pigeons peck in the absence of a contiguity between pecking and grain. In short, the operant level of the pecking response is high enough for the pigeon that it may follow different determinants from an act which occurs infrequently and for which the animal is not prepared.

Intentions. Intentions are of two kinds: specific and general. Acts correspond to *specific intentions.* When a subject tries to reach his mother on the phone, he lifts the receiver, dials, listens for the dial tone, and so on. This pattern of acts is organized, sequential, and specific to his goal. Several specific intentions may be manifestations of a *general intention*. For example, the general intention "to show concern" may be expressed in the specific intention "to call mother." Or, the general intention "to obtain help" might be expressed by the same specific intention. General intentions are sufficiently few in number to permit an adequate scientific analysis.

We must note now that there are several dimensions of such intentions, resulting in several types of intentions. The several types of intentions will be discussed in greater detail later. They were extracted through factor analysis (Triandis, 1964, 1967). Three dimensions were found in Greece, India, Peru, Taiwan, Japan, and the United States (Triandis et al., 1972b), while each cultural group also had culture-specific dimensions (Triandis, Vassiliou, and Nassiakou, 1968). The three culture-common dimensions were *seeking versus avoiding solidarity, seeking versus avoiding intimacy,* and *superordination versus subordination.* These three dimensions suggest a classification of intentions according to high versus low on solidarity, high versus low on intimacy, and high superordination, no superordination or subordination, and high subordination. This is a 2 x 2 x 3 or 12 cell classification. Examples: in the high, high, high cell, "to take care of," "to protect"; low, high, high cell, "to laugh at"; low, low, high cell, "to ignore," "to inspect work of"; low, low, low cell, "to plan ways to put him down."

Such general intentions are sufficiently few to allow us to develop a theory concerning when they occur. Fishbein (1967) has pointed out, however, that the more specific the intention, the better the prediction of behavior. We, therefore, propose a two-stage prediction of the behavior: first, by predicting the general intention; second, by predicting the specific. The general intention depends on the *social situation*. If two individuals, P and O, have promotively inter-dependent goals, so that when one reaches his goals the other does also, then solidarity tends to increase. When the relationship between them has been promotively interdependent over a long period of time, then the intentions have the additional attribute of intimacy. When the interdependence is contrient, so that when one reaches his goals the other does not, the intentions are both low in solidarity and formal. Special social situations, such as placing P and O in isolation in a small booth for three days (Altman and Haythorn, 1965) tend to compress time, and result in high levels of intimacy, although they do not reach the level typical of best friends.

The social situation is also characterized by each individual's control of resources. If one person has access to more resources than the other, he is likely to act in a superordinate manner, while the reverse is true if his resources are more limited than those of the other. Thus, three parameters of the social situation—type of goal interdependence, length of time of relationship, and relative access to resources—result in the 12 types of general intentions mentioned above.

The paradigm described here is an open system in which the antecedents involve the type of interdependence, the length of the relationship, and the relative access to resources. These parameters result in general intentions. Specific intentions depend on *previous learning* of particular responses, the *ability* of the person to carry out an act, his *affect* toward the act, and his *perception of the consequences* of the act.

Relationships Among the Concepts and Their Mathematical Representations

The reader will quickly get lost in the complexities of the paradigm unless he is helped by some simple mathematical statements, which will allow him to pay attention to essentials. We propose to use a set of simultaneous equations to represent the major relationships among the primitive terms of the paradigm. We will utilize Latin letters for the primitive terms, and Greek letters for the weights attached to these terms.

The Probability of an Act (P_a)

$$P_a = [\alpha H + \beta (BI)] (F) \qquad (1)$$

where P_a = the act potential, a measure that predicts the probability of an act
  H = the "habit" of the organism to emit this act
  BI = the behavioral intention to emit the act
  F = facilitating conditions, such as the person's ability to perform the act, relative to the difficulty of the act.

Equation 1 states that the act potential is higher, the greater the "habit," which can be indexed by the frequency of occurrence of the act in the previous history of the organism. Such a "habit" may be high for several reasons. The act might be naturally occurring for the particular animal, in the sense that pecking is a frequent response for a pigeon; or the animal might have received much reinforcement in the past for emitting this act; or the animal in the past might have developed expectations that acting in this way would lead to reinforcement or the size of the previously received reinforcement was large, and so on. For our purposes the causes of high H are not important. It is sufficient to know that the organism has frequently emitted this act in the past. We might obtain the best measurement of H by counting the number of times, in the life of the organism, that the act has appeared. Because obtaining this information for humans is impractical, we may have to settle for a self-report, by the subject, of how frequently he has done something. Thus, we might ask, "Did you ever spit in somebody's face?" If he says, "Yes," we might ask, "How many times, in your life, do you think you have done this?" If we obtain this information from many subjects, and convert the scores to standard score form, we might enter Equation 1 with a score that has no "units." The obtained P_a, then, would also be in standard form and would predict the relative probability of the act for the observed population of subjects.

Equation 1 also indicates that the act potential is proportional to the behavioral intention (BI) corresponding to the act (e.g., the intention to spit in somebody's face). Finally, the person's ability to carry out the act relative to the difficulty of the act is multiplied by the sum of the habit (H) plus behavioral intention, (BI) terms. If the person is gagged, for instance, he may not be able to spit in anybody's face, no matter how frequently he has done it in the past or what his level of behavioral intentions might be.

The two coefficients, alpha and beta, reflect the extent to which the act is overlearned, automatic, or deliberate, or requires thought, planning, and so on (the more deliberate, the larger the beta). Alpha is also a function of the social situation and may reflect individual differences. The more the social situation resembles situations in which the act has occurred in the past, the larger the alpha. Some individuals may be more "creatures of habit" than others, so we might predict better if we use a larger alpha in the case of these specific individuals. The betas also depend on the social situation and on individual differences (personality). When the social situation is novel and the behavior has not yet become "automatic," the beta weight will be larger; some individuals intentionally try "new ways" and value new behavior patterns, thus suppressing the relative size of alpha in relation to beta.

When the subject is highly aroused, as in situations of social facilitation or anxiety, the size of the alpha weight becomes much larger than the size of the beta weight. As stated earlier, behaviors that are overlearned have a large alpha weight. Arousal increases it further, so that, for these behaviors, arousal leads to improved performance. Novel behaviors have nonsignificant alpha weights, and when arousal increases the alpha weight, there is interference with the novel behavior, hence a deterioration in performance. This is consistent with Zajonc's (1965) analysis of social facilitation, as well as with observations of behavior under panic. In the latter case, typically, people "do not think," but behave according to overlearned patterns, which might often be counterproductive.

The way α and β may vary from moment to moment is illustrated from the writer's experience with a Japanese lady psychologist. Here behavioral intentions and habits mixed to determine walking in an interesting pattern. On a previous trip to Japan, the writer had met this Japanese psychologist. Recognizing her, he began a conversation while walking toward the hotel where an international congress was to take place. But we soon stopped walking. Analysis of the circumstances suggested the reason. The lady, in the proper Japanese manner, was in the habit of walking behind men; the writer, in the proper Western manner, was in the habit of walking at the same level or slightly behind a lady.

Result: A clash of habits, which resulted in a standstill. At once the writer's behavioral intentions took hold of his walking behavior: "In Rome you do as the Romans do," hence he walked slightly ahead and progress was normal, until his attention to this matter no longer focused on walking and the well-established habits "unintentionally" again controlled his behavior. Again we came to a standstill. Again, the writer's behavioral intentions took hold of the behavior and again we made normal progress toward the hotel.

Here, then, we have an example of increasing and decreasing relative influence of behavioral intentions and habits, which could best be explained by a complex mathematical model, with feedback loops, and a switch from habits to behavioral intentions after every stop. Much behavior may well be under similar influences, and its mathematical description may require such a complex set of considerations.

The Determinants of Behavioral Intentions. In the next equation we follow closely Fishbein's (1967) adaptation of Dulany's (1964) theory. We propose that

$$I = \gamma (S) + \delta (A) + \epsilon (C) \tag{2}$$

where S = the social determination of the behavioral intention

A = the affect attached to the behavior itself

C = the value of the perceived consequences of the behavior.

By social determinants of the behavior (S) we mean the norms, roles, and general behavioral intentions that derive from the relationship between our subject and other people. In addition, we include the "contractual arrangements" made by our subject with other people, and his conceptions of behavior consistent with his self-concept.

For a specific example let us return to "spitting at another." In some cultures a simulation of this act is a method used to protect the other from the "evil eye." While only socially determined roles allow one to engage in this behavior (e.g., priests may do so in the Greek orthodox church), it is also engaged in by other people in specifiable roles (e.g., old ladies spit at young children who appear unusually cute). *Norms* are beliefs that certain behavioral patterns are appropriate for a specified group of people. *Roles* are beliefs that certain behaviors are appropriate for persons holding a particular position in a social system. Thus, norms apply to all members of a group, while roles apply only to some. A *custom* is a pattern of recurring socially approved behaviors. *Norms* are typically related to some *value*. A *value* is a desirable state of affairs. For example, when the old ladies spit at the child, the underlying value is the child's good health and welfare. The belief is that this act will lead to this value. The behavior is normative among Greek villagers and particularly appropriate for certain roles (priest). Thus, all these elements combine to provide one form of social determination of the behavioral intention.

General behavioral intentions are also part of the determination of specific intentions. As discussed earlier, general intentions depend on the type of interdependence, length of the relationship, and relative access to resources between two individuals. If the general intention is "to help," when other social determinants are consistent one might get the behavioral intention "to spit in his face." On the other hand, if the general intention were "to ignore," the latter behavioral intention would not occur.

Contractual arrangements are often very specific. An agreement between P and O to meet at 8:00 p.m. is an example of such an arrangement. Such arrangements can become goals which guide a chain of behavioral intentions, such as to walk to the car, enter, start the ignition, and so on, all done a few minutes before 8 p.m.

The *self-concept* consists of self-attributed traits and behavior patterns. If a person considers himself "kind," he would be more likely to use behavioral intentions consistent with this self-concept than if he thought of himself as "aloof." Eisen (1972) found that high self-esteem boys behave honestly. Certain behaviors appear to be more consistent with a person's self-concept than others. For example, the behavior "typing an article" is more consistent with this writer's self-conception than the behavior "hitting somebody." In short, a person might think of himself as the sort of individual who does type articles, but not the sort who hits others. These conceptions, then, facilitate or inhibit particular behavioral intentions.

Cues associated with any behavior, including the cognitive representation of the behavior as a behavioral intention, become associated, probably under the laws of classical conditioning, with certain pleasant or unpleasant outcomes. Thus, a particular configuration of emotions becomes activated at the thought of the behavior. This is the affect (A) associated with the behavior. Bolles (1972) represents this component with $E_{s-s*} \cdot V_{s*}$, where E_{s-s*} is the expectancy that a certain situation will be contiguous with an outcome s*, and V_{s*} is the value of this outcome. The more pleasant the situation associated with the behavior, the more positive the emotions (affect) associated with the behavior.

The value of the perceived consequences (C) is a function of the sum of the products of the subjective probability (P_c) that a particular consequence will follow a behavior, and the value of (or affect attached to) that consequence (V_c). Thus, following the decision theorist, as well as Peak (1955), Rosenberg (1956), and Fishbein (1963), we propose that:

$$C = \sum_{i=1}^{n} P_{c_i} V_{c_i} \qquad (3)$$

where n = the number of consequences that a subject perceives as likely to follow his particular behavior.

It should be clear that the greater the frequency of contiguity of an act and an outcome (f_{R-s*}), the larger the P_c terms. The larger the value of the outcome V_{c_i}, the larger the C.

$$P_c = \theta\, f_{R\text{-}s*} \tag{3a}$$

A number of personality variables might be reflected in particular relationships between the variables of Equation 3. Thus if a person sees valuable outcomes as occurring infrequently, the correlation between V_{c_i} and P_c values would be negative. For some superoptimistic individuals, however, the correlation may be positive. Steiner (1970) has provided a most interesting analysis of the relationships among components of this equation. He considers the costs of a behavior separately. These would be negative outcomes. Some individuals may see a positive correlation between such costs and the value of outcomes (e.g., hard work leads to wealth), that is, they correlate some negative aspects of the consequences of the behavior to valuable outcomes.

An alternative way to state the relationship between C and outcome is to use Equation 3b. This form is most useful when we have a complete record of the history of reinforcements of an organism.

$$C = \Sigma\, E_{R\text{-}s*}\, V_{s*} \tag{3b}$$

where $E_{R\text{-}s*}$ = the expectation that the response will lead to a particular outcome $s*$

V_{s*} = the value of this outcome.

Hence,

$$C = \sum_{i=1}^{n} \theta\, f_{R\text{-}s*}\, V_{s*} \tag{3c}$$

where θ is an individual differences parameter.

The C term represents a "quantity of affect," because it is the sum of affective (values) states. Adding this to A gives a total quantity of affect that increases the strength of the behavioral intention. However, the *direction* of the behavioral intention will depend on the S component. Social pressures (i.e., the S component) occur toward solidarity, intimacy, superordination, or their opposites. In short, social pressures can be represented by vectors in a three-dimensional space, defined by the dimensions of solidarity, intimacy, and superordination. Behaviors are also coded on solidarity, intimacy, and superordination. Thus there is an isomorphic relationship between social pressures and behaviors. Each occurs in a three-dimension space. The goal interdependence, length of the social relationship, and access to resources determine where two individuals will find themselves in the space of social pressures. Roles and interpersonal agreements shift their position in that space still further. Those behaviors which are coded at corresponding points of the behavior space are "most appropriate," and the greater their appropriateness the stronger the behavioral intention to perform the behavior (for more details, see Triandis, Vassiliou, and Nassiakou, 1968).

The three coefficients of Equation 2 again reflect situational and individual differences variance. Certain social settings evoke relatively large gamma co-efficients. For example, in most religious establishments there is a detailed specification of the norms, roles, and contractual expectations. A person may be "bored to death," but he will probably do what is expected of him in a church. He certainly .also sees strong negative consequences for those of his behaviors that are inconsistent with these norms. Hence, in church settings we would expect relatively large gamma and epsilon coefficients, but relatively small delta coefficients. When the norms, roles, and social arrangements have a large weight, the *behavior setting* (Barker, 1968) is a very important determinant of the behavior. Wicker (1972) has examined a number of theoretical perspectives which may account for the consistency between behavior and social environment. On the other hand, at a party, the delta coefficients may be the largest, while in a battle, the epsilon coefficients may be the largest.

Individual differences in the size of these coefficients can also be noted. There is a type of person who tends to do the "right thing" (high gamma). The compulsive type in Freudian theory is such a sort. There is also the impulsive type who does not do what is expected of him, or what maximizes good consequences, but rather what is most pleasant during a brief moment of time. He would be a high delta. Finally, there is a deliberative, calculating, rational, and intellectual type. Perhaps a high Machiavellian (Christie and Geis, 1970) is a high epsilon.

The Perception of the Situation. Selectivity in perception is well-documented. In intercultural encounters it is particularly important because, when people use different language, they encode reality in different ways. Current analyses, relevant to the Whorfian hypothesis, suggest that we encode that for which we have a term in our language, and the presence of the term facilitates such encoding. Different languages lead to the cutting of the pie of experience in relatively arbitrary ways (Triandis, 1964), which can lead to different maps of reality. A cue is likely to be perceived to the extent to which it fits such arbitrary ways of encoding reality, to the extent that it is vivid and associated with pleasant rather than unpleasant events, and if it is familiar (Campbell, 1967). Expectations, needs, and values create filters through which cues are selectively processed.

A more detailed analysis of perceptual processes (Gibson, 1969) suggests that perceptual selectivity is a function of the extent to which stimuli contain both familiar (previously learned) stimulus patterns and distinctive features.[1]

In person perception any interpersonal behavior or attribute that stands out is likely to be selected, particularly if it permits greater predictability of the environment. Thus, if, in a given culture, blacks behave just like whites and people never discriminate a person who is black from one who is white, there will be no information carried by a person's racial characteristics. In such a society people would probably not notice a person's race, but would instead focus on other characteristics of persons. Klineberg (1954) claims that one of his Brazilian roommates did not notice the race of persons he encountered.

The interpersonal behaviors of individuals differ in thousands of ways, but only some of these cues are meaningfully related to social events. Those dimensions are learned, and individuals learn to look for them in new situations. Thus, a person who has been robbed by a thief wearing a red and blue tie might learn to attend to red and blue ties as a cue to possible "trouble." In short, what is attended to can be arbitrary; but the point is that, if the distinctive feature reduces uncertainty (can discriminate thieves from honest people), it will be attended to. Once a person has learned to make a discrimination, he is likely to transfer it to new situations. The trouble with intercultural experiences is that the features that are valid in one setting are usually invalid in other settings. The contrived example mentioned above clearly points to the arbitrariness of the discriminations: If we take to another culture the expectation that people wearing red and blue ties are thieves, the likelihood of correct behavior is just about zero.

In sum, what is selectively perceived, according to Gibson, is the distinctive, familiar feature of the other, which has reduced uncertainty in previous situations.

Once the cues have registered in perception, they are integrated, probably according to some approximation of the additive model extensively studied by Anderson (1971). The affect toward a social situation is a function of the sum of the affects associated with the situation.

$$A = n + \sum_{i=0}^{\lambda} w_i s_i \qquad (4)$$

where n = a constant

$w_o s_o$ = the initial affective response to the social situation, and i goes from 1 to λ and represents the number of cues processed.

Cues filter through if they are differentiated from other stimulus patterns by reducing uncertainty (Gibson, 1969). Cues that are familiar or have distinctive features are especially likely to be selected, particularly if they have some characteristic such as unusual loudness, vividness, or protrusiveness.[2]

We, therefore, define the properties:

distinctiveness of the cue (D) (including loudness, protrusiveness, association with previous rewards)

familiarity (F) previous utilization by organism

relevance (R) to the present state of the organism, including relevance to internal drives.

When a cue has D.F.R. values greater than a threshold, it will be registered and will become one of the cues that is considered in Equation 4. Thus we write:

$$k < D.F.R. \qquad (4a)$$

where k is a parameter which measures the threshold needed to be surpassed for the cue to register. It is clear that there might be individual differences in k.

An alternative way to state Equations 4 and 4a is Equation 4b which relates $E_{s\text{-}s*}$, the expectation that the cue will lead to the outcome, and V_{s*}, the value of the outcome, to experienced affect:

$$A = E_{s\text{-}s*} \cdot V_{s*} \tag{4b}$$

Research is needed to determine whether Anderson's (1970) approach to functional measurement can be used in the determination of the weights. If this approach proves useful, we could also have the additional equations:

$$\alpha + \beta = 1 \tag{5}$$

$$\gamma + \delta + \epsilon = 1 \tag{6}$$

$$\sum_{i=0}^{\lambda} w_i = 1 \tag{7}$$

Empirical procedures that might be used to obtain values for the principal variables of the model are:

Variable	Suggested Method
P_a	Place subject in a situation that allows a finite number of responses. Observe the frequency with which he chooses one particular response, as you change the parameters of the situation.
H	Either observe how subject has acted in similar situations in the past, or ask him to report how he remembers he has acted in the past. The observation is preferable, but might be impractical.
F	Ask judges to view the social situation and task, and also measure the relevant abilities.
BI	Use the behavioral differential (Triandis, 1964).
S	The basic question is "What should you do?" This question can be asked from the perspective of several reference groups, and several *others*. A form of the role differential (Triandis, Vassiliou, and Nassiakou, 1968) can yield scores comparable to those obtained for BI.
A	The evaluative factor of the semantic differential may be used, with the particular behavior as the "concept" to be rated on evaluative scales.
C	Is computed from Equation 3

P_{c_i} Probability judgments of the extent to which a behavior is having particular consequences as in the antecedent/consequent method, described by Triandis et al. (1972b).

V_{c_i} The evaluative factor of the semantic differential may be used to obtain ratings of the outcomes (consequences).

A   Is computed from Equation 4.

s_i These are obtained from Thurstone scalings of the affective value of particular cues.

W_i These weights should be determined as prescribed by Anderson (1970).

It should be clear that the particular method suggested above for measuring each construct is only one of several possible methods. Multimethod measurement of each variable is highly desirable.

To illustrate these measurements we will consider the prediction of a teacher's criticism of students who do poor work in her classroom. We can set up some observers in the classroom who can classify the teacher's behavior into several categories, including the category "criticizes students." These observations would yield a measure of P_a. Observing the teacher's behavior on previous occasions would give us a measure of H. Such a measure can also be obtained by asking, "How frequently do you criticize your students?" However, the observation of previous behavior is a far better measure of H than the subject's answer to a question.

Facilitating conditions can be established by having the observers indicate how difficult it is for a teacher to criticize students in her classroom. For example, in the event that the classroom is so noisy that students would not be able to listen to the criticism, F would be rated as very low. The BI can be obtained from an item such as:

Would you criticize students who do poor work in your classroom?

probable ____: ____: ____: ____: ____: ____: ____: improbable

The norms require specification of various reference groups who might conceivably send norms, such as fellow teachers, the principal, her husband, and the like. An item might be:

Other teachers believe that it is a good idea for you to criticize your students.

definitely true ____: ____: ____: ____: ____: ____: ____: definitely false

Roles might be obtained with reference to several plausible, relevant role relationships in which the particular teacher might be involved, such as teacher-student, adult-child, female-male, and so on. One item might be:

teacher-student

should ____: ____: ____: ____: ____: ____: ____: should not

criticize poor work

Self-concept information might be obtained by asking:
Are you the type of person who criticizes others who do poor work?
The affect might be studied with an item such as:

Criticizing students who do poor work is

good ____: ____: ____: ____: ____: ____: ____: bad

unpleasant ____: ____: ____: ____: ____: ____: ____ pleasant

desirable ____: ____: ____: ____: ____: ____: ____ undesirable

The perceived consequences of the behavior might be studied with an item such as:

Criticizing students who do poor work improves their performance

strongly agree ___: ___: ___: ___: ___: ___: ___ strongly disagree

The value of the consequence might be studied with this item:

Improving the performance of students who do poor work is

good ____: ____: ____: ____: ____: ____: ____ bad

unpleasant ____: ____: ____: ____: ____: ____: ____ pleasant

desirable ____: ____: ____: ____: ____: ____: ____ undesirable

By adding (taking account of direction) the values of the evaluative scales, one obtains a measure of affect. Appropriate use of Equation 3 leads to estimates of C.

One point that is not discussed above is how to compute the weights. These can be determined in at least three different ways, with method selection being dependent upon the type of prediction desired. As noted earlier the weights are conceived to vary with the persons, the behaviors, and the social situations. One purpose of the paradigm is to describe how subjective culture variables are related to behavior. If the purpose is purely descriptive, the weights might be obtained as follows: consider a cube of data with N individuals, n behaviors, and m social situations. There are Nnm observations in the cube. These can be subjected to a three-mode factor analysis (Tucker, 1966). The analysis will yield types of people who do particular types of behaviors in particular types of social situations. By selecting the people who respond homogeneously to a particular behavior and situation, we can compute the weights, across people, that would be invariant with behavior and situation. Of course, every type of person requires a different set of weights.

Another need might be to predict the behavior of a given individual. If this is required, the weights can be obtained by examining how this individual responded to different behaviors and situations. The data can consist of the nm observations obtained from each individual, and a multiple regression analysis will yield the weights.

Still another purpose might be to predict who, from among a sample of individuals, will be most likely to behave in a particular way. Here the analysis concentrates on a single behavior, and examines the responses of the N individuals to the particular behavior-social situation combination. Again multiple regression analysis can be used.

The Dimensions of Interpersonal Behavior. Interpersonal behavior involves exchanges that are specific to it. Some anthropologists, such as Levi-Strauss (1963), have argued that there are three kinds of human exchanges: (1) of symbols, myths, and knowledge; (2) of affiliative and affectionate bonds, including the exchange of women by tribal groups; and (3) of goods and services. Foa (1971) has argued that there are six such exchanges, love, status, information, money, goods, and services,[3] and has offered empirical evidence that subjects perceive a circular order in these six exchanges. Turner, Foa, and Foa (1971) showed that reinforcers proximal in the order are perceived as similar and are substituted for one another more than the distal ones; for each resource, there is one resource that is more frequently exchanged than any other, and the probability of chosing to exchange the other resources is inversely proportional to their distance from the preferred exchange; and, the intercorrelation pattern among resources is invariant across exchange situations. All these findings can be interpreted as supportive of the circular order shown in Figure 1.

Other empirical work is consistent with these findings. Triandis (1964) found, through factor analyses, five factors summarizing the behavioral intention ratings of American students. The behavioral intentions were sampled from interpersonal behaviors utilized in American novels. Such behaviors tended to be extremely particularistic, and hence the density of behaviors was much greater in the particularistic section of Foa's exchange circle (Figure 1). The obtained factors reflected variations of Foa's particularistic exchanges. In particular, there was a factor that corresponds to respect (giving both status and affect), one that represents marital acceptance (exchange of love), one representing friendship (a mixture of giving love and status, as well as services), one described as social distance (denying status, love, and services), and one labeled superordination (denying status) versus subordination (giving status, but not affect).

It is likely that Foa's factors are the basic dimensions of interpersonal exchanges, and the ones extracted by Triandis are naturally occurring combinations of these basic dimensions found in the ecology of American students. This

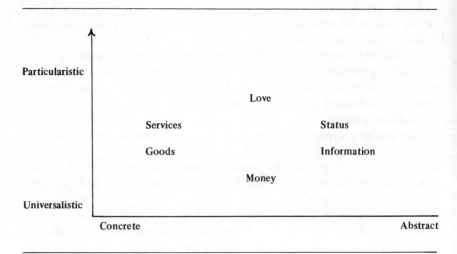

Figure 1. The Circular Order of Foa's Theory of Interpersonal Exchanges

viewpoint is supported by the cross-cultural work later undertaken by Triandis and his associates (Triandis, Vassiliou, and Nassiakou, 1968; Triandis et al., 1972b). In this work, done in Greece, India, Taiwan, Japan, and Peru, there appears to be a set of universal factors which Triandis labeled genotypic: giving versus denying affect, giving versus denying status, intimacy versus formality. However, each culture appears to utilize factors that are mixtures of these genotypic factors, which Triandis labels phenotypic. The latter are subject to influences from the specific sampling of subjects, behaviors, and stimulus persons or roles which the subjects are asked to think about when giving their behavioral intentions.

It should be recalled that in our earlier analysis we argued that cultural training involves becoming more cognitively differentiated. We now turn to a closer examination of the meaning of cognitive complexity, within the framework of our discussion of interpersonal exchanges.

ANALYSIS OF STRUCTURE

Cognitive Complexity

The concept of psychological differentiation has a considerable research history. The most recent history includes the contributions of Werner (1948), who conceived of human development as consisting of increased differentiation and better integration of the differentiated parts. With development, advanced action systems which are more differentiated and integrated dominate primitive systems.[4]

At a similarly high level of abstraction, but backed by a most impressive empirical research program, is Witkin's analysis of psychological differentiation (see Witkin et al., 1962). This approach utilizes a number of perceptual tests, such as the rod-and-frame test, the tilted chair, and the embedded figures test, and finds rather high correlations among these tests. The pattern of correlations implies that there are two kinds of people: those who perceive the world wholistically without differentiation of figure and ground, and those who discriminate, analyze, and differentiate. The former are called field dependent (FD), and the latter, field independent (FI).[5]

The Witkin research program shows that children begin by being FDs and become FIs. Men are higher in FI than women in several societies (Witkin, 1967). Mothers of FI children train them for independence (hence the high n Ach), are sure of themselves, have clear standards, praise a lot, stimulate the child to explore, and do not take care of the physical needs of the child when that is not necessary. High FI children are likely to have high FI mothers and to see their parents as supportive.

This approach has generated a good deal of research. There appears to be both a physiological basis and a cultural basis (Witkin, 1967) for differences in FI scores. Dawson (1967) has found that lack of protein in childhood is associated with gynaecomastia (i.e., big breasts in the male child), which is a feminine characteristic, and also with FD scores. Persons showing mixed hand-eye, auditory dominance are FD (Dawson, 1972). Societies that emphasize conformity have higher mean FD scores, while those emphasizing independence have higher FI scores. Generally, agricultural societies require much cooperation and emphasize obedience and conformity; fishing and hunting societies emphasize independence. Thus, Berry (1966) found that the Temne had FD and the Eskimo FI scores. Dawson (1972) has pointed out that having high FI scores is helpful in mechanical work, but is an obstacle to good relations with authority figures; hence, people from a hunting and fishing background, such as the Eskimos, are very good mechanics, but poor organization men. Because the latter quality may be more important for adjustment to the modern industrial world, Dawson sees FI as an obstacle to modernization. On the other hand Gruenfeld (1972) found a high correlation between FI and the mean standard of leaving of the country from which a person came to a management training school in Italy. Managers with high FI scores came from the more prosperous countries.

Berry (1972) showed that field independence is related to personality characteristics such as reserve, control, and independence. He examined scores of East Cree Indians from three Canadian communities. He concluded that such personality characteristics are helpful in avoiding stress and marginality during acculturation. High field independent individuals have been found by Bottenberg (1971a) to have integrated perceptions of events occurring in the past, present, and future, and to be more emotionally relaxed, balanced, and stable (Bottenberg, 1971b).

Amir (1972) found that individuals raised in the Israeli kibbutzim were significantly higher in field independence when compared with non-kibbutzim-raised individuals, Jewish subjects from Western countries are higher in field independence than Jewish subjects from the Arab countries, and Israeli subjects are higher in FI than Iranians, who in turn were higher than the Arab samples. Finally, FI correlated .33 with ratings of effectiveness received by officers in the Israeli army. All these results were statistically highly significant.

These findings apparently can be accounted for by the kinds of socialization practices employed in various societies. When parents emphasize obedience, the child is likely to be FD; when they emphasize independence, the child is likely to be FI. Differences in emphasis have been found by Kohn and his associates (1969) in both Italy and the United States to be strongly related to social class. In both countries, the lower classes emphasize obedience, while the middle and upper classes emphasize independence. Kohn suggests that industrial workers realize the importance of conformity to the demands of the supervisor, and train their children to be "good" workers, while upper middle-class parents realize that creativity is likely to lead to success in life and train their children accordingly.

Both the Werner and Witkin approaches deal with a broad psychological tendency. This tendency appears to become manifest in two ways: at the perceptual and the ability inputs in our paradigm. High FD would merge self and ingroup and perceive ingroup norms as part of the self. Hence, we expect a large γ weight for the high FDs. High FI implies better scores in mechanical ability tests. Because the latter are not particularly relevant to interpersonal relations, we can ignore them. Thus, the only implication of this work for our paradigm seems to be that high FD is probably related to a larger weight for variable S, that is, the correlation of FD and γ is probably positive.

Cognitive complexity is a term that apparently appeals to psychologists. The proof of this is that it is used by different writers to refer to entirely different entities. While Werner and Witkin use it to denote psychological differentiation, as revealed in perception, others use it to denote other constructs. We can distinguish four "schools" of usage: (1) Werner-Witkin; (2) Kelly-Bieri and others; (3) Harvey, Hunt, Schroder, Driver, and Streufert; and (4) Scott. The first school looks at it as a perceptual variable, which has major influences on other psychological functions. The second sees it as an interpersonal, cognitive variable; the third, as a personality variable; and the fourth, as a general cognitive variable which applies to different cognitive domains differently.

The Kelly-Bieri tradition usually uses some adaptation of Kelly's (1955) REP test, in which a subject lists traits or attributes of significant others and indicates the extent to which each attribute is an appropriate description of each significant other. Crockett (1965) has summarized much of this literature, which shows differences in differentiation that can be determined by counting the number of independently utilized constructs that characterize the responses of subjects. There is some evidence that amount of information is related to this type of cognitive differentiation (Miller, 1968). Highly complex individuals are more able to assimilate contradictory information, employ unbalanced cognitions with greater frequency, and make more use of favorable and unfavorable constructs (Crockett, 1965).

The third tradition is concerned with the way people process information. This is viewed as a broad personality variable. Schroder, Driver, and Streufert (1967) distinguish three aspects of complexity: differentiation (number of dimensions used), discrimination (the fineness of use of each dimension), and integration (the organization of the several dimensions into coherent structures). The work of Conrad and Dickenson (1972) suggests that Scott's (1969) R, derived from a job sorting task, or the number of significant beta weights, in a policy judgment task, are the best measures of differentiation. Fiedler's (1967) LPC measure is the best estimate of discrimination, and the F scale (high F is low integration) is the best measure of integration. Streufert and Fromkin (1970) showed that subjects chose, in sociometric situations, others who were similar to them in complexity. The simple persons chose simple others; the differentiators chose differentiators and the integrators chose integrators.

The last research program, on cognitive complexity, to be reviewed here is Scott's (1969). He uses a very large number of distinctions and multiple methods for the assessment of each of the aspects of complexity. The amount of information a person has about a cognitive domain is related to Scott's measures of *dimensionality* (differentiation) and *attribute articulation* (discrimination). Several cross-cultural studies showed stability in the correlations among the various aspects of complexity measured by Scott.

It seems useful at this point to guess at some of the relationships between our paradigm and the measures of cognitive complexity. It seems intuitively likely, for instance, that large differentiation (dimensionality) will be related to the number of significant (nonzero) weights in our paradigm. Simple persons might use only one or two of the primitive terms of the paradigm. It might also be related to λ since that parameter is concerned with the number of independent cues considered in Equation 4.

From the point of view of cross-cultural training, the examination of the literature summarized in the above discussion suggested that the most promising concept is that of differentiation. We now consider the kinds of differentiation that are likely to be important in intercultural relations.

Differentiation can be approached either at the interpersonal level or at the cultural level. There are analyses at both levels; Foa (1971) published one at the interpersonal, and Lomax and Berkowitz (1972), at the cultural. They suggest that differentiation is the most important dimension characterizing social relationships or cultures.

Differentiation in Interpersonal Relationships

Foa's (1971) analysis suggests that a person might differentiate a great deal, or not at all, on each of the modes of exchange presented in Figure 1. For example, consider the status mode. A person might assign much higher status to a Herr Universität's Professor Dr. Dr. than to a Herr Universität's Professor Dr. In short, an additional doctorate results in a discriminably larger amount of status for one person but not for another.

Another kind of differentiation concerns the six modes. An exchange in one mode might be seen as having direct implications for other modes. For example, exchanging love might imply exchanging status. In more developed countries there appears to be greater differentiation among modes than in more traditional societies (Foa and Chemers, 1967).

One reasonable guess is that there is a limit to the human capacity for differentiation, so that when humans differentiate very much in one domain, they may not differentiate much in other domains. From this consideration we conclude that, because there is much greater differentiation in highly economically developed societies in the exchanges of money, goods, and information, there is probably less differentiation in the exchanges of love, status, and services. Examination of the evidence seems consistent with this observation. Consider the multitude of money exchanges (banks, monetary units, stocks, bonds, checks, etc.), the tremendous diversity of goods (see the Sears-Roebuck catalogue), and the size of our libraries, plus the complexity of the mass media. On the other hand, our services tend to be poorer than in less developed societies, and there is reason to suspect that the Indians of the Kamasutra knew as much (if not more!) about love as modern urban Europeans or Americans. Foa has correctly pointed out that some exchanges require more time than others, and this might be the cause of the "unbalanced development" of differentiations. Specifically, the more particularistic exchanges require much more time than the more universalistic. In economically developed societies, we differentiate the universalistic at the expense of the particularistic exchanges.

Role differentiation is higher in urban than in rural environments (Stephan and Stephan, 1971). Similarly, in more traditional societies, roles are fewer in number. In traditional societies role complexity is high in ingroup roles; but in relations of ingroups to outgroups, the social behavior is generally uniform—suspicious and even hostile. In modern societies there is differentiation in both ingroup and outgroup roles, and the tremendous complexity is handled by bureaucratic principles, such as the idea of treating everyone equally well.

These comments can be formalized by considering a typology of differentiations:

(1) Among types of people: In traditional cultures people behave particularlistically, and hence relate to people in very different ways. In modern cultures there is a tendency toward equal treatment for all.

(2) Among modes of exchange: Traditional societies are low on this differentiation.

(3) Within mode of exchange: In traditional societies there is more differentiation with particularistic and less differentiation within universalistic modes of exchange.

(4) Of time: In traditional societies time is less differentiated than in modern cultures. The result is that there is less concern for planning, punctuality, and living by the clock.

Differentiation in Cultures

We just have seen that differentiation seems to be an important dimension for the characterization of human relationships; it is also important as a dimension of characterization of cultures.

A most interesting paper by Lomax and Berkowitz (1972) examines a taxonomy of cultures. The authors employ both behaviors recorded in the Human Relations Area File and analyses based on the distinctive features of musical expression (cantometrics) found in cultures around the globe to classify cultures. Using factor analyses based on behavior profiles from about 1000 cultures, and 4000 recorded song performances from about 400 cultures, these authors clustered cultures into a broad taxonomy. The most important dimension of this taxonomy was differentiation. A differentiation scale was used in which African Gatherers had a score of 1.6 and Europe and Old High Cultures, a score of 8.0. Two clusters of cultures were intermediate in differentiation. The Australian Gatherers, Siberian cultures, and most American Indian cultures averaged around 3.0, and the Polynesian, Melanesian, and Black African cultures, around 5.0 in degree of differentiation.

In the cultures low in differentiation, food is obtained mostly by gathering and fishing, while in the high cultures it is obtained through agriculture and cattle milking. In the low, settlements are small (villages of around 50 persons); in the high, they are large. In the low, there is no social stratification; in the high, there is. High gods are not found in the low, but they are found in the high. Corresponding to these behavioral differences, there is more complexity in the song of the highly differentiated. Finally, distinctive patterns of social integration are found to correspond with differentiation. Most integration is found at intermediate levels of differentiation. High integration is indexed by high levels of within ingroup solidarity, community organization, and a division of labor in which women contribute more than half to the main productive task. In the very differentiated cultures, males are the chief contributors, and there is less solidarity and little community organization. The authors also offer a list of variables loading on 19 orthogonal factors. The factor that accounts for more of the variance than any other is differentiation. Other factors include caloric value of produce, types of social organization, level of cohesiveness, matrilineal versus partilineal society, type of family, and so on. They argue, however, that two attributes (differentiation and integration) are sufficient to account for the evolution of cultures. They also show a correspondence of types of dance movements to these two features of cultures, with high differentiation associated with more manipulative dance styles.

Familial complexity corresponds to social integration, as described by Lomax and Berkowitz. Thus, in an examination of data from the *Ethnographic Atlas,* Blumberg and Winch (1972) found support for the curvilinear hypothesis that familial complexity is minimum at the extremes of societal complexity (hunting-gathering and urban-industrial). The maximum in familial complexity occurs in societies engaged in intensive agriculture without irrigation, whose largest towns house 200 to 5,000 persons, who have a system of hereditary aristocracy, and whose political hierarchy extends only one or two levels beyond the local community.

Societies with high familial complexity probably also have strong ingroups, and discriminate very clearly between those who are ingroup members and those who are not. Thus, tribalism is very strong and provides a major determinant to the pattern of human relationships in economic or political exchanges in the highly intergrated cultures.

From these considerations we can extrapolate that when person P comes from a culture that is similar in differentiation and integration to that from which person O comes, the two persons will be most likely to make isomorphic attributions and hence to find it easier to establish a good or effective human relationship. On the other hand, persons who come from societies with different levels of integration or differentiation will have difficulties in their relationship unless one is trained to differentiate the way the other is differentiating. Our hypothesis is that people who utilize a particular mode of differentiation and integration create a characteristic *social environment.* People who have learned to relate to others in one social environment will have trouble relating to others in another social environment unless they have been trained to make the differentiations that people in the other environment are usually making. To illustrate this point we will now consider a number of examples of poor fit (i.e., nonisomorphic attributions) between the social environment and a given individual.

Examples of Intercultural Difficulties as a Function of Different Types of Differentiation

Some Americans find Greeks extremely rude (Triandis, 1967). They come to this conclusion from observations of Greeks in public settings—subways, busses, streets. They fail to realize that Greeks have two sets of social behaviors; one set is used with their ingroup, and another with their outgroup. In an ingroup, which a Greek defines as "family and friends and other people who are concerned with my welfare" (Triandis and Vassiliou, 1972), Greeks are extremely polite. In outgroups they are rude. If the sample of behavior to which a foreigner has access is limited to outgroup social behavior, he will mistakenly assume that all Greek social behavior is rude. This will, of course, have consequences for his own social behavior. Once he assumes that the other person is rude, he is likely to behave in a rude way toward him, which will elicit rude behavior, thus confirming his preconceptions. A cycle of poor relations can then be generated. This is an example of a situation where one culture treats people very differently, while another culture treats them more evenly, with the difference in differentiation resulting in intercultural difficulties.

In the earlier example of the supervisor who encouraged participation and the subordinate who expected to receive orders, we discovered differences in the definition of the exchanges. The boss thought he was exchanging information; the subordinate thought he was receiving orders (the status difference was salient for him). Such misunderstandings can easily occur when cultures differ in the way they assign behaviors to the particular modes of exchange.

Differential differentiation among modes of exchange can be illustrated with another Greek-American misunderstanding found by Triandis (1967). Americans frequently complain that Greeks "pry into their personal affairs." The explanation is that Greeks who exchange love with others (are friends) also expect to exchange information. Americans are more differentiated in their exchanges, so that one does not necessarily discuss his sex life with his friends, and one does not necessarily reveal his income. For the Greeks such secrets are incomprehensible between friends.

Still another example concerns time. "What time should we come to dinner?" asks the American. "Anytime," answers the Greek villager. This can lead to a real misunderstanding, because the American use of the expression "anytime" is reserved for those noninvitations people give to be polite, but which they hope will lead to nothing, while the Greek villager *actually means* that the American would be welcome anytime. The villager believes that putting limits on when a guest can come would insult the visitor.

Still another cultural difference concerns the frequency of use of each exchange. Particularistic exchanges are used rarely in the United States and frequently in many traditional societies. For example, a person's work is infrequently complimented in great detail in the United States but more frequently in more leisurely environments.

The amplitude of the response can also differ. In one culture the level of exchanges is very loud and members of another culture might conclude that there is a fight, when in fact people are having fun arguing loudly.

Inappropriate exchanges are another problem. Trying to pay for a service for which one is supposed to give a compliment can lead to great embarrassment.

Returning to the paradigm we note that the differentiations we have discussed so far involve mostly *actions, time* and *place*, and types of *people* dimensions. However, the paradigm itself has several elements. These elements may be viewed as independent influences or as highly interrelated ones. Thus a person might assume that affect, cognition, and norms are always consistent with habits and hence there is but one input to consider to predict behavior. Another person might consider each of these influences as acting quite independently of each other and hence would be much more differentiated.

Our earlier hypothesis concerning isomorphic attributions implies that the person who discriminates and differentiates the same way as the other will be most effective in relating to the other. The empirical data presented by Streufert and Fromkin (1970) and Slack and Cook (1973) are consistent with this expectation. An extensive study by Lieberman, Yalom, and Miles (1973) on encounter groups found that the majority of such groups has few behavioral consequences; however, effective leaders who do create conditions of improvement in such groups can be found on some occasions. When they are found, they turn out to be concentrating on the making of "meaning attributions," that is, they redefine concepts and experiences. This is similar to what is done in the culture assimilator (Fiedler et al., 1971).

In sum, we have shown that there are numerous ways in which a person can differentiate and discriminate in domains involving interpersonal relations. Isomorphic attributions imply a similar pattern of differentiation and discrimination between two individuals. Cultural training probably increases isomorphic attributions.

SUMMARY OF ANALYSIS

Culture training, according to the analysis we presented in the previous pages, should accomplish the following goals:

(1) It should familiarize the student of culture with the "dimensions that

make a difference" in interpersonal behavior in the other culture. It will be recalled that Gibson (1969) pointed out that this can best be done if distinctive features are emphasized in the training. The learning of differences can be facilitated by presenting contrasting instances, in short, by presenting situations in which what is likely to happen in the learner's culture differs a good deal from what is likely to happen in the other culture.

(2) It should make possible the transfer of learning of the new information, concerning what is important in the other culture, to new situations. Maximum transfer occurs when the new situations contrast the features of the correct and incorrect discriminations in a maximal manner, when distinctive features are enhanced, and when new stimuli are familiar. In short, the learner must become familiar with the distinctive features of the other culture and the cues of what is important.

(3) It should increase isomorphic attributions. This means the learner should make judgments about the causes of the other's behavior that are similar to the judgments made by members of the other's culture. If the paradigm described in the previous sections is useful, it would be useful to present the learner with the following kinds of information:

(a) norms for different kinds of situations in the other culture,

(b) role structures, and in particular the way role perceptions differ in his culture and the other's culture,

(c) the way behaviors express general intentions in the other culture, e.g., in Egypt to compliment the hostess after the dinner, you belch,

(d) the kinds of self-concepts that are frequently found in the other culture,

(e) the kinds of behaviors that are valued and disvalued in the other culture,

(f) the kinds of antecedents and consequents of these behaviors that are frequently conceived in the other culture,

(g) the kinds of differentiations that are common in the other culture, among types of people, within modes of exchange, and between modes of exchange, as well as across time and place,

(h) the strength of the connections between norms, roles, the self-concept, general intentions, affect toward the behavior, and instrumentality of the behavior to behavior in the other culture, i.e., the weights of the paradigm, for that culture,

(i) the amplitude of the responses that people in the other culture generally make in various social situations,

(j) the kinds of reinforcement that people expect in different situations and the appropriateness of the exchange of particular reinforcements, e.g., that you can exchange love for status, but not money for love.

(4) It should familiarize the learner with typologies of culture, and the implications of dealing with persons from a more or less differentiated culture, in particular domains of interpersonal exchanges.

CULTURE TRAINING

A training approach that can accomplish these goals is the *culture assimilator*. This form of training was suggested by Stolurow and Osgood and developed by Fiedler and Triandis in the course of a research project in which these four psychologists collaborated. An account of the first validation studies involving this approach is presented by Fiedler, Mitchell, and Triandis (1971) and Mitchell, Dossett, Fiedler, and Triandis (1972).

Briefly, the student of intercultural events is presented with one or two hundred "items" which give information about the other culture. Each item consists of six sheets of paper. On page 1 there is a journalistic description of an intercultural episode (incident) in which alpha, a member of culture A, interacted with beta, a member of culture B, and there was some sort of interpersonal difficulty or misunderstanding. Page 2 presents four interpretations of what went wrong. These interpretations can be considered as attributions of the observed behavior. Only one of these attributions is correct, from the perspective of culture B. Thus a member of culture A has to find the one correct attribution in a set of four, in which the other three are plausible and usually consistent with the attributions made by naive members of his own culture, but unacceptable and inaccurate from the point of view of the other culture. The trainee selects the alternative that he considers correct and is then instructed to turn to one of the remaining four pages. If he selects the correct answer, when he turns to the appropriate page he is praised and told why it is correct. If he selects the wrong answer, he finds on the appropriate page a mild criticism, such as "you did not read the episode sufficiently carefully," and he is instructed to read it again and select another answer.

This procedure clearly increases the extent to which a member from culture A makes attributions that are isomorphic with the attributions made by members of culture B. Furthermore, as he learns to make correct attributions, it is probable that he becomes more and more able to predict the behavior of members of culture B.

Note that this procedure has much in common with the recommendations which would stem from Gibson's analysis. The procedure trains the reader to discriminate the correct and distinctive features of the other's behavior. As the reader of the assimilator goes through the items, he learns to what features in the episodes he should attend, and which aspects he should ignore (discrimination learning). The episodes are selected so that they expose the trainee to situations that emphasize the distinctive features of social situations which he must learn to discriminate. The items are also selected to give the trainee contrasting experiences with situations differing sharply on such features. The training, then, emphasizes the distinctive features of events which make the situation in the other culture most different from the situations that the trainee has already learned in his own culture. As he receives more and more training with related items, he can abstract features which such items have in common. We call such invariances "cultural principles." After the trainee goes through half a dozen items featuring the same principle, he is presented with a summary sheet in which the principle is stated as a conclusion. Thus, if he has not abstracted the principle by that point, it is given to him.

As an example, consider some recent work on black/white subcultural differences. Triandis, Weldon, and Feldman (1972c) found that black subjects have a tendency to assume that all white persons are prejudiced against blacks. This has major implications for social perception in interracial encounters. Almost any behavior of the white *can* be misinterpreted, if the context in which it is seen reflects prejudice. For instance, P smiles, and he is accused of "ingratiation"; P tries to help, and he is accused of "being forced to be nice by the government." One dimension of differentiation for the training of blacks is pointing out that there are differences in the degree of prejudice and the *kind* of prejudice (Goldstein and Davis, 1972; Triandis and Davis, 1965) among whites. Such information can help blacks improve their attributions of white behavior.

It is worth noting that in the last example we implied that cultural training results in increased cognitive complexity. When a black learns to discriminate one kind of white from another and vice versa, there is increased differentiation. However, correct attributions will also involve the use of more of the terms of Equations 1 through 4. It is reasonable to assume that the results of the Jones and Nisbett (1971) analysis will also apply to cross-cultural situations; in fact, they should occur even more strongly. These writers summarized numerous studies which showed that an actor tends to attribute his behavior to external causes, while an observer tends to use internal-to-the actor causes. This means that an actor is likely to emphasize variables such as S and C (Equation 2) and an observer, variables such as H (Equation 1) and A (Equation 2). Of course, variables like H are implicated in the concept of *trait* or of a *personality* variable. If in fact the actor's behavior is under the control of all four of these variables, then when the observer learns to make isomorphic attributions he learns to emphasize variables S and C in addition to H and A, hence to use all four variables. According to our assumptions this would also be more accurate. This implies, because he uses four instead of two variables, that he is cognitively more complex.

Another approach to cultural training is presented by David (1972). He argues that intercultural adjustment problems occur because alpha finds the other culture (B) unable to give him as many reinforcements as he is used to and likely to provide him with stimuli that he considers aversive. Thus, he proposes the utilization of training which can help alpha (1) attain reinforcements and avoid punishment, (2) transfer and modify present reinforcing systems, (3) develop new reinforcers, and (4) change, neutralize, or avoid punishers. He proposes the use of (1) modeling, (2) simulation of host culture conditions, and (3) desensitization by counterconditioning procedures.

There is little doubt that such approaches can be effective. The question is whether the expenditure of training time involved in such procedures can be reduced by providing the kinds of "cultural principles" that assimilator training makes readily accessible. Clearly, 10 hours of assimilator training will be like a "drop in the bucket" when compared to six months of language and culture training, as described by David. The question is whether there are any 10 hours of language and culture training that can increase the traveler's effectiveness as much as 10 hours of assimilator training. In short, assimilator training is claimed to be effective, but limited by its relatively short and specific focus.

SUMMARY

A paradigm for the study of intercultural relationships is presented and some of the empirical studies relevant to it are reviewed. In general, there is much empirical support for this paradigm. The paradigm suggests that effective intercultural behavior requires the development of isomorphic attributions. A number of theoretical considerations suggest that the kinds of cognitive changes that are likely to take place in cultural training involve an increase in differentiation, which is an aspect of cognitive complexity. The analysis suggests the probable optimal ways to develop cross-cultural training. The use of culture assimilators is consistent with these ways.

Author's Note: This paper was written while the writer held a Guggenheim Fellowship and an appointment to the Center of Advanced Studies of the University of Illinois. Much of the empirical work on which the paper is based was done under a grant from the Social and Rehabilitation Service, Department of Health, Education and Welfare, Grant No. 15-P-55175/5.

NOTES

1. The organism if exposed to extremely rich stimulation, which already contains homogeneities and inhomogeneities (i.e., the stimuli are highly patterned). The organism learns to discriminate the distinctive features of the stimulus array. As perceptual learning takes place, what is meaningless becomes differentiated, meaningful, and readily recognizable. Stimulus generalization decreases as stimulus differentiation increases. During perceptual learning, the organism extracts dimensions of difference across stimulus arrays and

learns to identify the distinctive features that characterize different events. Once a stimulus pattern has been undifferentiated from other patterns, this new skill can be transferred to new situations, with the transfer being best when the new situations allow for maximum contrasts and provide several sharp and distinctive features, as well as several clues of similarity to previously learned stimulus patterns. Thus, the mechanisms of perceptual learning involve abstraction of the distinctive features of stimulus arrays and the filtering out of irrelevant variations of stimulus input. Neither reinforcement nor knowledge of results are essential. What is important, according to Gibson, is the reduction of uncertainty.

2. While Gibson does not consider the association of a cue with previous reinforcements necessary, it seems that such associations would increase distinctiveness by providing more meaning to the cue, and hence would also increase the probability that it would be perceived.

3. It is obvious that these overlap with Levi-Strauss's, since the latter's category (1) is equivalent to Foa's exchange of information, his category (2) is the same as Foa's exchange of love, and his category (3) is the same as Foa's exchanges of goods and services. Levi-Strauss does not explicitly consider exhanges of status and money, but these are obviously important.

4. Werner emphasizes that acts differ in kind, from reflex, to trial and error based behavior, to assimilation controlled behavior, to practical judgment, to conceptual thought, and finally logicomathematical analysis, which has rules of its own, and where behavior would be under the control of these rules. He emphasizes the detachment of thought from motor and affective influences at the higher levels of development.

The more complex a highly developed person is, the more detached he is from motor and affective influences. In Werner's system, then, our paradigm is dealing with an intermediate level of behavior. Cultural training, presumably, allows the individual to make better practical judgments concerning the other's behavior. While Werner's system is most inclusive, it seems too abstract to test, and not directly relevant to the needs of the present analysis.

5. The FDs take a long time to locate familiar figures in complex figures, conform to authority, and are low in need for achievement. But they are often faster in learning and do well in verbal tests; they like people and understand the meaning of authority relationships. The FIs have an articulated view of their own body; they can distinguish the figure from its background and use intellectualization as a major defense mechanism (the FDs use regression). The FDs are more likely to be alcholic, obese, and suffer from ulcers and asthma; the FIs suffer from manic-depressive and delusional psychoses more than the FDs.

REFERENCES

ALTMAN, I. and W. W. HAYTHORN (1965) "Interpersonal exchange in isolation." Sociometry 28: 411-426.

AMIR, Y. (1972) "Inter- and intra-ethnic comparisons of intellectual functions in Israeli and Middle Eastern populations." Paper presented at the International Congress of Psychology, Tokyo. (See also p. 175 of Abstract Guide of the Congress.)

ANDERSON, N. H. (1970) "Functional measurement and psychophysical judgment." Psychological Review 77: 153-170.

——— (1971) "Integration theory and attitude change." Psychological Review 78: 171-206.

BACK, K. W., S. BUNKER, and C. B. DUNNAGAN (1972) "Barriers to communication and measurement of semantic space." Sociometry 35: 347-356.

BANDURA, A. and R. H. WALTERS (1963) Social Learning and Personality Development. New York: Holt, Rinehart & Winston.

BARKER, R. (1968) Ecological Psychology: Concepts and Methods for Studying the Environment of Human Behavior. Stanford, Calif.: Stanford University Press.

BERGER, S. (1962) "Conditioning through vicarious instigation." Psychological Review 69: 450-466.

BERGER, S.M. and W. W. LAMBERT (1968) "Stimulus-Response theory in contemporary social psychology," pp. 81-178 in G. Lindzey and E. Aronson (eds.) Handbook of Social Psychology. Vol. 1. Reading, Mass.: Addison-Wesley.

BERRY, J. W. (1966) "Temne and Eskimo perceptual skills." International Journal of Psychology 1: 207-229.

——— (1972) "Possession of typical cognitive and personality traits and resistance to acculturation stress," p. 581 of Abstract Guide, International Congress of Psychology, Tokyo. (See also Berry's chapter in this volume.)

BLUMBERG, L. and R. F. WINCH (1972) "Societal complexity and familial complexity: evidence for the curvilinear hypothesis." American Journal of Sociology 77: 896-920.

BOLLES, R. C. (1972) "Reinforcement, expectancy and learning." Psychological Review 79: 394-409.

BOTTENBERG, E. H. (1971a) "Der kognitive Stil von Feldabhängigheit-Feldunab-hangigkeit und det Modus des Zeiterlebens." Psychologie und Praxis 15: 138-141.

——— (1971b) "Feldunabhangigkeit, Cattells Persönalichkeitsfaktoren und Kompononten der Selbstaktualisierung." Revue Swisse de Psychologie pure et Appliquee 30: 312-319.

BYRNE, D. (1969) "Attitudes and attraction," pp. 35-89 in L. Berkowitz (ed.) Advances in Experimental Social Psychology. Vol. 4 New York: Academic Press.

——— (1971) The Attraction Paradigm. New York: Academic Press.

CAMPBELL, D. T. (1963) "Social attitudes and other acquired behavioral dispositions," pp. 94-172 in S. Koch (ed.) Psychology: A Study of a Science. Vol. 6. New York: McGraw-Hill.

——— (1967) "Stereotypes and the perception of group differences." American Psychologist 22: 817-829.

CHRISTIE, R. and F.L. GEIS (1970) Studies of Machiavellianism. New York: Academic Press.

CONRAD, K. A. and T. L. DICKINSON (1972) "Least squares regression model indices of the cognitive structural characteristics of job desirability ratings." Unpublished manuscript.

——— (1972) "A multitrait-multimethod investigation of measures of cognitive complexity." Unpublished manuscript.

CROCKETT, W.H. (1965) "Cognitive complexity and impression formation," in B. A. Maher (ed.) Progress in Experimental Personality Research. Vol. 2. New York: Academic Press.

DAVID, K. H. (1972) "Intercultural adjustment and applications of reinforcement theory to problems of 'culture shock.' " Hilo, Hawaii: Center for Cross-Cultural Training.

DAWSON, J. L. M. (1967) "Cultural and physiological influences upon spacial-perceptual processes in West Africa." International Journal of Psychology 2: 115-128, 171-185.

——— (1972) "Effects of ecology and subjective culture on individual-modern attitude change, achievement motivation and potential for economic development in the Japanese and Eskimo societies." Paper presented at the International Congress of Psychology, Tokyo.

DEUTSCH, M. (1968) "Field theory in social psychology," pp. 412-487 in G. Lindzey and E. Aronson (eds.) Handbook of Social Psychology. Vol. 1. Reading, Mass.: Addison-Wesley.

DULANY, D. E. (1964) "The separable effects of the information conveyed by a reinforcer." Paper read at the Psychonomic Meetings.

——— (1968) "Awareness, rules and propositional control: A confrontation with S-R theory," pp. 340-387 in T. Dixon and D. Horton (eds.) Verbal Behavior and General Behavior Theory. Englewood Cliffs, N. J.: Prentice-Hall.

EISEN, M. (1972) "Characteristic self-esteem, sex and resistance to temptation." Journal of Personality and Social Psychology 24: 68-72.

FARINA, A., B. CHAPNICK, J. CHAPNICK, and R. MISITI (1972) "Political views and interpersonal behavior." Journal of Personality and Social Psychology 22: 273-278.

FESTINGER, L. (1957) A Theory of Cognitive Dissonance. Stanford, Calif.: Stanford University Press.

FIEDLER, F. E. (1967) A Theory of Leadership Effectiveness. New York: McGraw-Hill.

FIEDLER, F. E., T. MITCHELL and H. C. TRIANDIS (1971) "The culture assimilator: an approach to cross-cultural training." Journal of Applied Psychology 55: 95-102.

FISHBEIN, M. (1973) "An investigation of the relationship between beliefs about an object and the attitude toward that object." Human Relations 16: 233-240.

——— (1967) "Attitude and the prediction of behavior," in M. Fishbein (ed.) Readings in Attitude Theory and Measurement. New York: John Wiley.

FOA, U. G. (1971) "Interpersonal and economic resources." Science 171: 345-351.

——— and M. CHEMERS (1967) "The significance of role behavior differentiation for cross-cultural interaction training." International Journal of Psychology 2: 45-58.

GIBSON, E. J. (1969) Principles of Perceptual Learning and Development. New York: Appleton-Century Croft.

GOLDSTEIN, M. and E. E. DAVIS (1972) "Race and belief: a further analysis of the social determinants of behavioral intentions." Journal of Personality and Social Psychology 22: 346-355.

GRUENFELD, L. (1972) Personal communication.

HEIDER, F. (1958) The Psychology of Interpersonal Relations. New York: John Wiley.

HOMANS, G. (1961) Social Behavior: Its Elementary Forms. New York: Harcourt, Brace & World.

IRWIN, F.W. (1971) Intentional Behavior and Motivation: A Cognitive Theory. New York: Lippincott.

JONES, E. E. and R. E. NISBETT (1971) The Actor and the Observer: Divergent Perceptions of the Causes of Behavior. New York: General Learning Press.

KELLY, G. A. (1955) The Psychology of Personal Constructs. New York: W. W. Norton.

KLINEBERG, O. (1954) Social Psychology. New York: Henry Holt.

KOHN, M. L. (1969) Class and Conformity: A Study in Values. Homewood, Ill.: Dorsey.

KUHN, T. S. (1962) The Structure of Scientific Revolutions. Chicago: University of Chicago Press.

LEVINE, R. and D. T. CAMPBELL (1972) Ethnocentrism. New York: John Wiley.

LEVI-STRAUSS, C. (1963) Structural Anthropology. New York: Basic Books.

LEWIN, K. (1951) Field Theory in Social Science. New York: Harper & Brothers.

LIEBERMAN, M. A., I. D. YALOM and M. B. MILES (1973) Encounter Groups: First Facts. New York: Basic Books.

LOCKE, E. A. (1968) "Toward a theory of task motivation and incentives." Organizational Behavior and Human Performance 3: 157-189.

LOMAX, A. and N. BERKOWITZ (1972) "The evolutionary taxonomy of culture." Science 177: 228-239.

MCGUINESS, E. (1970) Social Behavior. Boston: Houghton Mifflin.

MILLER, A. G. (1968) "Some determinants of cognitive complexity." Dissertation Abstracts 28: 3901.

MILLER, G., E. GALANTER and K. PRIBRAM (1960) Plans and the Structure of Behavior. New York: Henry Holt.

MITCHELL, T. R., D. L. DOSSETT, F. E. FIEDLER and H.C. TRIANDIS (1972) "Culture training: validation evidence for the culture assimilator." International Journal of Psychology 7: 97-104.

NUTTIN, J. R. (1972) "The outcome of a behavioral act–its reinforcement and information functions in human learning and perception," p. 8 in Abstract Guide, presented at the International Congress, Tokyo.

PEAK, H. (1955) "Attitude and motivation," pp. 149-188 in M. R. Jones (ed.) Nebraska Symposium on Motivation. Lincoln: University of Nebraska Press.

ROSENBERG, M. (1956) "Cognitive structure and attitudinal affect." Journal of Abnormal and Social Psychology 53: 367-372.

RYAN, T. A. (1970) Intentional Behavior: An Approach to Human Motivation. New York: Ronald Press.

SARBIN, T. R. (1954) "Role theory," pp. 223-258 in G. Lindzey (ed.) Handbook of Social Psychology. Vol. 1. Reading, Mass.: Addison-Wesley.

––– and V. L. ALLEN (1968) "Role theory," pp. 488-565 in G. Lindzey and E. Aronson (eds.) The Handbook of Social Psychology. Vol. 1. Reading, Mass.: Addison-Wesley.

SCHEERER, M. (1954) "Cognitive theory," in G. Lindzey (ed.) Handbook of Social Psychology. Vol. 1. Reading, Mass.: Addison-Wesley.

SCHRODER, H.M., M.J. DRIVER, and S. STREUFERT (1967) Human Information Processing: Individuals and Groups Functioning in Complex Situations. New York: Holt, Rinehart & Winston.

SCOTT, W. A. (1969) "Structure of natural cognitions." Journal of Personality and Social Psychology 12: 261-278.

SELIGMAN, M. E. P. (1970) "On the generality of the laws of learning." Psychological Review 77: 406-418.

SHERIF, M., O.J. HARVEY, B.J. WHITE, W.R. HOOD, and C. SHERIF (1961) "Intergroup conflict and cooperation: the Robbers Cave Experiment." Norman, Okla.: University of Oklahoma Institute of Group Relations.

SKINNER, B. F. (1953) Science and Human Behavior. New York: Macmillan.

SLACK, B. D. and J.O. COOK (1973) "Authoritarian behavior in a conflict situation." Journal of Personality and Social Psychology 25: 130-136.

STEINER, I. (1970) "Perceived freedom," pp. 187-249 of L. Berkowitz (ed.) Advances in Experimental Social Psychology. Vol. 5. New York: Academic Press.

STEPHAN, W.G. and C. STEPHAN (1971) "Role differentiation, empathy and neurosis in urban migrants and lower-class residents of Santiago, Chile." Journal of Personality and Social Psychology 19: 1-6.

STOTLAND, E. and L. K. CANON (1972) Social Psychology: A Cognitive Approach. Philadelphia: Saunders.

STREUFERT, S. and H.L. FROMKIN (1970) "Cognitive complexity and persuasion." Technical Report No. 28. Lafayette, Ind.: Purdue University.

THIBAUT, J. and H. H. KELLEY (1959) The Social Psychology of Groups. New York: John Wiley.

TOLMAN, E. C. (1951) "A psychological model." Pp. 279-359 of T. Parsons and E. A. Shils (eds.), Toward a General Theory of Social Action. Cambridge, Mass.: Harvard University Press.

TRIANDIS, H. C. (1959) "Cognitive similarity and interpersonal communication in industry." Journal of Applied Psychology 43: 321-326.

––– (1960a) "Cognitive similarity and communication in a dyad." Human Relations 13: 175-183.

——— (1960b) "Some determinants of interpersonal communication." Human Relations 13: 279-287.

——— (1964) "Exploratory factor analyses of the behavioral component of social attitudes." Journal of Abnormal and Social Psychology 68: 420-430.

——— (1967) "Towards an analysis of the components of interpersonal attitudes." pp. 227-170 in C. and M. Sherif (eds.) Attitudes, Ego Involvement and Change. New York: John Wiley.

——— and E. E. DAVIS (1965) "Race and belief as determinants of behavioral intentions." Journal of Personality and Social Psychology 2: 715-725.

——— and V. VASSILIOU (1972a) "A comparative analysis of subjective culture," pp. 299-335 in H. C. Triandis et al. (eds.) The Analysis of Subjective Culture. New York: John Wiley.

——— V. VASSILIOU, and M. NASSIAKOU (1968) "Three cross-cultural studies of subjective culture." Journal of Personality and Social Psychology Monograph Supplement 8(4): 1-42.

——— G. VASSILIOU, Y. TANAKA, and A. SHANMUGAM (1972b) The Analysis of Subjective Culture. New York: John Wiley.

——— D. WELDON and J. FELDMAN (1972c) "Black and white hardcore and middle-class subjective cultures: a cross-validation." Technical Report No. 14, SRS No. 15-P-55175/5. Champaign, Ill.: University of Illinois, Department of Psychology.

TUCKER, L.R. (1966) "Some mathematical notes on three-mode factor analysis." Psychometrika 31: 279-311.

TURNER, J. L., E. FOA, and U.G. FOA (1971) "Interpersonal reinforcers: classification, interrelationship and some differential properties." Journal of Personality and Social Psychology 19: 168-180.

VASSILIOU, G. and V. VASSILIOU (1966) "Social values as a psychodynamic variable: preliminary explorations of the semantics of philotimo." Acta Neur. Psychiat. Hell 5: 121-135.

WERNER, H. (1948) Comparative Psychology of Mental Development. New York: International Universities Press.

WICKER, A. W. (1972) "Processes which mediate behavior–environment congruence." Behavioral Science 17: 265-277.

WITKIN, H.A. (1967) "Cognitive style approach to cross-cultural research." International Journal of Psychology 2: 233-250.

——— R. B. DYK, H. F. FATERSON, D. R. GOODENOUGH, and S. A. KARP (1962) Psychological Differentiation. New York: John Wiley.

ZAJONC, R. B. (1965) "Social facilitation." Science 149: 269-274.

——— (1968) "Cognitive theories in social psychology," pp. 320-411 in G. Lindzey and E. Aronson (eds.) Handbook of Social Psychology. Vol. 1. Reading, Mass.: Addison–Wesley.

Chapter 2

COGNITIVE DIFFERENTIATION AND CULTURE TRAINING

A N D R E W   R.   D A V I D S O N

Battelle Human Affairs
Research Centers, Seattle

Contacts between individuals with diverse cultural backgrounds have multiplied as efforts toward political and economic integration, international cooperation, and technical assistance have increased. These cross-cultural contacts have frequently led to substantial difficulties on the part of the participants in working together harmoniously and effectively (see, for example, Davidson and Feldman, 1971; Fiedler, 1966; Kelman, 1963). Problems of this nature have stimulated a substantial body of research designed to improve the adjustment and effectiveness of heterocultural groups by means of culture training (for a survey of many of these approaches, see Wight, 1969).

The majority of these culture training programs have been commissioned in response to some specific heterocultural problem, for example, the need to improve the interpersonal effectiveness of American military advisors working in Iran. And, as is frequently the case with problem-oriented research, the initial research emphasis was on doing whatever seemed intuitively reasonable to solve the immediate problem. Theoretical and substantive issues were de-emphasized. The result has been an accumulation of nomological studies designed to test intuitive hypotheses about the effects of procedural variations in culture training programs. As previously witnessed in other scientific fields (Meehl, 1967), research of this kind has tended to be noncumulative and has failed to produce a systematically integrated body of knowledge.

In response to these trends, Triandis, as outlined in the preceding chapter, has attempted a theoretical re-analysis of the role that culture training can play in abating the poor interpersonal relationships among individuals from different cultures. On the basis of this re-analysis, Triandis suggested that the most

Author's Note: The work was carried out while the author was a National Science Foundation Predoctoral Fellow at the University of Illinois. The research was partly supported by a grant from the Social and Rehabilitation Service, Department of Health, Education and Welfare, Grant No. 15-P-55175/5, Harry C. Triandis, Principal Investigator.

significant cognitive change that takes place in culture training involves an increase in cognitive complexity. That is, training increases the trainee's cognitive complexity about the target culture, which in turn enables him to behave more effectively in that culture. The relation between complexity and cross-cultural effectiveness is assumed to exist because a cognitively simple person has a single framework within which to evaluate the observed behavior of others in the target culture. Thus, when a behavior which he does not understand takes place, he is likely to evaluate it ethnocentrically. A complex person, on the other hand, has several frameworks for the perception of the same behavior. He might, for example, suspend judgment and obtain more information before evaluating the behavior.

The relation between culture training and complexity is assumed to exist because training is thought to increase the trainee's knowledge about the target culture. This increase in knowledge leads to greater differentiation of stimuli within that cultural domain. Although no research has demonstrated this relation using stimuli from the cultural domain, there are data from other cognitive domains documenting a positive correlation between familiarity and differentiation. For example, Scott (1969) reported that a comparative government course increased the dimensionality of students' judgments of nations (on several different measures). Scott also reported significant correlations between information measures and dimensionality. Friendly and Glucksberg (1970), in a study of Princeton University students, used a multidimensional scaling (MDS) approach to establish that seniors had a higher dimensional solution for the use of Princeton slang terms than did freshmen. Similarly, another MDS study (Green and Morris, 1969) found that music majors' judgments of musical groups yielded a higher dimensional solution than business majors' judgments. Therefore, it can be hypothesized that a cultural training technique designed to increase the trainee's familiarity and knowledge of the target culture should also increase the trainee's cognitive differentiation concerning significant elements of the target culture. Consequently, if this hypothesis is confirmed, increased complexity could serve as a "proximal" test of the validity of culture training.

As previously noted, however, to date no research has investigated the relation between knowledge of a cultural domain and differentiation of stimuli within that domain. Accordingly, a necessary first step in checking the validity of complexity as a proximal criterion variable is the demonstration that members of a culture are more differentiated concerning significant elements of their own culture than are untrained members of a foreign culture. The research presented in this chapter represents an attempt to demonstrate this relation. Specifically, it is hypothesized that black subjects will be more differentiated than white subjects in their judgments concerning characteristics of black culture in the United States. This hypothesis examines a cognitive difference that is purely structural in nature.

In addition, it can be anticipated that not only will black and white subjects differ in cognitive *structure* but also that they will differ in terms of the *content* of their cognitions about the culture domain. Consistent with this expectation are the results of an experiment by Warr, Schroder, and Blackman (1969). They conducted a MDS study in which subjects of left, right, and middle-of-the-road political orientations judged various national governments. It was found that "centerists" had slightly higher average dimensionality and that the nature of the dimensions differed among the three groups. Following Warr et al., it is predicted that not only the complexity, but also the content of dimensions of the cultural domain will differ for members of different cultural groups.

The research presented in this chapter is one aspect of a larger culture training project (Illinois Studies of the Economically Disadvantaged) whose goal is the construction of two culture training devices, that is, cultural assimilators (cf., Fiedler, Mitchell, and Triandis, 1971). One, a black cultural assimilator, is for white foremen and workers preparing for on-the-job contact with hardcore unemployed blacks. The second, a white assimilator, is for unemployed blacks preparing for contact with white workers and foremen. Corresponding to the theoretical approach to culture training outlined above, we have attempted to develop a proximal test of the validity of assimilator training employing cognitive complexity as the criterion variable.

A recent development in nonmetric MDS proposed by Rosenberg, Nelson, and Vivekananthan (1968) appears, at least at an intuitive level, to provide a task that is ideally suited for achieving the goals of the present project. That is, the dimensionality of the MDS solution provides a frequently used index of differentiation. In addition, by comparing the content differences between MDS solutions based on the judgments of black and white respondents, it will be possible to locate cultural differences in the perception of black culture. These content differences can then be incorporated in the culture training program.

Rosenberg and his colleagues utilized a trait-sorting task. The subject's task was to put those traits that tend to go together in the same individual in the same category. Each subject was instructed that, in making these judgments, he should think of a number of different people he knows who are quite different from one another. A category then corresponds to one person. To make this task applicable to the study presented in this chapter, black and white subjects were asked to sort primarily physical characteristics representative of the black community into categories representing subgroups within black culture.

METHOD

Overview

Rosenberg et al.'s (1968) procedure was applied to a sample of primarily physical characteristics representative of the black community. Details of the rationale for using the trait-sorting technique can be found in Rosenberg et al. Following an outline of the Rosenberg procedure presented by Friendly and Glucksberg (1970), the method entails: (1) selecting characteristics to be studied; (2) obtaining distance estimates between the items; (3) obtaining a MDS solution to represent the distances spatially; and (4) obtaining ratings of each of the characteristics on a number of undimensional, bipolar scales and using multiple regression techniques to determine the location of the axes in the hypothetical geometric space corresponding to the inferred dimensions of the space.

Selection of Black Characteristics and Subjects

The 32 black characteristics employed are listed in Table 1. The traits were selected by black consultants[1] to represent a wide range of possible characteristics existing within the black community.

Twenty-one black and 32 white subjects, all from the University of Illinois, performed the sorting task. The white subjects were enrolled in an elementary psychology course and received course credit for their participation. The black subjects were all volunteers from university residence halls and were paid $2.00 for their services. All subjects were tested in small, homogeneous racial groups of 4 to 8 subjects. The race of the experimenter corresponded to the race of the subjects.[2]

Sorting Task for MDS

Each subject was given a packet of 32 randomly ordered cards. Each card contained one of the characteristics from Table 1. Using a slight variation of Rosenberg et al.'s instructions, subjects were told to sort the cards into an arbitrary number of categories, with each category representing some real black person or group of black people. Subjects were informed that if there were any characteristics that they felt could go equally well into more than one category, they should request an additional copy of that card from the experimenter. Subjects were also allowed to use a miscellaneous category for characteristics which could not appropriately be placed into any other category. Subjects were allowed to reassign traits among their categories until they signaled that they had completed the task. They were then asked to write down a few phrases describing the "type" of person that each category represented.

Distance Measure

The degree of dissimilarity between any two characteristics was assessed with the disassociation measure (δ_{ij}) developed by Rosenberg et al. As summarized by

TABLE 1

LIST OF CHARACTERISTICS USED IN THE STUDY

1. Clean-cut and clean shaven.
2. Flashes the peace sign when greeting friends.
3. Believes that progress can be made within the system.
4. Says, "Blackness bro!" when greeting black friends.
5. Individualistic behavior.
6. Wears a dashiki.
7. Wears conventional work clothes.
8. Believes in revolution rather than gradual change.
9. Dresses like a hippie.
10. Has a well-groomed natural.
11. Has a beard.
12. Gives black power sign when greeting other blacks.
13. Says, "Hello, how are you, " when greeting friends.
14. Does not talk about the black-white situation.
15. Believes in money power not black power.
16. Embraces blacks in long, black handshake.
17. Says, "Say, baby, what's up?" when greeting black friends.
18. Embraces blacks in regular handshake.
19. Speaks grammatically correct English.
20. Believes he should be concerned only with self.
21. Says, "What's happenin'!" when greeting black friends.
22. Believes blacks are responsible for their present status.
23. Says, "How are you, John, Bill, etc." when greeting black friends.
24. Embraces blacks in short version of black handshake.
25. Has a long natural.
26. Dresses according to current black fashion.
27. Conforms to employers' expectations.
28. Says, "Hey now, whatta you in to?" when greeting black friends.
29. Says, "What's going on?" when greeting black friends.
30. Imitation of white language frowned upon.
31. Believes in getting blacks better jobs within the system.
32. Says, "What are you into?" when greeting black friends.

Friendly and Glucksberg (1970), the δ_{ij} measure reflects the number of times any two characteristics, i and j, are not assigned to the same person. The measure is derived from (1) a disagreement score, d_{ij}, the number of subjects in a group who place characteristics i and j into different categories, that is, attribute them to different people, and (2) a measure of indirect association, which takes into account the disagreement scores of i and j with the other items. Essentially, the measure of indirect association can best be thought of as an indicator of the base line frequency with which i and j are associated with other traits. Details of the derivation of Equation 1, which was used to obtain δ_{ij} for each trait pair, may be found in Rosenberg et al.:

$$\delta_{ij} = \sum_{k \in T} (d_{ik} - d_{jk})^2 \qquad (1)$$

where T is the set of items.

Unidimensional Scales

Each subject, upon completion of the sorting task, was asked to rate each of the 32 characteristics on five seven-point bipolar adjective scales. These scales were each scored 1 to 7; liberal-conservative, conformist-nonconformist, militant-nonmilitant, old-young, and good-bad. Subjects were told to be very careful to make each judgment in terms of a black person who has the characteristic being rated. Subjects were also given the standard instructions for semantic differential judgments (Osgood, Suci, and Tannenbaum, 1957).

Means were calculated separately for black and white subjects for each characteristic on each of the five scales. For white subjects, the intercorrelations of the mean scale ratings are presented in Table 2. Similar intercorrelations for black subjects are presented in Table 3. Unfortunately, all correlations within both tables are relatively high and significant at less than the .01 level; therefore, because the various unidimensional scales selected (representing our hypotheses as to the identity of the potential dimensions within the solutions) are so highly intercorrelated, they will all probably be correlated with the same dimensions in the MDS solution.

Tables 2 and 3, however, yield one very interesting finding. Using Peabody's (1967) distinction between evaluation and descriptive aspects in trait inferences, the magnitude and sign for the intercorrelation among the four descriptive scales are almost identical for black and white subjects. However, correlations involving the evaluative good-bad scale show consistency across subject populations with regard to magnitude of correlation, but the sign of the correlation is reversed. For example, if the characteristic "Believes in revolution rather than gradual change" is rated as liberal, there is a strong possibility that both black and white subjects will also tend to rate it as nonconformist, militant, and young. However, white subjects will tend to rate the characteristic as bad, whereas black subjects will rate it as good. Thus, characteristics *evaluated* quite differently by black and white subjects were *described* in very similar ways by both subject groups across a number of scales. This finding is contrary to expectations based on theories of affective or evaluative consistency, but consistent with Peabody's notion that trait inferences are determined more by descriptive than evaluative similarity.

TABLE 2

INTERCORRELATIONS OF UNIDIMENSIONAL SCALES FOR WHITE SUBJECTS

Unidimensional Scales	Liberal-Conservative	Conformist-Nonconformist	Militant-Nonmilitant	Old-Young
Conformist-Nonconformist	-.97			
Militant-Nonmilitant	.96	-.96		
Old-Young	-.97	.95	-.93	
Good-Bad	-.55	.63	-.71	.54

NOTE: The five scales ranged from 1-7.

TABLE 3

INTERCORRELATIONS OF UNIDIMENSIONAL SCALES FOR BLACK SUBJECTS

Unidimensional Scales	Liberal-Conservative	Conformist-Nonconformist	Militant-Nonmilitant	Old-Young
Conformist-Nonconformist	-.80			
Militant-Nonmilitant	.75	-.87		
Old-Young	-.83	.84	-.79	
Good-Bad	.53	-.61	.79	-.62

NOTE: The five scales ranged from 1-7.

RESULTS AND DISCUSSION

Multidimensional Scaling

A version of TORSCA, a nonmetric multidimensional scaling computer program developed by Young and Torgerson (1967), was used for the multidimensional scaling. The program computes a geometric representation of a data matrix such that the distances between the points in the representation best reproduce the *order* of the entries in the matrix. This program also computes Kruskal's (1964) measure of goodness of fit, termed "stress," for each solution and expresses it as a percentage.

Dimensionality

The appropriate dimensionality is, in terms of Kruskal's stress measure, estimated by obtaining a one-dimensional solution, a two-dimensional solution, a three-dimensional solution, and so on, until (1) the fit is satisfactory, and (2) no real improvement is obtained by adding dimensions. Based on experience with other kinds of data, Kruskal (1964) suggests that a stress of 5% is "good," while 10% is "fair." Kruskal's stress measure was calculated separately for the black and white data.

A three-dimensional solution for white subjects and a four-dimensional solution for black subjects were selected as the best solutions. The stress values indicated that the three-dimensional solution for white subjects (stress = 5.2%) and the four-dimensional solution for black subjects (stress = 5.5%) yielded stress values that were very similar and quite close to Kruskal's "good" criteria. There is little decrease in stress values with higher dimensional solutions for either group. In addition, examination of other dimensional solutions (2 to 5 dimensions) for both black and white data by the author and a number of black and white consultants indicated that the three-dimensional solution for whites and the four-dimensional solution for blacks provide the highest dimensional solutions in which all dimensions are psychologically meaningful. Therefore, attempts at interpretation will be limited to the three-dimensional solution for whites and the four-dimensional solution for blacks.

Interpretation of Dimensions

Table 4 presents the values for each of the 32 characteristics on the four dimensions of the black subjects' solution and the three dimensions of the white subjects' solution. An attempt was made to identify these dimensions in terms of the unidimensional scales with which they had the highest correlations. Correlations between the five unidimensional scales and dimensions defining the black and white subjects' spaces are presented in Tables 5 and 6, respectively.[3] As can be seen in these tables, the unidimensional sclaes are all highly intercorrelated. Thus, in general, all the unidimensional scales tend to correlate with the same dimensions.

TABLE 4

VALUES OF EACH OF THE CHARACTERISTICS ON THE FOUR DIMENSIONS OF THE BLACK SUBJECTS' SOLUTION AND THE THREE DIMENSIONS OF THE WHITE SUBJECTS' SOLUTION

Character-istics	Dimensions of the Black Subjects' Solution				Dimensions of the White Subjects' Solution		
	1	2	3	4	1	2	3
1	-.279	-.023	-.299	-.501	.487	-.436	-.877
2	.012	-.165	.015	.022	-.032	.449	.039
3	-.231	-.040	-.237	-.479	.759	-.069	-.331
4	.679	-.064	-.119	.630	-.979	.022	.272
5	-.147	-.033	-.191	-.299	-.226	.060	.075
6	.349	.483	.713	.269	-.690	.183	.401
7	-.289	-.130	-.006	-.208	.495	-.298	-.275
8	.546	.428	-.029	.732	-.706	.189	.658
9	.062	-.452	.047	-.040	-.318	.345	.058
10	-.017	.627	.171	.114	.003	.116	-.356
11	-.060	-.300	.319	.095	-.254	.133	.317
12	.334	.207	.331	.944	-.769	-.256	.537
13	-.295	.099	-.313	-.751	.637	-.549	-.469
14	-.519	-.236	-.212	-.405	.405	-.113	-.311
15	-.518	-.115	-.297	-.289	.467	-.231	-.653
16	.726	.417	.255	.160	-.554	-.081	.734
17	.286	-.223	.201	.241	-.465	.222	.250
18	-.826	.042	-.161	-.257	.858	-.257	-.468
19	-.633	.391	-.157	-.402	.874	-.307	-.174
20	-.151	-.165	-.476	-.147	.067	.061	.011
21	.689	.073	.399	.256	-.170	.151	.134
22	-.389	-.379	-.207	-.433	.326	.009	-.206
23	-.697	-.152	-.254	-.676	.612	-.145	-.533
24	.316	-.014	.169	.201	.090	.372	-.123
25	.588	-.049	.080	.123	-.437	.229	.450
26	.143	.093	.179	.307	-.397	.028	.219
27	-.632	.097	-.473	-.464	.603	-.085	-.318
28	.198	-.085	.342	.135	-.437	.073	.369
29	.398	-.116	.078	.282	-.074	.077	.066
30	.337	.153	-.113	.511	-.403	.197	.779
31	-.073	-.183	-.052	-.081	.372	-.319	-.346
32	.093	-.184	.299	.410	-.145	.231	.073

NOTE: The characteristics that correspond to the numbers 1-32 can be found in Table 1.

TABLE 5

CORRELATIONS BETWEEN THE FOUR DIMENSIONS OF THE BLACK SUBJECTS' SOLUTION AND THE UNIDIMENSIONAL SCALES

Unidimensional Scales	Dimensions			
	I	II	III	IV
Liberal-Conservative	-.69	-.05	-.60	-.72
Conformist-Nonconformist	.81	.15	.61	.80
Militant-Nonmilitant	-.83	-.40	-.65	-.91
Old-Young	.83	.22	.64	.80
Good-Bad	-.64	-.51	-.47	-.69

NOTE: The five scales ranged from 1-7.

TABLE 6

CORRELATIONS BETWEEN THE THREE DIMENSIONS OF THE WHITE SUBJECTS' SOLUTION AND THE UNIDIMENSIONAL SCALES

Unidimensional Scales	Dimensions		
	I	II	III
Liberal-Conservative	.92	-.69	-.87
Conformist-Nonconformist	-.94	.68	.89
Militant-Nonmilitant	.94	-.63	-.93
Old-Young	-.91	.72	.81
Good-Bad	-.67	.37	.68

NOTE: The five scales ranged from 1-7.

In an additional attempt to investigate the interrelations among the dimensions of the two MDS solutions, the four dimensions of the black subjects' solution and the three dimensions of the white subjects' solution were intercorrelated. These correlations were computed by comparing the value for each stimulus characteristic on each of the seven dimensions. The intercorrelations indicated that there was a significant amount of common variance shared by four of the seven dimensions: Dimensions I and IV from the black solution and Dimensions I and III from the white solution. All intercorrelations among these four dimensions were significant at less than the .01 level, indicating that the stimulus characteristics aligned themselves similarly along these four dimensions.

A canonical correlation computed between the two stimulus spaces provides additional support for this observation. There was only one significant canonical correlation (R = .91, p < .01, using Bartlett's chi-square approximation test); and as expected, in the formation of these significantly correlated canonical variates, Dimensions I and III from the white subjects' space and Dimensions I and IV from the black subjects' space had the highest loadings. With these interrelationships in mind, let us turn to an interpretation of the dimensions.

Dimension I for the black subjects' solutions was interpreted as an *overt militancy-nonmilitancy* dimension. It correlated -.83 with the militant-nonmilitant scale, .83 with the old-young scale, and .81 with the conformist-nonconformist scale. Characteristics aligning themselves on the militant, young, nonconformist end of the dimension include: Embraces blacks in long black handshake; Says, "Blackness Bro!" when greeting black friends; Has a long natural; and Says, "What's happenin?" when greeting black friends. Characteristics falling on the nonmilitant, old, conformist end of the dimension include: Embraces blacks in regular handshake; Says, "How are you, John, Bill, etc." when greeting black friends; Speaks grammatically correct English; and Conforms to employer's expectations. The emphasis in this dimension is on overt miltant and nonmilitant behaviors.

Dimension IV, which, as mentioned previously, is highly correlated with Dimension I, was interpreted as a *covert militancy-nonmilitancy* dimension. In this dimension greater emphasis is placed on private militancy-nonmilitancy, for example militant and nonmilitant beliefs, than on overt militancy-nonmilitancy. Dimension IV was correlated -.91 with the militant-nonmilitant unidimensional scale. Focusing specifically on those items with very high values on Dimension IV but with only moderate or low values on Dimension I, at the militancy end of the dimension we find: Believes in revolution rather than gradual change; and Imitation of white language frowned upon. Both of these characteristics can be considered beliefs. The nonmilitancy end of this dimension also includes a number of belief statements including: Believes that progress can be made within the system; and Believes blacks are responsible for their low status.

Dimension II for the black subjects' solutions was interpreted as a *slick dude-jive, out-of-it* dimension. Among the unidimensional scales, the good-bad scale correlated best with this dimension (r = -.51), indicating that the slick dude end of the dimension is considered by black subjects to be the good end of the dimension. Stimuli falling at this end of the dimension include: Has a well groomed natural; Speaks grammatically correct English; and Wears a dashiki. The stimuli characterizing the jive, out-of-it end of the dimension include: Dresses like a hippie; Has a beard; and Believes blacks are responsible for their low status. It is significant to note that, of the four dimensions in the black subjects' solutions, this dimension correlates most poorly on the average with the four descriptive unidimensional scales. The present author, who selected the unidimensional scales, did not anticipate this dimension; however, on the basis of an informal content analysis of the short descriptions that black subjects wrote about each of their categories, it appears that this dude-jive dimension is very salient among black subjects.

Dimension III was designated as a *self oriented-black movement* and *black experience oriented* dimension. This dimension correlated about ± .60 with each of the four descriptive unidimensional scales. The nonmilitant, old, conformist, conservative pole of the dimension was interpreted as the more traditional self-oriented end of the dimension. Stimuli characterizing this pole of the dimension include: Believes he should be concerned only with self; Believes in money power, not black power; and Conforms to employer's expectations. Stimuli located nearest the black experience oriented pole include: Wears a dashiki; Gives black power sign when greeting other blacks; and Embraces other blacks in long black handshake. Let us now turn to a discussion of the white subjects' stimulus space.

As previously mentioned, Dimensions I and III from the white subjects' solution and Dimensions I and IV from the black subjects' solution are all significantly intercorrelated. As might be expected by this pattern of inter-correlations, actual inspection of the configuration of characteristics suggest that Dimension I for white subjects was quite comparable to Dimension I obtained for black subjects. Both dimensions appear primarily to be tapping a dimension of overt militancy-nonmilitancy. Thus, Dimension I for white subjects has also been labeled *overt militancy-nonmilitancy*. Further inspection of the configuration of characteristics suggested that Dimension III from the white subjects' solutions was measuring the same covert militancy-nonmilitancy dimension as Dimension IV for black subjects. Thus, Dimension III for white subjects was labeled *covert militancy-nonmilitancy*.

Dimension II from the white subjects' solution was designated *establishment-antiestablishment*. The dimension correlated significantly with each of the descriptive scales (range, ± .63 to ± .72). The more militant, young, non-conformist, liberal pole of the dimension was interpreted as the anti-establishment pole. Stimuli characterizing this end of the dimension include: Dresses like a hippie; Flashes the peace sign; and Has a long natural. Stimuli characterizing the establishment end of the dimension include: Clean-cut and clean shaven; Wears conventional work clothes; and Speaks grammatically correct English.

CONCLUSIONS

The initial hypothesis, that MDS would reflect differences in the structure of black stimulus characteristics as a function of race of subject, has been confirmed. As expected, black subjects, having, in general, greater familiarity with aspects of black society than white subjects, exhibited greater differentiation between black characteristics. This was indicated by the higher dimensionality of the black subjects' solution. Two dimensions, *overt militancy-nonmilitancy* and *covert militancy-nonmilitancy,* were common to both the black and white solutions. One dimension, *establishment-antiestablishment,* was unique to the white solution. Two dimensions, *slick dude-jive, out of it* and *self oriented-black movement oriented* were unique to the black solution.

This study provides a number of implications for improving both black and white cultural assimilators. White subjects should be taught that, in addition to making distinctions between militant and nonmilitant blacks, they also need to distinguish between jive and dude blacks and between blacks who are self-oriented and those who are black movement-oriented. In addition, it should be made more salient to both black and white subjects that their evaluations of subgroups within the black culture are diametrically opposed. The incorporation of these principles in an assimilator, however, should be contingent on validation of the importance of distinguishing between these subgroups using a behavioral criterion (e.g., behavioral differential). Research investigating these relations is currently being conducted at the University of Illinois.

The present research, in accord with the previous research of Warr, Schroder, and Blackman (1969), illustrates the usefulness of MDS methodology in cross-cultural research. This methodology allows for a compromise solution to the emic-etic dilemma (Pike, 1966) found in most cross-cultural research. That is, it is possible to extract a set of pan-cultural (etic) dimensions and an additional set of culture-unique (emic) dimensions. However, as in factor analysis, the interpretation of the dimensions is left to the judgment of the researcher and his consultants.

In conclusion, it seems worthwhile to anticipate a frequent reaction to research of the present type. Namely, to what extent can we solve the real world problem of poor intercultural relations on the basis of the information gained in this esoteric laboratory study. With solely the data from the present research, one could do little more than make an enlightened conjecture as how best to solve our real world problem. Solving a problem, however, was not the purpose of this study. Rather, the present research was designed to test one link in a general model of intercultural disagreements, presented by Triandis in the preceding chapter. A number of laboratory and field studies are currently testing other aspects of this theory. If, in this programmatic research effort the model receives support, we will have some evidence that the model provides an accurate description of the underlying process of intercultural disagreements. The descriptive model can then be used as a logical basis for determining what kinds of culture training will be most effective and at what stage in the process they should be administered. In addition, because the emphasis of the present work is on testing a general model rather than on solving a specific heterocultural problem, the knowledge gained in this research program should be applicable to a wide variety of intercultural disagreements.

NOTES

1. The author is primarily indebted to Freddie Lambert for selecting the 32 black characteristics.

2. Jerry Crayton, who served as the black experimenter, was also in charge of recruitment of black subjects and aided greatly in preliminary data analysis and interpretation of the black multidimensional space.

3. Multiple correlations (regressing the value of each characteristic for each dimension on to the mean unidimensional scale score for that characteristic) were also computed. They are not reported because the multiple correlation was never significantly higher than the highest zero order correlation.

REFERENCES

DAVIDSON, A.R. and J. FELDMAN (1971) "An attribution theory analysis of interracial conflict in job settings." Report No. 11, SRS No. 12-P-55175/5. Champaign, Ill.: University of Illinois, Department of Psychology.

FIEDLER, F. 1966) "The effect of leadership and cultural heterogeneity on group performance: a test of the contingency model." Journal of Experimental Social Psychology 2: 237-267.

––– T. MITCHELL, and H. TRIANDIS (1971) "The cultural assimilator: an approach to cross-cultural training." Journal of Applied Psychology 55: 95-102.

FRIENDLY, M. and S. GLUCKSBERG (1970) "On the description of subcultural lexicons: a multidimensional approach." Journal of Personality and Social Psychology 14: 55-65.

GREEN, P. and T. MORRIS (1969) "Individual difference models in multidimensional scaling: an empirical comparison." Working paper. Philadelphia: Univeristy of Pennsylvania.

KELMAN, H. (1963) "The reaction of participants in a foreign specialists seminar to their American experiences." Journal of Social Issues 19: 61-114.

KRUSKAL, J. (1964) "Nonmetric multidimensional scaling: II." Psychometrica 29: 115-129.

MEEHL, P. (1967) "Theory testing in psychology and physics: a methodological paradox." Philosophy of Science 34: 103-115.

OSGOOD, C., G. SUCI, and P. TANNENBAUM (1957) "The measurement of meaning." Urbana: University of Illinois Press.

PEABODY, D. (1967) "Trait inferences: evaluative and descriptive aspects." Journal of Personality and Social Psychology Monograph 4: (Whole No. 664).

PIKE, K. (1966) "Language in relation to a unified theory of the structure of human behavior." The Hague: Mouton.

ROSENBERG, S., C. NELSON, and P. VIVEHANANTHAN (1968) "A multidimensional approach to the structure of personality impressions." Journal of Personality and Social Psychology 9: 283-294.

SCOTT, W. (1969) "Structure of natural cognitions." Journal of Personality and Social Psychology 12: 261-278.

WARR, P., H. SCHRODER, and S. BLACKMAN (1969) "The structure of political judgment." British Journal of Social and Clinical Psychology 8: 32-43.

WIGHT, A. (1969) A Draft Handbook for Cross-Cultural and Community Involvement Training. Estes Park, Color. Center for Research and Education.

YOUNG, F. and W. TORGERSON (1967) "TORSCA, a Fortran IV program for Shepard-Kruskal multidimensional scaling analysis." Behavioral Science 12: 48.

Chapter 3

A BEHAVIORAL ANALYSIS OF CULTURE LEARNING

G E O R G E   M.   G U T H R I E

Pennsylvania State University

Learning to live in an alien society is much more than learning to speak a strange language, to eat unfamiliar food, and to observe different social customs. It involves a subtle but important change in one's expectations of oneself and of others and in the controls one feels over his emotions. One has to learn to do many new things and to stop a number of actions that are of long standing. But, more important, one has to cope with a loss of identity and familiarity and to get along without some of the social events that provide encouragement, direction, and meaning in our lives. Those who became discouraged or angry in the new setting can teach us a great deal about everyone's problems of learning, especially if we can get their reports of their experiences before they return to the shelter of home.

What sorts of difficulties do people who try to live in alien settings encounter? There is a sameness, almost a monotony about Americans' difficulties. It's not the physical environment, the heat, the food, nor the risk of infection. It's the people:

> There wouldn't be many problems if these people would just behave sensibly and honestly. Although we try to set an example by a forthright and open statement of our goals, they continue their devious ways. These people have to learn not to say one thing and mean something else, and not to promise things they have no intention of fulfilling. The problem, of course, is that this is what they have learned, but with education they can learn more effective methods of problem solving, learn to face issues more objectively, and be less influenced by emotions and old prejudices.

Those who have worked in alien settings have heard or uttered such statements until they are as familiar as their passport number.

People were not always so charitable in their analyses of misunderstandings in cross-cultural contacts. Interpretations used to be primarily moral: good guys and bad guys, civilized men and barbarians, chosen people and gentiles, and Christian and heathen. Eighteenth- and nineteenth-century Western travelers were quite outspoken in their reactions as a cursory reading of Fraser's *Golden Bough* will indicate.

This sort of writing no longer appears, but the emotional turmoil that prompted it is still experienced. Few authors express the moral superiority which permeated earlier reports, but this does not mean that value judgments and moral reactions are no longer important. It is quite possible that a refusal to recognize these reactions leads to a good deal of the confusion people may encounter in their attempts to live and work in alien societies. We have become so accustomed to the I-love-their-differences approach that Colin Turnbull's recent book (1972) caused reviewers to express surprise that a thoroughly unlikeable group of people had been found and that someone would say so· in writing.

Living and working in an alien society involves a profound challenge not only to one's problem-solving abilities and to one's ability to maintain emotional composure but to one's gastrointestinal and immunologic processes as well. There is also an evaluative or moral component which is often overlooked, which has to do with differences between the hosts' and the visitor's habits of approving various activities. In this paper I propose to review some observations which have been reported by sojourners, to analyze some of their experiences using behavioristic concepts, to cite some experiments that may enhance our understanding of the processes sojourners undergo, and to suggest some implications for those who work in alien societies. In this analysis of culture learning I will draw heavily on my experience with Americans living in the Philippines and on training efforts and research data from the Peace Corps. As the title of my paper suggests, I plan to approach the problem as a social behaviorist, which means that I will speak a certain dialect, worship certain ancestors, utter certain incantations, and hold certain truths as revealed.

The need to understand members of other societies has become imperative: some of them possess weapons that could wipe us out in less time than it takes me to deliver this paper. The sentiments of my early paragraph are hopelessly out of date. At one time, and not too long ago, peoples who were in contact related to one another largely as conquerors and enslaved; at least the strong demanded tribute from their weaker neighbors. More distant peoples were candidates for trade. The ideological invasions, primarily of Christian missionaries, and the era of colonies which is still with us required more knowledge about alien culture patterns. The alliances and assistance relationships of the twentieth century required still more understanding than the empire building of the eighteenth and nineteenth centuries. But we now face a situation in which communication satellites, rapid travel, and nuclear weapons have made us all more or less equal and more or less neighbors. While understanding one's neighbor will not guarantee that one will not do him in, misunderstanding him certainly raises the likelihood that one will see him as a threat. The ongoing accommodations necessary for peace are less likely to occur if we misinterpret the premises of others' actions.

Living in an alien culture can be emotionally exhilarating; it can also be an emotionally shattering experience. Probably most who live for more than a short interval among people with different culture patterns would say that both things happened to them. The difficulties one encounters vary depending on one's age, previous experience, role in the new setting and, I believe, one's experiences during the first few days and weeks in the new setting. Failure to learn to live effectively in an unfamiliar culture may have serious or trivial consequences depending on whether one is the ambassador or a student on a 3-month exchange visit.

There are certain indications that learning is not going well: increased irritability, impatience, depression, loss of appetite, poor sleep, and vague physical symptoms. This has been described as *culture shock* by Oberg (1960), but I have suggested that it might be more appropriately called *culture fatigue* (Guthrie, 1967). Certainly satisfaction falls off, but performance and willingness to stay on the job may not change. Performance, satisfaction, and tenure are lowly correlated in industry at home (Brayfield and Crockett, 1955); there is no reason to expect them to covary in an alien setting, with the exception that satisfaction may be an essential element in performance in some folk societies. Lynch and Maretzki (1966) report that Filipino villagers considered happiness for Peace Corps volunteers in the Philippines an essential element in good performance. Of course, if dissatisfaction becomes too intense at home or abroad, an individual drops out altogether and performance falls to zero.

Because Brein and David (1971) have provided a very comprehensive review of the adjustment of sojourners and Brislin (1970) has surveyed training strategies, I will not review these areas of research. Although a good deal is known about how to train a person to perform the duties that may be expected of him abroad and to speak the language, there is very little systematic information about methods by which he can be prepared to cope with the extraordinary demands of a new culture. Some very thoughtful people insist that no preparation in a formal sense is possible; one learns to cope with the new demands by experiencing them. Each individual has to master the situation from the beginning. I do not agree with this position, but I do acknowledge that no training program can convey the full meaning of the second culture. I am convinced that, by offering certain kinds of information and by helping trainees develop certain attitudes, the likelihood of their success on the job can be increased. The position taken is that much of the variance in performance abroad can be attributed to factors in experiences during training and especially during the early stages of life in the second country, and that relatively less of the variance can be accounted for by the character structure and deeper personality factors of the individual. Because the new experience is in so many ways noncontinuous with previous experiences, one's behavior is probably determined more by recent events and less by long-term patterns and habits.

Training and initial experiences in the new society may have much more to do with performance in the society than they would if one were accepting a new assignment in old haunts.

Moving into a new culture can be a profound and hard-to-describe experience. One is deprived of familiar cues and controls. The subtle, unspoken conventions that one has learned from childhood are changed; familiar gestures take on new meanings; many of the old experiences from which one derived satisfaction and support are no longer there. It is analogous to the experience of sensory deprivation, an experimental condition in which one is progressively denied sensations from his various sense organs until, sensing nothing, he becomes frightened and disoriented. In a way, it is like that brief interval upon awakening when we do not know where we are. One can experience this only if he cuts himself off from the familiar and goes into the new situation alone. The tourist, or anyone who works abroad in a large city, rarely has this experience because he takes with him enough of the familiar things of home, such as food and clothing, so that he is always firmly anchored to a reality he understands. These same things that make life more tolerable for him also cut him off from the people around him so that he continues to live and feel and think as he always has. As long as he can maintain this pattern, he will probably meet his responsibilities and wonder why others get so upset. For many assignments, this may be the optimum strategy.

I would like to draw further on the reports of Peace Corps volunteers. Although they are not representative of all who are faced with culture learning problems, they do represent a rich source of information because volunteers did try to learn to come to terms with unfamiliar cultures and also because Peace Corpsmen were accessible, numerous, and articulate.

David Szanton (1967), who served in the second group in the Philippines, has described a sequence of experiences through which many volunteers appeared to pass. There was the initial flush of excitement produced by the warm welcome of the Filipinos and by the novel environment. After a few weeks this subsided and the volunteer set about trying to develop his assignment so that he could feel useful. This was accompanied by an increasing awareness that the society was different in spite of the warm and familiar feelings aroused by the initial reception. At this point, several months after arrival, volunteers almost without exception reacted with vigor and made some serious efforts to master the intricacies of the new situation in which they found themselves. Progress, however, was halting, and not all persevered. Some ultimately reacted to this situation by limiting their contact with the society, by concentrating on their jobs, and by seeking their relaxation in their own American ways, often with other Peace Corpsmen. They were not critical of Filipinos. but they were often quite bitter about all phases of the Peace Corps. Others managed to achieve considerable competence in the language and in the subtleties of the society. Rather than move away from the people, they moved toward them and began to experience life something the way Filipinos do. Both groups may have performed equally well, but those who withdrew missed learning the meaning of life to the Filipino and the insight that such knowledge can offer about oneself.

One of the early experiences reported by many volunteers was feeling that Filipinos had cooled in their relationships with them after the first extravagant welcome. This is an example of the American's failure to differentiate between a social form and the expression of personal feelings. Filipino hospitality is a tradition. This does not mean it is insincere, but it does not carry the same meaning that it does for the American. The Filipinos said they were very happy to have the Americans among them. The Americans in effect said, "We are very happy to be here, now let's get to work." The second step simply did not follow in the Philippine way of thinking. Americans found it extremely hard to grasp that just having the American there was enhancing to the town but that some of his ideas about work were almost embarrassing. Different values regarding the importance of work, and the Americans' overwhelming urge to "do something" played an important role in difficulties early groups had with their job definitions.

After volunteers has been on the job for a few months and had begun to develop some perspective on themselves, a number of them began to experience some conflicts about the degree to which they should change their behavior patterns to be like those of the Filipinos. Many felt that they were being insincere and not honest to themselves. To accommodate to Philippine ways was seen as compromising and denying one's own identity: "I was born and raised an American, I can never be a Filipino no matter how hard I try." Because these volunteers made every effort to understand Filipino ways, they expected Filipinos to understand them and make adjustments to their American ways. Besides, if reassurance were needed, they felt many American ways to be more efficient, as American progress bears witness. Many began to raise seriously the question, "How can we help them if we define our task as adopting their ways?" It would appear that some volunteers were experiencing their attempts to come to terms with Philippine ways as a loss of personal values, a price they began to question.

Some were overtaken by an acute self-consciousness which was partly a result of being stared at and partly the result of continual vigilance in an attempt to reduce the possibility of social errors. In an attempt to avoid blunders they were sure they would make, these struggling individuals had given up their spontaneity and were as self-conscious of every move as one is of every word when he is trying to learn a new language. It is not hard to see that such an effort proved exhausting and more difficult the longer it was practiced. The role of the learner can be most unpleasant, particularly if one finds it hard to acknowledge the inevitability of mistakes. What appears to be needed is some humility about one's own social competence and enough self-confidence to keep trying.

Closely related to learning new modes of behavior were anxieties about personal identity. In a situation where one is different from everyone else, one looks at oneself much more closely than ever before. Conflicts of this sort appear elsewhere in life, but usually there are familiar models available to calm the uncertainties that are aroused. In the loneliness of a new and different group of people and in a situation where the familiar ways of doing and feeling do not seem right, one begins to wonder what sort of person he really is: "If I can't be my old familiar self, what kind of person will I become?" In pondering this problem many volunteers felt that they came to some remarkable insights and developed a new awareness of their strengths and limitations. Facing oneself in strange surroundings may be far from an assuring experience: one will not like nor understand all that he sees, and one may change his view of himself in ways he did not think possible.

An untold number of volunteers endured the anxiety of uncertainty until both they and their hosts became more predictable. This opened a new world, one in which it was possible to know something of the deeper feelings of another people and to communicate in both their spoken and unspoken languages. Those who achieved this transition have offered a number of beautiful statements of their feelings, statements which to paraphrase is to destroy. These experiences have an ineffable, religious quality about them. Many found that they could describe the depth of their emotions only in religious terminology, a terminology they had not previously used because they were not actively religious (see Szanton, 1967: 51-53).

In the same vein, those who were most articulate about the deep personal significance of the encounter observed that learning to cope with the mysteries of another society was inevitably stressful. They contended that those who had said they enjoyed every moment of it had really never come to grips with the meaning of meeting another people on their terms. This is not the kind of material that lends itself to questionnaires, nor is it shared with strangers. It is, rather, a deeply personal adventure filled with adversities and triumphs. The costs involve some painful insights into oneself, and the rewards include a new capacity for human relationships. It means something different for each person, but for all it involves fulfillment of oneself and a new appreciation of others.

Not only does living in an alien culture have a profound effect on one's emotions and values, it affects one's body as well. Each individual develops resistance and immunities to many of the disease organisms in his environment, but these protections do not necessarily extend to new environments nor to new bacterial agents. Tuberculosis and measles, for instance, decimated native populations who had none of the acquired immunities of the Europeans who carried the diseases to them. Similarly, Europeans may fall victim to cholera and other disorders to which the Europeans have not been exposed. Beyond that, and of greater significance here, is the complex relationship that exists between life changes and illness. Holmes and Rahe (1967) and Rahe and his colleagues

(1972), in an extended series of studies, have shown that there is a small but significant relationship between magnitude of life changes and somatic illness. Both variables have been very general—many different life changes are added— and the sum of all somatic symptoms regardless of locus, duration, or severity make up the dependent variable.

One could multiply these observations because each person who has lived abroad has reports of his own experiences or those of others. A note of caution needs to be introduced, however. Self-reports in this situation, as in many others, are likely to be distorted. We found that those who had worked abroad reported colleagues' difficulties in culture learning but almost invariably denied their own (Guthrie and Spencer, 1965). We believe that anecdotal and other material must be collected in the field because no one likes to recall past difficulties. By the time a sojourner has arrived home, he is no longer beset by many of the annoyances that beset him abroad and he recalls mostly the pleasant things about his experience.

We also acknowledge the qualitative, impressionistic, imprecise nature of the foregoing material. Ideally one would obtain tabulations of various activities or, less desirable in our opinion, ratings by participants on various scales so that one could give a more numerical indication of who did what. Such "hard data" may be ideal from some perspectives in certain situations: for our purposes here the personal accounts of participants are more productive of insights and suggestive of strategies whose effectiveness can be subjected later to careful counting. Numbers are for testing; they may get in the way of observation, especially when we do not know what to count.

ANALYSIS

Failures of learning to cope with a new culture have been matters of concern to many individuals and organizations; and, as with other human problems, many explanations and solutions have been offered. No one denies the central importance of language if one is going to achieve some depth of understanding of another society; but a good translator may be all that is necessary for many specialists with relatively short-term technical assignments (Guthrie and Spencer, 1965). There is a related area of nonverbal communication for which few instruction programs exist. One of the silent languages is proximity (Hall, 1959), but there are also cues and conventions which involve facial expressions, touching, posture, dressing, and the whole spectrum of paralinguistic cues of the volume, speed, and tone of speech. Finally, as is suggested by the Sapir-Whorf hypothesis, cognitive processes may differ in different linguistic systems. This is an intriguing suggestion, but I have not seen anyone work out its implications fully or demonstrate its operation under controlled conditions. Cole and his colleagues (1971) have made more progress than anyone in the general area of culture and cognitive processes with their studies of the learning of mathematics and of memory process by the Kpelle of Liberia.

Even with adequate communication, a newcomer to a culture faces differences in the ordering of values and acceptable modes of behavior. These differences may be especially difficult to identify because they are recognized only vaguely by those who hold them, who, in turn, have probably acquired their values through processes of imitation with a minimum of verbal mediation. Violations of values similarly may not be interpreted as a failure of understanding, as happens when a newcomer mispronounces a word or uses a strange phrase, but as signs of moral or ethical shortcomings. For instance, Filipino students give and receive a great deal of help from one another in classroom situations; one society's cooperativeness is another's cheating. Americans say they value frankness, but Filipinos experience this as insensitive behavior. The newcomer finds that he is disapproved of for reasons he does not know and that he fails to please others with strategies that always worked at home.

One can acknowledge the fact that values differ, but one cannot get along without approval. It is probably the loss of approval that precipitates the alienation and identity crises sojourners report. A group of Peace Corps volunteers in a West African country told me that one of their greatest problems was the failure of local people to say thank you for services rendered. They recognized that the Africans did not thank each other but that Africans were aware of services they rendered and received. But the failure of verbal acknowledgment which the Americans had been taught in their highchairs was most upsetting.

I tried on an earlier occasion (Guthrie, 1963) to show the parallels between learning to speak a second language and learning to live in a second culture (Table 1). This analysis reminds one that communication and culture are inseparable and that a major component of differences in cultures is differences in communication.

It may be useful to think of placing an individual in a novel cultural setting as an experiment. What happens to an individual if you put him in a new setting where people treat him differently, expecting new things from him, denying him the right to do some things he has done in the past, and reacting differently to things than past experience has led him to expect? Now, of course, this is not a conventional experiment in which all factors but one are held constant in order to determine the effect of the factor that is varied. In this situation many situational variables are changed, but the person—his language, body, memories, skills, and identity—is left constant. In a sense this is an experiment to determine the relative contributions of inner and social determinants of behavior. This, of course, has been one of the unsolved problems of personality theory in which some theorists have emphasized long-term, internalized, unconscious determinants while others have paid more attention to current, social factors as determinants of behavior.

TABLE 1

PARALLEL PRINCIPLES OF SECOND LANGUAGE
AND SECOND CULTURE LEARNING

Language	Culture
1. Acquired early, relatively fixed by the age of five.	1. Acquired early, relatively fixed by the age of five.
2. New language learned more easily by younger children.	2. New culture patterns are learned more easily by children than adults.
3. First language structures habits of thinking.	3. First culture determines habits of valuing.
4. A new language has a new set of pitch levels which one must learn.	4. A new culture has a new range of gestural and other expressive movements which are interpretable by the participants.
5. First language determines most of the errors in learning the second.	5. First culture introduces errors in interpretation of second culture.
6. An accent remains which reveals the first language.	6. Patterns from the first culture continue to distort and influence the expression of patterns from the new.
7. In instances of severe frustration or illness one reverts to his first language.	7. When the life is difficult one reverts to his childhood or early patterns of relationship.
8. One can usually express best his deepest feelings in his first language.	8. One can express best his deepest values in overt behavior patterns that are of long standing. It is more difficult to learn a new way of expressing love than a new style of clothing
9. One ponders his deepest personal values and problems in the words and concepts of his first language.	9. One feels most deeply either favorably or unfavorably in terms of his first learned value system. One's first culture determines one's most profound emotions.

In the usual formal social psychological experiment we can manipulate only some of the social variables which we believe are important determinants of behavior and we can do so only for a few minutes or an hour at best. We can manipulate size of group, knowledge of results, type of message, favorability of evaluation, and other social influences, but we know that the duration and intensity of these treatments are slight compared with the social pressures of everyday life. And the subject knows it too, well enough that he apparently tries to help us by playing the role of the good subject. These factors have prompted a renewed interest in naturalistic field studies and in nonreactive measures. What I am suggesting is that placing a person in an alien society constitutes a massive manipulation of important social psychological variables, a manipulation of greater magnitude and duration than we have achieved in laboratory studies. In contrast also to laboratory situations, the subject does not look upon the treatment as an experiment and distort his reactions to please the experimenter. Some shortcomings must be acknowledged: when many variables are changed, we may not be able to sort out the sources of main effects or identify the interactions, and we may have trouble collecting data on dependent variables because subjects are not confined. In addition, response biases of various sorts will continue to operate if we rely exclusively on verbal reports.

I propose, then, to look upon living in an alien society as a massive social psychological experiment in which independent variables are manipulated more extensively and pervasively than they are in typical experiments. From this perspective, by extrapolating from experiments others have reported, we may be able to understand some of the changes we have observed. Observations in alien settings may also suggest some new ideas which could be tested in new experiments.

Before we turn to the experiments, however, I would like to recall some empirical data which prompted much of the thinking of this paper. In 1961-62 Penn State trained the first four groups of Peace Corps volunteers bound for the Philippines. As part of that program we collected a great deal of data on each trainee, and we were able to collect information on their performance in the Philippines. In Table 2 we report the correlations among various predictors and the final overall performance rating obtained from American staff members. We were able to obtain criterion data from Filipinos for some 70 of the volunteers, data which were collected in another study by Lynch and Maretzki (1966). The correlations among American predictor and criterion and Filipino criterion data are given in Table 3. Until we got the Filipino data, we felt that our selection procedures might have some merit—not much, but some. The American selection board's ratings, however, correlated .004 with the Filipino's overall end-of-tour evaluation. Our Filipino training staff's predictions correlated .003 with their countrymen's final judgments, so it was not a matter simply of Filipinos and Americans looking for different qualities. What impressed us most was the noncontinuity of performance from the United States to the Philippines. How well one functioned in the United States did not predict how well he would do in a different cultural setting.

Further evidence of the noncontinuity of performance from the United States to other cultural settings is implied in the summary of Peace Corps attrition over the decade 1961 to 1971 supplied by Harris (1973). The percentage of volunteers who prematurely terminated their stay in their assignment, in short, those who quit or were sent home, climbed steadily from 10% to 37%. Some of this rise was due to increasing disillusionment with American foreign

TABLE 2

CORRELATIONS BETWEEN PREDICTORS' AND AMERICANS' FINAL PERFORMANCE RATING
(N = 278)

	Variable	1	2	3	4	5
1	Final performance					
2	Selection board	361				
3	Filipino training staff	226	466			
4	Peer choice	175	172	080		
5	English vocabulary	180	194	122	006	
6	Discussion group leader	317	457	248	056	087

SOURCE: Guthrie and Zektick (1967)

TABLE 3

CORRELATIONS BETWEEN PREDICTORS AND RATINGS FROM AMERICANS AND FROM FILIPINO
(N = 70 except variable 7, N = 36)

Variable	1	2	3	4	5	6	7	8	9	10	11
Americans' ratings											
1 Final performance											
2 Selection board	325										
3 Filipino training staff	229	540									
4 Peer choice	114	350	301								
5 English vocabulary	-005	022	103	-127							
6 Discussion group leader	288	476	405	041	-191						
7 Dialect proficiency	512	011	-078	147	100	075					
Filipinos' ratings											
8 Overall performance	-375	004	003	-049	061	-021	269				
9 Dialect proficiency	354	021	018	166	-002	-029	594	070			
10 Liked by community	420	180	283	192	-167	252	505	451	247		
11 Known in community	304	209	092	015	-047	173	645	458	241	534	
12 Effective in community	336	125	127	245	-135	069	544	361	389	408	453

SOURCE: Guthrie and Zektick (1967)

policy on the part of volunteers. It is also quite clear that selection processes had failed to improve and that no one had found a way to prevent culture fatigue. My contacts with different volunteers in the field during that decade lead me to believe that neither selection nor preparation improved or deteriorated significantly, but that it became acceptable to volunteers in the field and to Peace Corps staff to admit that they were miserable, that they lacked any feeling of accomplishment, and that they might as well go home.

In consultation with psychiatrists, we approved at final selection meetings a half dozen trainees who could reasonably have been dropped as too unstable for the stress of foreign assignments. All of them completed their tours without psychiatric mishap while at least three others without histories of instability had to be evacuated. The numbers do not prove our contention, but they suggest that patterns of instability are rooted in the environment as much as in the dynamic makeup of the individual. Shall we found a Travel School of Psychotherapy?

Still dealing in impressions, Spencer and I found that Americans who had worked abroad as technical assistants and specialists often commented on how different their American colleagues were in Nigeria or India and how they reverted when they returned to the home campus (Guthrie and Spencer, 1965). Both the selection and the clinical data emphasize the lack of continuities of the behavior of the same individuals from one society to another.

We believe it would be very useful to examine the change a sojourner experiences as a change in reinforcement contingencies. In the new setting, well-established behaviors are no longer reinforced, previously punished behavior no longer leads to aversive consequences, new behavior is acquired through imitation and because of new reinforcement contingencies. Of equal significance, because learned reinforcements are different from one society to another, the newcomer gets little satisfaction from many of the episodes that are deeply satisfying to the members of the host society. Not only have reinforcement contingencies and models been changed but so have the values of the tokens. It is as if some mischievous person switched the experimental animals from one study to another about the time that the experimenter had gotten his animals at stable rates of responding. Following this line of reasoning, we will examine some instances where changes in reinforcement contingencies have been imposed in controlled experiments. In short, what does the laboratory say to real life?

SOME ANALOGOUS EXPERIMENTS

I have suggested that we look upon an encounter with an alien society as an experimental situation in which the social determinants of behavior are changed extensively. In behavioral terminology, the sojourner faces a massive shift in reinforcement contingencies, a greater change than is usually imposed in experiments. More specifically, I would suggest that reinforcement for some behavior is terminated altogether; ratios are thinned for other activities; symbolic reinforcements are modified so that what is reinforcing for members of one society is aversive for those of another; and discriminating stimuli are changed, reducing the predictability of reinforcement. It is as if someone shifted the wires on the control panel after a stable pattern of responding had been established. The subject experiences these changes not as a loss of cues, as in sensory deprivation studies, but as a confusion of cues, a massive input of misinformation.

In alien settings just as at home, most new behavior is acquired through processes of imitation. We see someone do something and we do something similar, especially if the model was successful or reinforced. Behavior and attitudes in new settings are acquired primarily through observational learning. For this reason the first few weeks in a new setting influence greatly the later behavior patterns of the sojourner. It is said that an American oil company in the Middle East quarantines its newly arrived personnel with selected employees whose behavior toward Arabs the management would like the new arrivals to acquire. The evidence is anecdotal but persuasive and in keeping with learning principles which emphasize primacy. By the same token, the complaints of unhappy overseas Americans about their living conditions and social experiences are so monotonously similar that they were clearly learned from one another rather than from direct contact with the natives. Not only are attitudes and other overt behavior patterns learned from others, but so are people's physical reactions.

The analysis I am trying to develop is that moving to a new society is like changing the reinforcement program, changing the position of the bar to be pressed, even substituting a new required response for the press of the bar. To make matters more complicated, reinforcements may be changed and may be administered adventitiously. Worse than that, the sojourner and the natives may be administering reinforcements and /or negative consequences to each other without being aware that they are doing so.

I was disappointed when I examined the literature to find out what happens under these massive changes because no experimenter would or could publish findings based on such a chaotic procedure. Quite to the contrary, experimenters in this field try to achieve errorless automation. There are some experiments, however, which may help us understand better what happens to our non-naive subject who finds himself in an unfamiliar Skinner box. Following this line of thought we might fruitfully differentiate schedule-dependent and schedule-induced behavior (Gilbert and Millenson, 1972: xi). The former refers to patterns the experimenter is seeking to manipulate, and the latter to qualitative behavior changes incidental to certain stages of learning.

In the following paragraphs we would like to point out some of the parallels that exist between the experiences of living in a foreign culture and the behavior observed in the operant conditioning laboratory. Specifically we will look at extinction-produced aggression, changes in reinforcers, changes in secondary reinforcers, accidental reinforcement, and the reinforcement of novel behavior. Following that we will mention modeling and finally discuss some testable replications of the analyses for orientation programs.

One of the most common and readily apparent effects of being placed in an alien environment is the loss of familiar pleasant events. Deprived of friends, familiar food, and the usual entertainment, we may feel desperately lonely even though we are surrounded by people. The loss of learned reinforcements can be studied in the laboratory. Azrin, Hutchinson, and Hake (1966) introduced a second pigeon into the experimental apparatus at the same time as they began to reduce greatly the frequency of reinforcement of the first and found what they called extinction-produced aggression. They summarize their experiment as follows:

> Pigeons were conditioned to peck a response key under a procedure that alternated periods of food reinforcement with periods of extinction. The pigeons attacked a nearby pigeon at the onset of extinction. Some also attacked a stuffed model of a pigeon. The duration of attack was an inverse function of the time since the last food reinforcement and a direct function of the number of reinforcements. The pigeons attacked after the last food delivery whether or not the conditioned pecking response was required and whether or not the extinction period was signaled. Prior satiation reduced attack. The phenomenon was not attributable to a past history of competition between pigeons since socially deprived pigeons also attacked. Superstitious reinforcement of attack was not found to be a factor. The results indicated that the transition from food reinforcement to extinction was an aversive event that produced aggression. [Azrin, Hutchinson, and Hake, 1966]

Living in an alien culture, one experiences a loss of approval (reinforcement) for many activities that have been approved at home. During this extinction phase, which may go on for a long time because one is still periodically reinforced by peers or by communications from home, the sojourner, like the pigeon, may aggress against innocent bystanders. Because the bystanders are not restrained, as Azrin's pigeons were, we have a situation where a cycle of aggression and retaliation can appear. This corresponds rather well with anecdotal accounts of sojourners.

In addition to extinction, one experiences changes in rewards. Different societies have different social forms of approval. Touching another person has markedly different implications, for instance. In the Philippines one man touches another as a friendly gesture, but he keeps his hands off members of the opposite sex because of the sexual connotations of such a gesture. It is almost the reverse in North America. Laboratory studies of shifts in reinforcements are hard to find because such a shift disrupts the precise control sought by the experimenter. Many years ago, Tinklepaugh (1928) reported that his monkeys showed marked behavior disruption when reinforcement substances were changed.

Another element in the confused reinforcement contingencies of an alien culture is the tendency of a sojourner to see approval or disapproval (translated as reinforcement or punishment) in cues that do not mean the same to host and sojourner. Laughing and smiling are prime sources of confusion. We smile approval and withhold smiles or other expressions of disapproval. Filipinos laugh with an embarrassed person so that he will not feel too isolated. They may smile and laugh when they are very angry, and they interpret a failure to greet as a sign of disapproval. I recall that I was not reinforced when all the seats were taken on the bus and my Filipino friends were laughing at me so that I would not feel the inconvenience too acutely. Similarly, lost in thought, I was administering very aversive treatment to colleagues when I failed to greet them cheerily every time we met on a crowded campus. Clinicians who apply reinforcement strategies in school or home situations encounter frequently situations in which a child's behavior is being reinforced by other children without awareness by the teacher or the parent. Disruptive classroom behavior, for instance, is reinforced by the attention of classmates even though it may be punished by the teacher. Both teachers and parents inadvertently extinguish desirable behavior by failing to reinforce it and strengthen other behavior by giving attention, irritable though it may be. Much the same occurs in alien settings where the sojourner has not learned to benefit from the hosts' reinforcers nor to emit appropriate discriminating stimuli to his hosts.

What may be closer to our social situation is the research on accidental reinforcement. Beginning with Skinner (1948), there have been a number of studies, summarized by Staddon and Simmelhag (1971), in which reinforcement has been administered on a fixed interval schedule regardless of what the pigeon was doing. The birds were reinforced in some odd activities, actions which they repeated. Skinner called this "superstitious," noting the relationship with gambler's incantations and other situations in which the individual has no control over outcomes. In the complexity of social relationships in alien societies, one person's different behavior may be very reinforcing to a recipient. In many societies individuals agree with proposals, keeping reservations to themselves. Social forms in one society are taken literally by visitors from another which makes for a lot of inadvertent reinforcement and unintended aversive consequences. Because of different learning histories, a good deal of unplanned reinforcement, both positive and aversive, goes on in cross-cultural learning situations.

The immediately foregoing discussion considered the role of adventitious positive reinforcement. Similar research has not been done, as far as I can recall, on FI noncontingent shock. Some people who have had unpleasant experiences abroad are probably convinced that such a situation would be very much like living in an alien society.

In a variation from the traditional shaping strategy, Pryor, Haag, and O'Reilly (1969) at Sea Life Park in Hawaii reinforced porpoises whenever they emitted a not-previously-seen action. The procedure produced a pair of most creative porpoises. Certainly our porpoise-sojourner often finds himself in precisely this set of reinforcement contingencies, particularly if he is in any way responsive to children. In this case, instead of adventitious reinforcement, we have the reinforcement of adventitious behavior. Sojourners frequently report the feeling that their welcome has worn out; actions that earned approval on arrival are no longer valued. We would suggest that their foreigner's behavior was initially reinforced but that reinforcement by the hosts diminished as the novelty wore off. They pass from a situation in which all actions and suggestions are applauded to one in which nothing seems to work.

The research of Schachter and Singer (1962) sheds a good deal of light on the intense emotional experiences of the sojourner, experiences which may lead to psychosomatic symptoms in the gastrointestinal, cardiovascular, and other organ systems. Injecting epinephrin or a placebo, Schachter and Singer showed that stirred up states were interpreted and experienced in markedly different ways depending on cognitive factors, particularly the subject's interpretation of the present situation as induced by the remarks and behavior of the experimenters' confederate. A newcomer to a foreign setting is similarly stirred up by the injection of novelty as it were and possibly by jet fatigue. The experiences he undergoes will be determined in large part by the cognitive set imposed by confederates, the people whom he meets in the new situation. It is my impression, and I don't know how I would prove it, that much of the anger and irritation one can observe in fatigued sojourners could also be experienced as fear or even happiness given a different shared cognitive set. We need to remind ourselves again of the First Law of Social Psychology that attitudes are learned through contact with attitude holders and not in contacts with the object of the attitudes.

In addition to cognitive factors and emotional reactions, there is the problem of cognitive factors and social controls. The new freedom of an assignment in a foreign setting may be experienced as dangerous, but the danger may come from within the sojourner. Zimbardo's studies of social controls and roles (Zimbardo 1970, 1973) shed light on the problems of alienation and identity of the sojourner. In a series of experiments and naturalistic observations, Zimbardo showed that individuals can engage in marked outbursts of destruction and sadism merely as a result of watching others or of putting on the uniform of a prison guard. In the latter experiment men were assigned randomly to prisoner and guard roles and, with no measurable differences in personality, became such submissive prisoners and sadistic guards that the experiment had to be terminated prematurely. These experiments demonstrate that novel role assignments can lead to behavior that no one would expect from the earlier history of the individuals involved.

Zimbardo suggests (1970) that reinforcements may increase the rate of responding to socially inappropriate levels. In our case, the "gung-ho syndrome" of American Peace Corps volunteers and of other self-styled agents of change may be the result of the effects of reinforcement on rate of responding. The local people are on stable DRL schedules while the sojourner is differentially reinforced for a high rate of responding. A DRL schedule is one in which a subject is Differentially Reinforced for a Low rate of responding; not only does he not receive reinforcement for speeding up his rate but he actually postpones reinforcement by responding immediately or frequently. The result is the familiar situation of the sojourner's impatience with the natives' resistance to change, and inherent conservatism, if not laziness.

In addition to gaining control over one's emotions and developing new self-controls over behavior, the sojourner is confronted with the problem of acquiring behavior patterns appropriate to the host society. We know that frequent reinforcement is necessary in the early stages of acquisition, and the ratio of reinforcement can be lowered as acquisition proceeds. In a new society the ratio may be too thin for acquisition for the newcomer but strong enough to maintain behavior which oldtimers have already acquired.

A periodic reinforcement which is also poorly timed, characteristic of many societies, can also produce and maintain ineffectual or superstitious behavior. Individuals are especially prone to repeat whatever works in an unfamiliar setting. This seemed to be what was happening in Szanton's account of the extravagant welcome given to volunteers with the subsequent change in the ratio of reinforcement.

At the same time as newly acquired behavior faces an early extinction for lack of reinforcement, older behavior patterns that are not valued in the new setting are also being extinguished. As ratios are extended, requiring more and more activity to gain a reinforcement, an experimental animal shows longer and longer pauses after each reinforcement. The research of Azrin and his colleagues (1966) indicates that the transition from reinforcement to extinction also produces aggression. Withholding reinforcement can make a human subject very angry; the Azrin research suggests that this reaction may be rooted far down the phylogenetic scale.

IMPLICATIONS FOR CULTURE LEARNING

I have offered some observations on the processes of learning to live in an alien culture, and I have suggested that it may be fruitful to look upon a second culture as a massive change in reinforcement contingencies. We may be able to deduce a few suggestions of ways in which culture learning can be enhanced. Again, we assume that language instruction is emphasized. Beyond that, models can be important in the form of native informants, role playing, films, movies, and the accounts of those who have mastered the second culture. In our case, the best models were Americans who were doing a good job of learning to cope with Philippine culture patterns and not Filipinos themselves. The reason, in our instance, was that we were trying to help Americans to become effective Americans not to become Filipinos, which was impossible.

David (1972) has described the application of reinforcement principles to intercultural adjustment. Based on extensive work in a Peace Corps training center, his paper offers the most sophisticated and extensive outline of this approach which is available. Unfortunately, in his case, as in ours, and in most other training efforts, we are long on theory, principles, and practices but deficient on criterion data. There is still one hypothesis that cannot be rejected: training doesn't make any difference.

Beyond models, our analysis suggests that supervisors try to fill the reinforcement gap in the early stages. There will be mistakes and uncertainties to be sure, but there will be little learning if the neophyte has to rely on the alien social situation which is busily reinforcing him for being a passive curiosity.

Recognizing that reinforcements from the new social enviornment may be infrequent, the sojourner needs to give more thought than at home to the establishment of attainable goals and the mapping of the steps necessary to attain them. In this way self-reinforcement can become a significant element in the maintenance of effective behavior. Just as the host culture may not offer sufficient reinforcement to maintain effort, so the sojourner may fail to respond appropriately to his hosts' efforts. He should identify those situations in which his hosts approve or reinforce one another and he should join in the approval even though he may not think that the occasion is important. For example, a sojourner in the Philippines should recognize the importance to Filipinos of birthdays, death anniversaries, and victories at the cockfights, even though these events are not high on his scale of values.

Some of the strategies used in systematic desensitization could be adapted to training for living in an alien culture. The gradual introduction under pleasant circumstances of strange food is a good example of this approach and contrasts sharply with an implosive experience in which one eats his last American meal with Pan Am and then tries to survive on rice and fish. Similarly, American trainees can be introduced in gradual, controlled steps to different customs of housing, sleeping, bathing, and sanitation.

The prospective sojourner needs also to understand that he will experience some intense emotions due to the novelty of the situation and to his own anxiety which he may wish to deny. As the Schachter and Singer (1962) study suggests, he can experience the same stirred up state as anger or positive exhiliration, depending on his outlook. This information may be used by the sojourner on himself and especially in his relationship with his fellow visitors who are also experiencing surges of adrenalin.

In summary, then, I would like to suggest that a behaviorally oriented training program could draw with benefit from laboratory studies of modeling, reinforcement management, self-reinforcement, and desensitization. The extension of social learning theory to include cognitive elements increases the range of phenomena to which this approach has immediate significance. One should also bear in mind that these techniques, as traditionally practiced, involve careful monitoring of effectiveness. Not only would we have a theoretically cohesive program which is not new, but clear indications of its effectiveness, which is.

CONCLUDING REMARKS

I have suggested that we look at culture learning from the perspective of a social behaviorist. I have applied selected concepts to an analysis of the difficulties that sojourners encounter, and I have indicated some training strategies which follow from this perspective.

There are theoretical implications in the psychology of cultural learning which have not received the attention they deserve. Social behaviorism has led to a shift in personality theory away from such inner variables as traits and also from the intrapersonal, unconscious determinants of psychodynamic theories. As exemplified in the approach developed by Mischel (1973), there is a growing interest in a cognitive social learning theory of personality which emphasizes external determinants of behavior. The role of social factors cannot be determined unless they are extensively altered while traits and dynamic factors remain the same. This cannot be done readily in brief social psychological experiments where the subject knows about the experiment and the experimenter has relatively little power to manipulate significant independent social variables. Plunging an individual into an alien environment for months or years is a rather untidy experiment, but there is little doubt that more than trivial and transitory changes in social factors have occurred. Techniques to exploit this natural experiment have not been developed. Anecdotal information suggests, however, that trait theory takes quite a beating in such a situation because the meek may become dominant, the stable, unstable, and the achieving, apathetic when they move to a different society. Furthermore they tend to get their old traits back when they come home.

Social behaviorism is a rapidly developing theoretical outlook with a significant accumulation of experimental support. It offers a useful analytical approach to cultural learning and suggests some testable techniques of training for second culture living. Living in an alien setting, in turn, presents an unusual opportunity to observe the effect of marked changes in the social context of an individual's behavior.

REFERENCES

AZRIN, N., R. HUTCHINSON and D. HAKE (1966) "Extinction-induced aggression." Journal of the Experimental Analysis of Behavior 9: 191-204.

BREIN, M. and K. DAVID (1971) "Intercultural communication and adjustment of the sojourner." Psychological Bulletin 76: 215-230.

BRAYFIELD, A. and W. CROCKETT (1955) "Employee attitudes and employee performance." Psychological Bulletin 52: 396-424.

BRISLIN, R. (1970) "The content and evaluation of cross-cultural training programs." Paper P-671. Washington, D.C.: Institute for Defense Analyses. Also available in D. Hoopes (ed.) Readings in Intercultural Communication, Vol. III. Pittsburgh: Regional Council for International Education, 1973.

COLE, M., J. GAY, J. GLICK, and D. SHARP (1971) The Cultural Context of Learning and Thinking. New York: Basic Books.

DAVID, K. (1972) "Intercultural adjustment and application of reinforcement theory to problems of culture shock." Trends 4: No. 3.

GILBERT, R. and J. MILLENSON (1972) Reinforcement. New York: Academic Press.

GUTHRIE, G. (1963) "Preparing Americans for participation in another culture." Peace Corps and Behavioral Sciences Paper presented at the conference, Washington, D.C.

——— (1967) "Cultural preparation for the Philippines," in R. B. Textor (ed.) Cultural Frontiers of the Peace Corps. Cambridge, Mass.: MIT Press.

——— and R. SPENCER (1965) "American professions and overseas technical assistance." University Park, Pa.: Pennsylvania State University, Institute of Public Administration.

GUTHRIE, G. and I. ZEKTICK (1967) "Predicting performance in the Peace Corps." Journal of Social Psychology 71: 11-21.

HALL, E. (1959) The Silent Language. Garden City, N.Y.: Doubleday.

HARRIS, J. (1973) "A science of the South Pacific." American Psychologist 28: 232-247.

HOLMES, T. and R. RAHE (1967) "The social readjustment rating scale." Journal of Psychomatic Research 11: 213-218.

LYNCH, F. and T. MARETZKI (1966) "The Philippines Peace Corps survey." Honolulu: University of Hawaii, Social Science Research Institute.

MISCHEL, W. (1973) "Toward a cognitive social learning reconceptualization of personality." Psychological Review 80: 252-283.

OBERG, K. (1960) "Culture shock: adjustment to new cultural environments." Practical Anthropology 7: 177-182.

PRYOR, K., R. HAAG, and J. O'REILLY (1969) "The creative porpoise: training for novel behavior." Journal of the Experimental Analysis of Behavior 12: 653-661.

RAHE, R., E. GUNDERSON, W. PUGH, R. RUBIN, and R. RANSON (1972) "Illness prediction studies." Archives of Environmental Health 25: 192-197.

SCHACHTER, S. and J. SINGER (1962) "Cognitive, social, and physiological determinants of emotional state." Psychological Review 69: 379-399.

SKINNER, B. F. (1948) " 'Superstition' in the pigeon." Journal of Experimental Psychology 38: 168-172.

STADDON, J. and V. SIMMELHAG (1971) "The 'superstition' experiment: a reexamination of its implications for the principles of adaptative behavior." Psychological Review 78: 3-43.

SZANTON, D. (1967) "Cultural confrontation in the Philippines," in R. Textor (ed.) Cultural Frontiers of the Peace Corps. Cambridge, Mass.: MIT Press.

TINKELPAUGH, O. (1928) "An experimental study of representative factors in monkeys." Journal of Comparative Psychology 8: 197-237.

TURNBULL, C. (1972) The Mountain People. New York: Simon & Schuster.

ZIMBARDO, P. (1970) "The human choice: individuation, reason, and order versus deindividuation, impulse, and chaos," in W. Arnold and D. LeVine (eds.) Nebraska Symposium on Motivation, 1969. Lincoln: University of Nebraska Press.

――― (1973) "Pirandellian prison." New York Times Magazine (April 8): 38. (See also International Journal of Criminology and Penology (1973) Vol. 1: 69-97.)

Chapter 4

ADJUSTMENT PROBLEMS OF FOREIGN
MUSLIM STUDENTS IN PAKISTAN

S. M. H A F E E Z Z A I D I

University of Karachi, Pakistan

In recent decades there has been a growing interest in the scientific analysis of culture learning in order to enhance cross-cultural understanding. Unfortunately, however, implicit in the scientific interest in the study of culture contact has been the assumption that the less developed nations need civilizing. This assumption has often become apparent in the writing of many Western social scientists (e.g., Doob, 1960). Moreover, the postwar appearance of concepts like "modernization" and "development" have implicity been understood as being synonymous with Westernization. Social scientists in the so-called developing countries seem to suspect that behind every facade of modernization there is an attempt to impose the Western and, more specifically, the American concept of development which, as we now know, may or may not be appropriate for a given country (Bennet, 1968; Inayatullah, 1967). This academic and technical imperialism and overzealousness for a civilizing mission have even been noted by American social scientists and effectively described by Campbell (1968).

Cross-cultural participation and encounter is a postwar phenomenon which has been growing and will probably grow further in different directions as communication and space research draw the world closer. Angell (1967), in his categorization of various types of cross-cultural participation, has analyzed in detail the category of *participation through study abroad.* Looking at cross-national interactions from the viewpoint of the degree of development, it appears that contacts among developed Western nations and those between developed and underdeveloped nations have been the most frequent and possibly fruitful. Research on such interactions has also mostly focused on the interfaces either between developed nations themselves or between developed and underdeveloped nations. Studies of the American community in India (Useem and Useem, 1967) and of the Western-educated man in India (Useem and Useem, 1955) represent this kind of interface between a developed and another developing nation.

There is a dearth of information on cross-cultural contacts between underdeveloped nations, possibly because such contacts have been assumed to be less

[118]   LEARNING ANOTHER CULTURE

fruitful and also because one underdeveloped nation holds little attraction for persons from another underdeveloped nation. Although cross-cultural contacts among underdeveloped nations have been taking place for the past few decades, very little is known about problems of culture learning or adjustment in such contacts. The present study, therefore, is unique in the sense that an attempt has been made to analyze problems of adjustment of a group of Asian and African students in a country whose degree of development is similar to that of their own country and, in certain aspects, may even be less.

Academic institutions in Pakistan have been receiving foreign students for the past two decades. Foreign students are now studying in almost all the universities and in several big colleges in Pakistan. A rough estimate of the total number of foreign students in Pakistan is about one thousand. Karachi, being the largest city in Pakistan, has more than 30% of all foreign students. These students come from the Philippines, Malaysia, Thailand, Jordan, Palestine, Yemen, Iraq, Saudi Arabia, Abu Dhabi, Iran, Nepal, Burma, Tanzania, Uganda, Ghana, and Mauretina. There are more males than females, and their concentration is in medical and engineering colleges. Those who cannot get into these professional colleges go for degrees in the Faculty of Science.

Pakistan came into being as an ideological state and soon became a center of attraction for most of the countries with large Muslim populati ns. The government of Pakistan, realizing the attraction to Pakistan Muslims everywhere, made liberal scholarship grants available to them. Thus a beginning was made for the cross-cultural contacts between Pakistan and those Asian and African countries.

One major feature of Pakistan society and culture, her religious orientation, is most relevant in the present context. Pakistan was carved out of the Indian subcontinent for the specifically stated purpose of enabling Muslims to live their own life in the light of their religious and cultural demands. This made Pakistan an ideal for Muslims everywhere and particularly for those in Asia and Africa. Pakistan thus became psychologically attractive for Muslims, and a visit and stay in Pakistan became the cherished desire of Muslim families in Asia and Africa. This desire even ignored the fact that Pakistan was an underdeveloped country. Religious and cultural affinity became the dominant link between these countries and Pakistan. In the present survey, I asked foreign students why they had come to Pakistan. Table 1 lists the different reasons they gave for choosing Pakistan as a place of study. Each respondent gave more than one reason for his choice, although the majority of them (73.5%) indicated that their choice was determined by the fact that Pakistan is a Muslim country. The other frequent reasons for coming to Pakistan relate to academic facilities and ease of getting admitted to colleges and universities.

An additional factor in the attraction Pakistan holds for foreign students is historical. Any student of Indian history in the early twentieth century knows that Indian Muslims, even during the colonial days, were ready to sacrifice their

TABLE 1

STATED REASONS FOR COMING TO PAKISTAN
(In percentages)

Reasons	Yes	No
Pakistan is a Muslim country	73.5	26.5
Admissions are easy	58.5	40.5
Relatives are in Pakistan	22.0	78.0
Due to friends' suggestions	35.5	64.5
Received scholarship	30.0	70.0
To improve English	42.0	58.0
To learn Urdu	17.0	83.0
Academic attraction	51.0	49.0

all for the Muslims of Asia and Africa. It is a fact of recorded history that Indian Muslims felt the pinch whenever any Muslim country in Asia or Africa was in trouble. This long record of fraternal interest of Muslims of the Indo-Pak subcontinent in the welfare of Muslims in other countries made Pakistan a symbol of Muslim regeneration. In most instances, therefore, when foreign Muslim students came to Pakistan, they brought goodwill and high expectations for their stay. The basic question in terms of their adjustment to the academic, social, and physical life in Pakistan, therefore, was Pakistan's ability, or lack of it, to meet their expectations and sustain their motivation during their stay.

DESCRIPTION OF SURVEY POPULATION

For this study the subjects were 102 male and 21 female foreign students. No sampling was necessary because we contacted all those available in Karachi at the time of the survey. Some students were vacationing outside Karachi or had gone home, and so could not be interviewed. About 80% of them were below 25 years of age. Female students were younger than their male counterparts. A 43-item questionnaire was administered to each participating student individually.

The family pattern in most of the countries represented in the survey seemed to be very similar to the Pakistani family configuration. In most cases, the father was the only earning member of the family, and the mother was a housewife. The literacy percentage among the mothers was as low as that in Pakistan. A majority of the parents of this foreign student sample were engaged in business, and very few were doctors, engineers, or civil servants. Most of them belonged to the middle or upper middle income groups. About half the families were joint-extended, and the other half were nuclear families.

The female foreign students resided either with their parents or in the university girls dormitory, whereas a majority of the male foreign students resided in rented houses in the city and were generally independent of any supervision. It is reported that most males spent their evenings in the city cinema halls or hotels.

The majority of the foreign students came from countries that have large Muslim populations. Students from Africa generally did not have language problems because the medium of instruction at the higher education level is generally English, as it is in Pakistan. However, students from the Middle East, Iran, and Southeast Asia were deficient in English and often had difficulty in following the lectures. Very few foreign students, however, knew Urdu, the language spoken all over Pakistan outside the university classroom.

THE SETTING

A new social situation is always beset with problems of adjustment. This happens everywhere and to everyone. The foreign students in Pakistan, in spite of their supposedly high motivation and attraction, cannot avoid facing a few adjustments in their life pattern. Immediately on arrival in Pakistan, they face a new language, different food preparations, and in most cases, different physical and climatic features. In addition to these, when they arrive at the academic institution, they may find different codes of behavior and a new system of educational administration, all of which may upset their expectations for and about Pakistan. Various other problems of living, such as access to medical facilities and the inevitable transport hazards, may add to their difficulties.

One aspect of Pakistani social life which may provide disillusionment to many foreign male students relates to the special position of girls in the Pakistani cultural context. Pakistan society, in spite of being developed in many fields, prescribes more restriction to girls than to boys. There is very little free mixing between the sexes and, therefore, social relationships paralleling those of Western or Westernized societies are very restricted. The foreign students are often heard complaining about the isolation and restrictions in their social life. They experience these restrictions both inside and outside the class. Because many of the foreign students have been accustomed to freemixing and un-restricted social contacts between the sexes, they find the situation in Pakistan most frustrating. As a matter of fact, they make no secret of their dislike for this aspect of Pakistani social life and express the feeling of having been cheated in coming to Pakistan.

In view of these problems, the present study focuses on three aspects of foreign student adjustment to life in Pakistan. These are (1) physical, (2) academic, and (3) sociocultural. It is assumed that the major difficulties faced by foreign students fall within these three categories.

PHYSICAL ADJUSTMENT

Food is a hazard in a foreign country, and the Pakistani cuisine is fairly spicy for the taste of many foreigners, including those from certain countries in Asia. The respondents, however, were divided in their likes and dislikes for Pakistani food. About 50% reported liking the food in the beginning and 22% never did like the food. However, many of those who reported liking the food in the beginning reverted to their native food preferences. Sixty-two percent of the respondents preferred to take their own native food, while 38% retained their liking for Pakistani food. It appears that food is not a major problem for foreign students in Pakistan, and sooner or later each one of them becomes adjusted to the variation in his food habits.

Pakistan does not have proper medical facilities for most of her own population. Both medical advice and medicines are costly, and Pakistanis often complain of poor medical facilities. However, academic institutions usually have their own medical officers and provide medical facilities and subsidized medicines to students. It is, therefore, expected that foreign students would face fewer difficulties in obtaining medical services than local students who live with their families. It is, however, likely that many of the countries in Asia and Africa have better medical facilities than those in Pakistan. Among the respondents, 60% found the medical facilities good, some (6%) even found them excellent, and 29% reported having received poor medical service during their stay in Pakistan.

One of the factors that gives a sense of security to life in a foreign country is the amount of money one has available for expenses. When one lives with the family, one can manage with a small amount; but when one is on his own, he should have sufficient funds to live and study undisturbed. It may be noted here that living in Pakistan is cheaper than in many of the Middle Eastern and African countries and, therefore, the allowance given to the foreign students either from the government of Pakistan or from their own families is only slightly more than would be given to a Pakistani student. This allowance, however, may appear small if compared with allowances given in several other countries. The amount of the scholarship is generally sufficient for living the life of an average student in Pakistan, and most of the students from Africa and Southeast Asia find it adequate; however, there are usually complaints of inadequate funds from students coming from the Middle East. Such complaints do not seem very genuine because most of them want money for their expensive social life. They want to rent flats, keep servants, and visit expensive hotels in Karachi. For this purpose, of course, the money is always insufficient. It is reported that most of the Middle East students supplement their allowances with money from their parents. In general, however, the allowance given foreign students in Pakistan is sufficient, and there is no financial worry to cause maladjustment in their lives.

ACADEMIC ADJUSTMENT

Academic success in a new social setting does not depend entirely upon the learner's preparedness and inner resources. To a large extent, success in learning is also determined by the learner's adjustment to new academic demands, institutional setting, and the people with whom he must interact. These include teachers, classmates, the administrative structure of the institution, and the academic program. The foreign students in Pakistan, though highly motivated, must adjust to new academic demands which may appear dissonant with their own expectations and earlier experiences. In the present survey, therefore, a part of the inquiry related to problems requiring academic adjustment. Self reports indicated that about 66% of the respondents found the administrative staff of the academic institutions quite cooperative. As for the academic programs, 49% found them easier than the courses in their own country; 37.5% found the syllabi no different, and 13.5% found them more difficult. In consonance with their perception of the academic difficulty, only 37.5% felt the necessity of special coaching in English outside the class. In this group, however, the majority (63%) were students from the Middle East.

We have already mentioned the difficulty in communication due to lack of proficiency in the local language. Urdu has affinity with Persian and Arabic, but most of the foreign students still find it difficult to learn enough to communicate in Urdu. This is quite a familiar problem in any cross-cultural contact, and the only way to solve it is to learn the language. However, language is a handicap for a majority of the foreign students, and the only vehicle of communication available to them remains English, in which most of them are somewhat deficient. Even if their English was good, the local people would not be able to understand them. A significant consequence of this difficulty is that they do not have frequent social contacts with either their teachers or their classmates. They are also prevented from having many Pakistani friends and, therefore, must confine their social contacts to other students from their own country.

The language difficulty is a significant factor in shaping their perception of Pakistani academic institutions, teachers, and students. Despite the fact that most of the foreign students found the teachers cooperative, helpful, and sympathetic, they complained of poor student-teacher relationships in which the teacher was perceived as inefficient, not caring about student problems, and not encouraging hard work. Epithets used about their classmates are both interesting and significant. These were: "conservative," "irresponsible," "aggressive," and "temperamental." Only 34.5% found their classmates good, cooperative, friendly, and hardworking.

In reply to the specific question on the difference in the academic life between Pakistan and their own countries, the responses indicated that the students tried to adjust to the different academic life in Pakistan; however, their ways of accommodating themselves in Pakistan were indicative of their frustration. About 28% reported a belief in the dictum "when in Rome do as Romans do." About 38.6% reported working hard, using the library facilities, and obtaining help from teachers, as well as bright students. About 17.7% were indifferent and "took it easy." They enjoyed life in the metropolis and waited for their time to go back home. The rest found it difficult to adjust to the academic life throughout their stay; however, they tried, and time often helped them to manage, although at a low level of adequacy.

The academic adjustment per se, therefore, does not appear to be a very serious problem. The only problem that seems to be significant is lack of proper communication because the foreign student does not know the language of the people. In such a situation, even the best academic setting will create difficulties for a student. Hence it is to be expected that, unless proper arrangements, either before coming to Pakistan or on arrival in Pakistan, are made for teaching Urdu, this will continue to be a hindrance in culture learning for foreigners in Pakistan.

SOCIOCULTURAL ADJUSTMENT

The general assumption of the present study is that the foreign student will find it more difficult to accommodate himself in the sociocultural life in Pakistan because in most cases it will be different from his own cultural conditioning and patterning of social behavior. The responses clearly substantiate our view that a majority of the foreign students (93%) were not satisfied with the social life in Pakistan. The response also indicates that only 47% had any social relationship, even with their classmates, and very few had any social relationship with Pakistani families. Thus it appears that the foreign student in Pakistan is very much on his own socially.

The main features of the difference between the social life in Pakistan and that in the respective countries of the respondents relate to dress, food, degree of Westernization, and of course, the language. In addition, the sharp reaction of foreign students focused on their dislike of restrictions on the freedom of girls and the absence of free mixing between the sexes. The people of Pakistan were perceived to be narrow-minded, conservative, formal, and poor in social relationships. There were also complaints concerning the social life and lack of entertainment on the campuses. The immediate consequence of a barren social life mixed with a different sociocultural pattern of behavior was that about 59% of the students felt homesick, among whom the majority were from the Middle East and Africa, where possibly the social life is more free and uninhibited.

The sharp cleavage in the sociocultural life between Pakistan and these Asian and African nations has made the life of foreign students generally difficult. They keep away from their classmates, visit the American Centre and British Council, go sight-seeing, and mostly try to get closer to other foreign students instead of coming closer to Pakistanis. Only very few female students have tried to adopt the Pakistani dress, learn the language, and seek the company of Pakistani friends. There are obvious restrictions for boys because their extraverted behavior is likely to be misunderstood in a restricted and inhibited social context; therefore, they try to concentrate more on their studies or spend time and money in clubs and on the cinema.

Sojourns in Pakistan for the foreign students thus presented a great challenge in their social adjustment. They were not very happy, and some of them even felt that they had become conservative, almost bordering on the unsocial, especially in relation to the opposite sex. This reaction of helplessness and apathy indicates a state of frustration where the individual gives up and may accept a situation as inevitable. This apathy may find expression in unwholesome behavior and neurotic reaction-formation. Some of the responses were significant, viz., "have become careless," "feel lonely, sometimes nervous," "have become less refined in behavior towards others." There is, however, a small group that "admires the culture," "has become more religious," and "has adopted the culture and become more responsible."

While analyzing the social life of the foreign students, it may be relevant and significant to know what they thought of Pakistan and her people before their arrival and how they perceived them after they had been in Pakistan for a while. Tables 2 and 3 summarize the responses of foreign students in terms of their knowledge about Pakistan and image of a Pakistani *before* they arrived in Pakistan and *after* they had been in Pakistan for some time. These tables are presented to provide a perspective for their social adjustment in Pakistan.

The responses reveal that 55% knew Pakistan to be a Muslim country carved out of Indian subcontinent, with love for Islam and Muslims in other countries. Many of them were familiar with the political life in Pakistan and appear impressed with her rate of development. Their image of Pakistanis was that of a friendly, hospitable, religious, and brave people who had worked hard and were politically promising. A small group of foreign students thought them to be simple, illiterate, and backward. On the whole, however, the foreign students came with a favorable stereotype about Pakistanis and a highly laudatory image of Pakistan as a Muslim country.

TABLE 2

FOREIGN STUDENTS' KNOWLEDGE ABOUT PAKISTAN AND IMAGE OF A PAKISTANI *BEFORE* ARRIVAL IN PAKISTAN

Knowledge	Percent of Respondents	Image	Percent of Respondents
Great Muslim country	55.0	Helpful, patriotic, and friendly	36.9.
Only as a political entity	13.5	Highly religious	21.6
Friendly and brave people	7.2	Advanced and smart	10.0
Cheap living and poor	8.1	Shy of opposite sex	3.6
Has academic facilities	2.7	Backward	9.0
Not much	13.5	Not much	18.9

TABLE 3

FOREIGN STUDENTS' KNOWLEDGE ABOUT PAKISTAN AND IMAGE OF A PAKISTANI *AFTER* HAVING BEEN IN PAKISTAN

Knowledge	Percent of Respondents	Image	Percent of Respondents
Know enough about its culture	29.4	Hardworking, progressive, and friendly	30.1
Nice country	11.0	Emotional and irresponsible	23.3
Life different from other countries	11.9	Lack unity, selfish, and illiterate	30.0
Has many problems	20.2	Shrewd and diplomatic	4.9
Corrupt and underdeveloped	27.5	Religious	4.9
		Not truly religious	6.8

Having come to Pakistan with high expectations about her people, the foreign student tried to match his preconceived image of the country with the real Pakistan. During his stay in Pakistan, he tried to learn more about her people and their culture. Some students found it to be a nice country, but most of them had difficulty in reconciling the ideal with the real as they perceived it. Theirs was a situation, in Festinger's (1957) terms, of cognitive dissonance. The realities as perceived by the majority of the foreign students were not what they expected to find. Some extreme responses may illustrate their disillusionment:

"underdeveloped and illiterate; people not religious, no middle class; people very rich or very poor; religion and politics mixed up; no discipline, lot of corruption; dirty country and inactive people." This is how they found Pakistan in reality. We are not concerned so much here with the objective reality as with the perception of the foreign students. Phenomenologically this is what they know and believe about Pakistan. Their image of the people of Pakistan as a religious, honest, and brave people may also undergo some change in the process of adjustment to the realities of the situation. Some of their responses indicate that Pakistanis are perceived as changing for the better, but on the whole their assessment is unfavorable. They find Pakistanis to be shrewd, selfish, unsocial, uncooperative, violent, and not true Muslims.

It is clear that the foreign student comes to Pakistan with a fairly high expectation about the culture and the people; but after his stay for some time, his favorable image of Pakistan undergoes a change that is generally one of disillusionment, disgust, and frustration. However, it is surprising that most of them do not feel any sense of loss. Each one seems to feel that he has gained something in Pakistan; their responses are significantly full of hope and fulfillment. With 28% no response and 26.7% indicating "nothing in particular," 45% confessed having a sense of achievement, even if it was only a personal gain. Some succeeded in selecting a wife, some were happy in their academic success, and a few found improvement in their health. Other responses related to general broadening of outlook, becoming more religious, learning the language, and becoming independent. Some also discovered their own potential dramatic and artistic talents because, as foreign students, they had easier access to radio and talent shows. Most of them, therefore, felt that, in spite of differences in language, food, and behavior, their stay in Pakistan had helped them in many ways. Sixty-five percent reported that they hoped to go back better educated and more qualified to obtain jobs at home. If nothing more, at least they gained in terms of experience in another culture which is sure to give them a broader perspective.

Adjustment to a sociocultural situation is directly related to one's feeling of being accepted by the people in the new situation. The total perception of the new situation is conditioned by the strangers' assessment of how the host group looks at them. There is no doubt foreign students are accepted by students, teachers, and the general public alike; however, what matters in their adjustment is their own perception. In reply to our inquiry about their feeling of being accepted, 51% felt that they were accepted, 15% did not feel so, and 34% were not certain whether they were accepted or not. It is not certain what degree of acceptance the 51% felt they had in Pakistan. As a reciprocal gesture, we wanted to know if the foreign students had accepted the Pakistanis, that is, what degree of sociocultural affinity did they on their part feel for their hosts. For this we used a sort of crude social distance scale. The responses, in terms of checking their choices, are given in Table 4.

TABLE 4

CLASSIFICATION OF CHOICES ON SOCIAL DISTANCE DIMENSIONS
(In percentages)

Willing to	Yes	No
Reside permanently in Pakistan	7.0	93.0
Marry a Pakistani	31.0	69.0
Take a Pakistani as a business partner	16.0	84.0
Never come back to Pakistan	34.0	64.0
Take up permanent career in Pakistan	13.0	87.0

The fairly crude data in Table 4 clearly point to the attitude of foreign students toward Pakistan. They find Pakistan good enough neither for residence nor for work. Some may agree to marry a Pakistani, but they will not generally trust a Pakistani as a business partner. About one-third of them seem determined never to return to Pakistan. These responses, though not entirely definitive, surely tend to indicate that Pakistan is not able to sustain the interest and attraction that it holds for foreign students who come with a fairly favorable impression of that country and her people.

However, these unfavorable stereotypes can also be explained in terms of Zajonc's (1952) prediction wherein he maintains that foreigners want to conform, but as the difficulties mount, frustration grows and finally results in "attitudinal aggression" against the host country and its norms. It may also be that entering Pakistan with high hopes and extreme admiration, the foreign student can only become disillusioned.

ADJUSTMENT AS A FUNCTION OF TIME

Traveling is generally thought to be a source of experience and maturity. A Persian poet recommends frequent travel and lengthy stay in foreign lands for maturity of experience. An Urdu poet assures the weary traveler that there are always cool spots on the way. These proverbial statements point to the general assumption that traveling affords useful and profitable experiences; however, sojourns in a strange land may not be all comfort and ease. The sojourner will often have a feeling of isolation and a sense of insecurity in the midst of unknown and strange people and places. Between the gain in experience and frustrating discomforts, however, the duration of stay in a foreign land may be a significant variable. Studies of the effects of foreign travel as a function of the duration of stay are either inconclusive or inadequately designed. It may also be pointed out that there is no uniform conceptualization of adjustment as a dependent variable in the studies of foreign travelers. Most of these (including this study) are atheoretical explorations of the effects of foreign travel on the travelers' attitudes, information, morale, social relations, and general well-being (Byrnes, 1965; Forstat, 1951; Riegel, 1953).

Louise Kidder (1973) has made a critical review of the various studies of foreign travels and cross-cultural contacts in order to arrive at an empirical understanding of the relationship between duration of stay and adjustment in a foreign land. Her review seems to indicate that there is no consistent pattern of adjustment as a function of the duration of stay. Foreign travelers show considerable ambivalence in their attitude to the host country and her people. The review concludes by presenting four rival hypotheses concerning the patterns of adjustment in living abroad. These are: a positive linear function; a negative linear function; a three-stage—spectator, adjustment, and coming-to-terms—U-function; and a nullhypothesis of no significant change in adjustment over time.

In light of the analysis presented by Kidder of the relationship between adjustment and duration of stay, we looked at the data of the present survey. Relating the duration of stay with the three aspects of our analysis, we obtain indications of no significant change in the level of physical adjustment over time. In respect to academic adjustment, however, the trend is toward the U-curve, indicating an initial high expectancy or spectator phase, then falling off to an adjustment phase, and going up to the third stage of coming to terms with the academic situation. In terms of sociocultural adjustment, the data show a negative function indicating a decreasing adjustment level with increase in the duration of stay. It may be noted that these relationships between duration of stay and the three categories of adjustments are mere approximations. It would appear that the respondents find their experiences neither consistently pleasant nor consistently disillusioning. We agree with Kidder's suggestion that the time dimension should be measured more carefully and rationale for careful questioning should be developed.

ANOTHER POSSIBLE EXPLANATION

It may be possible to find some explanation for the trend of responses in the recent sociopolitical history of Pakistan which has shattered even our (Pakistanis') dream of a strong and prosperous Pakistan. During the past decade, military rule with the facade of basic democrary brought the country almost to ruin while patriotic Pakistanis could do nothing but shudder at the possible consequences of military rule. Such a situation of despondency and frustration could not but affect the foreign students who have nothing but goodwill and hope for Pakistan. It is in this context that the bitter responses of the foreign students should be understood. It is surprising that even a few favorable stereotypes survived from their original image of Pakistan.

John and Ruth Useem (1967) use the concept of a binational third culture in their study of the American community in India, which they define as "the patterns generic to a community of men who stem from two different societies and who regularly interact as they relate their respective societies, or segments therefrom, within the physical setting of one of the societies." In the present study the conditions generating a third culture are present, but instead of a binational third culture we may suggest a multinational third culture which, however, does not seem to exist as indicated by the present study. In the first place, sociocultural interactions between the local people and the foreign students are neither frequent nor congenial. If there is any social encounter, it is "nonpersonalized, casual, and surface-like." Most foreign students have no identification of any type with either Pakistanis or other foreign students. Each national group of students is a unit, separate and isolated. There is, therefore, no indication at present of a third culture, binational or multinational.

There is no well-established psychological theory that can explain fully the varied and paradoxical results of the many studies, including this one, concerning the adjustment of foreigners in another culture. Besides many methodological difficulties in theorizing, one difficulty which seems unavoidable is the fact that, in all such studies, the investigator will necessarily be an outsider to the respondents. There are, therefore, two alternative sets of attitudes for the respondents toward the investigator. Either he is too polite to hurt the investigator's national self-image, or he is too brutally frank to be objective in his reactions. This is one of the constant limitations of the social psychological research methodology for any kind of research. It is suggested that one of the techniques that may lead to more reliable and fruitful results is the use of unobtrusive and nonreactive techniques of data collection (Webb et al., 1966) in combination with direct questions such as those used in this study.

REFERENCES

ANGELL, R. (1967) "The growth of transnational participation." Journal of Social Issues 23 (1): 108-129.

BENNET, J. (1968) "Tradition, modernity and communalism in Japan's modernization." Journal of Social Issues 24 (4): 25-44.

BYRNES, F. (1965) Americans in Technical Assistance: A Study of Attitudes and Responses to Their Role Abroad. New York: Praeger.

CAMPBELL, D. (1968) "A cooperative multinational opinion sample exchange." Journal of Social Issues 24 (2): 245-256.

DOOB, L. (1960) Becoming More Civilized. New Haven: Yale University Press.

FESTINGER, L. (1957) A Theory of Cognitive Dissonance. Evanston, Ill.: Row, Peterson.

FORSTAT, R. (1951) "Adjustment problems of international students." Sociology and Social Research 36: 25-30.

INAYETULLAH (1967) "Towards a non-western model of development," in D. Lerner and W. Schramm (eds.) Communication and Change in the Developing Countries. Honolulu: East-West Center Press.

KIDDER, L. (1973) "What befalls foreign travelers as they pass their time abroad? A critical review." Unpublished manuscript.

RIEGEL, O. (1953) "Residual effects of exchange of persons." Public Opinion Quarterly 17: 319-327.

USEEM, J. and R. USEEM (1955) The Western Educated Man in India. New York: Dryden Press.

––– (1967) "The interfaces of a binational third culture: a study of the American community in India." Journal of Social Issues 23 (1): 130-143.

WEBB, E., D. CAMPBELL, L. SECHREST, and R. SCHWARTZ (1966) Unobtrusive Measures. Chicago: Rand McNally.

ZAJONC, R. (1952) "Aggressive attitudes of the stranger as a function of conformity pressures." Human Relations 5: 205-216.

Chapter 5

UNOFFICIAL INTERVENTION IN
DESTRUCTIVE SOCIAL CONFLICTS

LEONARD W. DOOB

Yale University

Most social scientists, psychiatrists, and psychologists, including the contributors to this volume, quite rightly maintain that ordinarily the learning involved in social change (such as the acculturation of individuals or modification of institutions) tends to be both slow and difficult. This chapter stems from a contrary assumption or hope: under rare conditions key individuals can learn new modes of thinking or behavior that can significantly affect social conflicts. Only the parameters of this optimism can be explored not merely because space is limited—the usual unimpressive excuse—but because adequate knowledge to accomplish much more is lacking. Concrete data have been obtained from six interventions, the skeletal details of which are given in Table 1,[1] from academic research on war and peace (Kelman, 1965; Wright, Evan, and Deutsch, 1962), and from laboratory studies of conflict and group processes (cf. Collins and Guetzkow, 1964; Druckman, 1971; Thibaut and Kelley, 1959). In spite of these admitted defects and handicaps, it seems fruitful to try to push as far forward as possible in this potentially useful field of intervention.

All the concepts in the chapter's heading save the first word can be painlessly defined. The hallmark of *social conflict* is the existence of two or more groups, at least one of which includes persons who believe that one or more other groups are or will be depriving them of goals or values they would attain or preserve. Nations that would expand or protect their territory or their foreign trade, ethnic groups that feel subjugated or discriminated against (Bailey, n.d.), and labor unions that are convinced they do not receive their fair share of the employers' earnings are all clearly in conflict with other groups, whether or not

Author's Note: Gratitude is expressed to various donors who have enabled the writer, together with one or two colleagues, to organize three interventions: Edward W. Barrett and Dr. and Mrs. John S. Schweppe through the Communications Institute of the Academy for Educational Development; the James Marshall Fund, Inc.; the Carolyn Foundation; and the Concilium on International and Area Studies of Yale University (Joseph M. Goldsen, Director). In addition, the Carnegie Corporation of New York, though not directly associated with any of the projects, has permitted me to carry on the kind of research in Africa that indirectly has led to the pathway of workshops.

TABLE 1

SUMMARY DETAILS ABOUT THE WORKSHOPS

(1) Project Name	(2) Conflict	(3) Site	(4) Year	(5) Immediate Goal	(6) Participants
Controlled Communication	Cyprus	London	1966	Resolve	4 minor officials
Fermeda Workshop	Somalia vs. Ethiopia and Kenya	Italy	1969	Resolve	18 influen- tial elite
Friends	Arabs vs. Israel	No con- fron- tation	1967-72	Inform	Large number of leaders and cross-section
Intercession	Dominican students vs. U.S.A.	In situ	1965-66	Resolve	Large number of members and leaders
Belfast Workshop	Catholics vs. Protestants	Scotland	1972	Teach skills	56 non- elite influential
Pugwash	World Powers	Various	1957 then annually	Inform	10 to 36 scientists and scholars

TABLE 1

SUMMARY DETAILS ABOUT THE WORKSHOPS

(7) Duration	(8) Psychological Emphasis	(9) Methods[a,b]	(10) Reentry Aid	(11) Results[c]
1 week	Cognitive	5, 2	No?	1, 3
11 days	Affective, cognitive	5, 1, 2 3, 4	No	1, 4, 6
Indefinite	Cognitive	6 and circulate	---	5, 6?
Irregular continuous	Cognitive, affective	6, 5	Yes	1, 6, 7
9 days	Cognitive, affective	5, 2 3, 4	Yes?	1, 2, 4 5, 7?
1 to 2 weeks	Cognitive	1, 2, 5	No	1, 5, 6 7?

NOTES: (a) Order indicates decreasing priority (b) Methods: (c) Results:

(b) Methods:
1. Lecture
2. Meeting
3. Games
4. Observation
5. Small group
6. Interview

(c) Results:
1. Learn others' viewpoint
2. Learn group functioning
3. Learn principles
4. Bonds between members
5. Publicity
6. Diffusion
7. Change

those other groups recognize the hostility directed toward them or the losses that would occur if they were to yield the gains or privileges ascribed to them. The word *destructive* is inserted because some social conflicts are said to be desirable and to serve useful ends (Coser, 1956: 20). The writers of textbooks and scholarly articles (e.g., Holsti, 1966) usually include *intervention* among the modes of resolving conflict. *Unofficial* would suggest that the intervener has no formal status within the conflicting groups and indeed that he may not be called upon by them to intervene. A policeman seeking to stop two gangs from fighting on a street intervenes officially; a stranger who happens to be passing by, unofficially. A professional mediator or arbitrator who is asked by one or both sides or by government to try to settle an industrial controversy has an official role to perform; but someone who volunteers his services toward the same end, though he may be a government official, is functioning unofficially. An unofficial intervener may or may not be a professional intervener. Many so-called consultants or trainers devote full or nearly full time to intervening, sometimes officially when their services are called upon periodically or irregularly by institutions or organizations, at other times unofficially when they themselves discern situations in which they think their skills can be useful.

A few additional definitions, sans neologisms or acronyms, also seem necessary. The intervener brings the disputants together in a *workshop* where they confront one another. When the confrontation is relatively informal and unstructured, reference is made to an *interacting group,* a term that is employed to cover a variety of techniques variously known as encounter, laboratory, study, T (for training), National Training Laboratory (NTL), human relations, Bethel, Tavistock, and sensitivity groups. The behavior of the participants at a workshop consists of *overt activity* when they move about, speak, or write; *covert activity* when they overtly rest, listen, or read.

INTERVENERS

Motives

Although the intervener's motives can be as diverse as those involved in any complex act, two related continua can be distinguished. The end points of one are selfishness and altruism. The intervener may be driven by thoughts of the personal glory that can result from success to an honest desire to contribute to conflict reduction or the commonweal. Among the selfish motives are conscious and unconscious urges to dominate the participants in the conflict, to display one's own superiority in controlling or teaching them. In between is the desire to contribute to knowledge concerning the technique of bringing disputants together. The professional who stands by, ready to be called, is paid for his services, but remuneration and altruism are not necessarily incompatible.

The other continuum describes the origin of the motive to intervene. Here the impulse can spring from the social philosophy of the intervener's group or apparently from his own conviction which unwittingly may be an expression of that philosophy. In addition, the philosophy may reflect the ethical tenets of a religion, for—if I may quietly say so—every great religious figure has intervened unofficially for the sake of persons whose dire conflicts he has witnessed. Most probably, too, the intervener and his staff have motives that are either unconscious or somehow rationalized, and that range from sadism and the will to dominate the disputants to a wish to rescue them from their own destructive impulses.

Whatever the motive behind intervention, it must be strong enough to enable the intervener to carry on regardless of the obstacles and frustrations he endures, for obstacles and frustrations can appear at every stage. Usually money must be raised. Permission from government must sometimes be obtained for some of the disputants to participate, or at least to safeguard them against reprisals; and an unofficial intervener cannot tread easily through most bureaucracies. The intervener is likely to be cast in the role of the busybody Good Samaritan who is injecting himself into a conflict that is not his affair. Most forms of intervention involve face-to-face contact with participants who may displace upon him their hostility toward one another or indeed any of their own personal difficulties. Afterward, he may even feel he does not deserve whatever expressions of gratitude he may receive because, as explained later, he usually has no clearway to assess the role of the workshop in changing the participants. In any case, the intervener must be convinced that intervention can be useful, and that other methods of dealing with destructive conflicts (Galtung, 1965; Katz, 1965) are not being tried, are not succeeding, or supplement or complement what he is attempting. He must have faith as well as a theory—a valid one, it is hoped—which at least provides him with sufficient confidence to carry through the enterprise. Intervention is not a panacea and may be doomed to failure when the rewards of the status quo (particularly the gains from economic, political, or personal power) are so overwhelming that they cannot conceivably be relinquished. "Conceivably" ? Here is the challenging problem, for those in power have other, if weaker, motives that include perhaps religious or ethical principles, and that might be tapped by an intervention. If this be so, then intervention is never completely hopeless. Come, come, we say to each other, can one intervene after armed conflict has broken out?

Ethics

By taking the initiative the intervener assumes a responsibility to the participants and his own conscience, for most interventions involve risks and an expenditure of time. In my limited experience, professionals who direct interacting groups have supreme confidence in their methods and especially in themselves: their past experiences suggest that something useful must emerge from any workshop. But they have not always succeeded in resolving or diminishing conflict, and sometimes psychiatric casualties have resulted (Yalom and Lieberman, 1971).

Under these circumstances the intervener must seek informed consent. To the best of his ability he must inform disputants concerning the nature of the workshop, its possibility of failure, and the perils that may be involved. A written statement and perhaps some reprints or, when requested, even a bibliography may be useful because they can be studied at the disputants' leisure. Whether the intervener succeeds in accurately covering information about the workshop is another matter; but he must make every possible effort to do so. The inclination to be optimistic and to minimize the dangers is great when disputants hesitate to accept an invitation to attend a workshop; yet, even though recruiting becomes more difficult, that temptation must be stoutly and courageously resisted. Obtaining informed consent, moreover, may never be completely satisfying to all informants, some of whom may say, as patients do to their physicians after major surgery, "You never really told me it would be as painful as it was." Actually, of course, the intervener is seeking changes within the participants, but only those they themselves evolve. Does this mean that no manipulation is involved? No hard-and-fast line can be drawn between self-determination and manipulation, for the intervener disapproves of the destructive conflict and hence may suggest an exercise facilitating useful or relevant learning, without however being too specific. And in a sense the participants, if they suffer from the existing destructive conflict, want to be manipulated.

Attributes

The principal attributes of an intervener have already been implied: patience, the ability to withstand frustrations, a willingness to endure the experience of being a target for hate or displaced aggression. In addition, his own social or adacemic status is of crucial significance for three reasons. First, he must raise the money to plan and support the workshop; and those controlling the money—foundations, universities, private persons—usually contribute only to someone with an established reputation. Second, contacts in the conflict areas are facilitated when the intervener, literally or figuratively, can present a calling card conveying the prestige of his occupation and the organization to which he is attached. And third, his roles at the workshop are affected by the participants' appraisal of him as a symbol and a person.

The intervener, therefore, must somehow identify himself and his status. One without a conventional affiliation is likely to arouse suspicion and, if he is an American these days, the belief that he is working for the CIA, no matter how loud his protests. What is needed is an institutional connection, such as one with a university, or a sponsoring organization, such as a branch of the United Nations. So much the better if the intervener represents an organization like the Quakers or any group having the reputation of being impartial and trustworthy. In international disputes, it is helpful to have a team of interveners from several countries, or at least to have the blessing of a regional or international organization. The source of funds should be clean so that it can be revealed.

The intervener must possess the skills demanded by the roles he performs, four of which can be distinguished: that of administrator who attends to all the mundane, logistical details; the director who plans the workshop beforehand and who may also function as titular authority during its sessions; the professional staff (when required) who direct and control the sessions; and the researcher who observes, whether or not he also participates, and who eventually analyzes what has taken place. Obviously no one individual can effectively perform all these roles. Even when the number of participants is small, advice from colleagues and experts is needed if only during the planning stage. Pages would have to be written to provide an inventory of the required skills. For example, the personality traits facilitating the role associated with the Tavistock technique are different from those required by the NTL approach: the consultants or trainers (the titles the adherents, respectively, prefer) are called upon to behave differently and the followers perceive them differently (Harrow et al., 1971).

In any case there must be teamwork before, during, perhaps also after the workshop: the destructive conflict of the participants dare not diffuse to the staff. Someone, probably the intervener in the role of director, must ensure efficient coordination and strive for high morale. And there is no sure fire pathway to this goal, not even the charisma of the intervener or a let's-get-our-differences-out-in-the-open technique.

Goals[2]

The intervener's goal can be viewed on two levels, one temporal, the other in terms of content. Temporally the intervention may occur before, during, or after the conflict in order, respectively, to prevent its occurrence, to contribute to its solution, and to diminish the probability of its recurrence. The content has either a direct or indirect relation to the conflict. *Directly* the intervener seeks some kind of solution or resolution, or at least a useful contribution thereto. Many forms of solution are evident, ranging from a zero-sum outcome in which one side wins and the other loses; through a middle position that is a compromise; and all the way to a creative result in which both sides gain and neither loses, in which instead "a richer, more integrative relationship" (Boulding, 1964) between the disputants is achieved. *Indirect* intervention involves the attempt, intentionally or unintentionally, to influence the disputants' personalities or skills or to increase or change the information they have at their disposal. The range of possibilities is almost limitless, stretching primarily from individual psychotherapy to the teaching of group dynamics. I say *primarily* because an exercise designed at one level may affect some participants at a level not intended by the intervener. Therapy may aim to produce a change in the goals of specific persons so that as disputants, whether as leaders or followers, they subsequently behave differently in their own reference groups. In interacting groups, disputants are taught about groups and their function, so that the knowledge thus acquired, it is implied, will be somewhat useful in coping with the conflict.

Assumptions

Interveners assume, explicitly or implicitly, that their intervention will or can be successful. The definition of success involves their own motives and the postulated goals. Support for the assumption comes from historically minded scholars who have asserted, for example, that "local conflicts have a general, common structure rather than being always unique and random phenomena" and that some kind of "control measures," consequently, can prevent many conflicts, such as those arising since World War II, or at least mitigate them (Bloomfield and Leiss, 1969: 15, 32). At least five subsidiary assumptions are also made:

(1) The intervener himself does not suggest useful courses of action, at least at the outset, rather he hopes the participants can evolve their own proposals. This view in turn may reflect a conviction—whose truth or falsity in general or in particular situations must be left to historians to settle—that proposals originating with, or settlements devised by, the disputants themselves are likely to be more useful or lasting than those imposed by a third party (cf. Yalem, 1971). In fact, success is not considered the intervener's primary responsibility, although he may be motivated by the conviction that conventional approaches to conflict, through diplomacy and negotiation, have so frequently failed (Doob, 1968).

(2) Intervention is feasible in some kinds of conflicts and not in others, or perhaps at certain times but not at others. It may be impossible or doomed to failure after conflict has broken out or if a minority does not have its proportionate share of the society's total resources (Panagides, 1968). Also "when there is some desire for communication among the conflicting parties but the official channels for communication are unavailable, or their use entails unacceptable risks

at this point, a workshop may provide the needed alternative mechanism" (Kelman, 1972). Disputants from the side that seems to be winning a fierce conflict may feel they have nothing to gain from a workshop, or those from the losing side may wish to wait to negotiate or even interact until they can move into a more favorable position. A serious warning must be repeated: there are real conflicts in the real world that cannot be resolved by workshops but require negotiations by high policy-makers.

(3) Within a relatively short period of time, as suggested at the outset of this chapter, some disputants can learn new modes of behavior constructively related to mitigating or resolving the social conflict. This assumption stems from the view that, although early socialization has profound effects upon adult character and although "spectacular events" in the real world and "government efforts" ordinarily produce only slight changes in "human thinking and imagining" (Deutsch and Merritt, 1965), some persons under some conditions are sufficiently plastic and are available to be changed. Many believe, in the tradition of John Dewey and others, that such learning occurs only as a consequence of overt rather than covert activity. Inasmuch as the communications between the disputants in international conflicts are likely to be fragmentary and misleading, moreover, a workshop may be able to provide direct, face-to-face contact and hence promote some kind of useful understanding. There are of course numerous international organizations whose aim is to do just that (Evan, 1962).

(4) The intervener can arrange optimum conditions that facilitate learning. Laboratory and real-life research suggest that persons from different ethnic groups are changed by contact with one another, but that there is no magic in the contact per se: unless conditions are "right"—"right" cannot be precisely defined, though we can derive hints galore from research (Amir, 1969)—the outcome may turn out to be unfavorable. As has been declared again and again, sometimes though not by reality but by their own perception of that reality (Boulding, 1964)—and perceptions can be altered.

(5) The new learning can and will be utilized under real-life conditions in ways that constructively affect the social conflict. The utilization, it is further assumed, can occur in one of two ways, or in both:

  (a) The participants utilize what they have learned because they themselves are influential within their own society or group.

  (b) The participants communicate or diffuse what they have learned to those who are influential or, as a result of changes within them induced by the workshop, they behave differently or affect influential persons or groups.

induced by the workshop, they behave differently or affect influential persons or groups.

PARTICIPANTS

Attributes[3]

Potentially all disputants are qualified to participate in a workshop since virtually every individual can be changed in some respect and has some influence within his society if only with his family. To facilitate success, however, the most promising persons must be discovered, assessed, and recruited. Promise can be viewed in terms of availability, influence, interest, and personality.

Availability is to be taken literally: can the individual free himself from his normal responsibilities during whatever period the intervention requires? A mother with small children, the leader of an organization, a teacher with regular classes may not be able to pry herself or himself loose. Someone who knows that sanctions will be brought against him by his own group or the other side if it is known that he has participated will not or should not consider himself available—and sanctions range from social ostracism to physical harm and assassination. Not all available persons, however, are desirable. If the workshop is held outside the disputants' territory, some may be attracted for the sake of the trip, the social opportunity, or personal prestige.

Then individuals must be uncovered who are influential either directly or indirectly. Leaders may be able to implement directly what they learn at the workshop. Others may have access to leaders and thus indirectly affect policies.

The other two criteria are less sociological and more psychological in nature. Potential participants should be eager to learn something new; they must not have a vested interest in the status quo, especially in any aspect of the conflict. Ideally they should not be rigid, but be willing and able to try to devise and utilize innovations. They should also be emotionally stable in order to be able to suffer the strains and tensions often engendered by intense intergroup activity. With our present knowledge and techniques and under real-life conditions, systematic screening is difficult, like trying to reach an important destination without a compass. It is to be doubted whether the following generalization is applicable to genuine groups interacting over time: personality factors "have not been shown to affect behavior" in laboratory settings resembling international negotiations, rather factors in the immediate situation are of much greater significance (Druckman, 1971: 116-117).

The intervener is faced with a dilemma when he tries to weigh the influence of potential participants against their psychological readiness to participate in a workshop. If they are socially or politically important, they can transmit and perhaps carry out the positive recommendations emerging from the workshop; but such persons are seldom available for any length of time or, if available, they are not likely to be psychologically detached from the policies they represent. And if they are not important, they may be emotionally detached but less influential afterward.

Can the intervener attract disputants by suggesting that they will thereby be contributing to mankind's knowledge concerning workshop procedures and their utility? Very often not, I think, for people resent being guinea pigs. And yet participating in an enterprise with a pioneering flavor can appear somewhat glamorous, especially if the disputants can be made to believe that they themselves will also learn something and conceivably affect the conflict usefully. In those rare instances in which the research design requires and can obtain controls who do not participate in the workshop and whose behavior is compared with those who do, it may be especially difficult to explain or justify approaching them: "Why do you want to talk to me?" (McClelland and Winter, 1969: 206).

Since disputants agreeing to participate have expectations concerning the workshop, the intervener finds himself in a variant of the ethical dilemma already mentioned. On the one hand they must have sufficiently favorable anticipations if they are to be motivated to attend. On the other hand, they cannot be made to feel too optimistic, for then disappointment and disillusionment may eventually result. Obviously these expectations affect morale and behavior during the workshop itself: Somehow, therefore, recruits must be encouraged to believe that the workshop has potentialities, but is not likely to produce miracles.

Ideally, after being invited, participants should be willing and able to prepare themselves intellectually for the experience. Depending on the conflict, the preparation can range from becoming acquainted, in effect anthropologically, with the values or viewpoints of the opposing side to studying the so-called principles of conflict or conflict reduction. This criterion comes from our knowledge of how mental sets affect perception and behavior and from experiments on groups (Druckman, 1971: 36, 38), but again I think we have no precise data from real-life confrontations. By establishing standards for recruitment and selection, however, do we not obtain persons of good will and hence do we not weed out the hardcore disputants, the very persons who need to be changed? Yes, the answer must be, for the goal is not to affect a representative sample of the disputants but an unrepresentative collection who have the potentiality of being useful afterward. There is, however, no danger that all discordant persons can be detected beforehand: no matter how thorough the screening process, it must be cynically or realistically stated that one or more participants are likely to create difficulties during the workshop by their very presence or as a result of their behavior.

Recruitment

To attract disputants who satisfy the criteria just mentioned, the recruiter must possess almost infinite anthropological-sociological as well as psychological-psychiatric insight and wisdom. Selecting influential persons, for example, requires a knowledge of the areas in conflict, since the really influential may not be immediately apparent. Then somehow the emotionally unstable must be screened out and invitations issued only to bright, eager, reflective persons.

But how are such paragons to be found? Insight into the areas can be obtained by living there and absorbing the relevant sociological information formally or informally. The intervener, being an outsider by definition, is not an inhabitant; hence he can identify potential participants either by settling down in the areas for some length of time or by consulting informants. Practical reasons may exclude the first approach: the intervener cannot afford the time; he may arouse suspicions in one group of disputants as he investigates the other; he may not be temperamentally suited for field work. Using informants as an alternative provokes problems in its own right. In some way or other they must first be found, hence the intervener must know something about the areas if his selection is to be sagacious. His status within his own society may be helpful; thus a member of some profession, a scholar, or a scientist is part of an international network through which at least letters of introduction can be arranged and the initial contact established. Informants obviously must be trustworthy and reliable; being human, they have their own biases and hence give advice that is more or less slanted in some respects.

A tempting solution to the recruiting problem is to enlist the services of a deputy or several deputies who are inhabitants of the areas and hence have the same advantages and disadvantages as informants. Their motivation can come from being paid or, in addition, from their interest in the workshop. Clearly they must be most carefully instructed concerning not only the kinds of persons to be recruited but also the exact nature of the workshop. Deputies, however, may not be able to convey accurate information to potential participants unless they themselves have already experienced a workshop—something like trying to comprehend how it feels to be in love or under the influence of a drug if you have never been in love or ingested the drug.

Professional psychiatrists and clinical psychologists, as the honest ones always and the less honest ones occasionally admit, have no magic ray which infallibly distinguishes the emotionally stable from the unstable, the alert from the inert, the resilient from the rigid. The intervener or his deputy, therefore, is likely to make one or more mistakes in selecting participants. These mistakes can disrupt in small or large measure the workshop. If practical, it would be desirable to conduct a preliminary workshop on a small scale in each of the conflict areas in order to observe potential participants in action and then to select only the more promising ones.

PROCEDURE

Site and Duration[4]

For optimum learning and creativity one condition is assumed to be essential: the participants must be temporarily removed from the conflict so that some of the pressure they normally feel is diminished, hence they will not be distracted and can concentrate upon the workshop's tasks. Such isolation can be variously attained, perhaps most satisfactorily at a site some distance from the normal milieu. A neutral location is obviously necessary for disputants from two nations. At the site itself some degree of isolation is also desirable to avoid other, in this instance, dangerous or tempting distractions. The danger can result from being overseen by hostile persons; the temptation, from the opportunity to meet or mingle with nonparticipants. In addition, the participants should have comfortable living quarters and be well fed: when not concentrating upon the problem at hand, they require rest and relaxation. Liquor? As ever, this can be a problem when hard drinkers have not been eliminated during the recruiting process. There must also be a meeting room large enough to accomodate all the participants and the staff, in addition to smaller meeting rooms when group interaction techniques require them. A fairly luxurious hotel or lodge in a rural area or, when space is available, a dormitory in a university usually satisfy all or most of these requirements.

On the whole it is better to have the participants not accompanied by spouses or children, so that they can be free from normal obligations and devote themselves completely to the workshop. Some, however, may refuse to participate if they are separated from their wives, husbands, or children; and others may be anxious about their families, particularly if the conflict involves violence. Here, in brief, is another petty but important problem to which there is no dogmatic solution.

The workshop's duration should depend upon the learning method that is employed. A workshop in which "ideas" are exchanged may last only a long weekend; one based on various forms of interacting groups may require two weeks or even more. Actually, however, few persons, especially those who are politically or socially important, can afford to be away from home too long. And so a balance may have to be struck between optimum and available time.

An additional, compelling reason why the site should be isolated, the living arrangements comfortable, and the duration relatively long is that significant learning may also take place *between* the formal sessions of the workshop; while talking, walking, drinking, or otherwise relaxing, for example, the participants may come to like and even trust one another.

Methods[5]

Intervention methods depend, or should depend, completely upon the interviewer's goals, which can be roughly classified as *cognitive* when they involve changes in information, stereotypes, or opinion; or *affective* when they are directed toward feelings, attitudes, or the bonds of trust or mistrust between the disputants. All of them operate during two stages which may or may not be kept quite separate. Through various devices which engender a facilitating atmosphere, participants are encouraged to learn something new about themselves, about one another, and sometimes also about the bases of conflict. Then they seek new ways to deal with the conflict.

The methods themselves may be viewed in four dimensions:

(1) *Degree of overt activity:* the extent to which overt rather than covert behavior is provoked. Usually a reciprocal relation exists between the overt activities of the intervener or staff and the participants: the greater the overt activity of one, the less that of the other.

(2) *Degree of involvement:* the extent to which the participants' central goals or values are aroused by the activity.

(3) *Degree of participation:* the number of participants engaged in overt or covert activity.

(4) *Degree of structure:* the extent to which the participants determine the nature of their own overt activity; what happens to them covertly, of course, cannot be directly controlled.

These four dimensions are inextricably intertwined. The structure of a setting is likely to determine the overt activity which in turn affects the degree of involvement and participation; this is the sequence ordinarily planned by the intervener. But highly involved participants may determine their own structure and overt activity as well as the number who participate in the setting.

Six general methods can be distinguished and characterized modally in terms of the dimensions:

(1) *Lectures,* formal or informal in character. The flow of information is to the audience from the speaker who is usually the intervener but may be a participant. Only he is overtly active; the audience is passive. The audience's central goals or values may be evoked by his words, but not by their own activity. The speaker is the authority; the structure is all-powerful.

(2) *Meetings,* large or small, with or without adherence to parliamentary procedures, but always with some specific topic or topics to be discussed. Few or many participants engage in overt activity which may be superficial or deep. The structure, whether prescribed by the intervener or not, is affected by the rules of behavior the participants bring to the setting.

(3) *Games:* a variety of exercises employed especially in interacting groups. The participants, by following the arbitrary rules of the game, usually engage in some form of *simulation*: they interact by imitating or displaying the behavior they imagine would be appropriate or efficient in a specified situation; they play the role they think they themselves or someone else would play in that situation. In order to act out the role of someone else, his viewpoint or assumptions must be comprehended and internalized, as a result of which the actor may question his own assumptions. Unless you would make a fool of yourself, you are able to act like the enemy only by taking him seriously. Participants may also be given an opportunity to practice roles they may or will play back home. The role players are overtly active; as the game progresses, they may become highly involved.

(4) *Observation.* In one sense the participants and the interveners inevitably observe one another throughout a confrontation; in addition, they may be more formally instructed to make such observations, for example, in a so-called fishbowl when one group of participants watches another in action or engaging in role-playing or in other forms of simulation. Seeing and hearing one member of the group explode and reveal his own intimacies, as fostered by Gestalt therapy (Perls, 1964), falls under this heading but, dedicated as the technique is to individual therapy, it is not likely to be deliberately utilized in behalf of disputants concerned with a destructive social conflict. Observation can be facilitated by means of film, tape, or videotape, media that communicate the behavior of others or play back the participants' own words or deeds. With any of these methods, overt activity is close to zero, the structure is more or less overpowering, and the degree of involvement fluctuates from boredom to full absorption.

(5) *Small, arbitrary groups* that are formed during the confrontation. Some are planned by the intervener or the staff, especially in the case of interacting groups. In one tradition, T-groups train the participants to interact with one another, to learn to communicate, to recognize their own problems. In another tradition, that of Tavistock, different kinds of groups are formed by the intervener with no stated objective (study groups), with a general one (application groups), or with a specific one (planning groups); and at some point the participants are told to build their own groups ("intergroup exercise"). Although the

size and composition of these groups, except for the intergroup
exercise, are externally imposed, the participants themselves almost
completely determine what they shall say and do in the course of the
interaction. In fact, there may be no agenda, and the intervener or
staff members may remain silent when he is called upon for guidance
or direction, a state of affairs frequently leading to so much discomfort among the participants that they begin to communicate information about themselves and their organizations back home. Other
informal groups or cliques, furthermore, are likely to be brought into
existence by the participants during the periods when the workshop is
not formally in session. Degree of overt activity is high, and usually
involvement is too; there are always some participants who deviate
from the modal tendency which is to participate.

(6) *Interviews.* Any form of direct or indirect questioning may be used by
the interveners to obtain from the participants or disputants expressions of attitude, opinions, or facts concerning the conflict.

No one of the above methods is or should be always preferred over others.
Each method, however, has its own adherents who are inclined to consider what
they do a panacea for many if not most human and social ills, as a result of
which reasonable well-founded criticisms of interacting groups (e.g., Back, 1972)
have arisen. Usually, moreover, a workshop does and should employ a combination of methods. Pugwash concentrates upon lectures and meetings, which
probably are the best devices to employ when distinguished natural scientists
and others assemble to learn about arms developments and to make recommendations concerning, for example, the control of nuclear weapons. In "Controlled
Communication," the disputants interact with one another while seated in the
center of the room (a small meeting) and eventually are given specific information about their conflict or the principles of conflict by social scientists who
are stationed as observers behind them (a form of lecturing). Tavistock interveners are convinced that learning about groups in general occurs through
participating in the small, arbitrary groups formed throughout the workshop,
but infrequently at the outset and more frequently later they indicate, by brief
comments, what they assert to be the meaning of the participants' actions in the
here-and-now, a form of didactic lecturing in miniature form.

The problem for intervener and staff, consequently, is to arrange the mixture
of one or more methods that seems more likely to produce the required learning.
The solution in turn depends upon the intervener's goal and the participants'
cultural background. Reactions to innovative methods, such as those associated
with interacting groups, are affected by that background, but apparently the
methods can be employed cross-culturally (Doob, 1968: 347). The effectiveness
of any mixture can be determined in part by the feedback (the fashionable word
to which the professionals are addicted) provided by the participants not only to

the intervener but also to themselves. Unstructured groups are usually not disinclined to criticize what they are experiencing in the here-and-now. The unexpected, the surprising, the dazzling may suddenly appear—such as coalitions against persons considered unacceptable or undesirable for any imaginable reason—so that any one of the principles carefully deduced from laboratory situation often finds anecdotal validation.

When the participants have learned more about themselves and their opponents both individually and politically, they are ready, it is hoped, to work on the destructive conflict that has brought them together. They may be able, it is hoped, to communicate more effectively: they know one another's points of view and peculiarities, and they may also better appreciate their own short-comings. In a face-to-face situation, as they hurl words at one another, they appreciate their own "double standard of morality," namely, "exactly the same behavior is moral if we do it but immoral if they do it" (Osgood, 1962: 29). At this point some kind of give-and-take in the manner of a meeting may occur within the total group of participants or within one or more subgroups that have either functioned previously for some other purpose or that are specifically formed to work on the problem. Included among the techniques are ones that, in large part, are useful in the first stage of the exercise: injection of additional information by the intervener and his staff or by experts; simulation to discover the consequences of a course of action or the available alternatives, perhaps with the aid of a computer; role-playing to practice what has to be done in the real world outside the workshop; the sharp exchange or clash of viewpoints which can also be creative because, as John Dewey once suggested, "conflict is the gadfly of thought" and hence is "*a sine qua non* of reflection and ingenuity" (1930: 300); and, if need be, a return to one or more of the other techniques in order to increase insight. In addition, so-called brainstorming can be employed: some or all of the participants are encouraged to produce ideas, new or old, as quickly and as plentifully as possible without stopping to wonder how practical, feasible, or desirable they are.

No matter what the method, behavior in the workshop differs from normal behavior. Being out of their usual context, participants are less subject to the pressure of their own reference groups that usually prevent them from being innovative (Janis, 1972). Policy-makers in particular may feel somewhat liberated from the customary constraints of their office (Grinspoon, 1964). Coalitions during the workshop that resemble those back home, however, may enable participants to retain their protected covering and then innovation is stifled.

REENTRY[6]

Even before the workshop ends, other hazards appear in gloomy glory. In spite of the intervener's and the participants' best efforts, nothing especially useful may emerge. In interacting groups, participants may immerse themselves in the group (or in the study of group processes) very thoroughly, in order to avoid discussing the conflict. Everyone may pay lip service to peace, for example, and have genuine convictions on the subject; but that does not mean they necessarily agree on the means to be used to attain that praiseworthy end. There may be close to unanimity regarding the practical steps to be taken; but it may be simultaneously evident that the real world may not or cannot tolerate what seems desirable or needs to be done. The stresses and tensions resulting from the group exercises may prove distracting or may inhibit any semblance of creativity. The enthusiasms generated by being together in an isolated enclave may be diminished or may not survive at home. Will or can participants implement in another setting whatever useful information, techniques, or ideas they have learned in the isolated setting of the workshop?

Actually the participants themselves undoubtedly experience and also verbalize many of these very problems as the end of the workshop approaches. They realize that conditions there are not like the real world, and they know that their friends and enemies back home, without experiencing what they have experienced, will not or cannot appreciate what they have learned or the good or bad news they bring. This discrepancy may also plague them during the workshop itself. With some interacting-group methods, moreover, participants become emotionally attached or dependent upon the intervener or the staff (positive transference), a momentary bond that may be difficult to break. The tempo of interaction and even of creativity may be speeded up as participants appreciate the approach of the final day; and time, practitioners in the field of interacting groups point out, is also a scarce resource that cannot be taken for granted.

The problems of the real world facing the participants upon reentry cannot be neatly catalogued. They include all the general ones that have confronted converts to any religion who believe they have the solution but cannot implement what they are convinced is true, good, and sacred. Perhaps real dangers have to be faced, for disputants and particularly their leaders may consider the participants traitors who have consorted with the enemy. Money may be necessary and lacking to implement plans formulated during the workshop; and so on, and on and on and on. Under some circumstances difficult to specify, the intervener or a representative should be at hand or occasionally visit the participants to offer them advice or additional training, or to function as a loving father-figure.

RESULTS[7]

What is needed and is lacking is a detailed tabulation of the short- and long-term successes and failures of a variety of workshops. The information is lacking because few follow-up studies of workshops have been reported and also because the information is difficult or impossible to gather. Researchers are not ordinarily permitted to interrogate foreign offices or heads of institutions concerning what they have learned from workshop participants and which policies, if any, they have altered. The participants themselves cannot always be located and, if located, may be reluctant or unable to provide the information.

A baker's half dozen of possible results can be outlined:

(1) Participants become acquainted or better acquainted with their opponent's viewpoints and assumptions. The change here is basically cognitive. Immediately or eventually this information may be recalled and can lead to the conviction that deeply embedded attitudes are no longer tenable in some if not all respects. On theoretical and empirical grounds, there is good reason to anticipate that some of the learning will be of a latent character (Bunker, 1965).

(2) Participants learn more about the ways in which groups function as a result of the experiences they have had in the here-and-now groups within the workshop and the instruction of the interveners and the staff.

(3) Participants learn or formulate principles that seem to govern the reaction and behavior of themselves, other persons, or groups. Self-insight (a dignified way to refer to the razzle-dazzle currently associated with fashionable encounter groups in the West) is considered here to be a distinctly secondary gain.

(4) Bonds are established between or among the participants. The trust may involve persons on the same side of the conflict, or it may extend to disputants on the other side. Such an outcome is important since carrying out a plan of action is facilitated by the presence of others who share the same determination.

(5) Publicity concerning the existence or outcome of the workshop may have double-edged consequences. On the one hand, it may function as a way of disseminating information and thus exert pressure upon policy-makers; but on the other hand, it may endanger the enterprise or the participants, in the first instance because those in control may be convinced that conflicts can only be settled in secret, in the second because nonparticipants may seek to punish their peers for consorting with the enemy.

(6) Some information about the workshop always diffuses if only to the participants' immediate families. Foreign offices, and perhaps the police, are eager to know what has occurred (if they are aware of the workshop's existence) and debrief some or all the participants. The conditions under which policy-makers who receive this information are willing and able to accept and act upon it constitute a problem in

its own right beyond the present analysis. A schema outlining the "conflict regulating motives" (e.g., Nordlinger, 1972), if it is valid, can serve as a valuable introduction to that problem.

(7) Change, significant change, is obviously the most important consequence of all. The change may relate to the actual policy of the government or other important groups within one or both of the societies or factions in conflict, or it may involve the formation of groups or organizations which in the short or long run mitigate or, miraculously, resolve the conflict.

At least four caveats must be entered that spring in large part from the multivariant nature of destructive conflict. The first would suggest that any achievement or nonachievement cannot unequivocally be attributed to the techniques that have been employed, for almost always there is no control group, an equivalent collection of people from both sides of the conflict who have not attended the workshop; hence, we do not know whether they too might have changed as a result of forces in their societies which affected the participants. A pseudo-control might be squeezed out of the fact that, prior to the workshop, the participants had remained unchanged. Or it is perhaps reasonable to accept their own testimony that they have changed or feel different. Even if we believe that changes have occurred, however, we cannot attribute them to one or more specific methods employed in the workshop; for example, just being together in comfortable, isolated surroundings for some length of time may have been the decisive factor. Again an adequate control is lacking. Similar uncertainty exists when conscientious, rigorous attempts have been made either to determine whether two-week courses in India and Mexico aiming to strengthen a need to achieve higher or greater economic goals succeeded, or to provide an explanation for the success or failure (McClelland and Winter, 1969: especially 104-105, 252, 305, 324-326, 334, 364-366). One semiconsolation exists: because it is known that contact between disputants per se does not necessarily have useful results (Mishler, 1965), a desirable change may signify at the very least that the workshop has promoted the right kind of contact or that the contact has been sufficiently profound (cf. Pool, 1965: 117).

Second, even when a public policy affecting the conflict seems to resemble one that was discussed or evolved during the workshop, we may lack adequate information to determine the precise link. The existence of the SALT conferences between the United States and the Soviet Union, and some of the measures discussed and decided there, may have been inspired by resolutions previously adopted at Pugwash Conferences, but documentation is lacking.

The workshop, third, is likely to boomerang for some of the participants who threaten to leave while it is in progress (and some of them do, if leaving is feasible) or who berate it afterward (cf. Eurich, 1971: 62-63). Others do not feel hostile; they believe only that they have learned nothing important or have wasted their time by attending. What appears on the surface to be desirable or undesirable learning, moreover, may eventually have the opposite effect or no effect on overt action. Thus increased understanding of the opponent's viewpoint may possibly increase rather than decrease competition with him and make resolution more difficult, depending on the nature of the information (Druckman, 1971: 59, 84, 85).

Success or failure, finally, must also depend upon factors over which the workshop, the interveners, the staff, and the participants have no control. Shortly after the workshop attended by individuals from Ethiopia, Kenya, and Somalia ("Fermeda Workshop" on Table 1), for example, a coup d'etat occurred in one of the countries, as a result of which some participants were jailed and others became cabinet ministers.

CONCLUSION

Unofficial intervention in destructive social conflicts is a very risky kind of activity. The intervener who organizes a workshop must be highly motivated, must be concerned with the ethical implications of what he does, must possess a variety of skills, and must be aware of the goal he seeks as well as of his implicit and explicit assumptions. The participants to be recruited must be available, influential, interested, and stable; they are not easy to locate, recruit, and assess. It appears as though isolating the participants geographically for a relatively long period of time (e.g., two weeks) may be essential to facilitate the learning that is needed. In the workshop a variety of methods may be employed and should be selected by a reference to the goal being sought and to the participants who are present. A critical problem arises when the participants seek to utilize what they have learned in the real world back home. Results of a workshop are difficult or impossible to ascertain, but there are enough clues suggesting the possibility of limited success to justify the tentative, optimistic conclusion that intervention of this kind can be both useful and desirable.

N O T E S

1. Columns 1, 2, 3, and 4 in Table 1 contain the basic information about the workshops: the name by which they are known, the conflicts they sought to resolve or mitigate, the site at which they were held, and the year of their occurrence. Reference is also made to the remaining columns in footnotes attached to the appropriate headings of this chapter. Detailed information concerning each project can be obtained as follows: Controlled Communication (Burton, 1967, 1969); Fermeda Workshop (Doob, 1970, 1971); Friends (Eurich, 1971: 52-79); Intercession (Wedge, n.d.); Belfast Workshop (Doob and Foltz, 1973); Pugwash (Rotblat, 1967).

2. Cf. Table 1, column 5.

3. Cf. Table 1, column 6.

4. Cf. Table 1, column 7.
5. Cf. Table 1, columns 8 and 9.
6. Cf. Table 1, column 10.
7. Cf. Table 1, column 11.

REFERENCES

AMIR, Y. (1969) "Contact hypothesis in ethnic relations." Psychological Bulletin 71: 319-342.
BACK, K. (1972) Beyond Words. New York: Russell Sage.
BAILEY, S. (n.d.) Peaceful Settlement of Disputes. New York: United Nations Institute for Training and Research.
BLOOMFIELD, L. and A. LEISS (1969) Controlling Small Wars. New York: Knopf.
BOULDING, K. (1964) "Toward a theory of peace," pp. 70-87 in R. Fisher (ed.) International Conflict and Behavioral Science. New York: Basic Books.
BUNKER, D. (1965) "Individual applications of laboratory training." Journal of Applied Behavioral Science 1: 131-148.
BURTON, J. (1967) "The analysis of conflict by casework." Yearbook of World Affairs 21: 20-36.
——— (1969) Controlled Communication. London: Macmillan.
COLLINS, B. and H. GUETZKOW (1964) A Social Psychology of Group Processes for Decision Making. New York: John Wiley.
COSER, L. (1956) The Functions of Social Conflict. New York: Free Press.
DEUTSCH, K. and R. MERRITT (1965) "Effects of events on national and international images," pp. 132-187 in H. Kelman (ed.) International Behavior. New York: Holt, Rinehart & Winston.
DEWEY, J. (1930) Human Nature and Conflict. New York: Modern Library.
DOOB, L. (1968) "Facilitating rapid change in Africa," pp. 333-386 in A. Rivkin (ed.) Nations by Design. Garden City, N.Y.: Doubleday.
——— [ed.] (1970) Resolving Conflict in Africa. New Haven, Conn.: Yale University Press.
——— (1971) "The impact of the Fermeda workshop on the conflicts in the horn of Africa." International Journal of Group Tensions 1: 91-101.
DOOB, L. and W. FOLTZ (1973) "The Belfast Workshop." Journal of Conflict Resolution 17(3): 489-512.
DRUCKMAN, D. (1971) Human Factors in International Negotiations. New York: Academy for Educational Development.
EURICH, A. [ed.] (1971) Observation on International Negotiations. New York: Academy for Educational Development.
EVAN, W. (1962) Transnational forums for peace," pp. 393-409 in Q. Wright et al. (eds.) Preventing World War III. New York: Simon & Schuster.
GALTUNG, J. (1965) "Institutionalized conflict resolution." Journal of Peace Research 2: 348-397.
GRINSPOON, L. (1964) "Interpersonal constraints and the decision maker," pp. 238-247 in R. Fisher (ed.) International Conflict and Behavioral Science. New York: Basic Books.
HARROW, M., B. ASTRACHAN, G. TUCKER, E. KLEIN, and J. MILLER (1971) "The T-group and study group laboratory experiences."-Journal of Social Psychology 85: 225-237.
HOLSTI, K. (1966) "Resolving international conflicts." Journal of Conflict Resolution 10: 272-296.
JANIS, I. (1972) Victims of Groupthink. Boston: Houghton Mifflin.

KATZ, D. (1965) "Nationalism and strategies of international conflict resolution," pp. 356-390 in H. Kelman (ed.) International Behavior. New York: Holt, Rinehart & Winston.

KELMAN, H. [ed.] (1965) International Behavior. New York: Holt, Rinehart & Winston.

——— (1972) "The problem solving workshop in conflict resolution," pp. 168-204 in R. Merritt (ed.) Communication in International Politics. Urbana: University of Illinois Press.

McCLELLAND, D. and D. WINTER (1969) Motivating Economic Achievement. New York: Free Press.

MISHLER, A. (1965) "Personal contact in international exchanges," pp. 550-561 in H. Kelman (ed.) International Behavior. New York: Holt, Rinehart & Winston.

NORDLINGER, E. (1972) Conflict Regulation in Divided Societies. Cambridge, Mass.: Harvard University, Center for International Affairs.

OSGOOD, C. (1962) An Alternative to War or Surrender. Urbana: University of Illinois Press.

PANAGIDES, S. (1968) "Communal conflict and economic considerations." Journal of Peace Research 5: 133-145.

PERLS, F. (1964) Ego, Hunger, and Aggression. New York: Random House.

POOL, I. (1965) "Effects of cross-national contact on national and international images," pp. 106-129 in H. Kelman (ed.) International Behavior. New York: Holt, Rinehart & Winston.

ROTBLAT, J. (1967) Pugwash, the First Ten Years. London: Heineman.

THIBAUT, J. and H. KELLEY (1959) The Social Psychology of Groups. New York: John Wiley.

WEDGE, B. (n.d.) "A psychiatric model for intercession in intergroup conflict." San Diego: Institute for the Study of National Behavior.

WRIGHT, Q., M. EVAN, and M. DEUTSCH [eds.] (1962) Preventing World War III. New York: Simon & Schuster.

YALEM, R. (1971) "Controlled communication and conflict resolution." Journal of Peace Research 8: 263-272.

YALOM, I. and M. LIEBERMAN (1971) "A study of encounter group casualities." Archives of General Psychiatry 25: 16-30.

PART TWO.

EMPIRICAL STUDIES OF PERCEPTION AND COGNITION

Chapter 6

AN ETHNOGRAPHIC PSYCHOLOGY OF COGNITION

MICHAEL COLE

The Rockefeller University

SOME PRESUPPOSITIONS

Like many psychologists who currently engage in cross-cultural research, my introduction to this area of psychology was an accident of circumstances. Trained as a mathematical psychologist and possessing an active passport, I was available on short notice to go to Liberia on a project to improve the mathematics education of tribal children. At the time I embarked for Liberia, I had only a vague idea of its geographic location. My sponsors had an equally vague idea of my mission, and how it was to be accomplished.

As a graduate student, trained in the tradition of American psychology of learning, I arrived in Liberia with an invisible cargo of assumptions about human nature and human learning. Of course I knew a lot about the experimental method. I could properly design and execute a wide variety of experiments, collect the data in neat tables, and analyze those tables of numbers by a variety of statistical techniques. Like most of my colleagues, I was an environmentalist. I was willing to grant individual differences in all sorts of human attributes, including something loosely labeled intelligence, but I did not believe that any one race was likely to have more of that stuff than any other. More important, I was convinced that the psychological processes that people develop are very much a function of their early experiences; lacking certain experiences, various psychological processes are unlikely to develop, or at least, unlikely to develop fully. Finally, I knew that psychological tests and experiments are essential tools to understanding psychological processes. To learn about a child's level of conceptual development, I could use Piagetian conservation tasks that would tell me whether the child had made it into the concrete operational stage or not. Conservation performance also would indicate whether the child had developed such schema as "reversability." I could assess the development of mediated learning processes using one of several discrimination transfer designs. Subjects' abilities to classify and their abstract thinking abilities could be measured by a variety of classification tasks, and clustering in free recall would tell me about whether their memories were organized categorically. The number of experimental tools I could use and the number of hypothetical processes that I could study were legion. The only common denominator was the assumption that each experimental task was diagnostic of a particular cognitive process.

When I first arrived in Liberia, I spent a good deal of time traveling around the countryside asking people about the source of the mathematics difficulties which had prompted my trip. The answers I got from people who spent time around children (teachers, doctors, American mothers who had observed African children playing with their offspring) were consistent with expectations I had brought with me.

The list of things that the tribal children could not do, or did badly, was very long indeed. They could not tell the difference between a triangle and a circle because they experienced severe perceptual problems. This made the tribal child's task almost hopeless when it came to dealing with something like a child's jigsaw puzzle, explaining why "Africans can't do puzzles." I heard a lot about the fact that "Africans don't know how to classify" and, of course, the well-known proclivity of African schoolchildren to learn by rote came in for a lot of discussion.

The source of these difficulties? A college physics teacher suggested that AID buy tinkertoys for every child in Liberia. Almost everyone had a favorite deficit in the child's experience which, if rectified, would greatly benefit the educational products of Liberian schools.

Both the collection of assumptions that I brought to Liberia as a result of my graduate education and the diagnoses of my hosts concerning the learning difficulties of Liberian students were very much a part of the times. This was the era in which America "discovered" the disadvantaged child. In language very much like that applied to Kpelle children in Liberia, American scholars and educators offered explanations for the school difficulties of American minority groups and the poor (Riessman, 1962; Deutsch, 1967).

John Gay and I also sought the source of school difficulties in the child's home background. But it turned out, in retrospect, that we approached this problem with added assumptions that really were not a part of my psychological training and were not shared (or at least not taken into consideration) by the educators and psychologists with whom we talked. First, we assumed that, although Kpelle children lacked particular kinds of experiences routinely encountered by children, they were by no means lacking in experience. In fact, we explicitly began with the assumption that "we must know more about the indigenous mathematics so that we can build effective bridges to the new mathematics that we are trying to introduce" (Gay and Cole, 1967). This assumption led us into an exploration of the way that numbers, geometrical forms, and logical operations are expressed in the Kpelle language. We also investigated situations in which the Kpelle measure, engage in arguments, and organize situations for the education of their children.

Our second, somewhat unprofessional, assumption was that people would be skilled at tasks they had to engage in often. This statement may seem patently obvious or trivial, but its consequences are neither. Eventually, it led me to reformulate the problem of the relation between experience and the development of cognitive processes, as I shall attempt to make clear presently. In the 1960s, it led us to discover that Kpelle people are masters at measuring rice. For this area of their experience, they have a highly developed vocabulary and a system of measurements that is completely consistent. When measuring distances or lengths, however, the vocabulary is less detailed, and·we discovered that very often noninterchangeable units of length depended upon the kind of object or distance being measured.

Looking back at our early work, I find a great deal with which I can no longer agree. Too much of our thinking was imbued with the idea of cultural deprivation and its consequent cognitive deficits. Nevertheless, I can see now that our mixture of "scientific" and "common sense" approaches to Kpelle mathematical behavior pointed the way to our later work on culture and cognition. In particular, it led us to emphasize the situation-dependent nature of cognitive processes and the consequent need to combine ethnographic and experimental techniques in the study of culture and cognition.

COMMUNICATING: A PSYCHOLOGIST'S DEFICIT
IS AN ETHNOGRAPHER'S SKILL

To illustrate the kind of paradox that concerns me when I go beyond standard psychological inferences to consider ethnographic evidence, I will describe part of an unpublished study conducted among the Kpelle of Liberia.[1] Two adults are seated at a table. In front of each is a haphazardly arranged pile of ten sticks made of different kinds of wood of different shapes and sizes. A barrier is placed between the two men and one (to whom I shall refer as the speaker) is told to describe the sticks one at a time to his partner (the listener). One of the sticks is then chosen from a preassigned list, laid next to the barrier in front of the speaker, who describes the stick. After hearing the description, the listener tries to pick up the appropriate stick from his array. This process continues until all ten sticks have been placed by each man. They are then shown the array of ten pairs, errors are described and discussed, and the process repeated.

A set of sticks as I would describe them and as actually described by a Kpelle speaker is listed below in Table 1.

What is striking about this man's performance (and it is representative of the performance of the many traditional Kpelle rice farmers who participated in this study) is that he is failing to include features in his description which, given the

TABLE 1

English Description	Kpelle Description #1	Kpelle Description* #2
thickest straight wood	one of the sticks	one of the sticks
medium straight wood	one a large one	one of the sticks
hook	one of the sticks	stick with a fork
	one of the sticks	one of the sticks
thin, curved bamboo	piece of bamboo	curved bamboo
thin, curved wood	one stick	one of the sticks
thin, straight bamboo	one piece of bamboo	small bamboo
long, fat bamboo	one of the bamboo	large bamboo
short thorny	one of the thorny	has a thorn
long thorny	one of the thorny sticks	has a thorn

*NOTE: Actual order of presentation for Trial 2 was different from that for Trial 1.

nature of the array, must be communicated if the message is to be unambiguously received.

When such results are obtained with young American children, they are usually interpreted as evidence that the child has failed to develop the capacity to take the listener's point of view. Some investigators would attribute the speaker's inadequacy to his failure to have developed beyond the stage of egocentric speech (Piaget, 1926). In the work of Bernstein (1961), or Krauss and Rotter (1968), it is hypothesized that the difficulty of lower-class children relative to middle-class children in a communication task similar to this one arises because of the minimal interactions between child and adult and because of deficiencies in lower-class language when it comes to the expression of abstract ideas. Both of these theoretical approaches are applicable to interpretation of our Kpelle subjects' behavior. But are they reasonable? Do we really want to claim that a Kpelle adult is no more developed cognitively than a Genevan 6-year-old, or that the Kpelle language is deficient in its capacity to deal with abstract ideas?

These doubts are quickly reinforced by casual discussion with the subjects outside the experimental situation. They certainly seem to communicate very adequately, and about the time they have talked us into buying them a couple of bottles of beer, we may be very uncertain about just what was going on back in that experimental room.

Recourse to the ethnographic literature gives us even more cause for theoretical skepticism.

Among the many papers written by Evans-Pritchard about Zande culture is one entitled, "Sanza, a characteristic feature of Zande language and thought" (1963). In this paper, Evans-Pritchard describes the way in which the Zande exploit the potential for ambiguity in speech in order to protect themselves against their supposedly hostile tribesmen. Evans-Pritchard gives many examples of Sanza, but one which we can all appreciate readily is the following (1963: 211):

A man says in the presence of his wife to his friend, "friend, those swallows, how they flit about there." He is speaking about the flightiness of his wife and in case she should understand the allusion, he covers himself by looking up at the swallows as he makes his seemingly innocent remark. His friend understands what he means and replies, "yes, sir, do not talk to me about those swallows, how they come here, sir!" (What you say is only too true.) His wife, however, also understands what he means and says tartly, "yes, sir, you leave that she (wife) to take a good she (wife), sir, since you married a swallow, sir!" (Marry someone else if that is the way you feel about it.) The husband looks surprised and pained that his wife should take umbrage at a harmless remark about swallows. He says to her, "does one get touchy about what is above (swallows), madam?" She replies, "ai, sir. Deceiving me is not agreeable to me. You speak about me. You will fall from my tree." The sense of this reply is, "you are a fool to try and deceive me in my presence. It is me you speak about and you are always going at me. I will run away and something will happen to you when you try to follow me."

Evans-Pritchard's formulation for a successful Sanza is as follows (1963: 222): "The great thing . . . is to keep under cover and to keep open a line of retreat should the sufferer from your malice take offense and try to make trouble." So successful are the Zande in following this practice, and so ubiquitous is the use of Sanza in everyday Zande speech, that our renowned Oxonian colleague is led to lament at the end of his article: "It [Sanza] adds greatly to the difficulties of anthropological inquiry. Eventually the anthropologist's sense of security is also undermined, his confidence shaken. He learns the language, can say what he wants to say in it, and can understand what he hears; but then he begins to wonder whether he has really understood . . . he cannot be sure, and even they [the Zande] cannot be sure, whether the words do have a nuance or someone imagines that they do." He closes by quoting the Zande proverb, "Can one look into a person as one looks into an open-wove basket?"

It is important to mention that, while the particular form of ambiguous speech that Evans-Pritchard describes may have special features among the Zande, the use of rhetorical skills as a vehicle for controlling one's social environment is a very general feature of both nonliterate and literate societies alike (Albert, 1964; Labov, 1970).

I have picked these examples because they can serve as a vehicle for illustrating the ways in which anthropological and psychological approaches to the study of culture and cognition differ.

Consider first the example from Evans-Pritchard. It seems no more than good, common sense to recognize from the data presented that the Zande are subtle and complex thinkers who must consider a host of contingencies, including the viewpoint of their listeners, when deciding what they are going to say, to whom, and how. Assuming equal rhetorical skill among the Kpelle (and there is good evidence that this is so: Bellman, 1969), it seems equally obvious that there must be something wrong with the communication experiment. Perhaps the participants are deliberately shamming, or failing to understand what is expected of them. How could anyone who is an accomplished debator, a user of proverbs and subtle insults, be incompetent in such a simple task?

This style of interpretation has a long and honorable history in anthropology. Starting from the *assumption* of psychic unity, the anthropologist asserts that all human groups are sufficiently competent to carry out the many complex functions demanded of them by their culture and physical environment (Kroeber, 1948). Societies, of course, vary in the kinds of tasks that they pose their members, and environments vary in their physical features. The common-sense dictum that people will be skillful at tasks they experience often leads to the conclusion that there will be cultural differences in the activities eliciting skilled performance. But these are not differences in "cognitive processes" in the sense that psychologists seem to mean. They are only differences in emphasis.

It may be asked, how could anyone fail to agree? The fact is that psychologists generally do fail to agree, both on the interpretation of our two examples, and on the problem of the relation between culture and cognitive processes in general.

I cannot give a detailed account of how these differences arose (for a slightly more expanded account, see Cole et al., 1971: chaps. 1 and 6). The major points seem to be these:

(1) Psychologists as a group reject the use of naturally occurring behavior sequences as a source of evidence about learning and thinking processes. The major line of objection can be seen in an example taken from Cole et al., 1971: A man sees black clouds on the horizon and says it is going to rain. Did he make an inference, or did he simply remember the association, black clouds=rain? Complicate the example. Suppose that a man uses instruments to measure wind velocity and barometric pressure. A certain combination of wind velocity and barometric pressure is observed, and he says it is going to rain. Did he make an inference? It would seem more likely than in the first case, but it is still possible that he simply remembered this case from an earlier experience. In fact, it is impossible to determine, without

specific kinds of prior knowledge about the person and circumstances involved, whether a particular conclusion is a remembered instance from the past, or an example of inference based on present circumstances. Hence, evidence about the "logic of an inference" obtained from anecdotes or naturally occurring instances is always open to alternative interpretation. Just as there are ambiguities when trying to decide what processes are involved in the prediction of rain, there are problems in deciding exactly what people are doing when they use Sanza. Sanza, by its nature, is designed to be ambiguous, but the ambiguity of interpretation for the psychologist is twofold. We not only need to know what the person "really" meant, but we want to know if what he said represented "thinking" or memory. Perhaps people learn a set stock of Sanzas. As children they observe the application of Sanzas by adults and then emulate their elders when the appropriate situation arises. In effect, it might be argued that Sanza requires little more than recall of ambiguous formulas.

(2) These kinds of difficulties led psychologists to *define* thinking as a new combination of previously learned elements, among which problem-solving situations have been predominant. Bruner's (1957) definition of cognition as "going beyond the information given" captures the essence of this approach which is shared by psychologists of a wide variety of theoretical persuasions. Such a definition seems to require experimentation in order to make statements about thinking.

(3) The dominant pattern of inference in psychology is to use data from experiments as evidence about the psychological processes of individuals and, statistically, about groups. These processes are treated as properties of individuals that are "tapped" by the experimental procedures. It must be obvious from what I have said so far that I believe there is a very wide gulf between ethnographic and psychological approaches to the study of cognition. The two disciplines do not share the same data base: ethnographers rely for the most part on naturally occurring, mundane events, while psychologists rely on experiments. Ethnographers reject experiments as artificial, while psychologists avoid natural behavior sequences as ambiguous.

THE INTERPRETATION OF FAILURE TO PERFORM

In my opinion, the weakest aspect of current experimental psychological research in cross-cultural settings is the way that inferences are drawn from "poor performance," instances in which subjects give the wrong answer.

I am referring to instances such as the failure of our Kpelle subjects to specify the critical attributes of the sticks about which they are asked to communicate.

Given the pattern of inference current among developmental psychologists, we are led inexorably to the conclusion that Kpelle adults are egocentric, or in some other way deficient in the cognitive processes at their disposal. I believe this pattern of inference to be logically indefensible as it is ubiquitous. As one investigator stated recently: "Experiments in developmental child language can show you what children *can* do at various ages, but you cannot conclude from that what children *cannot* do" (see the discussion on Mehler in Ingram, 1971: 154). I can add only that this same principle applies generally to comparative research, whether age, culture, or species is the contrast of concern.

The reason lack of performance (or a low score) leads to the inference of lack of capacity is that the conclusion so often seems "reasonable." When applied to children in a single culture, the fact that an older child remembers more words, communicates more accurately, and in general behaves more competently is only to be expected. After all, the child has matured! He *must* have acquired some new cognitive apparatus.

In the same fashion, comparisons involving cultural institutions become plausible. Comparative statements are commonly made by psychologists and some anthropologists, usually in terms of a theory of general cultural advancement as cultures become more modernized. Rarely are the cultural insitutions and cultures compared viewed as "different, but equal." Schooling (Greenfield and Bruner, 1966), literacy (Goody and Watt, 1962), and acculturation (Doob, 1960) are all seen as providing people with new cognitive processes, new abilities, and new intellectual tools. It is claimed that, without extensive training, the mind is only capable of concrete thought; without writing, analytic thinking is not possible; without new technical challenges, culture and thought are stagnant.

The general consequence of this view that I have emphasized so far is that the "deprived" groups (who lack formal schooling, who have not learned to write, and who lack Western technology) are seen as uniformly lacking in particular, "developed" skills. Another consequence is that the cultural transition to the educated, literate, technological world is often conceived of as causing a *transformation* in cognitive processes. It is in this framework that Bernstein's ideas become plausible vehicles for explaining cultural differences in communication. And it is this framework which makes it possible for some people to suppose that traditional Kpelle adults are egocentric enough to be unable to take the point of view of their listeners.

It is on inferences of this type that the anthropologist and the psychologist part company. My objection to the anthropological treatment of experiments is that justified criticisms of the inference drawn from poor performance are combined with unjustified dismissal of culturally linked differences in performance. Data from psychological experiments, properly treated, are an important source of evidence about the applicability and limits of the doctrine of psychic unity. I also believe that proper cross-culture experimentation can greatly enrich our understanding of the development and structure of cognitive processes in general. But I do not believe that most cross-cultural experimentation fulfills our hopes for it.

SOME ILLUSTRATIVE EXAMPLES

Even anthropologists noted for their hardheadedness and acumen have been led to suppose that cultures may differ with respect to the mnemonic skills that they foster in their members. For example, Gregory Bateson's discussion of the cognitive aspects of Iatmul culture emphasize Iatmul memory skills and relates them directly to central features of the culture (1958: 200ff.). This idea has rather wide currency in the folklore of anthropologists, but it has received little explicit study (for reviews, see Cole et al., 1971; Cole and Gay, 1972).

A rather extensive research program using the technique of free recall illustrates one procedure that an experimental study of culture and memory can follow.

First, a series of studies was carried out using standard techniques borrowed from contemporary experimental psychology. Subjects were told to remember a list of common nouns consisting of familiar objects: clothing, food, utensils, and tools. They were read the list one item at a time and asked for recall in any order. This procedure was repeated five times for each subject with a single list.

These studies indicated that traditional Kpelle-Liberian farmers recalled relatively few items and failed to learn many new items with repeated presentations of the list. The sequence in which words were recalled conformed to no recognizable pattern of organization. This generalization held even though the experiment was modified to include monetary incentives, different kinds of words, concrete objects, and a variety of other stratagems aimed at producing good recall. I might add that an extensive investigation of the terms used revealed that they were indeed common and were categorized in the Kpelle language in the way we thought they were.

By contrast, Kpelle who attended high school remembered well, learned rapidly, and manifested a high degree of conceptual organization in the way they recalled the lists.

So far, this story is unusual only in that we seemed to have ruled out some obvious trivial explanations of the relatively poor performance of the Kpelle rice farmers. At this point we might well be tempted to draw some conclusions about deficient memory processes among Kpelle nonliterate rice farmers; we could seek an explanation in the small amount of information that they are asked to commit to memory each day, or the lack of books in their homes. But we still have not accounted for an important fact: in everyday affairs and in certain ritual contexts, the Kpelle exhibit normal, and perhaps even very good, memory by the standards of any reasonable ethnographer.

Happily, our work continued in search of conditions where experimentally measured Kpelle memory performance would be in line with common observation. We found several such situations. One occurred when we embedded the to-be-recalled list in a Kpelle-style folk story. Asked for the items, our subjects manifested highly organized recall consistent with the story of which it was a part.

In further studies, we were able to trace the difficulty of recall in the standard situation to a difficulty in finding information that was stored, but not effectively retrieved when the instruction to recall was given. Finally, we found still other, slightly altered, circumstances that spontaneously produced fine performance in traditional, noneducated people. This occurred, for example, where the objects to be recalled were associated with concrete objects, or when subjects were required to form their own groups during extensive exploration of the objects.

This series of experiments taken as a unit certainly seems to bear out the dictum that people will be able to perform well at tasks they find normal and which they often encounter. As such, it confirms anthropological doctrine. But it does more, I hope. It specifies somewhat more closely than usual what "normal" conditions are. And it turns out that "normal" in any simple way cannot be equated with "encounter often." Some of the experimental situations eliciting fine recall were *abnormal* in the sense of infrequently encountered. What the successful conditions seem to share with frequently encountered situations is a lot of structure. Where life or the experimental procedures do not structure the memory task, the traditional person has great difficulty. "Normal," in this case, refers to the presence of certain structural features.

Free recall is so named because it permits the subject to repeat back items presented in any order he likes, at any pace. We believe that skilled subjects learn such a task by providing structure (via mnemonic devices and rehearsal strategies) which they then use to retrieve stored information. Spontaneous production of such structures in free recall seems to be a learned behavior which is fostered in some cultures (or by some cultural institutions) and not in others.

In summary, this series of studies illustrates the following principles:

(1) Cultures differ in the situations that elicit skilled mnemonic performance.

(2) Cultures differ in the degree to which members will spontaneously produce structure as a device for enhancing recall of totally unstructured, disconnected material. Free recall is one such task.

(3) By pursuing the problem of poor performance—by whom and under what conditions it is manifested—we can tease apart cultural differences in the situations to which memory skills are applied from cultural differences in the development of general memory capacity.

The very tentative nature of these conclusions has to be immediately recognized. To give them greater basis, collaboration of anthropologists and psychologists aimed at exploring natural and contrived situations for the application of mnemonic skills is essential. This is a point to which I shall return.

Let me briefly recount one other example of a research program in which pursuit to the causes of poor performance was instructive. My example concerns inference.[2]

The enduring controversy over the existence or nonexistence of "primitive mind" involved, among other things, an argument over whether it was the premises or laws of inference that differ among "primitive" and "civilized" peoples.

Starting with a device used to assess inferential processes in American children, we set out to study the development of inferential processes among the Kpelle of Liberia. The device we used is pictured in Figure 1.

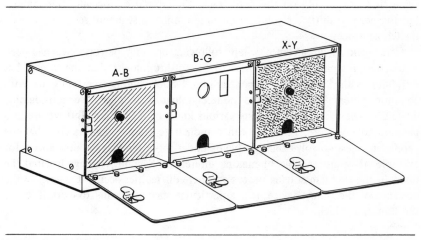

Figure 1.

The problem is presented as follows.

First, the subject is taught that pushing the button on the left-hand panel will yield him a marble. Then he is taught that pushing the button on the right-hand panel will yield a ball bearing. Then, with the two side panels closed, he is taught that putting a ball bearing in a hole in the center will yield him a piece of candy which he can see in a small window in the panel. Finally, all three panels are opened at once, and the subject is instructed to obtain the candy which he can keep and eat.

This problem has the nice feature of specifying the "premises" (the way to get a marble and a ball bearing) from which a solution (get the candy) is to be reached and of ensuring that the subjects know these premises very well before they proceed to make the required inference.

When this problem was first presented to groups of traditional Kpelle (children and young adults), performance was very unimpressive. For example, only 15% of the young adults spontaneously solved the problem and about half reached an incorrect solution.

Another experiment identified the general source of difficulty. When an analogous problem was constructed of matchboxes and a small locked chest, even small children were generally proficient performers. This suggests strongly that familiarity with the materials about which one is asked to reason is important if people are going to apply a cognitive skill they have.[3]

One additional study further localized the point in the problem where familiarity was important. Stages of the first two studies were pitted against each other. For example, keys were obtained from our fancy apparatus, one of which could open the locked box. It was shown that subjects who performed poorly did so because they did not deal effectively with the *first* link in the problem. Once they got started on the right track, the inference proceeded adequately, but the need to initiate a solution on an unfamiliar instrument seems to impede the whole process.

Here again is an instance where following up poor performance has been instructive. It comes as no surprise to the anthropologist that the subject has difficulty with "that foreign contraption." Such findings certainly fit with common observation that some nontechnological peoples have considerable difficulty when first encountering various kinds of machinery. But we are in a position to say more. First, we can demonstrate (rather than assert) that the people in question solve such problems under more familiar circumstances; for example, they are capable of making inferences. Second, we have isolated the point in the problem solving processes where difficulties occur: it is not just the presence of the funny device; it is a particular stage in having to work it that is the stumbling block.

PROBLEMS FOR THE FUTURE

Looking back over almost a decade of our research on culture and cognition, I can see that it has been dominated by two classes of questions. At the start we were led to make two inquiries: what kinds of experiences promote the development of what kinds of intellectual processes? Are these experiences linked to particular cultural institutions that are of special importance? In answering these questions, I proceeded on the assumption of a close relationship between experimental technique and psychological process. Implicitly, I was using the experiments as an assessment technique: how much of process X is present in culture Y?

In the past few years, the question changed. I began to ask: What kinds of cultural experience promote the manifestation of intellectual processes in particular experimental situations? This question led us to ask another: What kinds of nonexperimental situations yield clues about the existence of abstract thinking, inference, memory, and a variety of cognitive processes? I became much more skeptical about the relation between experiment and process, resorting to the generalization that "cultural differences in cognition reside more in the situations to which particular cognitive processes are applied than in the existence of a process in one cultural group and its absence in another" (Cole et al., 1971: 233).

I believe this statement to be true, but its acceptance should not obscure two important unresolved issues. First, are there identifiable deficits in cognitive processes arising from absence of specifiable experiences? Our methodological critique of current psychological experimental and inferential practices is not a denial of the possibility that there are cultural differences in the existence of cognitive processes. Such a blanket denial is not only premature, it is almost certainly wrong. Second, a demonstration that someone has the capacity to remember and form concepts is not a claim that there are no important cultural differences in cognition. Kpelle children often fail to remember well in school; they do not make "obvious" inferences about the cause of hookworm; they do not generalize from 2+2=4 and 4+4=8. These difficulties may all result from a failure to apply existing capacities to the problem at hand, but they are no less real problems on that account.

I will consider these two issues in turn, emphasizing my belief that their resolution will depend upon a combination of ethnographic and experimental approaches.

ON THE EXISTENCE OF PSYCHOLOGICAL PROCESSES

One of the really attractive aspects of cross-cultural research on cognition is that it seems to offer a natural laboratory in which to test a wide variety of hypotheses about the relation between experience and behavior. Because most of us accept the general proposition that adult cognition arises out of an interaction of organism and environment, what could be more natural than the impulse to introduce some meaningful variation on the environment side of this proposed interactional system? It is within this framework that my colleagues and I undertook our studies of the influence of education on cognitive development. And it is within this framework that most of the major programs of cross-cultural research have been conducted (e.g., Segall, Campbell, and Herskovits, 1966; Berry, 1971; Bruner et al., 1966; Dasen, 1972a,b and many others).

I very much want to see this kind of research effort continued and expanded.

I have been stimulated by the evidence that education, child-rearing practices, physical environment, and language can all influence cognitive behavior. But from my presentation thus far, you can anticipate the uneasiness with which I greet conclusions that equate poor performance with lack or less of some general cognitive process. I will discuss only one of many lines of research about which I have many questions.

I want to examine the conclusions we can draw from the enormous and growing body of cross-cultural work using Piagetian tasks which is putatively relevant to the issue of whether certain cultures push cognitive growth further and faster than others. Leaving aside the question of whether or not formal educational experience is crucial to the development of concrete-operational thinking among traditional, nonliterate peoples (Greenfield and Bruner's work, 1966, would lead us to believe it is; Dasen, 1972a,b, would lead us to believe it is not sufficient), I am left wondering about the cognitive status of people who do not conserve. Consider, for example, research done among people who live in semiarid locations where severe water shortages occur from time to time and natives' abilities to find scarce water are legendary (e.g., aborigines). Are we to believe that aborigine adults will store water in tall thin cans in order to "have more water"; do they think they lose water when they pour it from a bucket into a barrel? I am tempted to believe that they would have disappeared long ago were this the case. I also find it difficult to believe that they cannot think through an action and its reverse. Yet if we are to extrapolate the interpretations of poor performance from Genevan children to aborigine adults (note, I am not quarreling with the *fact* that many aborigine adults fail to make conservation responses in experimental situations), what else can we conclude?

Like Heron (1971), I am curious about the noncorrelation between performance on a Piagetian task and mathematical performance which takes for granted the operations assessed as absent. If schools promote cognitive growth, the tests which reflect this growth ought to discriminate between the relevant performances of the more and less developed students (according to the test criterion). Yet this was not so in the case of Heron's Zambian students, and we have no evidence that it is true in the other cases where conservation performance has been assumed indicative of cognitive development.

The failure of many aborigine (and African) young adults to make conservation responses is a fact, but the interpretation of this fact seems quite problematic to me. In Europe and the United States, where all normal children eventually come to respond correctly across the whole spectrum of conservation problems, such a statement as "55 to 60% of the 5- to 6-year-olds conserve" has a relatively clear interpretation: 55 to 60% of the children have entered the concrete-operational stage that *all* children *eventually* enter. The culture is homogeneous with respect to adult performance, but the various traditional societies we have been studying are *not* homogeneous with respect to their level of cognitive maturity as measured by conservation performance: some adults conserve, some do not.

What does it mean to claim that "Tribe X does not mature past the European 11-year stage" if 50% of the members of Tribe X conserve and 50% do not? No one in Tribe X is operating at the "11-year-old-level" and to speak of a "leveling off of cognitive development" as if the statement applies to individuals is a serious mistake. Until we have some better idea of what induces some members of traditional societies to solve conservation problems while their neighbors do not, we cannot be certain about the significance of conservation tests as a tool for understanding the relation between culture and cognitive development.

I do not think that current research practices will resolve these difficulties. It is going to be necessary to get a much more detailed idea of exactly what kinds of past experiences are linked to particular kinds of conservation. A few investigators have explored the influence of variations in content and procedures on conservation (e.g., Price-Williams, 1961; Greenfield, 1966; Price-Williams, Gordon and Ramirez, 1969). I think this is a step in the right direction, and the evidence so far clearly indicates that both procedural and content variations can have a marked effect on conservation performance (see also Dasen, 1972a,b). However, no one has carried out the systematic variations that Price-Williams (1967) advocates, and no one has made a study of a group's ecology and daily activities to determine if conservation-like principles are observable in any sphere.

ON SITUATIONAL VARIATION IN THE
MANIFESTATION OF COGNITIVE PROCESSES

Although I have emphasized the problems of research focused on cultural variations in the existence and amount of general cognitive processes, the situational approach to the study of culture and cognition is also fraught with conceptual problems and empirical gaps, all the more so because it has received so little attention.

To begin with, a good deal of hard thinking must be devoted to clarifying the concepts of *cognitive process* and *situation*. So long as we conceive of a cognitive process in the context of a particular theory and the experiments which have been accepted as diagnostic, these questions do not often arise. But our current analysis forces them upon us. In the literature on cognition, and on culture and cognition in particular, the variety of terms that can be grouped under the labels "process" and "situation" is bewilderingly large. It is not at all clear what distinctions, if any, are intended by different terms. At times "skill," "mechanism," "ability," "capacity," and "process" are used as if they were interchangeable. At other times there have been attempts to introduce systematic distinctions among these terms; Flavell and Wohwill (1969), for example, suggest a distinction between "mental operations" and "mechanisms for processing input and output"; Donaldson (1963) talks about "structural" and "executive" errors. Our distinction between the existence and application of capacities is in this latter tradition. But like others, I have been guilty of vagueness (as, for example, in the discussion of the "processes and skills" that underlie good free recall performance), and I will continue to be vague until we can specify criteria differentiating these terms.

Our problems with respect to the notion of situation are just as severe. At times situation has been used as roughly synonomous with "experimental manipulation." Here I would class the studies varying experimental materials (pictures versus objects, water versus soda pop), instructions, incentives, and the like. At other times, situation refers to the entire context of inquiry, as when we compare verbal dueling with a communication game. At present, we have no theory of situations to guide us; work from contemporary sociology (McHugh, 1968; Gumperz and Hymes, 1972) and perhaps some contemporary reserach in social psychology (Orne, 1970) might be used as a starting point.

In addition to definitional problems, we also need to consider what general form a theory of culture and cognition would take if situational factors are to be a part of the theory. At one extreme we can imagine a situational theory that is quite close to a general cognitive development or "factor" approach: some cultural institutions promote the widespread use of one particular process (e.g., abstraction) while others promote its application in only a few, selected situations. An example might be provided by Gladwin's (1970) description of Puluwat navigators, who use an abstract star compass to help them get from island to island, but who fail to respond with sufficient abstractness to a Piagetian seriation task. This approach will often assume that one process (abstract, generalized) is developmentally "higher" than another (concrete, rote).

A somewhat different approach to situational variations would emphasize differences in the application of cognitive skills to different domains of activity within a given culture in an attempt to determine what variables control the manifestation of different processes. A concrete example of the kind of research that I have in mind can be illustrated by reference to the work of Greenfield and Childs (1974) concerning whether or not learning to weave one of the three traditional Zinacantecan cloth patterns influenced a general ability to represent patterns. Research with girls (who know how to weave) and boys (who do not) demonstrated very little influence of weaving experience on any *generalized* ability to represent patterns, although girls were better than boys at copying details of given patterns. Greenfield and Childs also failed to obtain any marked influence of primary education on their pattern generalization task.

Why did learning to weave fail to have a generalized effect? Several possibilities exist. Citing Price-Williams, Gordon, and Ramírez (1969), Greenfield and Childs mention the possibility that the girls did not weave enough for their patterns to become generalized. Greenfield and Childs (1974: 29) prefer the explanation that "practical experience develops specific component cognitive skills ... whereas other more general cultural influences, economic activity for instance, develop generalized cognitive performance."

I am unhappy with this explanation because it does not specify what is special about economic activity except that it is "a general cultural influence." But one of our tasks is to discriminate and order cultural influences in terms of their generality. Is economic activity inherently general, or will any "general" activity do?

Let me make a suggestion which does not resort to invocation of general cultural influences, but which does offer some possibility of tying situational variation to a solid body of psychological data.

I would like to propose that the variety, as well as the amount, of practice with a particular subject matter is crucial to the wide application of cognitive skills. If there is a single, central lesson to be derived from years of research on learning sets, it is that animals (including man) learn generalized problem-solving skills through repeated experience with different problems of the same type. Weavers in Zinacantecan learn three patterns. That is all there are. As Bruner, Goodnow, and Austin (1956) pointed out, concepts are essential as a means of handling large quantities of information. But what is essential if the domain of information is small and constant? As a test of these ideas, I propose another experiment on weaving, but I seek an area where some people know only one or two patterns, others know five or six, and still others know 15 or 20. I know of no such place when we speak of weaving cloth, but in Yucatan, Mexico, where I have worked recently, I know there are great varieties of multi-colored patterns woven into hammocks. Some people know how to weave only a few patterns, some know how to weave many.

What I propose, then, is a study of the influence of weaving on pattern representation as a function of how many patterns a person can weave. I would be most interested in an outcome where the generality of pattern representation is a direct function of the number of patterns a person knows. Next I want to generalize this research strategy from the examples of ambiguous speech and communication performance which I presented at the outset of this paper. You can see that I am very impressed by the way traditional peoples seem to apply complex cognitive skills in social situations, while failing to use these skills in an experimental task. In the context of our weaving example, I would claim that social interactions provide for repeated practice with problems of the same type (getting someone to do a favor for you) but different content (different people, things, etc.). I would very much like some way to tie this speculation to experimentally replicable observations. This will require experiments that are *social* in content. I have no idea at the moment of how to proceed in this direction.

I am also anxious to explore other domains of daily activities with an eye to the variety of examplars that they involve. Ethnographic descriptions of traditional farming and handicrafts emphasize the rudimentary technology and paucity of tools. Might it be that an important dimension of cultural differences will turn out to rest on the variability of tasks and tools that people must deal with?

These are very broad theoretical questions indeed. I have discussed them at some length because they make interpretable my insistence on combining ethnography with psychology in the service of understanding culture and cognition.

NOTES

1. A brief report of this work, co-authored by J. Gay and J. A. Glick, was presented at the meetings of the Society for Research in Child Development, 1969.

2. For more details on this series of studies, see Cole et al. (1971: chap. 6).

3. It is almost certainly no coincidence that Wason and Johnson-Laird (1972) come to this same conclusion in their studies of reasoning among educated British adults.

REFERENCES

ALBERT, E. (1964) " 'Rhetoric,' logic, and poetics in Burundi: culture patterns of speech behavior," in J. Gumperz and D. Hymes (eds.) The Ethnography of Communication. Washington, D.C.: American Anthropological Association.

BATESON, G. (1958) Naven 2d ed. Stanford, Calif.: Stanford University Press.

BELLMAN, B. (1969) "Some constitutive factors of secrecy among the Fala Kpelle of Sucrumu, Liberia." Paper delivered at the meeting of the Liberian Research Association, Stanford, Calif.

BERNSTEIN, B. (1961) "Social class and linguistic development: a theory of social learning," in A. Halsey, J. Floyd, and C. Anderson (eds.) Education, Economy, and Society. Glencoe, Ill.: Free Press.

BERRY, J. (1971) "Ecological and cultural factors in spatial perceptual development." Canadian Journal of Behavioral Science 3: 324-336.

BRUNER, J. (1957) "Going beyond the information given," in Contemporary Approaches to Cognition: A Symposium Held at the University of Colorado. Cambridge, Mass.: Harvard University Press.

———J. GOODNOW, and G. AUSTIN (1956) A Study of Thinking. New York: John Wiley.

BRUNER, J., R. OLVER and P. GREENFIELD (1966) Studies in Cognitive Growth. New York: John Wiley.

COLE, M., J. GAY, J. GLICK, and D. SHARP (1971) The Cultural Context of Learning and Thinking. New York: Basic Books.

———and J. GAY (1972) "Culture and memory." American Anthropologist 74: 1066-1084.

DASEN, P. (1972a) "Cross-cultural Piagetian research: a summary." Journal of Cross-Cultural Psychology 3: 23-40.

———(1972b) "The development of conservation in aboriginal children: a replication study." International Journal of Psychology 7: 75-86.

DEUTSCH, M. et al. (1967) The Disadvantaged Child. New York: Basic Books.

DONALDSON, M. (1963) A Study of Children's Thinking. London: Tavistock.

DOOB, L. (1960) Becoming More Civilized. New Haven, Conn.: Yale University Press.

EVANS-PRITCHARD, E. (1963) "Sanza, a characteristic feature of Zande language and thought," in Essays in Social Anthropology. New York: Free Press.

FLAVELL, J. and J. WOHLWILL (1969) "Formal and functional aspects of cognitive development," pp. 67-120 in D. Elkind and J. Flavell (eds.) Studies in Cognitive Development: Essays in Honor of Jean Piaget. New York: Oxford University Press.

GAY, J. and M. COLE (1967) The New Mathematics and an Old Culture. New York: Holt, Rinehart & Winston.

GLADWIN, T. (1970) East Is a Big Bird. Cambridge, Mass.: Belknap Press.

GOODY, J. and I. WATT (1962) "The consequences of literacy." Comparative Studies in Sociology and History 5: 304-345.

GREENFIELD, P. (1966) "On culture and conservation," in J. Bruner, R. Olver, and P. Greenfield (eds.) Studies in Cognitive Growth. New York: John Wiley.

---and J. BRUNER (1966) "Culture and cognitive growth." International Journal of Psychology 1: 89-107.

GREENFIELD, P. and C. CHILDS (1974) "Weaving, color terms, and pattern representation: culutral influences and cognitive development among the Zinacantecos of southern Mexico," in J. Dawson and W. Lonner (eds.) Readings in Cross-Cultural Psychology: Proceedings of the First International Conference of the International Association for Cross-Cultural Psychology. Hong Kong: University of Hong Kong Press.

GUMPERZ, J. and D. HYMES (1972) Directions in Sociolinguistics: The Ethnography of Communication. New York: Holt, Rinehart & Winston.

HERON, A. (1971) "Concrete operations, 'g' and achievement in Zambian children." Journal of Cross-Cultural Psychology 2: 325-336.

INGRAM, E. (1971) "The requirements of model users" pp. 137-146 in R. Huxley and E. Ingram (eds.) Language Acquistion: Model's and Methods. New York: Academic Press.

KRAUSS, R. and G. ROTTER (1968) "Communication abilities of children as a function of age." Merrill-Palmer Quarterly 14: 161-173.

KROEBER, A. (1948) Anthropology. New York: Harcourt Brace Jovanovich.

LABOV, W. (1970) "The logic of non-standard English," in F. Williams (ed.) Language and Poverty. Chicago: Markham.

McHUGH, P. (1968) Defining the Situation: The Organization of Meaning in Social Interaction. Indianapolis: Bobbs-Merrill.

ORNE, M. (1970) "Hypnosis, motivation, and the ecological validity of the psychological experiment," pp. 187-265 in W. Arnold and M. Page (eds.) Nebraska Symposium on Motivation. Lincoln: University of Nebraska Press.

PIAGET, J. (1926) The Language and Thought of the Child. London: Routledge & Kegan Paul.

PRICE-WILLIAMS, D. (1961) "A study concerning concepts of conservation of quantities among primitive children." Acta Psychologica 18: 297-305.

---(1967) "Towards a systematics of cross-cultural psychology." Memorias del XI Congresso Interamericano de Psicologia, Mexico City.

---W. GORDON, and M. RAMIREZ (1969) "Skill and conservation: a study of pottery-making children." Developmental Psychology 1: 769.

RIESSMAN, D. (1962) The Culturally Deprived Child. New York: Harper & Row.

SEGALL, M., D. CAMPBELL, and M. HERSKOVITS (1966) The Influence of Culture on Visual Perception. Indianapolis: Bobbs-Merrill.

WASON, P. and P. JOHNSON-LAIRD (1972) Psychology of Reasoning: Structure and Content. Cambridge, Mass.: Harvard University Press.

Chapter 7

UNIVERSALS AND CULTURAL SPECIFICS
IN HUMAN CATEGORIZATION

E L E A N O R   R O S C H

University of California, Berkeley

The human visual system can discriminate some 7,500,000 different colors, but the most color names reported in any language are 4,000 English names of which only 8 are used very commonly (Brown and Lenneberg, 1954). No two plants—no two leaves, in fact—are identical, nor is any one plant quite the same on successive days; however, all cultures possess plant classification systems by which, at one or another levels of abstraction, billions of discrete, discriminable plants are rendered equivalent. There are an infinite number of perceptibly different things in the world, but no organism treats them all as different. In fact, one of the most basic functions of organisms may be the "cutting up" of the environment into classifications by which nonidentical stimuli can be treated as equivalent.

For humans, the major part of the classification system is probably neither biologically fixed nor created anew by each individual, but is provided by the culture and language into which the individual is born. It is the culture through which humans "see nature." Indeed, it is possible to define culture in terms of just its system of categories (the approach of "ethnoscience," cf. Tyler, 1969).

Where do such categories "come from"? By what principles of learning or behavior or "perception" do human groups segment variations among stimuli into classes? Why do we, for example, have "red" and "orange" which are considered two different colors and "cats" and "dogs" which are considered two different animals? Why do cultures cut up the world in just the ways that they do and not in other ways?

Surprisingly, such questions have received virtually no attention from the social sciences. Linguistics, psychology, and anthropology have commonly avoided the issue by means of the assumption that segmentation of the world is originally arbitrary. For example, a basic part of the hypothesis of "linguistic determinism" was that "the categories and types that we isolate from the world

Author's Note: This research was supported in part by a grant to the author (under her former name Eleanor Rosch Heider) by the National Science Foundation GB-38245X and the Grant Foundation and by a grant from the Foundations Fund for Research in Psychiatry No. G67-392.

[177]

of phenomena we do not find there because they stare every observer in the face; on the contrary, the world is presented in a kaleidoscopic flux of impressions which has to be organized . . . by the linguistic system in our minds" (Carroll, 1956: 213). Interestingly, it has been the "molding" effects of language rather than the arbitrary nature of the categories which has been challenged (Brown, 1958b). Whorf's view of categories is essentially mirrored in modern treatments. From psychology: "When the referents are not manufactured articles but are such things as dogs, people, flowers, and insects, it is clear that autochthonous factors in perception do not force any single scheme of categorization. The names applied must be the child's principal clue to the locally functioning scheme" (Brown, 1958a: 18). And from anthropology: " . . . the physical and social environment of a young child is perceived as a continuum. It does not contain any intrinsically separate 'things.' The child, in due course, is taught to impose upon this environment a kind of discriminating grid which serves to distinguish the world as being composed of a large number of separate things, each labeled with a name" (Leach, 1964: 34).

To assume that cultural categories are entirely arbitrary is rather like assuming that the distribution of different diseases among the populations of the world is arbitrary, an assumption it would make sense to maintain only in the total absence of any systematic knowledge about diseases. We are completely ignorant neither about principles of human learning and concept formation nor about the diversity of cultural classifications. Given the theoretically fundamental nature of the classification systems of cultures, it would seem eminently worthwhile to use and develop our knowledge to the point where we are able to explain and predict such systems.

The investigation of principles of classification is a truly interdisciplinary undertaking because cultural classifications can only have developed through the interaction of the principles of human learning and classification, the ecology of environments, and the dynamics of culture. Furthermore, the search for classification principles should reflect benefits back both to psychology and anthropology. Laboratory study of topics such as concept formation and free sorting of arrays of stimuli can be saved from sterility and provided with new dimensions for investigation when the psychologist considers the extent to which the concepts and categories produced by such experiments are really like those natural concepts and categories to which the words of actual natural languages refer. And anthropology can be saved from haphazard, cross-culturally noncomparable descriptions by hypotheses that direct the fieldworker's questions and provide a framework for meaningful cross-cultural comparison.

This chapter will explore two general issues of human categorization: the first concerns the nature of categories. It will be argued that the prevailing "digital" model of categories in terms of logical conjunctions of discrete criterial attributes is inadequate and misleading when applied to most natural categories.

An alternative "analog" model is presented which represents natural categories as characterized by "internal structure," that is, as composed of a "core meaning" (the prototype, the clearest cases, the best examples) of the category, "surrounded" by other members of decreasing similarity and decreasing "degree of membership." Evidence will be presented that, for most purposes, categories are processed both perceptually and linguistically in terms of the prototype and distance from the prototype and that, other things being equal, stimulus spaces will tend to become organized and categories develop around potential proto-types. The second issue concerns the role of the informational and predictive values of stimulus attributes in the formation of categories and of category prototypes; the basic argument is that categories become organized so as to maximize the correlation of attributes (redundancy) and, hence, predictability within categories. Taken together, the "principle" of salient prototypes and of attribute correlation serve both to indicate how domains at a given level of contrast (such as colors) may come to be partitioned in the way that they do and to generate tentative suggestions about the nature and evolution of tax-onomies and the related processes of sub- and superordination.

PART I: THE NATURE OF CATEGORIES

Any study of category learning and use within a culture, as well as any cross-cultural comparison of categories, will be conceived and carried out by methods which depend upon the investigator's prior concept of what a "cate-gory" is. The overwhelming preponderance of American studies, in attempting to treat categories scientifically, have defined and treated them as though they were "digital," that is, as though they were composed of discrete "units" which are "either-or" in nature. Thus, most studies carry the unexamined assumption that categories are arbitrary, logical conjunctions of criterial attributes which have clearcut boundaries and within which all instances possessing the criterial attributes have a full and equal degree of membership.

A. Some "Digital" Representations of Categories

The best example of "digital" representations of categories is the class of experiments known as concept formation or concept identification. Typically in such experiments (cf. the summary by Bourne, 1968), the subject sees an array of "artificial" stimuli: for example, squares, circles, and triangles, each form occur-ring once as red, once as blue, and once as green, each color of each form occurring once with one border and once with two, and so on. The subject must learn which of these stimuli are and which are not members of the "concept" which the experimenter has in mind. The concept may consist of any combina-tion of attributes, for example, "all the red things," or "red and square things," or "square or two borders or both." Note that stimuli for such experiments consist of discrete attributes (such as red versus green, square versus circle); the categories to which these attributes themselves belong are generally already well known to the subject (e.g., American college sophomores have already long since learned the concepts "red" and "square"); and the subset of attribute combinations which comprise the to-be-learned concepts can be formed *arbitrarily* out of any logically possible combination of attributes. For such concepts once the subject has learned the rule(s) defining the positive subset, boundaries of the concept can only be "well defined" (Minsky, 1961) and the concept has no rational basis for internal structure; that is, any one stimulus that fits the rule is as good an exemplar of the concept as any other. For example, if the positive subset consists of the conjunction "red square" with size as an irrelevant attribute, it makes no logical sense to ask the subject whether the small or large red square was a better example of the concept "red square." While the limited and controlled nature of the stimuli in concept formation tasks has made possible the collection of a large body of precise information about learning and problem solving, such tasks may not be representative of the majority of natural concepts. For example, color categories violate all of the characteristics of concepts in the concept formation paradigm: the physical properties of light, such as wavelengths, are not discrete (e.g., "long" and "short") but composed of continuous variation; a color name such as "red" does not refer to a logical combination of simpler, already-learned attributes (in fact, perceived colors are not "analyzable" into combinations of discrete dimensions; Garner, 1970; Shepard, 1964); boundaries between color categories are not well defined; and, as will be elaborated later, there are colors which are "better" members of particular color categories than other colors (a "good" red versus an "off" red).

In a number of fields, the semantic categories of natural languages are treated in a manner similar to the concept formation paradigm. A major trend in linguistics (cf. Katz and Postal, 1964) is to treat semantic categories as bundles of discrete "features" which determine how the words can be used in sentences. Features, loosely speaking, are those characteristics of nouns we can describe with adjectives. In these terms, the meaning of "girl" might be represented by such features as +animate, +human, +young, -male. These features clearly differentiate the category from all others and also render each category instance logically comparable to all others, in that instances are alike in possessing the defining combination of features. Studies of the nature of semantic representation in memory (both computer models and empirical studies of retrieval from memory, cf. the articles in Part II of Tulving and Donaldson, 1972) usually demonstrate indirectly by their choice of stimuli and testing methods that categories are assumed to be clearly bounded entities all of whose members are equivalent. Developmental studies have either treated concepts as equivalent to those of concept learning research (see virtually any concept identification study in a developmental psychology journal), or, within the Genevan tradition (cf. Inhelder and Piaget, 1958), have not been concerned with the internal structure of categories but rather with the development of deductive logical relations between classes.

It is not surprising, with the heavy emphasis on digital models of categories provided by linguistics and psychology, that anthropological studies of folk classifications (cf. Tyler, 1969) have tended to use a feature analysis of categories. Methods, such as componential analysis, seek to find the minimum basic criterial attributes by which folk use of the terms of a domain can be formally ordered. Thus, reports have tended to concentrate on a limited number of domains, such as kinship, perhaps because the domain on which kin terms are mapped does contain discrete attributes (e.g., sex, generational steps distant from speaker) which may be logically combined to give the formal meaning of the terms in much the same way that attributes are combined in the concept formation study. (That such formal meaning is not sufficient for a full exposition of the meaning even of kinship terms has been argued in several recent papers, cf. Kay, 1972.)

Undoubtedly, some categories and some kinds of processing of categories do involve digital codes. The "technical" criteria for membership in those categories that have technical criteria (explained below) are probably a case in point. However, the model of categories provided by artificial concept identification research may be pernicious in that researchers have, thereby, tended to neglect other types of categories and category codes which may be more appropriate to the way natural categories are formed and coded in cognition and more appropriate for cross-cultural comparisons.

B. "Analog" Representations of Categories: Prototypes

In fact, there is a small body of research which has attempted to treat categories and the process of categorization as "analog" functions ("non-Aristotelian" in the Cassirer sense of "Aristotelian"). Such attempts are important, not only in terms of impact on a conceptualization of categories, but also in terms of the long-range possibility of developing theories which attempt to embody, rather than "get around," the probably essentially analog nature of many mental processes.

Research dealing with "analog" categories has generally fallen under the heading of "schema" or "prototype" research. The term "schema" has been used to stand for a number of proposed codes or abstract mental representations by which people might be enabled to store and recognize members of categories given the infinite variations in the instances of the categories encountered. In its simplest form, a schema could consist of the elements common to all instances of a category along with notation about departures of individual instances

(Oldfield, 1954). In this form, a schema is digital and no different from a list of criterial attributes such as a subject might learn in a concept identification task; for example, the verbalized code ("anything red, form varies") might be the schema in a concept identification study for the concept "red." However, research on schemas has largely been concerned with more complex stimuli in which concepts cannot be identified by means of easily coded common elements or in which the mental representation, even of simple concepts, is proposed to be in a form other than a verbal list of elements, for example, in the form of an "image." (Note that Berkeley's claim was not that we could not verbalize that a triangle was a plane figure consisting of three straight joined lines; his claim was that we could not form an abstract image of a generalized triangle.)

There is considerable evidence that subjects can form mental schemas for types of artificial categories which do not lend themselves to a feature description. Most work on schema formation was performed on random visual patterns such as nonsense polygons (Attneave, 1957) and dot patterns (Posner, Goldsmith, and Welton, 1967). Such stimulus materials are used both because they can be carefully controlled and produced to order for the purpose of the experiment and because they are completely novel to the subject, thereby eliminating the prior history of learning of the actual concepts with which subjects come into the experiment. To produce categories from such materials, a set of patterns is generated by applying distortions to an initial random pattern, for example, by a random walk of the points forming the pattern. The initial pattern is, thus, the "central tendency" of a family of patterns; in a simple case, for example, it might be the mean of the patterns. The work of most relevance to our present purposes is that which indicates that, during classification and/or learning, subjects actually generate a mental representation of the schema pattern even when that specific pattern was never actually presented to them.[1]

Such prototype research demonstrates dramatically the capacity of the human mind for coping with analog categories; however, the categories used are still artifical and arbitrary. The schema patterns chosen and the rules for distortion of the schema are created at the will of the experimenter. One of the major claims of this paper is that natural categories can also be characterized in terms of prototypes and deviations from prototypes and that the nature and formation of such prototypes is not necessarily arbitrary.

1. *Universal Prototypes that Are "Biologically" Given.* The clearest, most unequivocal case for natural prototypes can be made for those categories in perceptual domains where there is reason to belive that prototypes are "given" by the perceptual system and that categories become organized around these perceptually salient prototypes. For such domains, not only are the *processes* of category formation probably universal (which may be true in all domains), but, in addition, the content of categories can be expected to be universal. The most completely documented case is that for the domain of color.

The color space is probably the real-world domain most obviously different from the kinds of attribute combinations used in digital artificial concept formation studies. Nevertheless, the color space was long considered a domain which, like all domains, languages could partition arbitrarily into color name categories. Because it was also obviously a domain of "uniform" variation whose physical characteristics (such as wavelength) could be measured by instruments indepently of "folk" color names, the color space was long considered an ideal domain in which to demonstrate the effects which the existence of language categories has on cognition (cf. Lenneberg, 1967). Thus, when an aspect of language (differences in "codability" among colors, cf. Brown and Lenneberg, 1954) was found to correlate with an aspect of cognition (recognition memory), it was presumed that it was the code that was affecting the cognitive process. Recent findings have challenged such a view.

Berlin and Kay (1969) argued that there are a limited number of "basic" color terms (defined by linguistic criteria) in any language: three achromatic (black, white, gray) and eight chromatic terms (red, yellow, green, blue, brown, orange, pink, purple). When informants from diverse languages were asked to choose the best examples of their language's basic color terms from an array of Munsell chips, they tended to choose the same areas of the color space. Berlin and Kay called these clusters of best examples of color terms "focal points," and argued that the previous anthropological emphasis on cross-cultural differences in color names was derived from looking only at the boundaries of color names, a more variable aspect of categorization than the focal points.[2]

Previous research by the present author (Heider, 1971, 1972b) provided evidence that the focal points of basic color terms represented areas of the color space which possessed a particular perceptual-cognitive salience "prior" to color naming. "Prior to naming" can be taken in two senses: developmentally, Heider (1971) showed that three-year-old American children oriented toward focal colors in preference to nonfocal colors and that four-year-old American children matched focal more accurately than nonfocal colors. Cross-culturally, Heider (1972b) demonstrated that the Dani of New Guinea, speakers of a language that lacks—at least for some speakers (Heider, 1972a)—all of the basic chromatic color names, remembered focal colors more accurately than nonfocal colors, both in a short-term recognition task similar to that used by Brown and Lenneberg (1954) and in a long-term memory task. Because it was the same colors that were the most codable in a large sample of languages which possessed the full complement of basic color names (Heider, 1972b) and because even speakers of a language for which these colors were not more codable remembered those colors better than nonfocal colors, it would appear that the color space, far from being a domain well suited to the study of the effects of language on thought, is rather a prime example of the influence of underlying perceptual-cognitive factors on the formation and reference of linguistic categories.

Of greatest relevance to the present theme are the mechanisms by which such saliencies can come to determine the nature of the categories. Rosch (1973) proposed the following account: There are perceptually salient colors which more readily attract attention and are more easily remembered than other colors. When category names are learned, they tend to become attached first to the salient stimuli, only later generalizing to other, physically similar, instances. By this means these natural prototype colors become the foci of organization for categories. Such an account has several testable implications. In the first place, it implies that is is easier to learn names for focal than nonfocal colors; that is, not only should focal colors be more easily retained than nonfocal in recognition over short intervals, they should also be more readily remembered in conjunction with names in long-term memory. In the second place, since a color category is learned first as a named focal color and second as the focal color plus other physically similar stimuli, color categories in which focal colors are central stimuli ("central" in terms of some physical attribute, such as wavelength) should be easier to learn than categories structured in some other manner (for example, focal colors physically peripheral or internominal colors central and no focal colors at all).

Such hypotheses are inherently cross-cultural for they obviously cannot be tested with subjects who already know a set of basic chromatic color terms provided by their language. In fact, these hypotheses suggest an important method of cross-cultural research which has seldom been applied: a learning paradigm. Many cultures lack codes (or a full elaboration of codes) for some domains. If an investigator has theories about that domain, instead of framing his hypotheses in terms of deficits in performance resulting from the lack of codes (with attendant problems in interpreting absolute differences between cultures), he can frame hypotheses in terms of learning the codes for the domain. Codes can then be taught, the input stimuli precisely specified and controlled within the context of the experiment in accordance with the relevant hypotheses. Because the variations are within culture, any general difficulty the people may have with the learning task per se will not influence the conclusions. It should be noted that this method is part of a more general mode of cross-cultural research for which the present paper argues and which it attempts to exemplify: choosing cultures to be studied for specific purposes, for example, in order to test specific hypotheses.

The Dani, with their two-term color language, provided an ideal opportunity to teach color names. Three basic types of color category were taught. In Type 1, the physically central (i.e., of intermediate wavelength or brightness) chip of each category was the focal color, and the flanking chips were drawn from the periphery of that basic name area. In Type 2, central chips lay in the internominal areas between Berlin and Kay's best-example clusters; flanking chips, thus, tended to be drawn from the basic color name areas on either side. Because two different, basic color name chips were included in the same Type 2 categories, these categories "violated" the presumed natural organization of the color space. Type 3 categories were located in the same spaces as Type 1; however, instead of occupying a central position, the focal color was now to one side or the other of the three-chip category.

Subjects learned the color names as a paired associate task: colors as stimuli, the same Dani word as the correct response for the three colors in a category. The results of the learning supported Rosch's account of the role of focal colors in the learning of color names. Focal colors were learned with fewer errors than other colors even when they were peripheral members of categories. Furthermore, the Type 1 categories in which focal colors were physically central were learned, as a set, faster than either of the other types. The Type 2 categories, which violated the presumed natural organization of the color space, were the most difficult of all to learn. Thus, the idea of perceptually salient focal colors as natural prototypes (rather like Platonic forms) for the development and learning of color names appears quite reasonable.

We have been referring to focal colors as "perceptually" salient; for colors, such terminology is more than a metaphor, for there is some evidence that the actual mechanisms of color vision may be responsible for the salience. McDaniel (1972) found that focal red, yellow, green, and blue corresponded reasonably well to the "unique hue points" for those colors proposed by Hering (1964) and somewhat substantiated by physiological data (De Valois and Jacobs, 1968). While unique hue points are not presently an unchallenged physiological theory, and while the theory as such fails to account for the other four proposed basic chromatic color terms (pink, orange, brown, and purple), it does lend considerable concreteness to the supposition that focal colors are, literally, physiologically salient.

However, color is not the only domain in which perceptually salient, natural prototypes appear to determine categories; there is evidence that geometric forms and facial expressions of emotion become structured in a similar manner. That there is something particularly "well formed" about certain forms, such as circles and squares, was long ago proposed by the Gestalt psychologists. Rosch (1973) tested the hypothesis that such forms act as natural prototypes in the formation of form categories just as focal colors do for color categories. The Dani also do not have a terminology for two-dimensional geometric forms, and some pilot studies showed that they neither possessed usable circumlocutions for referring to forms in a communication task nor did they tend to sort forms by form type. Thus, it was reasonable to teach Dani form concepts just as they had been taught color concepts. The logic of the form learning experiment was the same as that of the color learning. Circle, square, and equilateral triangle were taken as the presumed natural prototypes of three form categories. In the "naturally" structured categories, these "good forms" were physically central to a set of distortions (such as gaps in the form or lines changed to curves). In other categories, a distorted form was the central member, the good form, peripheral. The results mirrored those for color. The good forms themselves were learned faster than the distorted forms, and the sets of forms in which the good forms were central were learned faster than sets in which they were peripheral. Furthermore, for the forms (though not for the colors), Dani were willing, at the conclusion of learning, to point to which stimulus they considered the best example of the name they had just learned. The good forms tended to be designated as the best examples even when they were actually peripheral to the set; it was as though subjects were trying to structure the categories around the good forms even when the actual sets were structured otherwise.

Facial expressions of emotion are a surprising addition to the class of natural categories. Not only were they once not considered universal; but there was considerable doubt that, even within one culture, emotion could be judged better than chance from the human face (Bruner and Tagiuri, 1954). As had been the case with colors, such judgments seemed to stem from the unsystematic employment of miscellaneous facial expressions in judgment experiments. Ekman (1972) claimed that there were six basic human emotions (happiness, sadness, anger, fear, surprise, and disgust) and that each was associated with a quite limited range of facial muscle movements constituting a pure expression of that emotion; other expressions tended to be blends of emotions, or ambiguous or nonemotional expressions which could not be expected to receive reliable judgments. When Ekman put together sets of pictures of pure expressions of the proposed basic emotions, he found that these pictures were judged correctly by Americans, Japanese, Brazilians, Chileans, and Argentinians. Furthermore, two preliterate New Guinea groups with minimal contact with Caucasian facial expression, the Fore and the Dani, were able to distinguish which of the expressions was meant on the basis of stories embodying the appropriate emotion. Like color, universality was discovered in facial expressions of emotion only when an investigator thought to ask, not about all possible stimuli, but about the prototypes (best examples) of categories.

Although the content and the process of category formation of color, form, and facial expression of emotion categories may be universal, some aspects of categories, even in these domains, probably differ between cultures. The extent of elaboration of language codes for the categories, conceptual levels of categorization (are the basic categories divided into subordinate and/or combined into superordinate categories?), category boundaries, treatment of intercategory stimuli (such as blends of emotions), rules for use of the categories (such as aesthetic rules for colors and display and suppression rules for expressions of emotion)—all leave room for the development of cultural differences. What are those differences and how do they develop? At present, we have virtually no usable data for an explanation of such questions. What the present paper wishes to emphasize is that questions about cultural specifics in these domains can be reasonably asked and answered only in relation to the basic universal aspects of the categories.

2. *Prototypes of Semantic Categories.* Not all categories have an obvious perceptual basis, and many categories may be culturally relative. It is unreasonable to expect that humans come equipped with natural prototypes, for example, for dogs, vegetables, and Volkswagens. For colors and forms, internal structure and the concept of focal and nonfocal category members have a relatively concrete meaning; are such concepts more generally applicable to noun categories of other types? "Applicability" actually refers to two issues: can subjects make consistent, meaningful judgments about internal structure, that is, about the degree to which instances are "focal" members of categories, and can a reasonable case be made that internal structure affects "cognitive processing" of the categories?

(a) *Subjects' Judgments about Internal Structure.* In regard to the first issue, two normative studies have already been performed which show that subjects can reliably rate best examples of common semantic categories. Both studies used category names and instances taken from Battig and Montague (1969), a normative study in which American college students listed instances of categories such as "a flower," "an article of clothing," and the like. (The Battig and Montague norms consist of the frequency, in the whole population of subjects, with which each instance was given for the superordinate category name.) In both of our studies, subjects were asked to rate, on a 7-point scale, the extent to which the instances represented their "idea or image" of the meaning of the category name. In the first study (reported in Rosch, 1973), 113 subjects ranked six instances of 8 categories, the instances chosen to represent evenly spaced Battig and Montague frequencies. In the second study, subjects ranked all Battig and Montague instances appearing under the nine category terms (fruit, bird, vehicle, vegetable, sport, carpenter's tool, toy, furniture, and weapon); half of the subjects (approximately 50) received one random order of the instances, the other half a different random order. The results showed high agreement between subjects, especially in ranking the "best examples" of the categories; for example, from rankings made by approximately 200 subjects in which "1" was the highest rank, "robin" received a mean rank of 1.02 as a "bird," and "car," a mean rank of 1.02 as a "vehicle." Correlations within categories between ranks received in the two different orders of instances presented in the second study were high, the lowest being .87. Six categories occurred in both studies, making it possible to compare the rank order of the ratings which items received when they were the only six instances of the category present and when they were embedded in the total Battig and Montague list; for all six categories, all rank orders were identical! Since correlation between the two orders was high, the orders were combined and the data redivided on the basis of whether subjects had spent their first 10 years on the West or East coast of the United States. Correlations between those two groups of subjects were all in the .90s. All correlations between rankings and Battig and Montague order were significant but considerably lower than those of rankings with each other. Additional subject ratings of how much they liked the various instances were considerably more variable than rankings of goodness of example and were correlated with goodness of example rankings only in the case of the category "crime." In sum, it appears that prototypes and reliable "gradients" of category membership do exist for semantic categories in the sense that subjects consider it a meaningful task to rate members of such categories according to how well they fit the subjects' idea or image of the meaning of the category name and that there is high agreement between subjects concerning these rankings.

(b) *Evidence that Natural Categories Are Coded as Prototypes and Distance from the Prototype.* Although subjects agree on the goodness of example of instances of a category, such knowledge might well be irrelevant for the ways in which subjects "process" the category. If the "real meaning" of categories lies in a list of common attributes which a thing must have to belong to the category, it is quite possible that processes such as recognizing instances, judging category membership, searching categories, and the logic of the use of category terms in linguistic contexts are all derived from the common criterial attributes. We are presently engaged in a series of programmatic studies using diverse operations to determine the nature of the codes for categories; below is presented some of the evidence that natural categories are processed in terms of the prototype and distance from the prototype.

(1) Judging statements about category membership. Many studies of retrieval from semantic memory have used tasks that required subjects to respond "true" or "false" to statements of the form: "A (member) is a (category)," where the dependent variable of interest was reaction time. Rosch (1973) reasoned that the extent to which a category member represented the core meaning of the category (was a good member) should affect the time needed for subjects to judge that the member belonged to the category. Subjects were presented with statements of the form "An X is a Y" when X was a good example of Y, or a not very good example of Y, or where X was a good or not good example of some other category altogether. Results showed that it took longer for subjects to respond "true" to the true statements of category membership when X was a relatively poor member than when X was a "central" member of Y. No such difference occurred for the false statements, which argued that the "poor member" items were not, in and of themselves, more difficult to process. Furthermore, the differences were considerably more extreme for ten-year-old children than for adults, which argued that (like Dani learning of color categories) children learn category membership of prototypical members earlier than that of other members. Other recent studies have shown that several other

principles of ranking category members which correlate with or are implied by goodness of example also predict reaction time differences to statements verifying category membership (Loftus, 1973; Loftus and Scheff, 1971; Rips, Shoben, and Smith, 1973; Wilkins, 1971).

(2) The nature of the mental representation "generated" by a category name. Upon hearing a category name does a subject "generate" a list of criterial features, a "code" for the category prototype, an abstract "image," or what? A task that seems to offer considerable potential for the investigation of such questions is the type of "matching" paradigm described by Posner and Mitchell (1967). Because this technique is not well known outside cognitive psychology, it will be described in some detail. Subjects are required to decide as rapidly as possible whether two simultaneous visual letters are the same or different; under some conditions "same" is defined as physical identity (e.g., AA), under others as possession of the same name (e.g., Aa). Under all conditions, subjects were found to respond faster to letters which were physically identical than to those which had the same name. If a subject is provided with some of the information he needs to make the match in advance of presentation of the pair, matching speed should be facilitated. Beller (1971) "primed" subjects with a letter (presented the letter 2-seconds in advance of the pair) and found that response speed for physically identical, as well as same-name, pairs improved, even when physically identical pairs were in the opposite case from the case presented in the prime (e.g., if the prime was A, the pair aa, as well as AA, was facilitated). Beller (1971) and Posner (1969) argued that this showed that subjects were not simply retaining a literal representation of the presented letter but were "generating" (Posner's term) an abstract expectation or representation which did not depend on case.

This experimental paradigm is particularly suited for determining the precise nature of mental codes because a prime can only facilitate a match when it makes possible generation of a mental code containing within it some of the information needed to make the match. If the code generated by the category name is more like a list of criterial attributes, "same" responses to pairs of items of any degree of category membership should be facilitated since to be members at all, by definition, the items must possess the criterial attributes. On the other hand, if the code is more like a representation of the category prototype, "same" pairs closer to the prototype should be more strongly facilitated. Furthermore, if the generated representation is in the form of an abstract "image," physically identical pairs should be facilitated.

We have performed a number of priming experiments both with colors and members of semantic categories. Prototype colors were the focal colors derived from the previous color research. Chips representing the less good examples were determined by a pilot study in which subjects sorted chips into color name categories; the poor example chips were those farthest in saturation, or brightness from the focal chips which 90% of the subjects still labeled with the basic color name. Semantic category members were taken from the previously described norms for goodness of membership for the nine semantic categories; items were chosen to represent high, medium, and low ratings (for example, for "fruit" an example of high is "apple," medium is "grapefruit," low is "watermelon;" for birds an example of high is "sparrow," medium "owl," low "penguin"). Items in the semantic categories could be presented as pairs of pictures or as pairs of words. Colors, semantic categories represented as pictures, and semantic categories represented as words constituted separate experiments, administered to different subjects. Within a given experiment, each pair occurred twice, once preceded by (primed by) the category name, once preceded by the word "blank." The results of primary interest were possible interaction between facilitation by the prime and goodness of example of category membership. Results were clear and striking: for physically identical pairs of colors, pictures, and words, priming facilitated (speeded) responses of "same" to the high good example members and actually depressed performance (delayed "same" responses) for the low members. Such findings certainly seem to indicate that what is generated by the category name is not the attributes common to all members of the category but a representation coordinate with differing degrees of category membership. The fact that the interaction between goodness of membership and effectiveness of the prime occurred for physically identical pairs argues that the representation can be in the form of a "physical code" or "image." The fact that quite similar interactions occurred for pairs of words as occurred for pairs of colors and pairs of pictures argues that it is a very abstract and general "image" (see Rosch, 1972, for greater detail).

(3) The logic of natural language use of category terms: substitutability into sentences. The meaning of words is intimately tied to their possible uses in sentences; in fact, there have been many attempts to define meaning, synonymity, and semantic contrast in terms of substitutability of words into the same sentences without and with changes in the truth value of the sentences (see Fodor and Katz, 1964, for summaries). Certainly, judged similarity between words appears to be highly correlated with substitutability into linguistic frames (Stefflre, Reich, and McClaran-Stefflre, 1971). The claim of the present paper that categories are processed in terms of the prototype and distance from the prototype means that the better examples of the category should be closer to the core meaning of the superordinate term than the poorer examples. If this is the case, ratings of goodness of example should predict substitutability of category member terms for their superordinates and vice versa. On the other hand, if the core meaning of the superordinate terms consists of a list of criterial attributes common to all category members, substitutability should be equivalent for all members of the category. To test this, subjects were asked to generate sentences using the category names for some of the categories for which ratings of members had already been obtained (e.g., fruit, bird, weapon, vehicle).

The superordinate term was then replaced by member terms at five levels of goodness of example and other subjects rated the sentences as to their degree of naturalness-peculiarity and degree of truth or falsity. Both ratings, but particularly naturalness-peculiarity, showed a strong linear relationship between rated goodness of membership and substitutability. For example, in the sentence "Twenty or so birds often perch on the telephone wires outside my window and twitter in the morning," the term "sparrow" may readily be substituted for "bird" but the result turns ludicrous by substitution of "turkey." Similarly, in "A bowl of fruit makes a nice centerpeice," the substitution of "apples" but not "watermelon" produced a sentence which retains its naturalness and truth value.[3]

(4) The logic of natural language use of category terms: hedges. Although logic and psychology may treat categories as though membership is "either-or" and all members have a full and equal degree of membership, natural languages themselves possess linguistic mechanisms for coding and coping with gradients of category membership. In English there are qualifying terms and phrases which Lakoff (1972) calls "hedges" (terms such as "almost," "virtually"). Lakoff pointed out that even people who insist that statements such as "A robin is a bird" and "A penguin is a bird" are equally "true," would have to admit that different hedges were applicable to statements of category membership for the two birds. Thus, it is correct to say that a penguin is "technically" a bird but not that a robin is "technically" a bird because a robin is more than just "technically" a bird; it is a bird par excellence. Systematic study of some properties of hedges is now in progress.

Although the studies just recounted are only the first steps in the exploration of cognitive coding of categories, there is already consistent evidence of coding and use of categories in terms of prototypes and distance from the prototype. Such a finding is even more impressive when it is realized that these experiments have all been performed on educated Americans, probably one of the populations most likely to have available explicit, verbalizable lists of attributes and formal technical criteria for category membership. The concept of a category as a prototype and distance from the prototype may be even more applicable and more important in studying categories of other populations and other cultures. Most fieldworkers have probably experienced the frustration of an informant who seemed unable or unwilling to understand and comply with questions about why he called something an "X"; it may be that explicit formal criteria for membership not "available" at all for some categories and/or some cultures. Asking which "X's" are the most "X-like" may be a more universally fruitful way of approaching the issue. If people "really" code categories in an "analog" prototype manner, then we should be finding out about prototypes cross-culturally; that is, it is prototypes that may provide a "cognitively real" framework for cross-cultural comparison of categories.

We began with the question of why cultures segment reality into categories in the way that they do. We have argued that, for some domains such as color and form, categories form around perceptually given prototypes. We have further argued that even semantic categories which do not necessarily have "given" prototypes and whose prototypes may (or may not) vary widely between cultures, yet have a structure similar to that of perceptual categories for, like perceptual categories, have prototypes and gradients of category membership. The next questions are logically: (1) Where do prototypes of semantic categories "come from" (what are the principles of formation of prototypes) when they are not perceptually given? (2) Do such prototypes, once formed, play a role in the structuring and evolution of categories?

(c) *Formation of Semantic Category Prototypes.* Study of the characteristics of prototypes and the principles of prototype formation is barely begun. Below are listed seven tentative hypotheses about the nature and formation of prototypes. These are derived from the definition of prototype in the artificial category schema formation research, from observation of which members of semantic categories are most highly rated in the categories of our normative studies, and from general psychological principles.

(1) Prototypes will represent the mean of attributes of category members whenever such attributes have a metric on which means can be taken. Existing evidence concerning means is of three types. In the first place, schemas of artitifical categories, by definition, are central tendencies; thus, there is evidence that, at the very least, subjects *can* form representations of some kinds of categories based on the central tendency. However, because the stimulus sets used in schema formation research with artificial stimuli come with a "built-in" or readily definable central tendency, and because they are otherwise either random configurations or sets of overlapping cues, subjects can do little else but make judgments in terms of central tendency; that is, in such categories central tendency is a relevant and perhaps the only possible way to code the categories. Most natural categories, however, can and are normally considered to be coded in terms other than the means of attributes.

In the second place, there is some minimal evidence available that the best examples of natural semantic categories are items that possess mean values on those very attributes by which category members are seen to differ from one another. Judged similarity relations between different animals (Henley, 1969) and birds (Rips et al., 1973) have been used to determine the dimensions along which the human mind structures these categories. Henley's methodological study determined that the structures retrieved by mutidimensional scaling techniques are quite stable over many diverse methods for measuring perceived similarity. Both animals and birds appear to differ along two major dimensions which Rips et al. labeled "size" and "predacity." Birds are a category for which we have ratings of both goodness of example and substitutability for the category name in sentences. We found that, in fact, those birds that fell close to the origin in the Rips et al. scaling solution (i.e., those that had middle values on size and predacity) were birds high on our ratings of goodness of example. Furthermore, there were a number of cases in the sentence substitution task in which particular low membership birds could not be substituted into particular sentences because they violated size or predacity requirements inherent in the context attributed to "birds" by the sentence. It should be noted that neither size nor predacity is a formally or technically defining feature of birds.

The third type of evidence is one pilot study we have performed using artificial stimuli designed to see whether subjects have any tendency to encode and respond differentially to means of attributes which, in that task, are totally irrelevant. As pointed out earlier, in a standard concept identification task, there is no *logical* reason for the subject to do anything with irrelevant dimensions except learn that they are irrelevant. Our question was whether irrelevant dimensions would, nonetheless, affect subjects' ratings of the best example of the concept. Three sets of stimuli were constructed consisting of three levels of attributes. For one set, size (small, medium, large) was always defined as irrelevant to the concept; for the second set, number (one, two, or three repetitions of the stimulus figure per card) was irrelevant; for the third set, brightness (three levels of gray) was irrelevant. At the conclusion of learning (one perfect run through the 27 cards of the set), the subject was asked, among other tasks, to rank order the members of the positive subset according to how well each fit his idea or image of the concept. There was a significant effect of the irrelevant attribute with the middle level having a significantly higher rank as best example than either extreme for size and levels of gray. For number, the lowest level (the single stimulus form per card) and the intermediate card were both ranked more highly than the three stimuli per card.

Thus, coding a category in terms of central tendencies of category attributes appears to be one of the principles of formation of prototypes of natural categories, even when the dimensions on which means are coded are irrelevant to the formal definition of category membership. The precise parameters of this effect are yet to be determined (e.g., Will means be coded if the subject is presented only with positive instances? Does the tendency to code in terms of a mean increase as the category becomes more complex?). The generality of the effect has also to be determined. This is an extremely interesting area for cross-cultural comparison. Do differences between prototypes for corresponding natural categories represent differences in actual central tendencies of the categories? For example, might we find that a culture whose best examples of birds were larger and/or wilder than ours also had a distribution of types of birds which made those characteristics more the central tendency? To answer such questions, we need data both on the prototypes of categories for other cultures and on the actual incidences of category members. Hopefully, ethnographers or members of other literate cultures will be inspired to gather such data.

(2) The second "hypothetical" principle of prototype formation concerns the special salience of correlated attributes. Our hypothesis is that conjoint frequency (correlated attributes) will influence the prototype more than those attributes would affect it were they uncorrelated but occurred with the same frequency in the population at large. Because the correlation of attributes is the major topic in Part II of this chapter, this principle of prototype formation will not be discussed at this point.

(3) Frequency of particular members is a specific case of correlated attributes in which all of the attributes in the instances are correlated; that is what it means to say that an instance is repeated. The manner or extent to which the effects of frequency of particular members are different from effects of conjoint frequency of attributes is a matter upon which we presently have no data; however, there is evidence to believe that, in our own "folk" beliefs, we tend to overestimate the effects of frequency of instances. The author has repeatedly found that people, when told about the ratings of exemplariness of category members, respond with the suggestion that, obviously, it is simply a matter of the frequency of the items, a view which counterinstances (for example, that word frequency is correlated neither with goodness of example nor with frequency in the Battig and Montague norms; Mervis, Catlin, and Rosch, 1973) seem hardly to shake at all. A possibly relevant study by Kahneman and Tversky (1972) has shown that people do not have accurate knowledge of the probabilities of occurrence of events; specifically, it was shown, for a number of contexts, that people perceive events they consider representative or typical as more probable and, hence, more frequent than they are in reality. Perceived exemplariness of category members may, thus, be reflected back onto the world in terms of distorted views of the frequency of those items, a hypothesis we are presently testing.

(4) Attributes of particular interest or importance and the attributes with which they are correlated will have particular weight in forming prototypes. A hypothetical example might be that of a particular variety of sweet potato which is more tasty or easier to grow than other varieties whose leaves, growing characteristics, tuber color, and so on become heavily weighted in the formation of the prototype, in that culture, for sweet potatoes.

(5) Attributes of particular memorability and the attributes with which they are correlated influence the prototype with particular weight. For example (again hypothetical), Americans probably tend to think of jays as crested though only Blue and Stellar's jays actually are. The crest may be a distinctive mark in the domain of birds whose members are otherwise difficult to distinguish and remember.

(6) The nature of the prototype will be influenced by categories in the same "contrast set" as the category. That is, the prototype will tend to be defined as maximally different (as possible given the mean and other constraints) from

contrasting categories. Thus, means of attributes with metrics will be displaced away from contrasting categories when those categories contrast on those attributes, and the less a given discrete feature occurs in the contrasting category, the more it will be weighted in defining the prototype.

(7) Items first introduced (as members of the category) will be more heavily weighted. Once a prototype is formed for one set of items, it will be difficult to change to an expanded set.

All of the proposed seven principles are presently hypothetical. As argued for prototypes as means, all of the principles require cross-cultural investigation both of prototypes and of their relation to occurrences of category members.

(d) *Effects of Semantic-Category-Like Prototypes on the Structure and Evolution of Categories.* Although we do not yet have much data on how prototypes of semantic categories are formed, we may still ask whether such prototypes, whatever the true principles of their formation, play a role in the structuring and evolution of categories. That they do is suggested both by some cross-cultural findings from the field of ethnobotany and from some preliminary work in our own laboratory.

Berlin and his co-workers have been investigating the manner in which the lexical system for plant taxonomies evolves (Berlin, 1971; Berlin, Breedlove, and Raven, 1968). Berlin claims that there are certain fundamental natural perceptual groupings of plants which occur at the level of the genus (oak, maple), and he has amassed considerable evidence in support of the claim that the first plant names refer to this level (natural groupings and the nature of generic level classes will be discussed in Part II). Generic terms initially refer only to some members of the genus; over time, other "similar" plants become attached to the name "by the process of analogy." For example, Bright and Bright (1965) report that the Yurok and Smith River Indians have virtually no "depth" to their plant taxonomy but rather a set of loosely organized generic terms (glossed as "fir," "lilac," etc.) to which other plant terms are "tied" ("like the lilac," "like the fir," "small fir," "white fir"). Berlin (1971) claims that a frequent pattern of evolution is for the original referent of the generic term to become glossed as "Real X" or "True X;" in our terms, a prototype for the development of the category.

In our laboratory studies, we have been working with one- and two-dimensional arrays of stimuli such as lines differing in length, circles differing in radius, and a set of free forms developed by Shepard and Cermak (1973) which are continuously varying, low dimensional, unverbalizable, and dimensionally circular. We are interested in seeing how the introduction of "potential prototype" characteristics in some stimuli (such as darkening of the stimulus figure, repetition of the stimulus, and increasing the density of stimuli in one or more areas of the stimulus space) will change the ways in which subjects group the stimuli in free sorting tasks and the way in which they learn experimenter-determined divisions of the stimuli into categories. Specifically, the hypothesis is that potential prototypes will tend to become the centers of categories in free sorting and that predetermined categories will be easier to learn when the potential prototypes are at their centers. Unfortunately, data are not yet available from these studies.

In summary, in Part I it has been argued that an analog model of categories in terms of a prototype and distance from the prototype may be closer to the way in which categories are coded and processed in cognition than are the more usual digital models. Such an analog model has great potential usefulness for the understanding of category formation in cross-cultural perspective. In domains in which prototypes are biologically "given," categories can be expected to form around the salient prototypes and, thus, to have elements of content as well as principles of formation which are universal. Other semantic categories may have prototypes which are quite different cross-culturally. Both laboratory data on the principles of formation of prototypes and ethnographic data on cultural differences in prototypes and "related" differences in the content of categories are needed for a proper perspective on the formation and evolution of categories.

PART II: CORRELATIONS OF ATTRIBUTES

If natural categories were to consist of logical combinations of discrete features, the appropriate sets of stimuli for studying the origins of such classifications would consist of sets of items varying in discrete attributes. Numerous studies have been conducted in which subjects were asked to free sort (sort into groupings of their choice) sets of stimuli consisting of orthogonally varied separable attributes. By orthogonally varied, it is meant that a separate stimulus represents each of all possible combinations of all of the attributes. Thus, if the attributes were size (large, small), color (red, green), and form (square, circle), the set would consist of a small red square, a small red circle, a small green square, a small green circle, a large red square, and the like. For free sorts of such stimuli, repeated findings are: the overwhelming tendency is for subjects to sort on the basis of the levels of a single dimension (Handel and Imai, 1972; Handel and Preusser, 1969; Huang, 1945; Imai, 1966; Wing and Bevan, 1969). Thus, for the example given, subjects would typically sort into two groups based either on color or form or size but not on combinations of attributes. Both individuals and groups tend to have consistent preferences for sorting on one dimension rather than another; usually the preference is for color (Garner, 1966; Imai and Garner, 1965; Serpell, 1969; Suchman and Trabasso, 1966). For small sets of stimuli, subjects appear to have strong preference for creating categories containing equal numbers of stimuli (Imai, 1966; Imai and Handel, 1971; Wing and Bevan, 1969). A striking aspect of sets of stimuli with orthogonal separable attributes is that the confusions between stimuli which occur in tasks where subjects learn to pair each stimulus with an individual name do not predict the ease with which the stimuli can be learned as a group (paired with a single name) in a concept formation task (Shepard, Hovland, and Jenkins, 1961). Such findings do not go far toward developing principles by which we may explain how the world is "cut up"; indeed, a striking quality of such classifications is that they seem to correspond, not so much to "things" or noun classes, but to divisions of the world into qualities or adjective classes.

Just as was argued earlier for concept formation studies, free sorting studies may yield little information about natural categories because the stimuli lack some of the fundamental properties of natural categories.

A. Attributes of Natural Categories Are Not Orthogonal

The present paper began by pointing out that there were an infinite number of differences between stimuli, more than any organism could possibly cope with were it to try to respond differentially to all differences. Categorization occurs in order to reduce the limitless variation—the "uncertainty" of the world—to manageable proportions. What is the most useful form of grouping? Presumably that which enables the organism to reduce uncertainty as much as possible, which gives it as much information as possible. (For background on the technical uses of "uncertainty" and "information," see Garner, 1962.) In informational terms, a category is most useful when, by knowing the category to which a thing belongs, the organism, thereby, knows as many attributes of the thing as possible. Segmentation of the same domain would be progressively less useful the fewer properties of things predictable from knowing the category. Attributes and properties in the real world differ from those of typical free sorting stimuli in that the real-world attributes do not always occur orthogonally, but rather tend to occur in co-occuring sets. Creatures with feathers are far more likely also to have wings than are creatures with fur. In this sense, maximally useful categories would appear to be those that follow the lines of natural correlations of attributes, those that maximize the correlation and thus the predictability of attributes within categories.

Such a principle is, at present, hypothetical. And even if taken as a truism, it would not tell us anything about the form or parameters of the relationship between correlations and categories. This is partly because we do not have data on even the most elementary aspects of the cognitive effects of correlation. Is correlation of attributes, for example, a powerful principle affecting free sorting? We are presently undertaking some experiments in which attributes typically little used as the basis of sorting orthogonal arrays are presented in correlated format. The hypothesis is that when two attributes, such as size and angle of an interior line, which, for a particular array, are each in themselves unpreferred as a principle of sorting, are made redundant, that array will be sorted on the levels of both far more than the sum of the probability of sorting on either when they are separate. Is correlation of attributes a major factor in our judgments of how "good a unit" a category is? In general, it seems reasonable that categories will be judged to be "good units" the "more" correlated and "fewer" uncorrelated attributes they possess. For example, subjects presented with two categories, one of which contains two stimuli both of which are blue circles and the other of which contains two stimuli both of which are red squares will surely rate those as better units than two categories in which the same attributes are orthogonal (e.g., one contains a red square and a red circle, the other a blue square and a blue circle). Are such judgments a function of the total number of correlated attributes? Of the percent of correlated attributes? Is the function linear or does it change with increasing number of attributes? Is it the same for different kinds of attributes? As previously stated, correlations of attributes may be one of the major principles for the formation of prototypes for categories, but verification and establishment of the nature of that relationship has still to be performed.

Not only are we ignorant about rules, such as the above, but we lack any systematically formulated and gathered data concerning correlations in the real world—for our own as well as for other cultures. It is true that claims for universality in some aspects of correlations of attributes have been made in the field of ethnobiology. Although an initial claim that folk plant classifications mirrored the Linnaean system and were thus universal (Diamond, 1966) this has been shown to be largely a product of casual field observations and failure to distinguish loan words from indigenous classifications (Berlin, Breedlove, and Raven, 1966); anthropologists continue to assert that there is a level of biological classification which corresponds to "natural groupings" of organisms that possess "bundles" of correlated features and are "obviously" different from other groupings of organisms (Berlin, 1971; Bulmer, 1967; Bulmer and Tyler, 1968). However, support of the claim tends to be the casual and unsystematic listing of a few correlated attributes. What we need are: (1) a reasonable determination of what the attributes of "things" are—in order to be manageable, this kind of analysis will probably have to be performed first for a few relatively limited domains; (2) an environmental determination of actual rates of occurrence and of co-occurrences of those attributes; (3) such a determination should be performed for several different cultures whose categorization of corresponding domains is not identical. An analysis of the "predictive validity of cues" was an integral part of Brunswik's (1956) formulation; however, this often quoted work has never led to anything resembling a "survey" of real-world contingencies. Such data are probably vital to an understanding of categorization as well as many other cultural differences.

B. "Shape" as the Combination of "Integral" Attributes

We have argued that the stimuli used in the typical free sorting experiment do not represent real-world combinations of attributes. The first reason was that real-world attributes are not always orthogonal. A second reason may have to do with the quality of the attributes. Most sorting has been done with discrete, psychologically "separable" attributes; however, not all attributes appear to be of this nature. Garner (1970) has recently distinguished between "separable" and "integral" attributes. Operationally, the distinction was derived from "constrained" sorting tasks; for separable attributes, such as a dot above or below a form, subjects can sort on the basis of either attribute without facilitation or interference from the other; for integral attributes, such as hue and saturation of Munsell color chips, sorting on the basis of either attribute is facilitated if the irrelevant attribute is correlated with the relevant, and impeded if the irrelevant attribute is orthogonal. In phenomenological terms, for integral attributes, a change in one dimension appears to produce a stimulus which is different as a whole, rather than different in one attribute. In the free sorting of arrays of stimuli composed of orthogonal combinations of integral attributes, subjects do not typically sort according to the levels of a single dimension but on the basis of overall perceived similarity of the stimuli (Aiken and Brown, 1971; Handel and Imai, 1972). For most combinations of attributes, there are not yet data available to tell us whether they are separable or integral; however, one property of objects which is probably a major source of their perceived similarity is clearly integral, and the property is shape.

In a classic paper, Attneave and Arnoult (1956) discussed the problems of defining and measuring the shape of natural forms; however, those aspects of their discussion which appear to have had most influence were just those that could apply equally to nonsense patterns; for example, methods for generating random patterns and measures of attributes of the overall forms such as jaggedness or symmetry. Attneave and Arnoult's emphasis on the need for proper stimulus sampling in the analysis of natural form was translated into a procedure for adequate sampling of forms from a population of random forms generated by one particular method (Brown and Owen, 1967). Using this sample, all possible overall measures of the forms have been correlated and factor analyzed with the resultant derivation of dimensions such as compactness, jaggedness, and elongation along the vertical or horizontal axis. Many further studies on the "psychophysics of form" (cf. Behrmen and Brown, 1968; Forsyth and Brown, 1967) have demonstrated that, for this population of forms, those attributes seem to be the basic dimensions of sorting, similarity judgments, recognition, and scaled structure. Such measures do not, however, seem adequate to characterize perceived similarity of meaningful form. We have, for example, taken the outline drawing of a bird, reduced the curves to lines by connecting the points of maximum change of curvature (by the method described in Attneave, 1954), laid the resultant figure on a 1000-cell grid, and distorted the jaggedness, compactness, and elongation of vertical and horizontal axes dramatically while it retained both its recognizability as a bird and its perceived difference from the outline drawing of a cat when the cat underwent similar distortions; that is, a jagged bird looks more like a compact bird than a jagged bird looks like a jagged cat.

We are presently working on developing a technique that will more adequately measure the relationships of meaningful shapes. We find that a very simple measure, the correlation of the degree of each angle and correlation of the percent of the total perimeter of the figure taken up by each line segment, proves remarkably powerful in predicting the judged similarity of straight line figures composed of equal numbers of lines. It should be noted that this is neither a procedure of template matching nor an analysis of features (cf. Neisser, 1967), but rather an analysis based on correlation of the integral elements which compose shape. Some technical virtues of the measure are that it automatically normalizes for size differences. Normalization (actually matching) for orientation can be easily and automatically accomplished by taking all correlations generated by each possible match on orientation and using the highest. One major problem with the measure, even for straight line drawings, is normalization for unequal number of sides. Our present method is to reduce the greater number of sides to the lesser by finding the shortest pair of connected lines and then connecting the adjacent points, keeping track of the number of times the procedure is iterated and the percent of total perimeter eliminated in the process; however, it is not clear yet what the exact mathematical form of the equation incorporating this reduction should be.

C. The Generic Level Object as Correlated Attributes and as Prototype

This measure, in that it provides a means for the quantification of the perceived similarity of meaningful shapes, may provide a tool with which we can approach the final problem to be dealt with here, the relation of correlation of attributes to prototypes in natural categories. Our hypothesis is that such a relation occurs at the level of the "generic object." As previously reviewed, some anthropologists have asserted that the basic unit of division of plants and animals is on the level of the genus. In order to extend the definition of "generic" to inanimate objects and in order to avoid difficulties arising from technical versus folk classification of living things, "generic" can be broadened to mean that level, in a class inclusion hierarchy, at which a thing is most commonly named (linguistically, perhaps the most concrete level on which the name is monolexemic). The generic level unit may be basic not only because it is a bundle of correlated discrete attributes but because it is the unit at which things look most alike, that is, at which their shape is most correlated. More precisely the generic level is the unit at which there is the greatest gain in shape correlation when moving from the next higher (more abstract) classification. For example, the shapes of "chairs" are probably far more highly correlated than the shapes of all objects classifiable as "furniture"; however, relatively little gain in correlation is achieved when we go to the next more concrete level, to armchairs, rocking chairs, kitchen chairs, and the like. One important correlate of this may be that the generic level may be the most abstract and general level on which the "average" shape of the object (computed by our methods by taking the average of each angle and of the percent of perimeter per line segment for a set of the objects) is a meaningful shape, recognizable as the same type of object as the forms from which it was computed. An average chair probably looks like a chair; an average "furniture" shape is probably a nonsense form. And it may be that the generic level object is the most abstract level of classification which can be economically coded in cognition for it may be just the average shape which serves as the prototype (for those classes of objects for which the average shape is meaningful).

Thus, it may be the generic level object in which the two general principles of classification which the present paper has discussed "meet." Correlations of separable attributes (such as "has wings," "has a beak," "has two legs," etc.) may result in correlations of the integral attributes which define shape. If shapes are sufficiently correlated, an average shape is a meaningful representation of that class of objects and may become coded in cognition as the prototype.

CONCLUSIONS

This chapter has argued for the theoretical importance of an investigation of the principles of how categories are formed in human cultures. It has suggested two general principles of category formation which may be used as a framework for (1) cross-cultural comparison of categories and (2) determination of what aspects of categories are universal and what culturally specific. The first principle was that categories may be analog rather than digital in nature and may consist of a prototype (the best examples of the category) surrounded by other category members of decreasing distance from the prototype. Prototypes are important to cross-cultural investigation of categories, and they require such an investigation for their full understanding. Prototypes are important for several reasons: (1) Working in terms of prototypes enables the location and examination of domains where prototypes are perceptually or otherwise biologically determined and thus universal. Investigation of universal and culturally relative aspects of such domains can then be undertaken in proper relation to each other. (2) If categories "really are" "processed" in cognition largely in terms of a shorthand prototype, then cross-cultural comparison of categories must proceed in these terms. It is, in fact, quite possible that analog processes such as prototypes for categories are an even more prevalent mode of cognitive processing for preliterate cultures where technical criteria for category membership may not normally be a subject of conscious verbalized concern. Because categories have not normally been considered in these terms, there are few data available on prototypes for categories in different cultures; such data are clearly needed. (3) Once it is conceded that prototypes are an important aspect of the formation and cognitive processing of categories, it becomes important to determine the principles by which prototypes are formed for categories when they are not biologically determined as such. We have suggested some hypothetical principles for formation which may guide the type of data about categories and their prototypes which should be collected.

The second principle discussed was the importance of correlations of attributes as the basis for category formation. Less was said about this than about prototypes, not because it is not of equal importance, but because there are less data presently available. The relation of correlations of attributes to category formation, generic level objects, and prototypes cannot be studied without the collection of hard data on real environmental contingencies in different cultures.

NOTES

1. This evidence is: (1) After a number of distortions of prototypes are presented to subjects who must simply say whether each pattern is "old" (was previously presented to them) or "new," subjects erroneously believe they have seen the schema pattern previously (mistakenly identify it as "old"). They do not make this error for new nonschema patterns (Posner, 1969). (2) Subjects who are trained to discriminate patterns formed from different prototypes without being shown the prototype classify the prototype as rapidly and accurately as patterns they have seen and more rapidly and accurately than a new, nonprototype pattern they have not seen. This effect increases the more the need for memory comes into play (Frank and Bransford, 1971; Posner, 1969; Posner and Keele, 1968; Reed, 1972).

2. In fact, Berlin and Kay found that the designation of color category boundaries, even within a culture and within a given individual, were extremely unstable and unreliable. It is probable, therefore, that many anthropological reports of differences in color boundaries are based on unreliable data.

3. It may, at first glance, appear that such findings are simply a matter of frequency; that is, we frequently experience sparrows, but not turkeys, perched on telephone wires. However, the point is that, in the initial production of the sentences, subjects associated to

the superordinate term "bird" contexts which might frequently be experienced for good but not poor examples of birds. Note that subjects could also, logically, have produced sentences such as "She'd just put the bird in the oven when the guests came," for which "turkey" but not "sparrow" would be an appropriate substitution, but they did not.

REFERENCES

AIKEN, L. S. and D. R. BROWN (1971) "Feature utilization of continuously varying attributes in visual pattern classification." Perception and Psychophysics 9: 145-149.

ATTNEAVE, R. (1954) "Some informational aspects of visual perception." Psychological Review 61: 183-193.

――― (1957) "Transfer of experience with a class-schema to identification learning of patterns and shapes." Journal of Experimental Psychology 54: 81-88.

――― and M. D. ARNOULT (1956) "The quantitative study of shape and pattern perception." Psychological Bulletin 53: 452-471.

BARTLETT, F. C. (1932) Remembering: A Study in Experimental and Social Psychology. London: Cambridge University Press.

BATTIG, W. R. and W. E. MONTAGUE (1969) "Category norms for verbal items in 56 categories: a replication and extension of the Connecticut category norms." Journal of Experimental Psychology 80: Monograph Supplement 3, Part 2.

BEHRMAN, B. W. and D. R. BROWN (1968) "Multidimensional scaling of form: a psychological analysis." Perception and Psychophysics 4: 19-25.

BELLER, H. K. (1971) "Priming: effects of advance information on matching." Journal of Experimental Psychology 87: 176-182.

BERLIN, B. (1971) "Speculations on the growth of ethnobotanical nomenclature." Language-Behavior Research Laboratory Working Paper No. 39 (March). Berkeley: University of California.

―――, D. E. BREEDLOVE and P. H. RAVEN (1966) "Folk taxonomies and biological classification." Science 154: 273-275.

――― (1968) "Covert categories and folk taxonomies." American Anthropologist 70: 290-299.

BERLIN, B. and P. KAY (1969) Basic Color Terms: Their Universality and Evolution. Berkeley: University of California Press.

BOURNE, L. E. (1968) Human Conceptual Behavior. Boston: Allyn & Bacon.

BRIGHT, J. O. and W. BRIGHT (1965) "Semantic structures in northwestern California and the Sapir-Whorf hypothesis." American Anthropologist 67: 249-258.

BROWN, D. R. and D. H. OWEN (1967) "The metrics of visual form: methodological dyspepsia." Psychological Bulletin 68: 243-259.

BROWN, R. (1958a) "How shall a thing be called?" Psychological Review 65: 14-21.

――― (1958b) Words and Things. Glencoe, Ill.: Free Press.

――― and E. LENNEBERG (1954) "A study in language and cognition." Journal of Abnormal and Social Psychology 49: 454-462.

BRUNER, J. S. and R. TAGIURI (1954) "The perception of people," in G. Lindzey (ed.) Handbook of Social Psychology, Vol. 2. Redding, Mass.: Addison-Wesley.

BRUNSWIK, E. (1956) Perception and the Representative Design of Experiments. Berkeley: University of California Press.

BULMER, R. (1967) "Why is the cassowary not a bird? A problem of zoological taxonomy among the Karam of the New Guinea Highlands." Man 2: 5-25.

––– and M. J. TYLER (1968) "Karam classification of frogs." The Journal of the Polynesian Society 77: 333-385.

CARROLL, J. B. [ed.] (1956) Language, Thought, and Reality: Selected Writings of Benjamin Lee Whorf. Cambridge, Mass.: MIT Press.

De VALOIS, R. L. and G. H. JACOBS (1968) "Private color vision." Science 162: 533-540.

DIAMOND, J. (1966) "Zoological classification system of a primitive people." Science 151: 1102-1104.

EKMAN, P. (1972) "Universals and cultural differences in facial expressions of emotion," in J. K. Cole (ed.) Nebraska Symposium on Motivation. Lincoln: University of Nebraska Press.

FODOR, J. A. and J. J. KATZ (1964) The Structure of Language. Englewood Cliffs, N.J.: Prentice-Hall.

FORSYTH, G. A. and D. R. BROWN (1967) "Stimulus correlates of tachistoscopic discrimination-recognition performance: compactness, jaggedness, and areal asymmetry." Perception and Psychophysics 2: 597-600.

FRANK, J. J. and J. D. BRANSFORD (1971) "Abstraction of visual patterns." Journal of Experimental Psychology 90: 65-74.

GARNER, W. R. (1962) Uncertainty and Structure as Psychological Concepts. New York: John Wiley.

––– (1966) "To perceive is to know." American Psychologist 21: 11-19.

––– (1970) "The stimulus in information processing." American Psychologist 25: 350-358.

HANDEL, S. and S. IMAI (1972) "The free classification of analyzable and unanalyzable stimuli." Perception and Psychophysics 12: 108-116.

––– and D. PREUSSER (1969) "The effects of sequential presentation and spatial arrangements on the free classification of multidimensional stimuli." Perception and Psychophysics 6: 69-72.

HEIDER, E. R. (1971) "'Focal' color areas and the development of color names." Developmental Psychology 4: 447-455.

––– (1972a) "Probability, sampling, and ethnographic method: the case of Dani colour names." Man 7: 448-466.

––– (1972b) "Universals in color naming and memory." Journal of Experimental Psychology 93: 10-20.

HENLEY, N. M. (1969) "A psychological study of the semantics of animal terms." Journal of Verbal Learning and Verbal Behavior 8: 176-184.

HERING, E. (1964) Outlines of a Theory of the Light Sense. Cambridge, Mass.: Harvard University Press. (Translated by L. M. Hurvich and D. Jameson.)

HUANG, I. (1945) "Abstraction of form and color in children as a function of the stimulus object." Journal of Genetic Psychology 66: 59-62.

IMAI, S. (1966) "Classification of sets of stimuli with different stimulus characteristics and numerical properties." Perception and Psychophysics 1: 48-54.

––– and W. R. GARNER (1965) "Discriminability and preference for attributes in free and constrained classification." Journal of Experimental Psychology 69: 596-608.

––– and S. HANDEL (1971) "Hierarchical stimulus and preference structures in the classification of one-dimensional stimuli." Japanese Psychological Research 13: 192-206.

INHELDER, B. and J. PIAGET (1958) The Growth of Logical Thinking from Childhood to Adolescence. New York: Basic Books.

KAHNEMAN, D. and A. TVERSKY (1972) "Subjective probability: a judgment of representativeness." Cognitive Psychology 3: 430-454.

KATZ, J. J. and P. M. POSTAL (1964) An Integrated Theory of Linguistic Descriptions. Cambridge, Mass.: MIT Press.

KAY, P. (1972) "On the form of dictionary entries: English kinship semantics." Paper presented at the SECOL VIII Conference, Georgetown University (October).

LAKOFF, G. (1972) "Hedges: A study in meaning criteria and the logic of fuzzy concepts." Proceedings of the Chicago Linguistics Society.

LEACH, E. (1964) "Anthropological aspects of language: animal categories and verbal abuse," in E. H. Lenneberg (ed.) New Directions in the Study of Language. Cambridge, Mass.: MIT Press.

LENNEBERG, E. (1967) Biological Foundations of Language. New York: John Wiley.

LOFTUS, E. F. (1973) "Category dominance, instance dominance, and categorization time." Journal of Experimental Psychology 97: 70-74.

——— and R. W. SCHEFF (1971) "Categorization norms for fifty representative instances." Journal of Experimental Psychology 91: 355-364.

McDANIEL, C. K. (1972) "Hue perception and hue naming." Unpublished BA thesis. Cambridge, Mass.: Harvard College.

MERVIS, C., J. CATLIN and E. ROSCH (1973) "Relations among category norms, word frequency, and goodness of example." Unpublished paper. Berkeley: University of California.

MINSKY, M. (1961) "Steps toward artificial intelligence." Proceedings of the Institute of Radio Engineering 49: 8-30.

NEISSER, U. (1967) Cognitive Psychology. New York: Appleton Century Crofts.

OLDFIELD, R. C. (1954) "Memory mechanisms and the theory of schemata." British Journal of Psychology 45: 14-23.

POSNER, M. I. (1969) "Abstraction and the process of recognition," in G. H. Bower and J. T. Spence (eds.) The Psychology of Learning and Motivation. Vol. 3. New York: Academic Press.

———, R. GOLDSMITH and K. E. WELTON (1967) "Perceived distance and the classification of distorted patterns." Journal of Experimental Psychology 73: 28-38.

——— and S. W. KEELE (1968) "On the genesis of abstract ideas." Journal of Experimental Psychology 77: 353-363.

——— and R. F. MITCHELL (1967) "Chronometric analysis of classification." Psychological Review 74: 392-409.

REED, S. K. (1972) "Pattern recognition and categorization." Cognitive Psychology 3: 382-407.

RIPS, L. J., E. J. SHOBEN and E. E. SMITH (1973) "Semantic distance and the verification of semantic relations." Journal of Verbal Learning and Verbal Behavior 12: 1-20.

ROSCH, E. (1972) "The nature of the mental codes for natural categories." Paper presented at a meeting of the Psychonomic Society, St. Louis (November).

——— (1973) "On the internal structure of perceptual and semantic categories," in T. M. Moore (ed.) Cognitive Development and the Acquisition of Language. New York: Academic Press.

SHEPARD, R. N. (1964) "Attention and the metric structure of the stimulus space." Journal of Mathematical Psychology 1: 34-87.

——— and G. W. CERMAK (1973) "Perceptual-cognitive explorations of a toroidal set of free-form stimuli." Cognitive Psychology 4: 351-377.

———, E. I. HOVLAND and H. M. JENKINS (1961) "Learning and memorization of classifications." Psychological Monographs 75: Whole No. 517.

SERPELL, R. (1969) "The influence of language, education and culture on attentional preference between colour and form." International Journal of Psychology 4: 183-194.

STEFFLRE, V., P. REICH and M. McCLARAN-STEFFLRE (1971) "Some eliciting and computational procedures for descriptive semantics," in P. Kay (ed.) Explorations in Mathematical Anthropology. Cambridge, Mass.: MIT Press.

SUCHMAN, R. G. and T. TRABASSO (1966) "Color and form preference in young children." Journal of Experimental Child Psychology 3: 177-187.

TULVING, E. and W. DONALDSON [eds.] (1972) Organization and Memory. New York: Academic Press.

TYLER, S. A. [ed.] (1969) Cognitive Anthropology. New York: Holt, Rinehart & Winston.

WILKINS, A. (1971) "Conjoint frequency, category size, and categorization time." Journal of Verbal Learning and Verbal Behavior 10: 382-385.

WING, H. and W. BEVAN (1969) "Structure in the classification of stimuli differing on several continuous attributes." Perception and Psychophysics 6: 137-141.

Chapter 8

ECOLOGY, CULTURAL ADAPTATION, AND PSYCHOLOGICAL DIFFERENTIATION: TRADITIONAL PATTERNING AND ACCULTURATIVE STRESS

JOHN W. BERRY

Queen's University at Kingston, Canada

A long title requires some initial explanation: the first phrase merely indicates the three classes of variables upon which this study is based, while the latter portion refers to two phases in culture learning. The first of these, which may be termed "culture learning 1," indicates the universal and normal process of behavioral development within a particular context which in turn is adapted to its ecological setting; all mankind becomes enculturated, at least once. The second may be termed "culture learning 2" and indicates that, in addition to taking on a first culture, some people are subject to enculturation in one or more extra cultures; this process of acculturation is often stressful. One purpose of this paper is to show that culture learning 2 is not independent of culture learning 1; that is, the nature of the behaviors acquired in a traditional culture is a powerful contributor to the psychological distress which is often apparent during and after the acculturation process.

This chapter is an extension of a study which was reported in two articles (Berry 1966, 1971a) concerned with the examination of psychological differentiation (Witkin et al., 1962) across ecological and cultural settings. It is an extension along two dimensions: first, it expands the focus from differentiation solely in the perceptual domain (field independence) to include differentiation in the social and affective domains of psychological functioning; and second, it considers the adaptive function of psychological differentiation in preparing the individual to deal with problems accompanying acculturation.

Originally, Dawson (1963, 1967) transported the notion of *differentiation* to a different cultural setting from that which fostered it, and found considerable support for its generality (see Witkin, 1967). The concept was then carried across ecological settings and analyzed in terms of "ecological demands" and

Author's Note: For the Amerindian portion of this paper I gratefully acknowledge the general assistance of Bob Annis, the field assistance of numerous Native workers, and the financial assistance of the Canada Council (S70-0103, S71-0330, S72-0184).

adaptive "cultural supports" (Berry, 1966); this approach was later expanded (Berry, 1971a), and an overall model which has guided the present study was elaborated.

THE CONCEPT OF DIFFERENTIATION

Broadly the concept of *differentiation* refers to "the complexity of a system's structure. A less differentiated system is in a relatively homogeneous structural state; a more differentiated system in a relatively hetergeneous state" (Witkin et al., 1962: 9). With increasing differentiation there is implied an increasing degree of *specialization* (Witkin et al., 1962: 9) or separation of psychological functions (e.g., feeling from perceiving, thinking from acting, p. 10) from one another. Implied also is a degree of *integration* in the system, and this is postulated to increase with differentiation itself. It is a psychological analogy to the use of the term in biology where organismic differentiation is considered to increase both phylogenetically and ontogenetically.

This latter, developmental, aspect has proven to be its most obvious characteristic. "Development toward greater differentiation involves progress from an initial, relatively unstructured state, which has only limited segregation from the environment, to a more structured state, which has definite boundaries, and which is capable of greater specificity of function" (Witkin et al., 1962: 22). Further, "As children grow older, they tend to become more differentiated," although there are to be expected both individual differences and nonidentical differentiation in each of the "indicator areas" of psychological functioning (Witkin et al., 1962: 22).

The concept, since it has been employed to refer to the organism as a whole, should be useful in understanding many aspects of behavior; indeed Witkin has argued that there are substantial behavioral indicators in cognitive, social, and affective life, as well as in the often-studied perceptual domain (1962; chaps. 8 and 9). In these three areas of psychological functioning, an analytical approach to problem solving (requiring a restructuring of the situation), a sense of separate identity (involving social independence), and the use of structured controls and defenses in affective expression are all considered as indicative of a high degree of psychological differentiation.

Individual differences in differentiation have been widely studied by Witkin et al. (1962). A broad base for these individual differences has been found in the socialization practices in use in the family, particularly those used by the mother. Specifically, practices which emphasize the achievement of separation from the mother and autonomous functioning of the child tend to foster differentiation, as does a climate of warm, supportive socialization. On the other hand, practices emphasizing obedience and conformity (especially in coercive, physically controlled situations) tend to foster low levels of differentiation (Dyk and Witkin, 1965).

THE ECOLOGICAL MODEL

The school of cultural ecology (see Berry, 1971a for a brief overview) has advanced the point of view that cultures may be considered as a uniquely human form of adaptation to recurrent ecological press. Environmental determinism is eschewed, while maintaining that ecological variables constrain, pressure, and nurture cultural forms. This point of view is part of the functional tradition in social and behavioral science, and so is unable to assert cause and effect relationships; its major concern is to discover the principle lines of influence, linear, multilinear, and feedback, which best describe a functioning system. The model (Figure 1) which has guided the present research takes account of three classes of variables: *ecological, adaptive,* and *behavioral.*

Briefly the ecological variable may be specified by the combination of water, soil, temperature, and other natural resources which control the degree to which food may be accumulated in a central location. Typically, *high food accumulating societies* pursue agriculture or animal husbandry, or have a naturally provided abundance of food close at hand. Typically, *low food accumulating societies* pursue hunting or gathering as their main subsistence activities. The former are typically *sedentary* with a relatively *high population density,* while the latter are typically *migratory* with a relatively *low population density* (Damas, 1969; Vayda and Rappaport, 1968).

The adaptive variables may be separated into two sets, *sociocultural* and *organismic.* With respect to the latter, nutrition and disease have been well-demonstrated to vary as a function of ecological setting (e.g., Dubos, 1965), while the gene pool, from a traditional Darwinian point of view, is known to vary as a function of ecological press. These variables are not measured in the present study, although some pioneering work by Dawson (1966, 1967) has been done in this area.

With respect to the sociocultural variables, there is impressive evidence in the literature which illustrates the adaptive characteristics of these systems. In particular the original demonstration of socialization differences along this ecological variable (which led to much of the present formulation) by Barry, Child, and Bacon (1959) ties the Witkin research on differentiation to the school of cultural ecology. There are strong similarities between those practices considered to foster psychological differentiation (Witkin et al., 1962) and those found in the ethnographies of low food accumulating societies; the converse is also true, with those practices considered to hinder the growth of psychological differentiation found typically in high food accumulating societies.

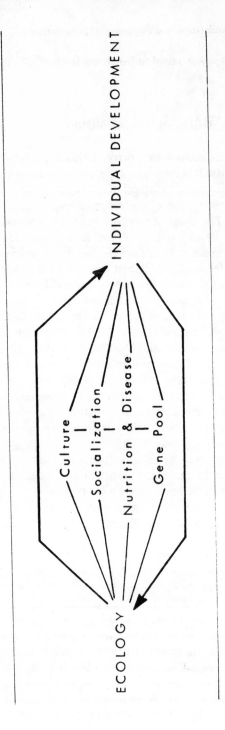

FIGURE 1 – ECOLOGICAL–CULTURAL–BEHAVIOURAL MODEL

Other sociocultural variables known to vary fairly consistently with this ecological dimension are family structure (Nimkoff and Middleton, 1960) social structure (Pelto, 1968) and social relations (Honigmann, 1968). A simple overview of these relations is provided in Figure 2.

FIGURE 2 - ECOLOGICAL MODEL - SOCIAL AND PSYCHOLOGICAL CORRELATES

1. ECOLOGICAL DIMENSION	LOW FOOD ACCUMULATION ◄──────► HIGH FOOD ACCUMULATION	
	(MIGRATORY, HUNTING GATHERING, LOW POPULATION DENSITY)	(SEDENTARY, AGRICULTURAL HIGH POPULATION DENSITY)
2. SOCIAL-CULTURAL (frequently observed)		
a) Socialisation (Barry, Bacon and Child, 1959)	LENIENT SUPPORTIVE	HARSH RESTRICTIVE
b) Family Structure (Nimkoff and Middleton, 1960)	NUCLEAR	EXTENDED
c) Social Structure (Pelto, 1968)	EGALITARIAN ATOMISTIC	HIERARCHICAL STRATIFIED
d) Social Relations (Honigmann, 1968)	RESERVED FRAGMENTED	MUTUAL DEPENDENCE INTEGRATED
3. PSYCHOLOGICAL (Predicted)		
a) Perceptual-Cognitive Differentiation (Cognitive Style)	FIELD INDEPENDENT ANALYTIC	FIELD DEPENDENT GLOBAL
b) Socio-Emotional Differentiation (Affective Style)	INDEPENDENT RESERVED CONTROLLED	GROUP RELIANT OUTGOING EXPRESSIVE
c) Response to Culture Contact (Acculturative Stress)	LOW STRESS (from A) HIGH STRESS (from B)	HIGH STRESS (from A) LOW STRESS (from B)

The behavioral variables considered have been chosen because of their apparent relationship to the concept of differentiation. They include measures of perceptual and cognitive functioning ("cognitive style"), of social and emotional functioning ("affective style"), and of problematic responses to the changes introduced by culture contact ("acculturative stress"); of course, other nonproblematic changes occur during acculturation, but being largely "shifts" from traditional levels of behavior, they have not been separately labeled. The first study to be guided by this model sampled only from the first set of behaviors (Berry, 1966, 1971a) while the second study has sampled from all three.

Study 1: Temne-Aborigine-Indigene-Eskimo Study

This study has been previously reported (Berry, 1971a); only the main outlines are included here. It was found that, across four eco-cultural settings (and in both traditional and transitional settings), there are systematic differences in group means on two tests of perceptual differentiation (Embedded Figures Test and Kohs Blocks) and one cognitive test which has a high perceptual (spatial) factor but involves the making of inferences beyond the perceptual display (Matrices). These differences were predicted from the model and are interpreted as supporting the model, and the usefulness of such a functional approach.

One finding, which had been reported only in part (Berry, 1967), was that an Asch-type test of independence of judgment (in the face of a suggested group norm) produced a similar systematic patterning across these four eco-cultural settings. This, too, had been predicted from the model, and was the first cross-cultural excursion into social aspects of differentiation. Witkin and his colleagues had shown that high differentiation (sense of separate identity) was associated with the maintenance of independence of judgment on a similar task. The degree of social stratification and social dependence (as well as a harsher, more restrictive pattern of socialization) often found in high food accumulation societies was argued as the basis for this systematic relationship between the ecological dimension and sample means on this social differentiation task (Berry, 1967).

Study 2: Amerindian Study

A larger study to incorporate these other dimensions of differentiation was launched in 1970. Specifically it retained two of the perceptual-cognitive tasks (Kohs and Matrices) and a variation of the one "social" task (Independence) while adding another "social" task (Reserve) and one "emotional" task (Control),[1] and a battery of scales to assess "acculturative stress" (Stress, Marginality, Deviance, and Attitudes Toward the Larger Society).

A major methodological aim was to attempt a test of the model by sampling along a necessarily more restricted range of ecological settings *within a single culture area* (Murdock, 1957). This aim was set in order to minimize variation due to extraneous variation which may derive from sampling across culture areas, and to maximize the possibility of cross-cultural comparability in behavioral observations (Berry, 1969). In this way one may also "test the limits" of a model.

The expectations, derived from the model, were that:

(1) When sampling across this more restricted ecological-cultural range, evidence for differences in perceptual-cognitive differentiation (field independence) could still be obtained.

(2) Evidence for differentiation in the social and affective domains would also be obtained, and that this would be related to levels of perceptual-cognitive differentiation. This expectation of consistency is based upon the assumption that differentiation is a characteristic of the organism as a whole.

(3) Evidence of acculturative stress would be obtained across all settings; between groups it may be higher or lower at either end of the ecological dimension depending upon the adaptive value of either perceptual-cognitive or social-emotional differentiation. Within groups, stress levels should be higher for those more dependent on their surrounding field.

These three expectations will be elaborated in the context of the ethnographic and descriptive material that follows.

Design and Samples

Because more than two observations are necessary to define a relationship (Campbell, 1961) in cross-cultural work, three ecological settings were selected; and within each setting two community samples were drawn from a "relatively traditional" and a "relatively acculturated" village. The design and samples are indicated in Table 1.

The "low food accumulating" setting is on the eastern and southern shore of James Bay. The Cree people who live in this area first came in contact with

TABLE 1

DESIGN AND SAMPLES–AMERINDIAN STUDY

Ecological Setting	"Relatively Traditional"	"Relatively Acculturated"
High Food Accumulating (Tsimshian) N = 115	Hartley Bay N = 56	Port Simpson N = 59
Medium Food Accumulating (Carrier) N = 121	Tachie N = 60	Fort St. James N = 61
Low Food Accumulating (Cree)[a] N = 121	Wemindji N = 61	Fort George N = 60

a. A more highly acculturated sample of Cree (N = 37) was taken in the historic community of Moose Factory; however, interview and testing difficulties led to an incomplete sample. A further comparison sample was drawn in the nonnative farming village of Westport (N = 48).

Europeans in 1668 when the Hudson Bay Company made its first voyage to Charles Fort (now Rupert House). At that time hunting and fishing were the main subsistence activities, with frequent moves being made during the yearly hunting cycle. Over these past 300 years there has been a shift from hunting for food to trapping for furs; however, this meshing with the economy of the larger society has not made serious inroads into basic Cree economic activity, and its associated cultural life-style.

The "medium food accumulating" setting is in the Rocky Mountain plateau area of northern British Columbia. The Carrier people were also hunters, but they have been strongly influenced by the coastal people in economic pursuits and other cultural factors. Major contact with Europeans began about 1800 when Fort St. James was established as the first capital of New Calendonia and a Hudson Bay post was opened. Further to the north, and relatively isolated is the more traditional village of Tachie, still pursuing some traditional hunting activities.

Finally the "high food accumulating" setting is on the Pacific Coast of British Columbia, adjacent to the Alaska panhandle. The Tsimshian people are part of the great Northwest Coast Indian Culture area, known for the economic abundance of their salmon supplies (often referred to as "marine agriculture"). Their villages were sedentary, but the people made seasonal relocations around their bays and islands. Port Simpson was the first Hudson Bay post established in the far Northwest and has frequent contact with the City of Prince Rupert. Hartley Bay is a village 100 miles south and is relatively isolated.

From ethnographic reports it is clear that the culturally adaptive variables all support, to varying degrees, the point of view of the cultural ecologists. With respect to socialization, lenient and supportive practices characterize the Cree, while more socialization pressure was exerted among the Tsimshian. So too we find nuclear family structure among the Cree, with extended families among the Tsimshian. And with respect to social stratification, there was little ranking of note among the Cree, while the Tsimshian were famed for their great chiefs and numerous slaves. A detailed ethnographic presentation is not appropriate here; suffice it to say that the literature on these three areas, as well as observations made during the present fieldwork, provide general support for this aspect of the model.

Sampling and Interviewing

For each community, a relatively complete census was available. The "Band Lists" were stratified into six cells: *Sex* (male, female) by *Age* (18-25, 26-40, over 40) to avoid the inevitable youth and sex biases that enter into fieldwork of this sort. An N of 10 for each cell was sought.

Interviewing was carried out, in all cases, by a member of the appropriate culture (Cree, Carrier, or Tsimshian). In the Cree study one male and one female

(19- and 20-year-olds whose brother was Chief at Wemindji) were trained at Queen's University for fieldwork. In the British Columbia studies, interviewer (three 20-year-old Tsimshian, and four Carrier, 20 to 30 years old) training was carried out in the home communities.

All sampling and interviewing was supervised by Bob Annis (a psychology student) in all three areas during the summers of 1971 and 1972. Continuity of procedure (and hence comparability of data) may be lower because of this method; however, the potential gain in this strategy of fieldwork is very great. Through constant supervision and standard materials and training, the loss of comparability is not considered to be great in this study; on the other hand culturally sensitive data, collected by "own-culture" interviewers, has been an advantage.

Interviewing and testing took place in a private "test center" in each community, although comfort and lighting conditions did vary from place to place.

Test Materials and Elaboration of Expectations

Because all three areas could not be visited for pilot work prior to the initiation of data collection, it should be noted that the Cree samples form the anchor, or baseline, for the study as a whole. For example, emic analyses (Berry, 1969) were made only in that area, and extensions made to the other two areas reflect this bias. Given this perspective, the test materials will be described in relation to published accounts and pilot field observations of Cree life.

With respect to perceptual-cognitive differentiation, it was expected that the Cree, like other low food accumulating samples before them (see Berry, 1971a), would provide evidence for high development in this area of functioning (estimated by Kohs and Matrices). The direct ecological requirements made of hunters, and the adaptive cultural responses reported in the literature (Hallowell, 1955; Honigmann, 1968) formed a solid base for this expectation. Being hunters, the Carrier were also expected to produce relatively strong scores on these tasks (Seward, 1963); however, their socialization practices and social structure, being influenced by the "tighter" (Pelto, 1968) coastal peoples, led to the expectation that scores may be slightly lower for equivalent degrees of acculturation. For the Tsimshian (Drucker, 1955), their lack of migration and hunting coupled with stricter socialization and social-structural characteristics led to an expectation of lower scores than in the two hunting samples; however, because their art forms are highly complex and because sea voyages were not infrequent over short distances, perceptual differentiation was expected to be much higher than that measured among other nonhunting, high food accumulation, high stratification societies (see Berry, 1971a). In all three areas, performance was expected to increase with exposure to Western life through education and experience with modern technology.

With respect to differentiation in social behavior, ethnographic reports of northeastern forest Indians (e.g., Hallowell, 1955, chap. 6, and Honigmann, 1968) led to a strong expectation of Independence and Reserve. The Independence task requires the respondent to make judgments on line length in the face of a suggested group norm and is an elaboration of a similar task used previously (Berry, 1967). Asch (1956) and Linton (1955) had earlier employed similar tasks to assess behavior on a dimension of independence-conformity. Accounts of northeastern migratory Amerindians strongly indicated high independence. Further, the performance of Eskimo samples on an earlier version of this test added weight to this expectation. The Reserve test is a modification of the Jourard (1971) "self-disclosure" questionnaire and consists of questions about whether the respondent would give information about himself to parents and to peers (ten questions each). Ethnographic reports suggest a high degree of reserve, generally for Amerindians, but in particular for the migratory peoples of the northeast. Although not previously connected to the notion of differentiation, it was considered that the degree to which a person retained information about himself would be another indicator of a "sense of separate identity" and be correlated with the tendency to maintain independent judgments.

In the other two ecological areas, there were no specific ethnographic accounts on which to base expectations. Although the model would predict lower social differentiation as the socialization practices become more restrictive and social stratification becomes more hierarchical, general views regarding typical Amerindian behavior would predict minimal variation. Thus, there was an expectation that social differentiation (scores on Independence and Reserve) would decline slightly across the ecological dimension from the low to the high food accumulation samples.

With respect to emotional differentiation, there appears once again to be a strong indication of emotionally controlled or restrained behavior among the northeastern migratory people (Hallowell, 1955) which has been termed "frozen affect" by Honigmann (1968). In Witkin's (1962) terms, affective differentiation is indicated by an elaborated system of defenses, one that rarely permits of massive emotional outbursts. Thus there was an expectation that differentiation in the affective domain would be high in the Cree area while there is an absence of psychologically oriented ethnographic reports on the other areas. The model, however, would suggest that the emphasis on *self-control* in the low food accumulation area would shift to an emphasis on *social control* in the high food accumulation area, given the shift in socialization practices and increased tightness in social structure. The task in this area (Control) was, after initial training on a maze, to attempt to return to the starting point (e.g., "bring the furs back down the water system") although a block had been placed in the way. The amount of time during which the respondent persisted without giving up or displaying loss of emotional control was taken as an indication of differentiation in the affective area of psychological functioning.

Expectations regarding "acculturative stress" levels between groups were equivocal. A basic assumption is that the more similar the behavior fostered in traditional life is to that demanded in Western wage-economy towns, then the less adjustment would be necessary for people or communities in transition. Two broad clusters of demands may be discerned in Euro-Canadian town life: the first is for a degree of perceptual-cognitive ability sufficient to permit the individual to participate in increasingly technological occupational roles; the second is for a degree of acceptance of control by others, on the job, on the street, and generally in urban life (Berry, 1971b).

Now, if differentiation is a characteristic of the organism as a whole, that is, if perceptual-cognitive and socioemotional differentiation tend to exist at roughly similar levels, then it is apparent that the adaptations necessary for the individual or community shift to Euro-Canadian life-styles are incongruent. The fostering in traditional life of high differentiation would adequately prepare individuals for one of the demands (technological role skills) but poorly prepare him for the other (acceptance of social control). On the other hand, the fostering of low differentiation in traditional life would adequately prepare individuals for the conforming demands of urban life, but would poorly prepare him for the more valued, technologically based occupational roles.

Thus across eco-cultural settings the adaptive value of differentiation, during the process of acculturation, cannot be clearly predicted. At best two alternatives may be established: if the greatest pressures are exerted upon individuals as part of specific skill expectations, in technologically based roles (and this would include most Western job-roles), then high differentiation would have adaptive value. On the other hand, if the greatest pressures are placed by the more general expectations of urban life (accepting social control, conformity, crowding, authority, etc.), then high differentiation would not have adaptive value.

However, within each sample, it may be predicted that those who are more field-independent (that is, are less reliant upon their immediate surroundings) would be less susceptible to the pressures to be encountered during acculturation; conversely, those individuals who are more field-dependent may be expected to be more strongly disturbed by such changes in their sociocultural environment.

The measures in this area have been termed those of *acculturative stress* (Berry, 1970); they include responses to the 20 item Cornell Medical Index (Stress) prepared for field use by Cawte et al. (1968); the 14 item Marginality scale prepared by Mann (1958), and the Deviance scale (called the Socialization scale in the California Psychological Inventory) by Gough (1957). In addition to these three scales, measures of Attitudes toward relations with the larger Euro-Canadian Society (Sommerlad and Berry, 1970) were assessed, and indexes of personal and community acculturation level, and of ethnic identification, were taken.

In summary, then, the eco-cultural variables are the degree of food accumulation in the traditional economy, along with population density, socialization pressure, and social stratification ("tightness"); and the behavior variables are perceptual-cognitive differentiation, (*cognitive style*), socioemotional differentiation (*affective style*), and response to culture contact (*acculturative stress*).

RESULTS AND DISCUSSION

Sample Characteristics

Both ethnographic evidence obtained prior to fieldwork and observations made in the field support the ranking of the three cultures on the ecological dimension. Among the Cree, the hunting and trapping economy is still dominant, as is the yearly migratory residence pattern associated with this economic base. The Carrier, too, provide evidence of this form of economic subsistence, although more influenced now by wage economy. The Tsimshian samples both maintain a strong reliance on the salmon economy, and live in very settled communities. There is thus little doubt that this dimension is sampled in the proper order. In the absence, however, of an exact index (quantification is extremely difficult in this area), it is not possible to assert how much more restricted the Cree to Tsimshian range is than, for example, is the Eskimo to Temne range (Berry, 1966, 1971a). The James Bay Cree are perhaps only a little more food accumulating than the Baffin Island Eskimo, while the Tsimshian are clearly much less food accumulating than those samples with annual or semi-annual harvests (Temne or Telefomin). A range of, perhaps, half the previous range may be reasonably suggested.

With respect to adaptive cultural characteristics, ethnographic material provides evidence of fairly clear differences traditionally (and still present to a lesser degree) in degree of social stratification and in socialization pressure. Data in this study on self-ratings of Mother and of Father socialization severity show that the Tsimshian rated parents most severe, the Carrier a little less, and the Cree the least severe.

The sampling for level of acculturation, however, was not so successful. The Cree samples were less acculturated on both years of education, and ownership of Western material goods (from radios to cars or boats and bank accounts) than the other two cultural groups. These acculturation level differences were unavoidable, and while they make many discussions of data quite difficult, we will argue later that they are in themselves psychologically significant.

However the sampling strategy of obtaining equal numbers of males and females, and in age categories 18-25, 26-40, and over 40, was fairly well met; thus a high degree of community representativeness may be claimed for these samples. And since the communities were in most cases the only ones representing the levels of acculturation sought, we may claim that these samples are highly representative of the three eco-cultural settings.

Differentiation: Sample and Individual Differences

With respect to perceptual differentiation (Kohs), there is fairly clear separation of the samples, as predicted from the model (5 of 6 multiple comparisons are significant at the .01 level). Indeed, the most acculturated Tsimshian sample (Port Simpson) does not quite reach the level of performance of the least acculturated Cree sample (Wemindji), and the traditional Carrier sample, combining both hunting and a high level of education has an even higher mean score. When considered in the light of earlier findings with Kohs across a wider range of settings (these scores all approximate the mean Eskimo performance in Berry, 1971a), these data are taken as further support for the model in the area of perceptual differentiation (field dependence-independence). This support derives both from the relatively high level of performance in all the samples taken from Amerindian groups in a single culture area, and from the ability to predict the differences, minimal but significant, among the three cultural groups.

The pattern of scores for Matrices, although all are fairly high, shows the opposite trend to that expected from the model and to that previously found (Berry, 1971a), and 4 of 6 comparisons are significant at the .01 level. The ranking of sample means on Matrices, however, is similar to their ranking on mean years of education, and correlations with education within samples (ranging from +.24 to +.66) provide support for an interpretation in terms of an acculturation overlay. However correlations between Kohs scores and education are equally high (ranging from +.32 to +.55) although Kohs means still come through the educational-acculturation process supporting the model. It is interesting to note that in those samples where hunting is still carried out (Wemindji, Fort George and Tachie), the Matrices correlation with education tends to be higher; in nonhunting communities, the Kohs correlation with education tends to be higher.

Quite clearly then, we have equivocal evidence for ecological relations with differentiation in the perceptual and cognitive domain (although it is fair to note that Matrices have no theoretical link with the concept of differentiation; they have an empirical link through a shared spatial factor). Depending on one's orientation, we could marvel at the persistence of differential Kohs scores through the education process, consider why Matrices appear to be more affected by the same process, and conclude some support for the model over this restricted ecological range. Alternatively, we could conclude that the equivocal evidence neither supports nor detracts from the model.

With respect to differentiation in the socioemotional domain, there are no overall trends in the sample means on the three tests (Independence, Reserve, and Control) across the three settings.

For Independence (where a higher score is indicative of lower differentiation), all scores are roughly comparable to means for the medium-low food accumulation samples in the earlier studies. Exact comparisons cannot be made because the task was expanded in the present study. This lack of trend across eco-cultural settings may be a valid finding, or it may be due to the fact that a different interviewer administered the task in each setting, and each may have had a different authority standing in the community. However, the generally high level of independence is consistent with ethnographic reports of prototypical Amerindian personal style.

For Reserve there are again no apparent trends across eco-cultural settings, for either Reserve with Parents or Peers. There has been no previous work with this specific test or in comparable situations; direct comparisons are thus not possible. However, comparisons with norms obtained in a nonnative community indicate that in four of the six samples, native respondents produce significantly more "no's" to questions such as "Would you tell your best friend what you are afraid of?" Such a response pattern may be termed highly reserved. This interpretation is again consistent with the ethnographic reports of prototypical Amerindian personal style.

For Control, a complete overview of trends is not possible since the task was administered in only three of the samples (Wemindji, Fort George, and Hartley Bay). For the data available, there is a decline across levels of acculturation between the two Cree samples, and there is a clear (and significant) drop in the comparison between the traditional Cree and Tsimshian samples (Wemindji and Hartley Bay). Both these observations are consistent with the model and with ethnographic reports.

Summarizing, there is no consistent support for the expected differences in socioemotional differentiation across these three eco-cultural settings; this is true for two of the tasks (Independence and Reserve), while differences in keeping with the model on the third task (Control) are only partial. Where levels of scores may be assessed, Independence scores approximate those previously found in medium-low food accumulating societies, while level of Reserve appears to be quite high; both of these are consistent with the ethnographic literature.

Thus, with respect to *differences* over this restricted range of eco-cultural settings, we find some support for the differences expected from the model in the perceptual domain (Kohs Blocks) and some in the Emotional domain (Control); there are essentially no differences in the two social tasks (Independence and Reserve), while differences are reversed in a cognitive task (Matrices). With respect to *levels,* we find that, where comparisons are possible with previous work (Berry, 1971a), perceptual and cognitive task means approximate those obtained by low food accumulating samples (Eskimo), while one task mean (Independence) approximates those found among medium-low food accumulating samples. Thus, given the general cultural characteristics of samples in this single culture area, *levels* of task means are much as expected, while there is only moderate support for expected *differences* across specific ecological settings.[2]

Although mean differences across eco-cultural settings are only partly confirmed, there is considerable variance on these tasks within each of the samples. Analyses of relationships within samples (Pearson correlations) can provide a check on the expectation that organismic differentiation would manifest itself in both cognitive style and affective style. The two perceptual-cognitive tasks (Kohs and Matrices) consistently correlate significantly (range +.36 to +.66) in all samples, and the two social tasks (Independence and Reserve) correlate significantly (+.30 and +.34) only in the Cree samples; however, Reserve and Control do not appear to be related nor do Independence and Control reveal consistent relationships.

Now, considering the relationships between the two classes of tasks (cognitive style and affective style) all (except 2) correlations are positive (8 of them significant) in the Cree samples, there is about equal division of positive and negative coefficients among the Carrier, and there is a preponderance of negative correlations (4 of them significant) among the Tsimshian samples. If there is a patterning of positive relations between these two domains of psychological functioning (as could be argued for the Cree), it is clear that it is not consistent across eco-cultural settings; the pattern is essentially zero among the Carrier, and emerges as slightly negative among the Tsimshian.

On the basis of these data, the notion of *differentiation* appears to be less unitary than the "characteristic of the organism" approach would suggest. Development of perceptual, cognitive, social, and emotional characteristics may be independently nurtured in particular eco-cultural settings, and may not need to "hang together." Ethnographic reports for the Cree (Hallowell, 1955; Honigmann, 1968) strongly suggest that the prototypical individual needs to be spatially-perceptually able, highly socially independent and reserved, and emotionally controlled; the patterning of relations among tasks is highly consistent with these field observations. For the Tsimshian, on the other hand, the prototypical person (from ethnographic reports) would have to be far less reserved and independent (for adequate performance of his social roles), while maintaining some level of spatial-perceptual ability (for coastal fishing and participation in fairly elaborate artistic activity). Although the sample *dif-*

ferences predicted from the model were generally not found, this patterning of generally negative correlations within both Tsimshian samples is consistent with an eco-cultural interpretation.

Relations with Acculturative Stress

There are equivocal expectations about the relationship between differentiation task scores and acculturative stress scores on both the sample and individual difference levels. There are, as previously outlined, good reasons to expect differentiation to aid or hinder adaptation to the acculturative process, depending upon which aspect is emphasized, and depending upon one's level of analysis.

Sample means for the three scales of acculturative stress (Stress, Marginality, and Deviance) may be examined both on the eco-cultural and acculturation dimensions. For two of the scales (Stress and Marginality) there is a consistent trend on the eco-cultural dimensions: Stress and Marginality both decline from the Cree, through the Carrier, to the Tsimshian samples (8 of 12 multiple comparisons being significant at the .01 level). And for Marginality there is a consistent decline, within each eco-cultural setting, from the more traditional to less traditional samples. Despite the lack of sample differences in measures of socioemotional differentiation, there appears to be some differential factor operative in the production of these aspects of acculturative stress. For Deviance, 3 of 6 multiple comparisons are significant, yielding a pattern across cultures similar to that of the other two variables.

With respect to Attitudes toward modes of relating to the larger society, further trends appear. There is a fairly marked increase (from Cree through to Tsimshian) in interest in Assimilation, and a consistent decrease in interest in Rejecting any relation with the larger society. For Integration, there is a consistent decrease across both the eco-cultural and acculturation dimensions.

Juxtaposing these two sets of data, we find the Cree experiencing the greatest Stress and having the greatest feelings of Marginality; and supporting these data, we find them with the least interest in assimilation and the greatest interest in rejecting contact with the larger society. The Tsimshian, on the other hand have a pattern of scores essentially opposite: low Stress and Marginality combined with a higher interest in Assimilation and no interest in Rejection. Two interpretations may be offered for this pattern of data; they may be due merely to existing differences in the degree to which acculturation has already proceeded among them, or they may be due to the expected differences in socioemotional differentiation. The latter interpretation is hampered because few eco-cultural differences were apparent on these tasks; however, the ethnographic descriptions cannot be entirely discounted. In one sense, these two interpretations are not alternatives, for if the Cree are Independent and Reserved, as so frequently described, then acculturation would have made fewer inroads on their lives, even though contact has been over a period about twice as long; the level of acculturation is, in itself, a measure of the attitudinal and behavioral distance they have maintained.[3]

When patterns of relations among the tasks are examined within samples, we find that Kohs, Matrices, and Reserve tend to correlate significantly negatively with Stress and Marginality within the Cree samples (Berry, 1972) and within the Carrier and traditional Tsimshian sample (Hartley Bay), but not in Port Simpson. However, the other two scores (Control and Deviance) do not display consistent or significant relations with the acculturative stress variables.

There is thus some evidence *within samples* that for the two Cree, the two Carrier, and the traditional Tsimshian samples, high scores on measures of differentiation tend to go with low scores on measures of acculturative stress. This generalization is opposite, however, to some of the evidence presented *across* eco-cultural settings, where the high (perceptually) differentiated Cree were fairly clearly displaying the highest Stress and Marginality. Although this paradoxical finding does not display the desirable property of "metric equivalence" (Berry and Dasen, 1973: 21), it is far from uninterpretable. At the level of cultural comparisons, we are dealing with aggregated sample means as features of groups, while at the level of within-sample comparisons among variables, we are dealing with individual differences. It is quite possible to argue that what may be the norm, and adaptive, for a community, may not be so for an individual; general levels of acculturative stress may be high in communities which display high levels of differentiation (and lower in low differentiation communities), while at the same time highly differentiated (field-independent) individuals, in *all* communities, may be less susceptible to acculturative pressures.

CONCLUSIONS

In a sense, the Amerindian study has attempted to test the limits of a model (for cognitive style) while at the same time extending it to include two new classes of variables (affective style and acculturative stress). These two aims should, ideally, have been carried out in two independent studies; however, the costs (in time, effort, and money) inherent in cross-cultural work encouraged the decision to attempt both simultaneously. It is appropriate, then, to examine the model separately from these two points of view.

First, it is fairly clear that we have once again obtained evidence for high field independence (Kohs) among low food accumulating, hunting societies. This emerging generalization has also been supported through work carried out in another research tradition (the Piagetian) by Dasen (1973a, 1973b). Detracting from this generalization, however, is the pattern of Matrices scores, although the interpretation in terms of acculturation differences is plausible. Thus we have some support for the model in the area of cognitive style, despite the greatly reduced range of eco-cultural variation. In such work, of course, it is quite possible to maximize the variation in one's antecedent (ecological and cultural) variables to ensure support for the model; conversely, one may seek to minimize such variation to discover the point where the model is no longer able to discriminate, or be predictive. This procedure is identical to the experimentalist's trick of varying the efficacy of his experimental manipulation to check the strength of his effects. In cross-cultural work, because of costs, this "testing the limits" (or treading close to the edge to see if you will fall off!) has not generally been carried out; however, it is a refinement, along with replication, which, despite the costs inherent in both procedures, will permit us a level of precision which has escaped us heretofore.

Reasons for finding fewer differences, or less extreme differences, predicted from a model may be considered under three headings: low level of variation in antecedent variables, not observing the parameters or assumptions of the model, and not sampling behaviors that theoretically flow from the model. In the first instance, we have already indicated that the present study set out to test the limits of the model at the risk of losing some of the effects. Three cultural groups which are all based upon similar economic pursuits (variations on fishing and hunting) and living within a single culture area, represent just such a minimal level of variation in antecedent variables; indeed, it is a wonder that all (not just some) differences were not wiped out, especially in the face of the acculturation covariable. For the second factor, one study has already been reported (Jones, 1972) which did not find the expected differences between fishing and urban communities in Newfoundland and Labrador. Our model, however, is explicitly limited to societies operating at a subsistence level economically, to those in adaptation to ecological press. This limitation stems from the study of Barry, Child, and Bacon (1959) where the demonstration of relationships between the economic base of a society and the socialization practices was limited to subsistence-level societies. Because their results form a crucial link between ecological setting and psychological differentiation in our model, we must also limit ourselves to these societies. Nonobservation of the parameters of a model can obviously lead to findings that are inconsistent with the model, but of course cannot reflect upon the model. Finally, one may sample behaviors that are theoretically unrelated to the model; such may be the case for Reserve and Control (and to a lesser extent for Matrices) in the present study; until further intracultural studies are carried out, this problem will remain unsolved.

Moving to our second focus for evaluation (the extension of the model to include two novel areas of behavior), with respect to affective style there are no clear differences in the patterning of scores across the restricted eco-cultural dimension. Either the ethnographic accounts are suspect, or our tests were not able to pick up these phenomena at the level of individuals. We may tentatively conclude then, that in a single culture area, with a restricted ecological range, scores from which differentiation in this area of psychological functioning may be inferred do not display consistent or systematic variation over this eco-cultural range.

Similarly, there is no consistent pattern of relationships between cognitive style and affective style across this range; however, there is some evidence for positive relationships at the low food accumulating end, zero relationship in the middle, and negative relationship at the high food accumulating end of the eco-cultural dimension. Such a pattern raises urgent cross-cultural research questions; the pattern does not shift intraculturally (Witkin et al., 1962), so that the relevant cultural factors now need to be sought. If such a shifting pattern is not merely due to the low level of variation in antecedent variables in the present study, and can be replicated across a wider eco-cultural range, then we will have to face an important issue in the theoretical and behavioral consistency of the concept of *differentiation.* Such a question has already been raised by Wober (1966) with respect to the sensory modalities involved with expressions (and measures) of cognitive style, but no data of substance have allowed judgments to be made. A study is now underway among Ojibway hunters and trappers in northern Ontario regarding differentiation in visual and auditory modalities; however, no data are yet available.

Finally there is evidence for higher acculturative stress in the low food accumulation samples, with scores declining across the dimension. At the same time, there is evidence that high differentiation (for some aspects of both cognitive style and affective style) may be related to lower levels of acculturative stress, at least in the two hunting societies (Cree and Carrier). As we have already argued, this paradox is not considered to be without some sense; at the cultural level, those communities possessing cultural and behavioral patterns least con-sistent with those in the larger society, may suffer the greatest social and psychological distress, while at the individual level, the more highly field-independent persons may be more independent of the sociocultural changes which induce such acculturative stress. This latter interpretation is now being checked with a sample of English and French Canadian university student volunteers who are spending four months in a field situation in India; the level of individual field-independence assessed prior to departure is expected to predict the degree of acculturative stress experienced; however, a good deal of future work with wider-ranging samples is necessary before any certainty may be claimed. Despite the limitations of present knowledge, we may venture the hypothesis for future study that culture learning 2 is not a uniform process among all peoples undergoing acculturation; rather it is a function both of the pressures placed upon a people by the larger society, and of the cultural and behavioral characteristics brought by a people to the acculturating situation.

More specifically, we venture to suggest that the greater the incongruity between the two cultural and behavioral systems, the greater the conflict and resistance associated with the transition, and the greater the resultant acculturative stress. Further, whatever the cross-cultural trend or relationship, individuals within each society who possess a high level of differentiation will be more independent of the incongruity and conflict, and thereby manifest less acculturative stress. In each instance, incongruity will be a function both of the actual cultural and behavioral differences, and of the pressures placed by the larger society upon a people to undergo acculturation. The first factor may be gauged by sociocultural analysis, while the second one may be assessed by examining social policy; if one or the other factor approaches the zero level, then acculturative stress will be minimal. In the case of a pluralist society, large real cultural differences may exist with little acculturative stress being apparent, while in an assimilationist society, even small real cultural differences may be associated with high levels of acculturative stress. If this general hypothesis is borne out by future research, then the clear policy implication for multi-ethnic societies lies in the pursuit of cultural pluralism (Berry, 1974), assuming that low levels of acculturative stress are preferable to high ones.

NOTES

1. Witkin (personal communication, 1973) does not accept that the Reserve and Control tasks unambiguously measure psychological differentiation.

2. These generalizations are based upon sample means only; further analyses for age, sex, and acculturation levels may reveal others.

3. These differential levels of Stress, Marginality, Deviance, and Attitudes toward the dominant society have been considered sufficiently reliable to offer court testimony based upon them. As noted in the introduction to this book, a planned hydroelectric project has recently threatened the cultural viability of these same Cree people; the probable psychological consequences in the form of even greater acculturative stress was pointed out at a hearing in application for an injunction to halt the project.

REFERENCES

ASCH, S. (1956) "Studies of independence and conformity." Psychological Monographs 70 (9): 1-70.

BARRY, H., I. CHILD, and M. BACON (1959) "Relation of child training to subsistence economy." American Anthropologist 61: 51-63.

BERRY, J. (1966) "Temne and Eskimo perceptual skills." International Journal of Psychology 1: 207-229.

——— (1967) "Independence and conformity in subsistence-level societies." Journal of Personality and Social Psychology 7: 415-418.

——— (1969) "On cross-cultural comparability." International Journal of Psychology 4: 119-128.

――― (1970) "Marginality, stress, and ethnic identification in an acculturated Aboriginal community." Journal of Cross-Cultural Psychology 1: 239-252.

――― (1971a) "Ecological and cultural factors in spatial perceptual development." Canadian Journal of Behavioural Science 3: 324-336.

――― (1971b) "Psychological research in the North." Anthropologica 13: 143-157.

――― (1972) "Possession of typical cognitive and personality traits, and resistance to acculturative stress." Abstract Guide, International Congress of Psychology, Tokyo.

――― (1974) "Psychological aspects of cultural pluralism: unity and identity reconsidered." in R. Brislin (ed.) Topics in Culture Learning, Vol. 2, 1974, pp. 17-22.

――― and P. DASEN [eds.] (1973) Culture and Cognition. London: Methuen.

CAMPBELL, D. (1961) "The mutual methodological relevance of anthropology and psychology," in F. Hsu (ed.) Psychological Anthropology. Homewood, Ill.: Dorsey Press.

CAWTE, J. (1968) "Personal discomfort in Australian Aborigines." Australia and New Zealand Journal of Psychiatry 2: 69-79.

DAMAS, D. [ed.] (1969) Ecological Essays. National Museums of Canada Bulletin, 230.

DASEN, P. (1973a) "The influence of ecology, culture, and European contact on cognitive development in Australian Aborigines," in J. Berry and P. Dasen (eds.) Culture and Cognition. London: Methuen.

――― (1973b) "Concrete operational development in three cultures." Paper presented at IACCP Regional African Conference, Ibadan, Nigeria.

DAWSON, J. (1963) Psychological Effects of Social Change in a West African Community. Doctor of Philosophy thesis. Oxford: Kebel College.

――― (1966) "Kwashiorkor, gynaecomastia and feminization processes." Journal of Tropical Medicine and Hygiene 69: 175-179.

――― (1967) Cultural and physiological influence upon spatial-perceptual processes in West Africa: International Journal of Psychology 2, parts 1 and 2: 115-128 and 171-185.

DRUCKER, P. (1955) Indians of the Northwest Coast. New York: American Museum of Natural History.

DUBOS, R. (1965) Man Adapting. New Haven, Conn.: Yale University Press.

DYK, R. and H. WITKIN (1965) "Family experiences related to the development of differentiation in children." Child Development 36: 21-55.

GOUGH, H. (1957) Manual for the California Psychological Inventory. Palo Alto, Calif.: Consulting Psychologists Press.

HALLOWELL, A. (1955) "Some psychological characteristics of Northeastern Indians," in A. Hallowell (ed.) Culture and Experience. Philadelphia: University of Pennsylvania Press.

HONIGMANN, J. (1968) "Interpersonal relations in atomistic communities." Human Organization 27: 220-229.

JONES, P. (1972) "Socialization practice and the development of spatial ability." Paper presented at the meetings of the International Association for Cross-Cultural Psychology, Hong Kong.

JOURARD, S. (1971) The Transparent Self. New York: Van Nostrand.

LINTON, H. (1955) "Dependence on external influence: correlates in perception, attitudes, and judgment." Journal of Abnormal and Social Psychology 51: 502-507.

MANN, J. (1958) "Group relations and the marginal personality." Human Relations 11: 77-91.

MURDOCK, G. (1957) "World ethnographic sample." American Anthropologist 59: 664-687.

NIMKOFF, M. and R. MIDDLETON (1960) "Types of family and types of economy." American Journal of Sociology 66: 215-225.

PELTO, P. (1968) "The differences between 'tight' and 'loose' societies." Transaction (April): 37-40.

SEWARD, J. (1963) Theory of Culture Change. Urbana: University of Illinois Press.

SOMMERLAD, E. and J. BERRY (1970) "The role of ethnic identification in distinguishing between attitudes towards assimilation and integration of a minority racial group." Human Relations 23: 23-29.

VAYDA, A. and R. RAPPAPORT (1968) "Ecology, cultural and non-cultural," in J. Clifton (ed.) Introduction to Cultural Anthropology. Boston: Houghton Mifflin.

WITKIN, H. (1967) "A cognitive style approach to cross-cultural research." International Journal of Psychology 2: 233-250.

――― et al. (1962) Psychological Differentiation. New York: John Wiley.

WOBER, M. (1966) "Sensotypes." Journal of Social Psychology 70: 181-189.

PART THREE.

CONTRIBUTIONS FROM HOLOGEISTIC STUDIES

Chapter 9

INITIATION CEREMONIES AND SECRET SOCIETIES AS EDUCATIONAL INSTITUTIONS

W A L T E R   E.   P R E C O U R T

State University of New York at Buffalo

PROBLEM

This study analyzes initiation ceremonies and secret societies as educational institutions.[1] While many attempts have been made to explain the functions of these institutions, little attempt has been made to investigate their *educational* functions. The reason for this is apparently because the notion of education as used traditionally has often been used in a very limited sense to refer to the direct instruction of substantive knowledge (see Herzog, 1962; Young, 1965). Because this form of education has been thought (often mistakenly) to be absent in initiation ceremonies, it was felt by many authors that little or no educational activity occurred during these ceremonies. Only recently has education been viewed with a broader perspective to encompass all forms of cultural transmission (see Gearing, 1972a, 1972b). It is, therefore, now possible to see the educational functions of initiations from many new and different perspectives. It is out of this latter conceptualization of education that the ideas presented in this chapter were conceived.

With this in mind, the conceptual basis of this paper can now be discussed. The key notion used throughout is that of *hidden curriculum.* This notion says essentially that in formal and informal social contexts there are two related but essentially independent phenomena operating that carry out educational functions. One is the explicit content of the activity that occurs in a particular context. For example, in a school classroom, this would include the substantive material present in textbooks. The second type of activity is much less obvious; it consists of those things that are usually inculcated without the conscious awareness of those involved in the social setting under consideration. In the example of the school classroom, an instance would be the activity based on the differences in the social positions of teacher and student. The transaction

Author's Note: I would like to thank the following persons for the assistance they gave me in conducting this study: Terrence Tatje, Keith Otterbein, Raoul Naroll, Frederick O. Gearing, Barry L. Isaac, and William T. Divale.

between the two can be seen as inculcating a basic notion of dominance-submission in the student, even though this is not explicit in the curriculum of that classroom. This latter type of phenomenon constitutes hidden curriculum.

Hidden curriculum is usually communicated nonverbally or paralinguistically. It sorts, directs, and censors human perception in ways that articulate persons to the structure of a particular cultural system. As such, it deals with dimensions of societal participation that are enacted widely in many social contexts, even though they are seldom recognized or verbalized.

In light of the notion hidden curriculum, the function and structure of initiation ceremonies is considered in two respects. First of all, it is theorized that in egalitarian tribal societies hidden curriculum will serve to articulate members of a society on a horizontal or equal basis. In chiefdom societies with incipient stratification, on the other hand, hidden curriculum will serve to articulate society members on the basis of social differentiation. It is argued that tribal initiations function in the former situation while secret societies function in the latter.

Hidden curriculum is also considered with respect to the actual mechanism of cultural transmission. It is theorized that the dynamic process of initiations conceptualized by Arnold Van Gennep (1960) as the structure of *rites of passage* is the second form of hidden curriculum. The passage rite structure includes the stages of separation, transition, and incorporation. It is argued that the structure formed by these three main events constitutes a mechanism of cultural transmission.

This study is also concerned with the relationship between explicit curriculum and hidden curriculum. In essence, this subject questions the extent to which the observable details of educational activity dictate or are dependent upon the hidden aspects of knowledge learning. This aspect of the study also provides a means of determining the extent to which substantive knowledge learning occurs during initiations.

While the major concern of the study is with investigating problems applicable to education generally, the study at the same time questions many of the theories that have been advanced to explain the function of initiations. By offering a somewhat different analytical framework, it is felt that the study sheds light on the many controversial issues that have arisen over attempts to explain the function of initiation ceremonies and secret societies.

PREVIOUS THEORIES

It is necessary to discuss briefly the various theories that have been advanced to explain the function of initiation ceremonies and secret societies. This will serve as a background and a point of departure for the ideas presented here.

Practically every imaginable explanation has been offered to account for the widespread occurrence of these institutions in stateless societies. While I shall not attempt to deal with each explanation separately, it is possible to include in several categories explanations that have essentially the same theme. Most explanations fall into one of the following categories: diffusionist, biogenic, religious, psychogenic, and sociogenic. Indeed, these categories are by no means mutually exclusive, but they provide a means of classifying, generally, the various modes of explanation.

Diffusionist explanations prevailed during the nineteenth century (see Allen, 1967). The worldwide presence of initiation ceremonies was explained as the result of diffusion from one, or possibly several, sources (Lowie, 1961). Often absent, however, is any indication of how the original ceremony developed.

Biogenic theories, while often used in conjunction with other explanations, are important in their own right. They usually argue that biological factors affect or are directly responsible for initiations. A good example of this approach is the notion advanced by Lionel Tiger (1969). He traces all male bonding groups (including initiation ceremonies and secret societies) to a time in man's evolutionary past when a genetically determined male "bond" was necessary for survival.

An explanation for initiation ceremonies that is biogenic in another respect is that of Whiting (1964). His causal chain starts with a tropical climate and protein deficiency and ends up with initiation ceremonies. The complete chain of causality is as follows: Tropical climate and protein deficient diet → prolonged lactation → post partum sex taboo → polygyny → patrilineal and patrilocal household → exclusive mother-infant sleeping arrangements → initiation rites.

Some explanations strongly emphasize the religious aspect of certain initiation ceremonies, and, in fact, consider this aspect to be of primary importance. Eliade (1965) sees all initiation and similar ceremonies as primarily having religious functions. Heckethorn (1965) regards secret societies as a link with man's spiritual evolution.

Sociogenic and psychogenic theories have by far been the most popular and controversial. Historically, sociogenic theories predominated in the early twentieth century, though they were to some degree replaced during the mid-twentieth century with Freudian and Neo-Freudian explanations. In the early 1960s, sociogenic theories again made their mark, and today both sociogenic and psychogenic theories prevail as essentially rival explanations for initiation ceremonies, although to some extent these approaches are converging (see Harrington, 1968).

Young (1965: 2) contrasts sociogenic theories and psychogenic theories. Sociogenic theories take as causal the structure of the social meanings held by the members of the group and interpret individual tendencies as operating within

such structures and having no independent effect. Psychogenic theories begin
with social structure, but assert the independent causal efficacy of intervening
modal personality tendencies in determining group-level phenomena.

Early sociogenic explanations include the one advanced by Radcliffe-Brown
(1948). He saw initiation ceremonies as mechanisms for transmitting from the
society to the initiate certain values and beliefs. Miller (1932; quoted in Allen,
1967: 2) felt that the function of initiations was to "rivet the individual to
society."

Psychogenic theories developed mainly after the publication of Freud's
Totem and Taboo (1952). Reik (1946) saw initiation rituals, such as symbolic
death and rebirth and circumcision, as attempts on the part of fathers to deal
with Oedipal rivalry. Thus, the purpose of initiation ceremonies was to prevent
and punish patricide and incest. Bettelheim (1954) argued that initiations were
mechanisms for resolving conflict between a child's pregenital desires and the
demands of his adult role.

The psychogenic theories that have recently had the greatest impact are those
postulated by Whiting, Kluckhohn, and Anthony (1958) and Burton and
Whiting (1961), although similar or related theories have been advanced by
Brown (1963) and Herzog (1962). These theories characterize what is known as
the "Neo-Freudian" approach. Whiting, Kluckhohn, and Anthony argue that
initiations function to resolve father-son conflict resulting from extended
mother-child sleeping arrangements. Burton and Whiting (1961) explain initiations along similar lines, although they modify the main theoretical argument.
Rather than explaining the need for initiations in terms of father-son rivalry,
they use the status envy hypothesis. They argue that initiations serve to resolve
sexual identity conflict.

Theories using primarily a sociogenic approach have also recently been
advanced. Those of Young (1962, 1965), Cohen (1964), and Allen (1967) are
perhaps the most significant and will, therefore, be considered here. Young
(1962) challenged the theory of Whiting et al. (1958), and by so doing questioned all of the explanations using a Neo-Freudian approach. He argues that
initiation ceremonies serve to inculcate male solidarity through status dramatization. This ensures that males will cooperate in organized activities that require
the loyalty of all males. Cohen (1964) suggests that initiations serve to anchor
individuals to a wider kinship or descent group when liability for unlawful acts is
not tied to the individual but is assumed by his entire kinship group. Initiations
will be absent when each individual is liable for his own actions. Allen (1967)
stresses that initiations are associated with strong sexual distinctions; that is, if a
society stresses differences between the sexes, then sexually exclusive organizations will exist.

The above review indicates that theories for explaining initiation ceremonies
are not only great in number but are very diverse and cover practically the whole
gamut of possible types of sociocultural explanations (see Naroll, 1970a:

1253-1255). The reason there are such a great number of different explanations is that, first of all, there is great diversity in the conceptions of initiation ceremonies held by different authors; second, authors are often preoccupied with trying to explain the details of particular ceremonies. With regard to the first factor, practically every author defines initiations somewhat differently. This often results in studies that are not comparable because the phenomena dealt with are of essentially different natures. For example, both Young (1965) and Allen (1967) offer explanations for initiation ceremonies and related activity, but their definitions of initiation are entirely different. With regard to the second factor, initiations frequently include blood-letting operations (circumcision, incision, nose-bleeding, eye-bleeding, and sacrification); representations of death and birth of the novice, bodily mutilation; name changing, changes in dress; ornamentation; and sometimes body painting (Van Gennep, 1960; Allen, 1967). If considered separately, each of these ritualistic details can potentially demand a different explanation. It is therefore no wonder authors have come up with a great variety of explanations for initiation ceremonies.

This study will differ from most previous studies in two respects regarding the above problems. First, the range of cultural activity categorized by various authors under the general heading "initiation ceremony" are defined in some detail. Both initiations per se and the various organizations into which novices enter will be considered separately, although both categories of phenomena will be subsumed within a single typology. Second, both the structure of an initiation and the various details associated with particular initiations will not be considered in isolation, but they will be seen as parts of a larger structure of cultural transmission, the components consisting of both hidden and explicit curriculum.

With respect to the different theories discussed above, my explanation of initiations is sociogenic in its emphasis. I feel, however, that it is impossible to pigeonhole a cultural phenomenon into a particular functional "slot" in a culture. Therefore, while I argue that certain forms of cultural transmission occur during initiations, this does not preclude the possibility that initiations may have other important functions. Thus, I feel that the theory advanced in this chapter does not necessarily rival any particular previous theory. On the contrary, I feel that it brings the other theories into better focus.

THEORETICAL BACKGROUND FOR THIS STUDY

Before discussing the various hypotheses that will be tested in this study, I shall consider certain important theoretical issues relating to my explanation of initiations. One notion crucial for my explanation is the conceptualization of societal organization put forth by Emil Durkheim that includes the notions of organic and mechanical solidarity. Mechanical solidarity means essentially that a society is organized on the basis of like parts or segments. Organic solidarity, on the other hand, is the organization of society on the basis of unlike parts, that is, specialization. Both of these notions lead to another closely related societal classification, the division of societies on the basis of egalitarianism and stratification. Mechanical solidarity is closely related to an egalitarian social structure, while organic solidarity is essentially a prerequisite for stratification. A fundamental concern of this paper is how cultural transmission operates in egalitarian societies (with mechanical solidarity) as opposed to stratified societies (with organic solidarity). The evolutionary classification put forth by Service (1962) categorizes societies into those integrated on the basis of mechanical and organic solidarity. Bands and tribes fall into the former category while chiefdoms and states fall into the latter. Applying the notions egalitarian and stratified to these societal types, it is found that both bands and tribes fall into the egalitarian category. Of the societal type chiefdoms and states, however, only states are truly stratified. For chiefdoms, a further breakdown of the notion "stratified" is necessary, which I have called "incipient stratified." I define this concept as follows: a society that is incipient stratified is one that is ideologically stratified, but which does not have social, political, and economic mechanisms to enforce the ideological principle of stratification. Still, however, the societal organization of chiefdoms is based on differentiation of function (i.e., organic solidarity).

In contrasting a chiefdom to a state we see the difference between a society that is incipiently stratified as opposed to a society that is fully stratified. In a chiefdom, enforcement of the principle of stratification is limited to the presence of sumptuary rules; in states, on the other hand, such institutions as a police force and an army back up the precepts of the stratification system, which in itself is often characterized by rigid economic classes.

Postulating the existence of three different types of societal organization—egalitarianism, incipient stratification, and stratification—is the basis for explaining the educational functions of initiation ceremonies and secret societies.

We are now ready to consider the part initiation ceremonies and secret societies play in cultural transmission. The assumption here is that all societies must have some mechanisms for the inculcation of knowledge. Children do not simply "absorb" knowledge, even though in certain instances, for example, language, a great deal of information apparently is acquired without any adult intervention. In fact, Jules Henry (1960) stresses that societies must actually teach society members *not* to see certain things, that is, things that would be deleterious to the individual and the society.

This raises the question as to what similarities and differences in cultural transmission exist at different levels of cultural integration. It is apparent that in all societies the family plays an important role in the process of cultural transmission. In primitive societies, the family is the locus for cultural transmission in the areas of material culture, language, values, knowledge of the physical environment, and, to a great extent, integration with the economic system (see Henry, 1960; Herzog, 1962). In certain areas, however, the family is not, in itself, adequate to complete the cultural transmission process: this is in the area of articulating the individual with the sociopolitical universe. Indeed, Cohen (1971) calls family-based transmission *socialization,* and reserves the term *education* for cultural transmission relating to the structure of the wider society.

In all societies, therefore, there must exist a mechanism for articulating a member of society into the broader sociopolitical universe. Although the family operates in most areas where cultural transmission is necessary, it does not suffice in most instances for purposes of this wider articulation. The main reason for this is that kinship is generally not broad enough in scope to inculcate the dimension of the wider society; it can teach wider social principles, but this is something quite different from articulation with the behavioral transaction dimensions of these principles.

The notion of "schemas" presented by Fortes (1936) exemplifies this situation. According to this idea, a child who is learning kinship terms, for example, learns at a very early age some of the various kinship categories and some of the terminology associated with these categories. It is not until the child gets older and actually becomes associated with the individuals represented in this kinship system, however, that the real meaning of the kinship terminology becomes clear, and the schema, as it were, are filled in. In extending this concept, at least as an analogy, to the wider society it becomes obvious that merely teaching a child the concepts associated with the wider social universe is not enough to make that child articulate into that universe.

In tribal societies, as was discussed above, sociopolitical organization is egalitarian; therefore, as an adult, the individual must function on an equal basis with members of the tribe, that is, he must articulate horizontally to members of his tribal group. An educational institution that could perform such a task would be expected to emphasize community solidarity and equality. It would be expected to bring the individual face-to-face, so to speak, with the community, that is, to interrelate the individual with the "public" as a unit. I hypothesize that in tribal societies such an institution in fact exists; this is the initiation ceremony. I further hypothesize that such ceremonies will be characterized by activity that emphasizes egalitarianism among those initiated and solidarity between the initiates and other members of the society. It is the theme of egalitarianism that I feel constitutes the essence of hidden curriculum as it operates in tribal initiations.

In chiefdoms, the sociopolitical structure is somewhat different from that found in tribal societies. At this level of cultural integration, the egalitarian principle no longer prevails, but there now exists what I have termed incipient stratification. In chiefdom societies, therefore, it would be expected that an educational institution would be present that would inculcate the notion of stratification. I hypothesize that the institution that carries out this function is the secret society and its associated initiations. A mechanism such as the secret society is necessary because there is no formal class structure with its institutionalized sanctions that can serve to integrate a society member according to the principle of differentiation. It can be noted that Webster (1968) observed that in some instances secret societies apparently have actually replaced initiations where a society's social integration has changed from the tribal to the chiefdom level.

Stratified state-level societies contrast to chiefdoms in that they usually have a formal class structure, either economic or political. As such, the mechanisms for articulating the individual with the wider sociopolitical universe are, to some degree, built into the structure of society. That is, one is articulated, at least initially, into the wider sociopolitical system by virtue of his family's social position. Thus, at birth, and via one's kinship group, one is "fitted" into the society's stratification structure. Furthermore, there are other secondary mechanisms for social articulation including, for example, formal educational institutions. It is argued here, therefore, that initiation ceremonies and secret societies do not exist as educational institutions at the state level because they are unnecessary, and in fact they are perhaps inappropriate. This does not rule out the fact that initiations and secret societies often exist in state societies. The function of such institutions, however, is often rather specialized and is of little significance when considered on a society-wide basis. It can also be noted that very often secret societies present at the state level come into direct conflict with official governmental principles and policies (see Webster, 1964). For these reasons, it is suggested that initiations that do exist in state societies will tend to be open and initiation will be into limited, nonsecret associations (see Note 3 on coding definitions). Subversive secret institutions are not considered in this study.

The other dimension to the process of hidden curriculum relates to the dynamics of the initiation per se. Van Gennep (1960) indicated that three fundamental steps occur in what he refers to as rites of passage (i.e., any ritualized recognition of a change in an individual social position). The three stages include removal from the previous environment, transition, and incorporation into former environment. It is suggested here that the presence of these stages in initiation ceremonies indicates another form of hidden curriculum. The actual step-by-step process constitutes a structure for the inculcation of knowledge associated with the general goals of the initiation. In initiation ceremonies the three-step process provides a mechanism for the inculcation of egalitarianism in tribal societies and the inculcation of stratification in chiefdoms. It is suggested, therefore, that the three-step initiation process transcends particular types of initiations and is universal to all initiations. In this study each initiation will be investigated regarding the extent to which the three-step pattern is present. If such a pattern does in fact exist in most of the initiations, it will be tentatively concluded that this pattern constitutes a universal structure for cultural transmission.

Initiation ceremonies and secret societies are also considered in light of explicit curriculum. Two primary questions are dealt with in this regard. The first considers the extent to which substantive instruction occurs during initiations, for example, direct instruction in tribal lore and customs, craft skills, and subsistence activity, and the like. Thus far, there has been little in the way of systematic analysis to determine the extent to which substantive knowledge learning actually occurs during initiations, and this study should help answer this question. The second question is concerned with the extent to which explicit curriculum is related to hidden curriculum. In essence, this provides a means of investigating whether or not certain patterns of explicit curriculum must function with particular patterns of hidden curriculum, or whether they are essentially independent forms of education.

HYPOTHESES AND OTHER RESEARCH PROBLEMS

The hypotheses that were tested can now be stated. The first is concerned with the relationship between type of initiation and level of cultural integration, and is as follows: Initiation ceremonies will exist at the tribal level of sociocultural complexity while secret societies will exist in chiefdoms. The second hypothesis is concerned with the structure of the various initiations and can be stated as follows: Initiation ceremonies will emphasize equality among the initiates, while secret societies will emphasize differentiation. It would also be expected that initiations that occurred in state societies would tend to be open and that the associations entered would tend to be limited nonsecret.

In addition to the main hypotheses, several other research problems bearing on the initiation ceremony data are dealt with. They are:

(1) The extent to which the three stages associated with rites of passage are present in the various initiations;
(2) The extent to which substantive knowledge learning occurs during the initiations;
(3) The relationship between explicit and hidden curriculum.

METHOD AND PROCEDURE

Hologeistic Method

Hologeistic method, the method of analysis used in this study, entails the comparison of a worldwide sample of societies. The rationale behind this method is that hypotheses dealing with sociocultural phenomena cannot be tested under ideal experimental conditions; that is, all the relevant cultural influences cannot simultaneously be controlled for. Furthermore, if it is hypothesized that two cultural traits are functionally related, their presence together in a single society does not necessarily support the hypotheses because their joint occurrence may be due to chance coincidence. Hologeistic method is designed to overcome both of these problems. First, the use of a worldwide sample of societies randomizes, and therefore controls for, the effects of cultural forces extraneous to the hypotheses being tested. Second, correlation coefficients are calculated to determine the extent to which hypothetically interrelated traits occur together in a large sample of societies. Correlation coefficients and significance tests help determine whether the traits are uncorrelated, correlated by chance, or significantly correlated (see Naroll, 1968).

Sampling

A worldwide sample of 37 societies was used to analyze the above hypotheses and other research problems. This sample was derived from the Quality Control Sample, a random sample of 60 societies drawn from the Quality Control Universe (Naroll, 1967). The sample of 37 societies was composed of Quality Control Sample societies that had data in one or more of the following Human Relations Area File (HRAF) categories: "Sodalities" (575), "Childhood Ceremonial" (852), and "Puberty and Initiation" (881). Thus, all Quality Control Sample societies that had data in any one of these categories were kept, while the rest were eliminated.

This selection procedure raises questions about the randomness of the derived sample. It may be argued that the remaining societies were biased with respect to initiations, that is, the societies in the sample would contain only societies with initiations present. For the following reasons, however, I feel that this procedure did not significantly bias the sample. First, the HRAF categories were used only as general guidelines to where pertinent data might be available. They give no indication of the exact nature of the data. Second, frequently, even when data were present on initiations, they indicated only that initiations were absent. Third, the 37 societies were distributed fairly evenly around the world geographically. They were also evenly distributed with respect to political complexities, that is, there were about an equal number of societies of low, medium, and high complexity.

Coding Procedure

Because there were no available codings for most of the variables used in this study (i.e., initiations, secret societies, rites of passage, differentiation, and explicit curriculum), it was necessary to construct coding rules for all of these variables. All of these codings were made with data from HRAF (see Moore,

1970). One exception to this, however, is the code for political complexity, which was based on the *Ethnographic Atlas* coding for "Jurisdictional Hierarchy" (Murdock, 1967). (See Note 3 for a brief summary of each of the coding rules.) I coded all 37 societies myself. Unfortunately, cost and time limitations precluded using additional coders for coding reliability checks.

Statistical Analysis

All of the statistical findings reported in this study were calculated either by hand or with the computer program ORDMAT.[4] To test the two main hypotheses, correlation coefficients were calculated between the variables level of political integration (tribe, chiefdom, and state), type of initiation and association entered, and presence or absence of differentiation. The extent to which the stages of passages rites were present was calculated by tallying by hand the presence or absence of such rites. Hand tallies were also made to determine the extent to which the two forms of explicit curriculum (ritual focus and secular focus) were present. The relationship between explicit and hidden curriculum was calculated using correlation coefficients.

Galton's Problem

Galton's problem is concerned with the effects of cultural diffusion among the societies used in a cross-cultural sample. Cultural diffusion is a problem in hologeistic studies because observed correlations among theoretical variables may be caused by diffusion, and hence may not be due to functional relationships. Naroll (1961, 1970b) and Naroll and D'Andrade (1963) have advanced various methods to test for Galton's problem. One of these, the linked pair test, is used here. The linked pair test helps determine whether or not cultural diffusion can explain away the correlations among the theoretical variables. (For discussion of the rationale and logic behind the linked pair test, see Naroll, 1961, 1970b, and Schaefer, 1969.)

The linked pair test was applied to the sample of societies used in this study. The results show that diffusion among the sample of societies was not significant with regard to this study's theoretical variables.

Data Quality Control

Data quality control is concerned with the quality of the ethnographic reports used to make cross-cultural codings, as well as the quality of the codings per se. Naroll (1962, 1970c) has found that several aspects of data analysis are pivotal for determining data quality. They relate to the three main aspects of data processing: the data source (i.e., native informant); the data gatherer (the ethnographer), and the cross-cultural analyst (the coder). Naroll has developed certain control factors which, when applied to an ethnographic report, help determine the accuracy of the report and provide an estimate of the accuracy of codings based on the report.

To test the accuracy of the codings for an entire sample of societies, Naroll et al. (1970) have constructed the Standard Ethnographic Sample. Using the Standard Ethnographic Sample, the sample of societies used in this study were tested for data quality. (See Naroll, 1962 for a discussion of the test for data quality.) The results show that the data used in this study meet an acceptable standard.

RESULTS

The statistical findings support the two main hypotheses. Public initiations tend to be associated with tribal societies, and secret societies tend to be associated with chiefdoms.[5] Furthermore, secret societies tend to be associated with differentiation while public initiations tend to lack differentiation. The correlation coefficients between these variables are presented in Tables 1 and 2.

TABLE 1

RELATIONSHIP BETWEEN POLITICAL COMPLEXITY AND TYPE OF INITIATION AND ASSOCIATION (N = 37)

Political Complexity	Initiation			Association			
	Public	Open	Secret	Society-Wide	Limited	Secret	Secret and Limited
Tribe	.3927[a]	-.2333	.0407	.3170	-.1808	.0036	-.0984
	(.0313)[b]	(.1613)	(.4338)	(.0643)	(.3764)	(.3527)	(.4154)
Chiefdom	-.1586	.2271	.2271	-.1898	.2891	.2782	.4249
	(.3045)	(.1593)	(.1593)	(.2121)	(.1247)	(.0943)	(.0133)
State	-.1935	.0625	-.2677	-.0166	-.1307	-.2862	-.3432
	(.3167)	(.4520)	(.1273)	(.3589)	(.5785)	(.0990)	(.0434)

a. Tau-B
b. Level of probability

The investigation of rites of passage revealed that 17 of the 27 societies with some form of initiation present had to some extent all three of the passage rite components (i.e., separation, transition, and incorporation). Of these, 12 had more than one of the five indexes for each separate stage present. Of the initiations that lacked all three of the formal stages of passage rites, 3 of them had evidence for at least one of the passage rite stages. Thus, only 7 of the 27 societies had no evidence whatsoever for these rites. It can be noted that where

TABLE 2

RELATIONSHIP BETWEEN DIFFERENTIATION PATTERN (HIDDEN CURRICULUM) AND INITIATION CEREMONIES AND SECRET SOCIETIES

Variable 1	Variable 2	Tau-B Correlation Coefficient	Probability	N
Differentiation	Public Initiation	-.5052	.0198	26
Differentiation	Secret Association	.4625	.0283	26

no rites were recorded, it was mainly due to insufficient data rather than clear evidence that no rites existed.

The analysis of explicit curriculum showed that in practically all of the initiations there was some form of training in substantive areas with a secular focus (see Note 2). Such training was present in 24 of the 27 initiations considered. It was also found that 10 of the 24 initiations with explicit curriculum (secular focus) had education in five or more of the subjects considered.

TABLE 3

RELATIONSHIP BETWEEN HIDDEN CURRICULUM AND EXPLICIT CURRICULUM

(Correlation between presence or absence of differentiation [Variable 1, Constant] pattern [hidden curriculum] and explicit curriculum [ritual and secular focus], Variable 2)

Variable 2	Correlation Coefficient	Level of Probability	N
Circumcision	.0706	.4424	23
Magical Cantations	.0952	.4925	23
Taboos	.0706	.4424	23
Dress Changes	.2114	.2900	23
Ceremonial Offerings	.2778	.1908	23
Games, Sports, and Singing	.1826	.3307	24
Tribal Lore and Customs	-.4667	.0350	24
Moral Code	.0216	.3780	24
Status or Position in Tribe	.1826	.3307	24
Magic, Witchcraft, and Religion	-.1826	.3307	24

It was also found that there tends to be no association between explicit curriculum and hidden curriculum (see Table 3). On the basis of correlating the presence or absence of the ten most frequent explicit curriculum elements (5 with a ritual focus and 5 with a secular focus) to the presence or absence of differentiation (hidden curriculum), it was found that in only one instance of ten was there any significant relationship between a form of explicit curriculum and hidden curriculum. The explicit curriculum element was the "teaching of tribal lore and customs," which tended to be negatively correlated to differentiation.

DEVIANT CASE ANALYSIS

Deviant cases are societies which have cultural traits that do not conform to the predictions of one or more of a study's hypotheses. Such exceptions must be explained because, as stated by Köbben (1967: 4), many deviant cases "may be either proved spurious or included in the rule. The latter method, besides making the 'law' statistically more significant, also adds to its value by increasing its subtlety." Furthermore, deviant cases may expose flaws in the original theoretical argument and may help disclose other sociocultural forces relevant to the theory.

This study's deviant cases fall into two main categories. The first contains tribes or chiefdoms which have no initiations or secret societies whatsoever. These societies include the Cuna, Kapauku, Trobrianders, and Tarahumara. The second category contains societies with initiations or secret societies present but which are at a level of cultural integration not predicted by the theory, that is, tribes with secret societies present and chiefdoms with public initiations present. These societies include the Cubeo, Kurd, Ojibwa, Ona, Santal, Tlingit, Toradja, and Bororo.

There are several other conceivable instances of deviancy though these cases do not directly conflict with the main theoretical argument and have been alluded to elsewhere. Therefore, I shall not consider them here. I shall discuss here only the four deviant societies that lack initiations or secret societies entirely, because they most strongly conflict with the theory.

The Cuna, Kapauku, and Trobrianders are all deviant for the same reason: they have petty chiefdoms (as measured by jurisdictional hierarchy) but lack secret initiations and secret societies. It is evident that the Cuna do not have secret societies because they had, up to the sixteenth century, a well-developed class system. In fact, according to the *Ethnographic Atlas* (1967), slavery existed during this earlier period. The traditional political structure was destroyed through European conquest. This case, therefore, actually supports the hypothesis, since societies with a class system are not expected to have secret societies.

The nature of the Kapauku economic system helps explain why they lack secret societies. According to Pospisil (1963) the Kapauku have a form of capitalism: there is a strong "profit" motive, and the accumulation of wealth is highly valued. It may be that individuals are articulated to the incipient differentiation structure through imitation of and participation in the Kapauku economic system, which emphasizes competition and "differentiation" through wealth accumulation. This may explain why the Kapauku lack secret societies: the economic exchange system serves as a functional equivalent.

A plausible explanation for why the Trobrianders are deviant is that they have a dual stratification structure, that is, a hereditary aristocracy and a lower class of commoners (Murdock, 1967). Thus, as in state societies, Trobrianders are born into one or another of the two classes. Secret societies are therefore not necessary because one is articulated to the political structure via membership in his kinship group, as in state societies.

The Tarahumara are deviant because they are a stateless "tribal" society but lack public initiations and society-wide associations. A plausible explanation for the absence of initiations among the Tarahumara is that they live in neighborhoods of dispersed family homesteads. Thus, the people are quite isolated from one another with respect to economic and political activity. In light of the theory, it is understandable why initiations are absent since it is not necessary to strongly integrate the individual to a community-wide political system. In fact, Bennett and Zingg (1935) suggest that no initiation ceremonies (or "societies") are present because of the "extreme isolation" of the people from each other.

CONCLUSIONS

The conclusion drawn with regard to the main hypotheses is that there are definite differences in initiations as they exist in tribal societies as opposed to how they exist in chiefdoms. The differences are not only in the general structure of the initiation, but they are also in the internal structure in terms of the presence or absence of differentiation patterns. It is therefore felt that the contrasting equality/differentiation characteristics of the initiations represent different forms of hidden curriculum.

The findings regarding the presence or absence of rites of passage indicate that the formal stages of removal, transition, and incorporation are present in most initiations. This lends support to Van Gennep's original theory concerning rites of passage. In addition, it suggests that another dimension of hidden curriculum must be seen as potentially operating in initiations. It is suggested here that the three-stage sequence of passage rites constitutes a structure for cultural transmission that is potentially operative in any educational context. It would be expected, though, that its presence would be most important in situations where the educational process involved a change from one social position to another.

Finally, the widespread presence of explicit curriculum with a secular focus suggests that, contrary to the opinions of many authors, there is indeed a good deal of substantive learning that occurs during initiations. Furthermore, the lack of positive or negative correlation between explicit and hidden curriculum suggests that these two forms of cultural transmission may operate independently of each other. If this is true, the implication of these findings for education in general is great. The implication is essentially that explicitly implemented forms of education are only part of what is inculcated in a learning situation. Thus, two identical, explicitly implemented curriculums may have far different educational outcomes depending upon what form of hidden curriculum is simultaneously present. Because it would be expected that hidden curriculum would be much more imbedded in the social-structural aspects of the learning environment, it not only would be much more difficult to control for hidden curriculum than it would be for explicit curriculum, but it would be a very significant factor when implementing any form of education cross-culturally since as cultural context changes there may be significant changes in underlying patterns of cultural transmission, regardless of the overt content of the education.

NOTES

1. In this study the terms initiation ceremony and secret society refer to cultural institutions that have particular theoretical relevance. (See Note 5, p. 248.) The term initiation ceremony refers in a broad sense to public initiations into a society-wide association, although in this particular paper the term is used to refer primarily to public initiations. Similarly, the term secret society broadly refers to secret initiations into a secret association, although it is used here to refer primarily to secret associations.

2. The following societies constitute the sample of 37 societies used in this study: Amhara, Andamans, Aranda, Ashanti, Aymara, Azande, Bemba, Bororo, Cagaba, Cubeo, Cuna, Dogon, Ganda, Gurani, Iroquois, Kanuri, Kapauku, Korea, Kurd, Lau Fijians, Lozi, Masai, Ojibwa, Ona, Pawnee, Santal, Saramacca (Bush Negro), Shiriana (Yanamamo), Siam, Somali, Tarahumara, Tikopia, Tiv, Tlingit, Toradja, Trobrianders, and Wolof.

3. SUMMARY OF CODING RULES. The original coding rules were approximately 20 pages long, and it is possible to give only brief summaries of the coding definitions here.

Coding for Initiation Ceremonies and Secret Associations. Both initiations per se and the associations entered as a result of the initiation were coded for. The initiations were classified as either public, open, or secret; the associations were classified as either society-wide, limited nonsecret, or secret. The coding definitions for each of these institutions are given as follows:

Public Initiation: These include initiations that occur in the context of the community as a whole, and the publicity of the initiation is emphasized. A key index for this kind of initiation is the presence of community involvement in the ceremony, whether in the actual initiation or in associated activities.

Open Initiation: These include initiations that are not actually public, that is, they do not stress community involvement. On the other hand, the initiation is not secret. Thus, such initiations are to some degree isolated from the public in that their publicity is not stressed. The activity, however, is not consciously shielded from public view.

Secret Initiations: These initiations are consciously shielded from public view. Physical activity and ceremonial lore are restricted from the public or the uninitiated.

Society-Wide Association: The limits of the association are defined horizontally by the limits of the society itself. Thus, in this definition we may speak of an association of all adult males, an association of all those of a particular age, or an association of all males excluding all females.

Limited Nonsecret Association: This refers to associations encompassing within their boundaries groups limited within age and sex divisions of the society; hence, not every member of a particular age or sex group belongs to such an association. The activities of the association are known to the public and the association does not stress secrecy.

Secret Association: This includes associations that are organized on the principle of secrecy. Most of the ritual activities are shielded from public view and the association's precepts are bound up in secrecy.

While all of the initiation and association variables were considered in this study, the ones that were most significant were the variables public initiation and secret association (see Note 5).

Coding for Hidden Curriculum (Differentiation). To determine whether an initiation emphasized equality or differentiation, several indexes were devised. The first considered whether recruitment for initiation was restricted or nonrestricted; the second considered whether the various activities that were present during the initiation were conducted equally or differentially; and, the third considered whether the initiation or the association was structured into a hierarchy, and whether or not certain parts of the hierarchy had restricted membership.

Coding for Rites of Passage. Several criteria were established in order to determine the presence or absence of the three stages of rites of passage. For each stage five separate indexes were considered; and if any one of the five indexes was present, it was concluded that the particular passage rite was present.

Coding for Explicit Curriculum. Two lists of explicit curriculum elements were compiled. One consisted of explicit curriculum with a ritual focus (22 elements) and a second consisted of explicit curriculum with a secular focus (25 elements). If any of the elements were present in a particular initiation, they were simply checked off on one of the lists of elements.

The ritual focus elements are: (1) circumcision, (2) superincision, (3) scarification, (4) body painting, (5) bodily mutilations, (6) ornamentation, (7) bleeding of any bodily part, (8) magical cantations, (9) taboos, (10) fasting, (11) tooth removal, (12) cannibalism, (13) tatooing, (14) beating, (15) dress changes, (16) hairstyle changes, (17) blood rites, (18) sexual activity, (19) immersion in dust or filth, (20) making ceremonial offerings, (21) smoking or burning, and (22) other.

The secular focus elements are: (1) responsibility and obedience to elders and parents; (2) bravery, courage, and discipline; (3) emancipation from natal household; (4) tribal lore and customs; (5) moral code and precepts; (6) taboos and avoidance patterns; (7) honesty, integrity, and courage; (8) games, sports, and singing; (9) learning tribal friends and enemies; (10) tribal unity and peaceful relationships; (11) food restrictions; (12) etiquette; (13) status or position in tribe; (14) methods of gaining sustenance; (15) crafts and craft specialization; (16) tribal duties and obligations; (17) marriage, kinship, or tribal rules of conduct; (18) sexual restrictions; (19) magic, witchcraft, religion, and sorcery; (20) nature lore; (21) kinship obligations; (22) warfare and use of weapons; (23) legal and political decision making; (24) rules of conduct related to association; and (25) other.

4. The computer program, ORDMAT, was developed by Dr. Raoul Naroll and Rolf Wirsing at the State University of New York at Buffalo. This program is designed specifically for hologeistic research.

5. In coding it was sometimes difficult to distinguish between secret associations and limited nonsecret associations. Furthermore, it was found that in some cases limited nonsecret associations were functionally equivalent to secret associations in the sense that they were characterized by differentiation patterns. Therefore, the study's conclusions were based on considering both secret associations by themselves and by lumping together the societies with secret associations and limited nonsecret associations.

State societies tended to lack initiations. When initiations did exist it was found that they were usually open. It was also found that the associations entered were usually society-wide. This finding confirms the prediction that state initiations would be open; the prediction that state associations would be limited nonsecret is not supported, however.

REFERENCES

ALLEN, M. R. (1967) Male Cults and Secret Initiations in Melanesia. London: Melbourne University Press.

BENNETT, W. C. and R. M. ZINGG (1935) The Tarahumara: An Indian Tribe of Northern Mexico. Chicago: University of Chicago Press.

BETTELHEIM, B. (1954) Symbolic Wounds. Glencoe, Ill.: Free Press.

BROWN, J. K. (1963) "A cross-cultural study of female initiation rites." American Anthropologist 65, 4: 837-853.

BURTON, R. V. and J. W. M. WHITING (1961) "The absent father and cross-sex identity." Merrill-Palmer Quarterly of Behavior and Development 7, 2: 85-95.

COHEN, Y. A. (1971) "The shaping of men's minds: adaptations to imperatives of culture," pp. 19-50 in M. L. Wax, S. Diamond, and F. O. Gearing (eds.) Anthropological Perspectives on Education. New York: Basic Books.

——— (1964) The Transition from Childhood to Adolescence: Cross-Cultural Studies of Initiation Ceremonies, Legal Systems and Incest Taboos. Chicago: Aldine.

ELIADE, M. (1965) Birth and Rebirth: The Religious Meaning of Initiation in Human Culture. New York: Harper & Row.

FORTES, M. (1938) "Social and psychological aspects of education in Taleland." Supplement to Africa, Vol. 11, No. 4. London: Oxford University Press.

FREUD, S. (1952) Totem and Taboo. New York: Norton. (Originally published in 1928.)

GEARING, F. O. (1972a) "Anthropology and education," in J. Honigmann (ed.) Sourcebook in Social and Cultural Anthropology. Chicago: Rand McNally.

——— (1972b) "Where we are: where we might go: steps toward a general theory of cultural transmission." Paper presented at the American Anthropological Society Convention, Toronto (November).

GOODENOUGH, W. [ed.] (1964) Explorations in Cultural Anthropology. New York: McGraw-Hill.

HARRINGTON, C. (1968) "Sexual differentiation in socialization and some male genital mutilations." American Anthropologist 70, 5: 951-956.

HECKETHORN, C. W. (1965) The Secret Societies of All Ages and Countries. New Hyde Park, N.Y.: University Books.

HENRY, J. (1960) "A cross-cultural outline of education." Current Anthropology 1, 4: 267-305.

HERZOG, J. D. (1962) "Deliberate instruction and household structure: a cross-cultural study." Harvard Educational Review 32, 3: 301-342.

KÖBBEN, A. J. F. (1967) "Why exceptions? The logic of cross-cultural analysis." Current Anthropology 7, 1 and 2: 3-34.

LOWIE, R. H. (1961) Primitive Society. New York: Harper Torch Books. (Originally published in 1929.)

MILLER, N. (1932) "Initiation." Encyclopedia of the Social Sciences 8: 49-50.

MOORE, F. (1970) "The Human Relation Area Files," pp. 640-645 in R. Naroll and R. Cohen (eds.) A Handbook of Method in Cultural Anthropology. New York: Natural History Press.

MURDOCK, G. P. (1967) Ethnographic Atlas. Pittsburgh: University of Pittsburgh Press.

NAROLL, R. (1961) "Two solutions to Galton's problem." Philosophy of Science 18: 15-39.

——— (1962) Data Quality Control. New York: Free Press.

——— (1967) "The proposed HRAF probability sample." Behavior Science Notes 2: 70-80.

——— (1968) "Some thoughts on comparative method in cultural anthropology," pp. 236-277 in H. M. and Ann B. Blalock (eds.) Methodology in Social Research. New York: McGraw-Hill.

——— (1970a) "What have we learned from cross-cultural surveys?" American Anthropologist 72, 6: 1227-1288.

——— (1970b) "Galton's problem," pp. 974-989 in R. Naroll and R. Cohen (eds.) A Handbook of Method in Cultural Anthropology. New York: Natural History Press.

——— (1970c) "Data quality control," pp. 927-945 in R. Naroll and R. Cohen (eds.) A Handbook of Method in Cultural Anthropology. New York: Natural History Press.

———, W. ALNOT, J. CAPLAN, J. F. HANSEN, J. MAXANT, and N. SCHMIDT (1970) "A standard ethnographic sample: preliminary edition." Current Anthropology 11, 2: 235-248.

——— and R. COHEN [eds.] (1970) A Handbook of Method in Cultural Anthropology. Garden City, N.Y.: The Natural History Press.

——— and R. G. D'ANDRADE (1963) "Two further solutions to Galton's problem." American Anthropologist 65: 1053-1067.

POSPISIL, L. (1963) The Kapauku Papuans of West New Guinea. New York: Holt, Rinehart & Winston.

RADCLIFFE-BROWN, A. R. (1948) The Andaman Islanders. Glencoe, Ill.: Free Press.

REIK, T. (1946) Ritual: Four Psycho-Analytic Studies. New York: Grove Press.

SCHAEFER, J. M. (1969) "Linked pair alignments for the HRAF quality control sample universe." Behavior Science Notes 4, 4: 299-319.

SERVICE, R. (1962) Primitive Social Organization: An Evolutionary Perspective. New York: Random House.

TIGER, L. (1969) Men in Groups. New York: Random House.

VAN GENNEP, A. T. (1960) The Rites of Passage. Chicago: University of Chicago Press. (Originally published in 1909.)

WAX, M. L., S. DIAMOND, and F. O. GEARING [eds.] (1971) Anthropological Perspectives on Education. New York: Basic Books.

WEBSTER, H. (1968) Primitive Secret Societies. New York: Macmillan. (Originally published in 1932.)

WEBSTER, N. H. (1964) Secret Societies and Subversive Movements. London: Britons Publishing.

WHITING, J. W. M. (1964) "Effects of climate on certain cultural practices," pp. 175-195 in W. H. Goodenough (ed.) Explorations in Cultural Anthropology. New York: McGraw-Hill.

———, R. KLUCKHOHN, and A. ANTHONY (1958) "The function of male initiation ceremonies at puberty," pp. 359-370 in E. E. Maccoby, T. M. Newcomb, and E. L. Hartley (eds.) Readings in Social Psychology. New York: Henry Holt.

YOUNG, F. W. (1962) "The function of male initiation ceremonies: a cross-cultural test of an alternative hypothesis." American Journal of Sociology 67, 4: 379-396.

——— (1965) Initiation Ceremonies: A Cross-Cultural Study of Status Dramatization. Indianapolis: Bobbs-Merrill.

Chapter 10

PARENTAL ACCEPTANCE-REJECTION AND PERSONALITY DEVELOPMENT: A UNIVERSALIST APPROACH TO BEHAVIORAL SCIENCE

R O N A L D   P.   R O H N E R

University of Connecticut

In this chapter I ask the question, Do the personality and behavioral characteristics attributed by Western psychologists to parental acceptance-rejection appear in all human populations under comparable conditions regardless of cultural context, physical type, geographic region, or other limiting conditions? A basic issue here is one of distinguishing culture-bound or culturally dependent responses from universal causal-functional relationships. The issue of course really refers to the identification of any limiting condition—not simply culturally conditioned responses—that influence the effects of parental acceptance-rejection. This effort to establish scientifically derived generalizations about human behavior, generalizations that are species-wide in their applicability, is what I refer to as *a universalist approach to behavioral science.*

The universalist approach rests on at least three assumptions. First, the researcher must make a supposition comparable to the one anthropologists often call "the psychic unity of man": He must assume that all normal (i.e., nonpathological) humans are subject to the same developmental tendencies, and that at birth all normal humans share the same general capacities for thought, feeling, and action. Such an assumption must be at least implicit in a search for panhuman regularities in behavior. Second, insofar as these universalist principles are to be genuinely species-wide in their application, they must be based on a worldwide or pancultural sampling design. Third, proper employment of the universalist approach requires a multimethod research format.[1] Every methodology has certain limitations and built-in potential bias. And, of course, each methodology has its own peculiar strengths and advantages; each gives us certain kinds of information and not others. Thus, specific research results are often a function of the methods employed, but it is essential that the conclusions in comparative, universalist research remain free of any important "method effect"; that is, it is important that the results are not an artifact of the discrete measures or of the general methodology employed. Therefore at least two and preferably three independent *methodologies* are needed to successfully *triangulate* the results (See Figure 1) in order to determine the extent to which the same conclusions emerge from the use of different methodologies, each with its own weaknesses and potential for bias. The point, of course, is that our confidence is raised in our conclusions when we get the same results from multiple, independent tests, especially when these tests are performed by different methodologies. By the term "methodology" I refer to distinguishable classes, traditions, or paradigms of research, each having its own natural history, employing a somewhat different logic and basic assumptions—epistemology, as it were—and each of which comprises one or more discrete methods (i.e., measures) such as questionnaires, behavior observations, or field schedules. In this sense, then, the cross-cultural survey method is a methodology; it is a class of research that has a different logic, requires different assumptions about "the world," and commits researchers to different concrete procedures from, for example, the experimental method often used in psychology, or from anthropological fieldwork.

I should note here that the universalist approach also generally assumes a probability or statistical model of behavior, not a mechanical model where a single exception to a theory is sufficient evidence to discredit the theory. I assume as a matter of course that exceptions will occur in the research of behavioral scientists. The best we can hope for—at least at the moment—is that these theories will lead us to make predictions with tolerably few exceptions.[2]

A UNIVERSALIST APPROACH TO
THE STUDY OF PARENTAL ACCEPTANCE-REJECTION

I want to illustrate and elaborate on this argument by drawing data from the Rejection-Acceptance Project (RAP), a multimethod, cross-cultural research program initiated in 1960. As noted above, the project has as its ultimate objective the establishment of scientifically derived generalizations about the panhuman (species-wide) causes and consequences of parental acceptance and rejection.[3] To deal with issues as complex as the one outlined above, we employ a research strategy that incorporates three distinct methodological components. Figure 1 shows that each of the methodologies used in our research—the cross-cultural survey component, psychological research component, and intra-cultural community studies component, described later—produces partly overlapping results. It is in the hatched area where all three methodologies converge that the results have successfully survived the onslaught of the universalist research strategy, and thus it is in this area that species-wide principles are found.

The first and most highly developed component of the Rejection-Acceptance Project is the cross-cultural survey component which utilizes a sample of 101 societies from around the world to explore the implications of parental accep-

FIGURE I

TRIANGULATION OF METHODOLOGIES

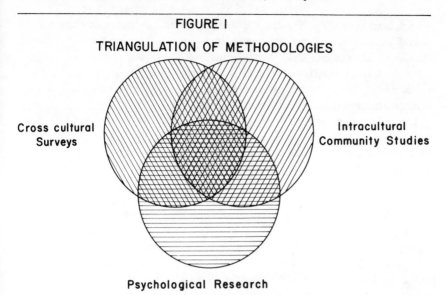

Cross cultural
Surveys

Intracultural
Community Studies

Psychological Research

tance and rejection for (1) aspects of personality development, (2) adult personality characteristics, and (3) institutionalized expressive systems including religious beliefs, certain medical beliefs, art forms, folklore and mythology—mainly nonutilitarian features of a social system that can be viewed as being expressive of personality. Finally, the cross-cultural survey component is used to (4) help discover the significant maintenance systems antecedents (including economic practices, political organization, and different aspects of social organization such as household size and composition) to parental acceptance-rejection.[4] The goal in both this component of the research and in the project as a whole is to develop a theory that will allow us to reliably predict specific environmental and maintenance systems conditions under which parents the world over reject or accept their children, as well as to predict the consequences of parental acceptance and rejection for personality development and for selected institutionalized expressive features of society.

The second component, the psychological research component, includes an intensive and systematic survey of the relevant psychological literature on the causes and consequences of acceptance-rejection. This survey also incorporates cross-species research on aspects of developmental psychobiology, ethological studies, and other disciplines relating to the maternal behavior of mammals (see for example, Denenberg, 1969; DeVore, 1963; Harlow, 1971). Moreover, this component involves our own research on topics of special concern to us such as research on child abuse, one dramatic form of parental rejection. Psychological research complements cross-cultural survey research in that the former deals with *interindividual* variability whereas cross-cultural survey research deals with *intercultural* variability. Scholars are often better able to manipulate and control variables experimentally in their psychological research within the United States than they can cross-culturally, but the cross-cultural survey component is also an essential part of this research because, among other things, it enables us to measure the extent to which conclusions reached in American psychological research are worldwide in their generalizability.

Intracultural community studies form the third component of the Rejection-Acceptance Project. This component involves anthropological and psychological field investigations of communities both within the United States and in culture areas outside North America. Sample communities around the world are studied in terms of the general cultural setting, parent-child relationships, personality assessment of children, and personality assessment of adults. Unlike the other two components, the community study component concentrates on *within-community* variability in behavior. That is, in every community some parents are warmer or more accepting than other parents, even though the general cultural norm may tend toward rejection. And we find similar variation in other relevant forms of behavior within all communities. The universalist theory in this research postulates that, regardless of the "culture" of a people, their physical type, or any other conditions that might alter their behavior, those children who receive significantly more warmth than others will develop specific characteristics that are like those children elsewhere—under widely different cultural or other conditions—who receive comparable amounts of affection. In fact, we expect children who are accepted in different societies (or under other conditions) to be more like each other in certain respects specified below, than they are like the other children in their own family who are rejected.

This technique of *subsystem replication* (i.e., testing within a single cultural system the results reached in cross-cultural surveys) contributes to the assessment of the validity and panhuman generalizability of results coming from our cross-cultural surveys and from the experimental and clinical research of Western psychology and allied disciplines. Because the results from this component are not yet in, the conclusions reached in this chapter only point in the direction we expect the ultimate "universalist principles" to take when the third component of the project is better developed.[5]

Nature of Parental Acceptance and Rejection. Parental acceptance-rejection is a unitary dimension of warmth and affection where rejection (i.e., the absence or significant withdrawal of warmth and affection) stands in opposition to acceptance (i.e., warmth and affection) on a graduated or continuous scale. The parental acceptance-rejection continuum is a universal dimension on which all humans can be placed because men everywhere, as children, experience more or less warmth and affection. I intend the concept of parental acceptance to be a descriptive, nonevaluative term referring to parent-child relationships that are characterized by displays of overt warmth and affection on the part of the parent to the child. Warmth and affection are revealed by parents playing with their child, comforting him, holding him, cuddling him, praising him, singing lullabies to him, caressing, fondling, consoling, and hugging or kissing him. Accepting parents generally like their child, and they take an interest in his activities and well being. They are not necessarily effusive or demonstrative in their affection, but they give affection without qualification. Parents are not necessarily warm, however, when they routinely care for or amuse their child as part of a schedule or as a matter of felt duty or responsibility. Parental rejection, on the other hand, is marked by the withdrawal or absence of warmth and affection on the part of the parent (PSA, see Note 3) toward the child.

Rejecting parents often dislike their child, disapprove of him, or resent him. In many instances they view him as a burden rather than as a pleasure, and they sometimes compare him unfavorably with other children. The absence of warmth and affection is revealed cross-culturally in two principal ways: by open or disguised hostility and aggression toward the child, or by parental indifference and neglect. Parental hostility is an internal reaction of anger, enmity, or resentment toward the child and may take the behavioral form of irritability, critical impatience, or antagonism toward the child. Such parents may make derogatory remarks to and about their child, and they often nag, scold, or ridicule him. They tell him how he gets on their nerves and they may curse him or speak to him in other harsh, deprecating tones of voice. Hostile parents may also be very rough or abrupt in their handling of their child, and they may punish their children often and severely.

Indifferent or neglectful parents are not necessarily aggressive toward their children; they may simply be unsympathetic, cold, and distant. Such parents often show a restricted concern for their child's welfare. They pay as little attention to him as they can, and they spend a minimum amount of time with him. When they are together they often ignore the child's requests for help, attention, or comfort. Not infrequently they forget promises they made to him and fail to attend to other details or needs important to his happiness or well being.

It is important to recognize that parental acceptance and rejection deal only with warmth and affection, and the various ways warmth and affection can be shown to or withdrawn from children such as in the form of aggression (hostility) or neglect (indifference). Other dimensions of parental behavior such as permissiveness (autonomy) and restrictiveness (control) must not be confused with acceptance-rejection. This latter dimension of parental behavior seems to be essentially independent of acceptance-rejection. That is, knowing that a child is accepted by his parents gives us little information about parent's permissiveness or restrictiveness. Very strict parents may accept their child, for example, or they may reject him; permissive parents may be equally variable in their warmth.

Studies within the United States suggest that rejection by itself seems to be sufficient to produce stark, massive, and often profoundly damaging consequences for growing children and for adults who were rejected as children. A review of the literature in the psychological sciences, for example, shows that, at least for Americans, parental rejection has profound consequences for personality development (see for example, Baldwin et al., 1949; Becker et al., 1962; Bowlby, 1951; Goldfarb, 1954; Sears et al., 1957; Wolberg, 1944), and that rejection is implicated in a wide range of personality and behavior problems such as various forms of psychopathology (see for example, Heilbrun, 1973; Kanner, 1949; Lidz et al., 1965; Lippman, 1956; Yarrow, 1961; but see also Farina, 1972); autism (see Kanner, 1949; Singer and Wynne, 1963); delinquency and conduct problems (see Becker, 1964; Becker et al., 1959, 1962; Cole, 1954; McCord and McCord, 1958; Shulman, 1949; Stagner, 1948; Symonds, 1939); psychosomatic reactions (see Miller and Baruch, 1948); poor concept formation (see Bender, 1947; Chambers, 1961); disturbed body image (see Schonfeld, 1966); stuttering (see Kinstler, 1961); intelligence (see Hurley, 1965); academic problems (see Levy, 1933; Rouman, 1956); anxiety (see Siegelman, 1965); insecurity (see Lowry, 1940; Siegelman, 1965). (For an expanded review of relevant literature on this problem see Rohner, forthcoming.)

Parental acceptance is associated with an utterly different constellation of traits in the United States. Describing a small part of these differences, Hartup and Yonas (1971: 372-373) conclude that

> An affiliative, person-oriented disposition is the outcome of nurturant attitudes and acceptance of the child by his parents. This pattern was found with the following dependent variables: (a) willingness to disclose things about oneself to others [Doster and Strickland, 1969], (b) expectations that the words, promises, and statements of other people are creditable [Katz and Rotter, 1969], (c) susceptibility to influence by both adults and peers [Medvene, 1969], (d) and attention to, seeking information from and compliance with maternal requests [Salmon, 1969]. Although none of the foregoing studies is strongly convincing by itself, the weight of the total evidence is substantial.

In this chapter I am principally concerned with a set of personality characteristics which we predict are *panhumanly* associated with parental acceptance-rejection. Specifically, I am most interested in six dimensions of behavior on which all humans can be located: (1) hostility, aggression, or passive aggression (or problems with the management of hostility and aggression), (2) dependence, (3) positive and negative self-evaluation, including feelings of self-esteem and self-adequacy, (4) emotional responsiveness, (5) positive and negative world view (evaluation of the world), and (6) emotional stability. These personality characteristics are operationalized below. It is important to keep in mind in the following definitions that we as individuals are not, for example, either dependent or independent, but that all of us are dependent (or independent) to a certain extent or in varying degrees. This continuum-like quality of the traits discussed below is not emphasized in the definitions, but this fact of variability among individuals should not be overlooked.

Hostility, Aggression, or Passive Aggression, and Problems with the Management of Hostility and Aggression

Hostility and (Active) Aggression. Hostility is an emotional (internal) reaction of anger, enmity, or resentment directed toward another person or situation. Hostility is expressed behaviorally (externally) in the form of aggression, an act that is intended to hurt someone or something, usually another person, but sometimes oneself. Active aggression may be verbally manifested, for example, in such forms as bickering, quarreling, telling someone off, sarcasm, or by making fun of someone, criticizing him, humiliating him, cursing him or by saying thoughtless, unkind or cruel things. Aggression may be physically revealed by fighting, hitting, kicking, biting, scratching, pinching, throwing things, or by other forms of destructiveness.

Passive Aggression. Passive aggression is a less direct expression of aggression in such forms as pouting, sulking, procrastination, stubbornness, passive obstructionism, bitterness, vindictiveness, irritability, and temper tantrums.

Problems with the Management of Hostility and Aggression. Sometimes an individual—adult or child—has conscious (recognized) or unconscious (unrecognized) difficulty coping with or managing his feelings of hostility, and he may have trouble expressing these feelings. In some social systems, in fact, adults are expected to inhibit almost all forms of aggression. Nonetheless these feelings of hostility are in one way or another likely to be expressed, at least in such disguised or symbolic forms as worried preoccupation about aggression, aggressive fantasies or dreams, anxiety over one's own real or fantasied aggression, unusual interest in hearing or talking about violent incidents, or by an unusual concern about the real or threatened aggression of others.

Dependence

Dependence is the *emotional* reliance of one person on another for comfort, guidance, support, reassurance, or decision making. Independence is the essential freedom from such emotional reliance.[6]

The goal of dependency behavior among children is usually the elicitation of warm, affectionate attention from an adult. Indicators of dependency among children include clinging to their mothers (PSA); seeking attention; becoming anxious, insecure, unhappy, weepy, or whiney when they are separated from their PSA; or waiting for or demanding the nurturant response of someone else (i.e., succorance).

Indicators of dependency among adults (as well as among children) include frequent seeking of comfort, nurturance, reassurance, support, approval, or guidance from others, especially those who are important to the individual, such as friends and family members including PSA. The dependent person attempts to solicit sympathy, consolation, encouragement, or affection from friends when he is troubled or having difficulty. He often seeks to have others help him when he is having personal problems, and he likes to have others feel sorry for him or to make a fuss over him when he is sick or hurt.

The independent person, on the other hand, does not rely heavily on others for emotional comfort, support, encouragement, or reassurance. He does not feel the need to evoke sympathy from his friends or family when he is troubled, and he does not often feel the need to seek reassurance, support, comfort, nurturance, or guidance.

Self-Evaluation (Self-Esteem and Self-Adequacy)

Self-evaluation consists of feelings about, attitudes toward, and perception of oneself, falling on a continuum from positive to negative. Self-evaluation consists of two related dimensions, self-esteem and self-adequacy.

Self-Esteem. Self-esteem is a global, emotional, evaluation of oneself in terms of worth. Feelings of positive self-esteem imply that a person likes or approves of himself, accepts himself, is comfortable with himself, is rarely disappointed in himself, and perceives himself as being a person of worth, or worthy of respect. Negative self-esteem, on the other hand, implies that a person dislikes or disapproves of himself, is uncomfortable with himself, is disappointed in himself, devaluates himself, perhaps feels inferior to others, and perceives himself as being essentially a worthless person or as being worthy of condemnation.

Self-Adequacy. Self-adequacy is an overall self-evaluation of one's *competence* to perform daily tasks adequately, to cope satisfactorily with daily problems, and to satisfy one's own needs. Feelings of positive self-adequacy imply that a person views himself as being a capable person, able to deal satisfactorily with his daily problems; he feels that he is a success in the things he sets out to do; he is self-assured or self-confident and feels socially adequate.

Feelings of negative self-adequacy, on the other hand, imply that a person feels he is an incompetent person, unable to meet or cope successfully with the demands of day-to-day living. He lacks confident self-assurance, often feeling inept, and he sees himself as a failure and as being unable to compete successfully for the things he wants.

Emotional Responsiveness

Emotional responsiveness refers to a person's ability to express freely and openly his emotions, for example, feelings of warmth and affection. Emotional responsiveness is revealed by the spontaneity and ease with which a person is able to respond emotionally to another person. That is, emotionally responsive people have no difficulty forming warm, intimate, involved, and lasting attachments. Their attachments are not troubled by emotional constriction or defensiveness. They are able to show spontaneous affection toward their friends and family, and they are easily able to act out their sympathy and other feelings on appropriate occasions. Interpersonal relations of emotionally responsive people tend to be close and personal, and such persons have no trouble responding emotionally to the friendship advances of others.

Emotionally unresponsive or insulated people, on the other hand, are able to form only restricted or defensive emotional involvements. They may be friendly and sociable, but their friendships tend to be impersonal and emotionally unexpressive. Emotionally unresponsive people may be cold, detached, aloof, or unexpressive, and they may lack spontaneity. They often have difficulty or are unable to give or receive normal affection, and under extreme conditions they may be apathetic or emotionally bland or flat.

Evaluation of the World (World View)

"World view" is a person's often unverbalized, global, or overall evaluation of life and the universe as being essentially a positive or negative place, that is, as being basically good, secure, friendly, happy, and unthreatening with few dangers (positive), or as being bad, insecure, threatening, unpleasant and hostile, or uncertain and full of dangers (negative). World view refers to one's conception of and feelings about the basic nature of the cosmos and of life itself; it does not refer to his empirically derived knowledge of the economic, political, social, or natural environment in which he lives.

Emotional Stability

Emotional stability refers to an individual's constancy or steadiness of mood and to his ability to withstand minor setbacks, failures, difficulties, or other stresses without becoming emotionally upset. An emotionally stable person is able to maintain his composure under minor emotional stress. He is not easily or quickly excited or angered, and he is fairly constant in his basic mood.

Emotionally unstable people, on the other hand, are subject to fairly wide, frequent, and unpredictable mood shifts which swing from such poles as cheery to gloomy, happy to unhappy, contented to dissatisfied, or friendly to hostile. Such persons are often easily upset by small setbacks or difficulties, and they tend to lose composure under minor stress. Many emotionally unstable people are excitable or get angry easily and quickly.

The personality characteristics just defined in no sense represent a complete roster of the consequences of rejection. These traits do serve as a point of focus, however, because in our cross-cultural survey data discussed below they appear to form an interrelated constellation within the rejected child and in adults who were rejected as children.

EVIDENCE REGARDING THE WORLDWIDE
EFFECTS OF REJECTION-ACCEPTANCE

With few exceptions the conclusions reached by American psychologists and psychiatrists in the psychological research component regarding the effects of parental rejection are supported by data in the cross-cultural survey component cited in Table 1. This is reassuring for the universalist theory in our research because as Dawson (1971), Jahoda (1970), Triandis (1964), and others have pointed out, the results of American and European psychological research cannot necessarily be assumed to have universal validity. Indeed the behavioral science literature is replete with cases where the results of tests among non-Western peoples are very different from the results found in psychological studies within the United States.

As shown in the cross-cultural data in Table 1, rejected children the world

TABLE 1

RELATIONSHIP BETWEEN PARENTAL ACCEPTANCE-REJECTION
AND PERSONALITY DEVELOPMENT

Personality Characteristic	Children			Adults		
	r	p <	N	r	p <	N
Hostility	-.48	.0001	60	-.31	.005	75
Dependence	-.30	.05	42	-.39	.01	40
Self-evaluation	.72	.01	11	.38	.025	33
Emotional responsiveness				.49	.0001	75
World view				.27	.025	68
Emotional stability				.62	.001	38
Generosity				.41	.005	42
Nurturance				.39	.025	35
Conflict over nurturance	-.36	.025	37			

NOTE: Correlations are Pearson r's. The first six traits were coded in the Rejection-Acceptance Project (see Rohner, forthcoming). Codes for "generosity" were taken from Bacon et al. (1963); codes and definitions for "nurturance" and "conflict over nurturance" are published in Barry et al. (1967).

over are hostile, aggressive, or passive-aggressive.[7] Numerous psychological studies in the United States support this conclusion (see for example, Becker, 1962; Feshbach, 1970; McCord and McCord, 1958; Stagner, 1948). Data in Table 1 also support the hypothesis explained in the next section that parental rejection is universally related to dependency in children, and again this conclusion is sustained by clinical and experimental research in Western psychology (see Brody, 1969; Finney, 1961; Maccoby and Masters, 1970; Wolberg, 1944). Dependency (and probably emotional unresponsiveness) may also be related to rejected children's "conflict over nurturance" reported in Table 1, that is, to their conflict over a positive desire to give succorance or love, on the one hand—especially to people in need—and to their fear or anxiety, on the other hand, about committing themselves emotionally and thus exposing themselves to the threat of further rejection. The correlations in Table 1 also show that rejected children tend panculturally to devaluate themselves, to dislike themselves, to be uncomfortable with themselves, and to perceive themselves as being worthless or worthy of condemnation. The research of Coopersmith (1967), Sears (1970), and other North American psychologists reinforces this conclusion.

We are unable to make reliable pancultural measures of children's emotional responsiveness, world view, and emotional stability—three personality traits discussed earlier—because anthropologists rarely report on these characteristics within the age range of special interest to us.[8] But by the same token, American psychologists have given only the most modest of attention to the relationship between rejection-acceptance and emotional responsiveness in children (e.g., Hattwick, 1936; Siegelman, 1965, 1966), and the association between parental rejection and emotional instability seems to be barely explored in the psychological sciences (see Feshbach, 1970: 218). Moreover, so far as I know, no psychological study in the United States has yet looked directly at the relationship between rejection and children's world views.

We do have adequate cross-cultural measures of all these personality characteristics in adults, however. Table 1 shows, for example, that adults who were rejected as children tend the world over to be emotionally unresponsive. That is, they encyst their emotions in a cocoon, as it were, and as a result they are unable to become deeply involved in affectionate, responsive relationships with others. Moreover they are less emotionally stable than accepted adults: they tend to lose their composure under minor emotional stress, and many adults who were rejected as children are subject to wide, frequent, and often unpredictable shifts in mood. In addition, Table 1 reveals that adults who were rejected as children are hostile, aggressive, or passive aggressive, and they are more emotionally dependent than adults who were accepted as children. They also tend to devaluate their feelings of self-adequacy and self-esteem (i.e., negative self-evaluation).

Additionally, as predicted by the universalist theory discussed below, several of these features, especially hostility and low self-evaluation, combine to produce a negative world view in adults who had been rejected as children. Such adults are inclined to view the world, life—the very universe itself—as being an unfriendly, uncertain, insecure, and often hostile place in which to live. Not surprisingly many of these adults around the world are nonnurturant in their relations with others—not simply with children but with other adults as well. They are less likely than adults who had been accepted as children to give sympathy, comfort, or support spontaneously to people who are in need, who are sick, lonely, or disabled. And they are, as shown in the cross-cultural data of Table 1, less generous than adults who had earlier been accepted. It is instructive to note here that two American psychologists, Rutherford and Mussen (1968), also find generosity related to rejection-acceptance: generous nursery school boys perceive their fathers as warmer and more sympathetic than nongenerous boys.

I should note here that cross-cultural survey research does not measure the actual development of children as they grow into adulthood; rather, measurements are made of the personality of children and of adults as they exist now, at a single moment in time, as it were. Thus, we could interpret the data regarding adults in the cross-cultural survey component of this research to mean that adults who are emotionally unresponsive tend, as parents, to reject their children more often than responsive adults (rather than interpret these data as showing that rejected children become emotionally unresponsive and continue to be unresponsive as adults). Indeed this conclusion is correct insofar as emotionally insulated adults are unable to give warmth and affection to their children. We know of no empirical data or theoretical rationale, however, to expect dependent adults to be more rejecting than independent adults, or, perhaps, for adults with a negative world view to be more rejecting than those with a positive world view. More important, we cannot explain why adults should have the total constellation of traits that we predict will emerge as a result of rejection if our data do not, for the most part, reflect a longitudinal continuity of personal characteristics.

This presumption of continuity is valid, however, only insofar as evidence can be marshaled that the child-rearing practices in the sample societies have maintained reasonable stability across at least two generations, that is, that the parents themselves were treated in about the same way as they now treat their own children. A careful review of the ethnographic literature shows that about 90% of the present sample for which measurements could be made had maintained appreciable cultural stability with regard to child training practices for about twenty-five years prior to the time of fieldwork. Given this information, along with the massive supporting evidence regarding the consequences of parental rejection in the psychological literature in America, we conclude that we are not in great danger of seriously misinterpreting the data when we conclude in the cross-cultural survey component of this research that the relationship between parental behavior and adult personality suggests a basic continuity over time.

THEORETICAL EXPLANATION OF TRAITS ASSOCIATED WITH ACCEPTANCE-REJECTION

The results reported in Table 1 were predicted in advance by our universalist theory in the Rejection-Acceptance Project. This theory begins with the basic assumption that all human beings have a profound, generalized need for positive response (love, approval, warmth, affection) from the people who are important to them. The bare, minimal care we as humans must have for physical survival is not enough for normal psychosocial development. I do not know whether this need for positive response is somehow rooted in man's biological-evolutionary development, or whether it is learned in the context of total infantile dependency, or indeed as I suspect, whether these two factors are interrelated. But whatever the explanation, the absence or significant withdrawal of warmth and affection is sufficient by itself to produce massive consequences for personality functioning. For example, rejection inhibits or distorts aspects of normal personality functioning such as feelings of positive self-esteem and self-adequacy (i.e., positive self-evaluation). All of us tend to view ourselves as we imagine "significant others" view us, and if as children our parents rejected us, we are likely to define ourselves as *unworthy* of love, and as unworthy and inadequate human beings. In this way we develop a sense of overall negative self-evaluation. Moreover, rejected children are likely to be more dependent—to seek parental approval, nurturance, attention, and physical contact—than the accepted child. As we noted earlier, all humans have a basic need for positive response, but if a child's "significant others" are rejecting, his needs for warmth and affection are unfulfilled and he will, *up to a point,* increase his efforts to get love and attention. That is, he will become dependent.

Beyond a certain point, however, the dependency response may be extinguished. That is, the seriously rejected child has not learned how to give love because he has never known a loving parent after whom he can model his own behavior; and, for reasons described below, even though he craves affection, he has difficulty accepting it. To protect himself from more emotional hurt, he tends to wrap his emotions in cotton, to encyst his emotions, and ultimately he stops trying to get affection from the people who are important to him (i.e., dependency responses disappear). Thus the rejected child becomes emotionally insulated, unable to freely and openly form warm, lasting intimate relations with others. His attachments tend to be troubled by emotional constriction or defensiveness; and in extreme cases, the rejected child may become apathetic or emotionally bland or flat. In addition, as a result of the massive psychological damage brought about by rejection, the rejected child is inclined to have less tolerance for stress, and he is therefore likely to be less emotionally stable than children who are accepted.

Resulting from the frustration of his dependency needs and other basic proclivities—and as a manifestation of his emotional instability—the rejected child typically becomes hostile, aggressive, or passive-aggressive. He is especially apt to be hostile and aggressive if rejection takes the form of parental hostility. Under these conditions the child is provided with a hostile model whom he may emulate, and thus his own hostile responses may intensify (see Bandura and Walters, 1963). In societies where persons are not allowed to express aggression overtly, however, rejected children are apt to have problems managing their hostility. Suppressed, over-controlled aggression, though, is often expressed in such disguised or symbolic forms as worried preoccupation about aggression, aggressive fantasies or dreams, or by an unusual concern about the real or imagined aggression of others.

Finally, the rejected child, one who is anxious, hostile, insecure, and emotionally unstable, and who devalues his feelings of self-worth and self-adequacy, is likely to generalize these feelings onto the nature of the world as being an unfriendly, hostile, unpleasant place in which to live. Any child who has experienced so much psychological hurt at the hands of the people who are most important to him comes to expect very little more from life itself. The very nature of life for him is threatening, dangerous, and an unhappy experience. That is, this child is likely to develop a negative world view.

In the absence of positive, counteracting experiences over time (such as rewarding peer group relations), these rejected children are likely to grow into adults who are hostile, insecure, dependent; who have feelings of low self-esteem and low self-adequacy; and who have a negative world view. Moreover, adults who were rejected as children tend to have strong needs for affection, but they are unable to return it because they have become more-or-less emotionally insulated or unresponsive to potentially close interpersonal relations. Adults who were unloved as children are also inclined to have less tolerance for stress and for this reason they are less emotionally stable then adults who were accepted as children. These adults who become parents are therefore much more likely to reject their own children than parents who were accepted. In this way the rejection cycle is perpetuated—and along with it the personality syndrome I have just described.

CONCLUSION

At the beginning of this paper the question was asked: Do the personality and behavior characteristics attributed by Western psychologists to parental acceptance-rejection appear in all human populations under comparable conditions regardless of cultural context, physical type, geographic region, or other limiting condition? The answer to this question now seems to be unequivocally, Yes, they do! Despite the enormous differences in culture, physical type, and other potentially limiting conditions in the 101 societies of our worldwide sample, almost all of the conclusions reached by psychologists and psychiatrists within the United States regarding the effects of parental acceptance-rejection are supported by our cross-cultural data. Thus, with these mutually supportive sources of information, the cross-cultural survey data and the psychological research data, we may conclude that in all likelihood we have identified several species-wide "principles" of human behavior. We cannot be unquestionably confident of the universal generalizability of these statements, however, until we have collected data from the intracultural community studies. If, as we fully expect, the community studies confirm the conclusions drawn from the other two components of our project, we will have decisive empirical evidence for making positive assertions about the "nature of human nature" insofar as this nature is revealed in the worldwide causes and consequences of parental acceptance and rejection.

NOTES

1. As an editors' note, the reader may see a striking resemblance between Professor Rohner's call for a multimethod research format (Figure 1) and the multitrait-multimethod matrix proposed by Campbell and Fiske (1959). Rohner is aware of the similarity, of course, but the subtle distinction to be noted in Figure 1 is that Rohner is recommending a multi(discipline) matrix which would unite psychological methods, survey methods, and perhaps even hologeistic methods (see Chapter 9 in this volume).

2. The serious scholar will naturally want to try to account for the exceptions to his theory, and thus he will continually revise his theory. The universalist approach and the other topics covered in this paper are described at greater length in Rohner (forthcoming).

3. Unless it is clear from the context that I am talking about the biological parents of a child, the term "parent" in this paper refers to a child's primary socializing agent (PSA), that is, whoever it is that assumes routine daily care or responsibility for a child. In many societies the PSA may be an older sibling or a grandparent.

4. The cross-cultural survey method is a technique where a worldwide sample of ethnographies (i.e., societies) is coded for specific variables in order to test hypotheses statistically about the pancultural workings of psychological processes, or of social and cultural systems. Readers who would like more detail about the methodological procedures, codes, and so forth used in the cross-cultural survey component of the Rejection-Acceptance Project (on which a substantial part of this paper is based) are encouraged to read Rohner (1970), Rohner (forthcoming b), and Rohner and Katz (1970). I (Rohner, forthcoming a) will later provide a comprehensive treatment of the methodological problems involved in the cross-cultural survey method, including this project. Many of the significant issues involved in the cross-cultural survey method are discussed in Naroll and Cohen (1970).

5. One community study is now being concluded in a peasant Turkish village; a second was terminated in Newfoundland. In time we plan to study approximately twelve communities around the world using the RAP community-study methodology. This paper concentrates on data from the cross-cultural survey component and from the psychological

research component of the project. Specifically, I focus on the implications of parental acceptance-rejection for *personality functioning* in children and in adults. This chapter does not deal with the important problem—especially to anthropologists—of the social and cultural contexts in which rejection-acceptance occur. Other writings (see especially Rohner, forthcoming) concentrate on this issue.

6. Some scholars (e.g., Beller, 1955; Heathers, 1955) prefer to conceptually distinguish "dependence" from "independence." They define the term dependence as we do, but they reserve the term independence for forms of behavior we call, but do not define here, self-reliance. The contrast between these usages is essentially one of *emotional* versus *instrumental* reliance (or dependence) of one person upon another, a distinction that is not always easy to make behaviorally.

7. We were unable to make confident judgments in the anthropological literature about disguised or symbolic expressions of aggression. Had we been able to reliably identify such behavior, the relationship between hostility and rejection-acceptance reported in Table 1 would probably have been much stronger than r = -.48.

8. In the cross-cultural survey component of our research, we are principally concerned with children from the ages of two to six, or for as long before two or after six as the parent-child relationship remains fairly stable. We chose these ages because, by the time a child is two, he has begun to learn complex symbolic skills, most notably language, and the effects of rejection become most clearly measurable in the ethnographic literature. In addition, parents or other socializing agents typically remain of fundamental importance to him until he reaches about six years of age. At this time his interests begin to expand and other people, such as peers, become increasingly important. It becomes difficult to sort out the effects of parental behavior from other social experiences when this happens. The variable "conflict over nurturance" reported in Table 1, however, relates to children from about ages five to twelve.

REFERENCES

BACON, M. K., I. L. CHILD, and H. BARRY, III (1963) "Cross-cultural study of correlates of crime." Journal of Abnormal Psychology 66: 291-300.

BALDWIN, A. L., J. KALHORN, and F. H. BREESE (1949) "The appraisal of parent behavior." Psychological Monograph 63: 4.

BANDURA, A., and R. H. WALTERS (1963) Social Learning and Personality Development. New York: Holt, Rinehart & Winston.

BARRY, H., III, M. K. BACON, and I. L. CHILD (1967) "Definitions, ratings, and bibliographic sources for child-training practices of 110 cultures," pp. 293-331 in C. S. Ford (ed.) Cross-Cultural Approaches. New Haven, Conn.: HRAF Press.

BECKER, W. C. (1962) "Developmental psychology," pp. 1-34 in Annual Review of Psychology. Vol. 13. Palo Alto, Calif.: Annual Reviews.

——— (1964) "Consequences of different kinds of parental disciplines," pp. 169-208 in M. Hoffman and L. Hoffman (eds.) Review of Child Development Research. Vol. 1. New York: Russell Sage Foundation.

———, D. R. PETERSON, L. A. HELLMER, D. J. SHOEMAKER, and H. C. QUAY (1959) "Factors in parental behavior and personality as related to problem behavior in children." Journal of Consulting Psychology 23: 107–118.

BECKER, W. C., D. R. PETERSON, Z. LURIA, D. J. SHOEMAKER, and L. A. HELMER (1962) "Relations of factors derived from parent interview ratings to behavior problems of five-year olds." Child Development 33: 509-533.

BELLER, E. K. (1955) "Dependency and independence in young children." Journal of Genetic Psychology 87: 25-35.

BENDER, L. (1947) "Psychopathic behavior disorders in children," pp. 360-377 in R. M. Lindner and R. V. Seliger (eds.) Handbook of Correctional Psychology. New York: Philosophical Library.

BOWLBY, J. (1951) "Maternal care and mental health." World Health Organization Bulletin 3: 355-534.

BRODY, G. F. (1969) "Maternal child-rearing attitudes and child behavior." Developmental Psychology 1: 66.

CAMPBELL, D. T. and D. W. FISKE (1959) "Convergent and discriminant validity by the multitrait-multimethod matrix." Psychological Bulletin 56: 81-105.

CHAMBERS, J. (1961) "Maternal deprivation and the concept of time in children." American Journal of Orthopsychiatry 31: 406.

COLE, L. (1954) Psychology of Adolescence. New York: Rinehart.

COOPERSMITH, S. (1967) The Antecedents of Self-Esteem. San Francisco: W. H. Freeman.

DAWSON, J. L. M. (1971) "Theory and research in cross-cultural psychology." Bulletin of the British Psychological Society 24: 291-306.

DENENBERG, V. H. (1969) "Animal studies of early experiences: some principles which have implications for human development," pp. 31-45 in John Hill (ed.) Minnesota Symposium on Child Psychology. Minneapolis: University of Minnesota Press.

DeVORE, I. (1963) "Mother-infant relations in free ranging baboon," pp. 305-335 in H. L. Rheingold (ed.) Maternal Behavior in Mammals. New York: John Wiley.

DOSTER, J. A. and B. R. STRICKLAND (1969) "Perceived child-rearing practices and self disclosure patterns." Journal of Consulting Clinical Psychology 33: 382.

FARINA, A. (1972) Schizophrenia. Morristown, N.J.: General Learning Press.

FESHBACH, S. (1970) "Aggression," pp. 159-259 in P. H. Mussen (ed.) Carmichael's Manual of Child Psychology. Vol. 2. New York: John Wiley.

FINNEY, J. C. (1961) "Some maternal influences in childrens' personality and character." Genetic Psychology Monograph 63: 199-278.

GOLDFARB, W. (1954) "Psychological privation in infancy and subsequent adjustment," pp. 397-403 in W. E. Martin and C. B. Stendler (eds.) Readings in Child Development. New York: Harcourt Brace Jovanovich.

HARLOW, H. F. (1971) Learning to Love. San Francisco: Albion.

HARTUP, W. and A. YONAS (1971) "Developmental psychology," pp. 337-392 in P. Mussen and M. R. Rosenzweig (eds.) Annual Review of Psychology. Vol. 22. Palo Alto, Calif.: Annual Reviews.

HATTWICK, B. W. (1936) "Interrelations between pre-school children's behavior and certain factors in the home." Child Development 7: 200-226.

HEATHERS, G. (1955) "Emotional dependence and independence in nursery school play." Journal of Genetic Psychology 87: 37-57.

HEILBRUN, A. B., Jr. (1973) Aversive Maternal Control: A Theory of Schizophenic Development. New York: John Wiley.

HURLEY, J. R. (1965) "Parental acceptance-rejection and children's intelligence." Merrill Palmer Quarterly 11: 19-31.

JAHODA, G. (1970) "A cross-cultural perspective in psychology." The Advancement of Science 27: 57-70.

KANNER, L. (1949) "Problems of nosology and psychodynamics of early infantile autism." American Journal of Orthopsychiatry 19: 416-426.

KATZ, H. A. and J. B. ROTTER (1969) "Interpersonal trust scores of college students and their parents." Child Development 40: 657-660.

KINSTLER, D. B. (1961) "Covert and overt maternal rejection in stuttering." Journal of Speech and Hearing Disorders 26: 145-155.

LEVY, D. M. (1933) "Relation of maternal overprotection to school grades and intelligence tests." American Journal of Orthopsychiatry 3: 26-34.

LIDZ, T., S. FLECK, and A. CORNELISON (1965) Schizophrenia and the Family. New York: International University Press.

LIPPMAN, H. (1956) Treatment of the Child in Emotional Conflict. New York: McGraw-Hill.

LOWRY, L. G. (1940) "Personality distortion and early institutional care." American Journal of Orthopsychiatry 10: 576-585.

MACCOBY, E. and J. C. MASTERS (1970) "Attachment and dependency," pp. 73-158, in P. Mussen (ed.) Carmichael's Manual of Child Psychology. Vol. 2. New York: John Wiley.

McCORD, J. and W. McCORD (1958) "The effects of parental role model on criminality." Journal of Social Issues 14: 66-75.

McCORD, W., J. McCORD and A. HOWARD (1961) "Familial correlates of aggression in non-delinquent male children." Journal of Abnormal and Social Psychology 62: 79-93.

MEDVENE, A. M. (1969) "Occupational choice of graduate students in psychology as a function of early parent-child interactions." Journal of Consulting Psychology 16: 385-389.

MILLER, H. and D. W. BARUCH (1948) "Psychosomatic studies of children with allergic manifestations: I, maternal rejection: a study of 63 cases." Psychosomatic Medicine 10: 275-278.

NAROLL, R. and R. COHEN [eds.] (1970) A Handbook of Method in Cultural Anthropology. Garden City, N.Y.: Natural History Press.

ROHNER, R. P. (1970) "Parental rejection, food deprivation, and personality development: tests of alternative hypotheses." Ethnology 9: 414-427.

——— (forthcoming a) The Cross-Cultural Method. New York: Holt, Rinehart & Winston.

——— (forthcoming b) They Love Me, They Love Me Not: The Universalist Approach to Behavioral Science.

——— and L. KATZ (1970) "Testing for validity and reliability in cross-cultural research." American Anthropologist 72: 1068-1073.

ROUMAN, J. (1956) "School children's problems as related to parental factors." Journal of Educational Research 50: 105-112.

RUTHERFORD, E. and P. MUSSEN (1968) "Generosity in nursery school boys." Child Development 39: 755-766.

SALMON, P. (1969) "Differential conforming as a developmental process." British Journal of Social and Clinical Psychology 8: 22-31.

SCHONFELD, W. A. (1966) "Body image disturbances in adolescence: IV. Influence of family attitudes and psychopathology." Archives of General Psychiatry 15: 16-21.

SEARS, R. (1970) "Relation of early socialization experiences to self-concepts and gender role in middle childhood." Child Development 41: 267-289.

———, E. E. MACCOBY, and H. LEVIN (1957) Patterns of Child Rearing. Evanston, Ill.: Row, Peterson.

SHULMAN, H. M. (1949) "The family and juvenile delinquency." Annals of the American Academy of Political and Social Science 261: 21-31.

SIEGELMAN, M. (1965) "Personality correlates of early parent-child relationships." Journal of Consulting Psychology 29: 559-564.

——— (1966) "Loving and punishing parental behavior and introversion tendencies in sons." Child Development 37: 985-999.

SINGER, M. T. and L. C. WYNNE (1963) "Differentiating characteristics of parents of childhood schizophrenics, childhood neurotics and young adult schizophrenics." American Journal of Psychiatry 120: 234-243.

STAGNER, R. (1948) Psychology of Personality. New York: McGraw-Hill.

SYMONDS, P. M. (1939) The Psychology of Parent-Child Relationships. New York: Appleton-Century.

TRIANDIS, H. C. (1964) "Cultural influences in cognitive processes," pp. 1-48 in L. Berkowitz (ed.) Advances in Experimental Social Psychology. Vol. 1. New York: Academic Press.

WOLBERG, L. R. (1944) "The character structure of the rejected child." Nervous Child 3: 74-88.

YARROW, L. J. (1961) "Maternal deprivation: toward an empirical and conceptual reevaluation." Psychological Bulletin 58: 459.

PART FOUR.

APPROACHES FROM DIFFERENT PERSPECTIVES

Chapter 11

RESOCIALIZATION INTO CULTURE: THE COMPLEXITIES OF TAKING A WORLDWIDE VIEW OF PSYCHOTHERAPY

JURIS G. DRAGUNS

Pennsylvania State University

In the foreword to a recent book of readings on cross-cultural psychology, Price-Williams (1970) commented on the autonomy of the two fields of cross-cultural study of normal behavior and of its psychopathological deviations. Each of these two new and growing subdisciplines has its journals, conferences, and citation circuits. This dichotomization in the cross-cultural investigation of normal and pathological variants of adaptation is consonant with the medical model that, in its crystallized variations, holds that the field of psychopathology is a matter of a finite number of qualitatively distinct afflictions and diseases to be counteracted by specialized medical procedures, one of which is psychotherapy (Draguns and Phillips, 1971; Price, 1972). The opponents of this view reject the notion of psychopathology as alien to, and discontinuous with, the person's premorbid adaptive pattern and his milieu's prevailing mechanisms of adaptation (Phillips, 1968). Instead, psychopathology is viewed as a continuation of adaptation by other means and one that exaggerates the normal techniques of adjustment and survival beyond their limits of functional usefulness. Abnormal behavior, then, is a caricature of its culture.

Within this framework, psychotherapy, the theme of this chapter, is not viewed as a set of specialized techniques of treatment, but as a much broader cluster of procedures aimed at redressing the balance between the individual and his society. Extending Precourt's formulation (see Chapter 9 of this volume), psychotherapy can be conceived as a series of reinitiation techniques for reentry into fuller, more efficient participation in society. Psychotherapy then is always a procedure that is sociocultural in its ends and interpersonal in its means; it occurs between two or more individuals and is embedded in a broader, less visible, but no less real cultural context of shared social learning, store of meanings, symbols, and implicit assumptions concerning the nature of social living.

These considerations, however, do not exhaust the cultural relevance of psychotherapy. Psychotherapy is the only global open-ended procedure for "changing people," that is, for modifying personalities, currently at the disposal of social scientists. To be sure, personality change occurs in, and is brought about by, personal trauma, coercive social pressure, thought reform, religious conversion, or political commitment (see Worchel and Byrne, 1964). In all of these instances, however, for a variety of ethical and practical reasons, the social scientist remains a bystander, at most an observer. In the case of psychotherapy, he is the agent and catalyst of personality change brought about in a voluntary and consenting client.

Of late, moreover, psychotherapy has crossed the invisible and shifting line between abnormality and normality in the guise of sensitivity training, encounter groups, marathon experiences, and similar developments, all of which can be legitimately regarded as derivations from psychotherapeutic techniques and procedures. There is ample justification for caution in appraising the status and promise of these new approaches, and especially of their numerous wild variants. There is, however, little reason to object to the general thrust of these new people-changing, global, open-ended, and hence, broadly therapeutic procedures beyond the mere alleviation of distress and toward the potentiation of personal growth and development. What this trend suggests is that psychotherapy is too broad to be confined within a psychopathological or a "mental health" framework. Potentially at least, psychotherapy is a procedure that is applicable in educational, employment, community organization, and other contexts. Its intercultural potential in the area of conflict management and resolution is illustrated in the work by Doob (1970).

Moreover, the objectives of all psychotherapeutic intervention are anchored to cultural goals. Broadly speaking, individuals seek psychotherapeutic help for two general classes of reasons: (1) they feel too confined, pressured, and inhibited by forces outside themselves, either actually experienced as such or internalized, or (2) their behavior is judged too rebellious, aggressive, or nonconforming to be tolerated by their social milieu. Historically, Freud's case material (e.g., Freud and Breuer, 1959) provides ample illustrations of the former class of therapy seekers: late Victorians excessively proper and oversocialized, paying in symptoms a high price for their precarious, if morally upright, adaptation. More recently, Mowrer (1960) has called attention to the latter category of candidates for psychotherapy: those with insufficient internalization of values and sanctions normally inculcated in the course of socialization, inadequately equipped with controls and scruples. While these two models of therapy seeking are sometimes polemically presented as general theories of psychopathology, any therapist or therapy supervisor with a sizable case load, at least in those social and cultural settings with which I am familiar, can easily provide exemplars of both of these broad classes of presenting problems in psychotherapy.

In the present context, the underlying similarities between these two classes of individuals are more significant than their readily apparent differences. In both instances, we are dealing with persons whose normal equilibrium between themselves and their social environment has been upset. Against this background, psychotherapy can be construed as an avenue of resocialization, an arena for completion or revision of social learning, aimed at bringing about a more stable and satisfactory relationship between the individual and his society. With symptom neurotics such as the ones that Freud typically treated, the objective is to increase the individual's experienced degrees of freedom in public behavior and private thought. In cases of character neurosis and personality disturbance that consume an even larger share of therapeutic energies, at least in the United States and other countries in the West, it is to regulate and control the behavior of the client more reliably, realistically, and efficiently than his incomplete or faulty socialization hitherto permitted him to do. In reference to the dichotomy recently brought to the fore by the French social psychologist, Vexliard (1967, 1968), the ends of psychotherapy are to make the client's behavior more alloplastic in the former and more autoplastic in the latter case. Thus, psychotherapy either strives to bring about a greater individuation, the liberation of the person to act upon his environment more actively and assertively than he thought possible, or a greater degree of socialization, a more complete acceptance of the social constraints thought to be desirable or even indispensable in a given social milieu. A special case is one that requires readaptation to abrupt or rapid social change, as with modernization sweeping away not only archaic technology, but a great many deeply ingrained values and beliefs, or with temporary confusion and disorientation faced upon first personal contact with an alien and different culture. Seward (1956) describes a great many instances of role conflict and value clash, revealed and externalized in the psychotherapy experience of those individuals who are products of two or more modes of culture heritage. A substantial literature has accrued on the uses of psychotherapy as an aid in the adaptation of individuals removed from their customary habitat to a new one as sojourners or immigrants (e.g., Murphy, 1955).

The main concern in this presentation is with the manner in which different societies discharge their therapeutic tasks. On a rational basis alone, it is to be expected that cultures would differ in their typical therapeutic techniques, and indeed they do. A rich anthropological and psychiatric documentation on this subject has accumulated over the past seventy years or more. This store of information is nowhere encyclopedically gathered or reviewed, although several recent writings (Kiev, 1964; Sanua, 1966; Torrey, 1972) have performed a much needed service by providing representative, if not exhaustive, coverage of this field. The use of this accumulation of reports for comparative and conceptual purposes is complicated by the difficulty of answering the following basic question: what is psychotherapy and what are its limits of cultural plasticity? In a narrow and concrete sense, it can be said that psychotherapy is both a recent and Western cultural product whose origins can be pinpointed in space and in time. In the broader and more speculative meaning of the term, the cross-cultural observer finds the techniques and insights of Sigmund Freud, Harry Stack Sullivan, and Carl Rogers antedated and paralleled by avenues of intervention strikingly similar to their contributions. The cultural anthropologist, Morris Opler (1936), has described the Apache medicine man as a intuitive psychoanalyst with an uncanny feeling for the personal and symbolic meaning of his clients' dreams; and Leighton (1969), more recently, has been impressed with the differential diagnostic acumen of the Yoruba healers in Western Nigeria as they formulated indications and counterindications for specific interventions within their repertoire of available treatments.

The answer as to where the limits of psychotherapy lie is further complicated by the unity of the medical, the psychological, and the spiritual in many cultures which disintegrated a long time ago in the West. A great many procedures that traditional healers employ are simultaneously and inextricably physical, mental, and sacral. Paranthetically, it is worth noting that the ingrained Western dualisms of mind versus body and secular versus spiritual are being questioned, and in part overcome, by attention to bodily experience in psychotherapy by some therapists (e.g., Gendlin, 1962) and by the noogenic approaches of others (e.g., Frankl, 1959), aimed at catalyzing the client's quest for his own synthesis of meaning. Despite these trends, most psychotherapy as practiced in the West remains focused upon only one of the three modes of human functioning as a secular, aphilosophical procedure, psychological in the narrow sense of the term.

Faced with these complexities, I despair of providing a rationally justifiable delineation of psychotherapy as a worldwide phenomenon. Somewhat ethnocentrically, I would like to proceed from Western psychotherapy as a prototype and restrict the coverage of this chapter to techniques of interpersonal intervention that are broadly similar to Western psychotherapy in both procedure and intent. To specify further, the concern of this chapter will be concentrated upon modes of intervention that (1) involve differential and asymmetrical roles of at least two individuals, one distressed and the other allegedly equipped with expertise to remove or alleviate such distress (2) by means of techniques that are principally verbal, interpersonal, and psychological in nature (3) with the general objectives of bringing about relief, reorganization of adaptive resources, and personality change. These specifications exclude from the scope of this discussion techniques that are primarily somatic in their mode of intervention or religious and magical in their character, even though there is no denying that either or both of these can produce dramatic psychological consequences. Similarly, those techniques of traditional, non-Western healing that aim directly and specifically at the change of particular circumscribed responses will only be skirted in this paper as they represent a topic more akin to behavior modifica-tion and worthy of separate and extended treatment.

On the other hand, the scope of this paper is not restricted to cataloging, or generalizing about, the procedures of non-Western psychotherapy. A subject worthy of equal note is the process and product of Western psychotherapy with non-Western clients. Historically, psychotherapy has been an avenue of tremen-dous heuristic importance in opening up the understanding of mainsprings of normal behavior and of its maladaptive deviation. Any lists of pioneering psychotherapists and of prominent personality theorists would necessarily be highly overlapping. The names of Sigmund Freud, Alfred Adler, Carl Gustav Jung, Harry Stack Sullivan, Carl Rogers, George Kelly, and Viktor Frankl exemplify both. I maintain that psychotherapy across culture lines can render a similarly significant service by bringing to light the culturally characteristic themes, preoccupations, sensitivities, fantasies, and conflicts. It has also been argued (Benoit, 1968) that such exploration in depth is peculiarly refractory to the superficial pull toward worldwide homogeneous modernization to which overt behavior often responds. Benoit's patients in Martinique were French on the surface—in their overt, public behavior—and Antillean inside—in their images, fantasies, fears, conflicts—the stuff psychotherapy is made of. Use of conven-tional psychotherapeutic techniques in combination with cultural sensitivity and awareness has already borne fruit in a number of other settings. Doi (1969), in Japan, has discovered in the psychoanalytic process the overriding role of deep-seated longings for passive dependent gratification, captured by the Japanese term *amae*. Similarly, the accounts of psychoanalytic therapy with the Dogon in West Africa by the Swiss psychoanalyst, Parin (1967; Parin, Morgen-thaler, and Parin-Matthey, 1963), have yielded rich information on the culturally characteristic modes of facing personal problems, making sense of one's own and other people's behavior, and of reducing external stress and internal conflict. In a form that unfortunately is partly fictionalized, Sachs (1947) in South Africa provided a fascinating account of psychoanalysis of an African medicine man that adumbrated by more than a decade the themes that were to erupt in overt behavior of Black Africans. Tseng and Hsu's (1969) recent account of the cultural structuring of conflictual and pathogenic experience in the traditional Chinese culture is heavily dependent upon material uncovered in anamnestic and therapeutic exploration. These accounts, although scattered, attest to the fruit-fulness of psychotherapy as an avenue of learning about culture, and one that deserves to be not only intensively, but extensively utilized. Brushing aside for the moment the very real and difficult problems of the range of intercultural applicability, the application of "standard" Western techniques of intervention, where they are appropriate and tolerated, is worth pursuing for descriptive and comparative research purposes. Instances may be rare where, from the practical social planning and public health points of view, imported therapy procedures would constitute techniques of choice. Yet, where they can be applied, the research data gathered might be useful as another avenue of penetrating the subjective culture of a group, in the conceptual, if not the operational, use of this term (Triandis et al., 1972).

Moreover, the concern with psychotherapeutic techniques of non-Western derivation is not exhausted by the provision of merely descriptive accounts of their procedures and modes of application. How a psychogenic conversion is traditionally treated in Korea, Thailand, or Ceylon is a matter of signal interest, but this information remains necessarily ambiguous and incomplete unless it is related to other prevailing modes of social and interpersonal influence practiced in that culture. In no social setting is the role of the therapist entirely autonomous; it represents but the specialization of more general patterns of social interaction. In the United States, the practice and the ideal of being a sympathetic "good listener" transcend by far the confines of psychotherapy. The continuities between the roles of confessor and therapist have been the subject of repeated commentary and scrutiny (e.g., Frank, 1961); and the prototypes of the therapist as physician, educator, and "behavioral engineer" have been influential in both the classical and contemporary periods of development of psychotherapy (Draguns and Phillips, 1971). What are the points of departure for the evolution of psychotherapy and how do they relate to the more generic influence that prevails in these settings? The accounts extant are too narrowly focused upon the behavior of the therapeutic agent to offer more than suggestive leads. Nonetheless, reading of recent integrative writings on traditional non-Western psychotherapies (Kiev, 1964; Torrey, 1972; Sanua, 1966) creates the impression of contrast between the elaborate, ceremonious character of psychotherapeutic procedures in complex, hierarchical, status-differentiated cultures, such as those of several major tribes of West Africa, and the more matter-of-fact, pragmatic, informal approach apparently characteristic of those cultures where such distinctions are minimally emphasized. It would seem that the healer has to validate his status by engaging in imposing ritual; and his effectiveness, moreover, may be closely linked with his maintaining and demonstrating his status. To put this tentative and intuitively deduced regularity differently, a socially powerless and prestigeless individual is ineffective as a psychotherapist in those settings where considerations of prestige are important.

Furthermore, the store of information on culturally characteristic variants of psychotherapy needs to be brought in relation to another body of knowledge, that concerned with intercultural variations in modes of psychopathological expression (Draguns, 1973; Draguns and Phillips, 1972; Pfeiffer, 1970; Wittkower and Rin, 1965). On the basis of data accumulated, it is safe to say that psychopathology is culturally plastic in its patterns of manifestation throughout the world. While there is probably no culture that is entirely free of psychological disturbance, the form that this disturbance takes is not only culturally variable, but continuous with prevailing adaptive patterns of behavior.

It therefore follows that change and amelioration of these culturally divergent pathways of maladaptation should be brought about by different means, subject to different rationales, embedded in different contexts. Yet, there is a paucity of empirical information that would substantiate this relationship, largely because cross-cultural research on psychopathology and on psychotherapy has been conducted independently and in isolation. In comparative studies of hospitalized United States patients and of their individually matched Argentine and Japanese counterparts, their authors (Draguns, Phillips, Broverman, Caudill, and Nishimae, 1971; Fundia, Draguns, and Phillips, 1971) have been repeatedly impressed by the parallels between their findings and the available fund of descriptive information on the therapeutic approaches favored in the countries in question. In the Japanese case, especially, the parallel was noted between the prevalence of nonintellectualized, immediate, spontaneous modes of symptom expression, and the preference for therapies either somatic in nature or behavioral and/or relationship-centered in conception, in contrast to procedures predicated upon reconstruction and analysis of past experience.

Even disorders identically labeled are experienced differently. A number of converging lines of evidence (Teja, Narang, and Arrgarwal, 1971; Tseng and Hsu, 1969; Pfeiffer, 1970; Wittkower, 1969) suggest that depression in the major cultures of the Far East is phenomenologically and dynamically different from depression in Europe or America. Kimura (1965, 1967) compared the manifestations of depression in Germany and in Japan and found a marked difference in the referents of guilt between the depressive patients of these two countries, with the themes of interpersonal failure prominent in the depressive ideation of the Japanese and the experience of violating an abstract and absolute principle characteristic of the Germans. In the culturally pluralistic setting of Hawaii, Marsella, Barker, and Johnson (1973) demonstrated that the wide discrepancy between the actual and the ideal self-concept, regarded as almost a defining criterion of depression in the West, is only characteristic of depressive patients of Caucasian descent and does not occur among their counterparts of Japanese and Chinese parentage. Certainly, the psychotherapist who went about "treating depression" as such, without reference to its culturally patterned meaning and mode of expression, would be faced with misunderstandings, gaps of communication, and obstructions of therapeutic process.

An even more basic issue concerns the nature of the active ingredients of psychotherapy. Can a common core be discerned in the kaleidoscopic variety of procedures that have been applied with therapeutic intentions throughout the world? Intraculturally, this question is linked to the controversy concerning the respective contributions of specific techniques of intervention versus general therapeutic experience as sources of therapeutic gain. The partisan claims of several schools of psychotherapy have increasingly been giving way to the recognition that psychotherapy works, if it does, for reasons both different and more general than those advanced by the proponents of the several theoretical positions (Berenson and Carkhuff, 1967; Goldstein, Heller, and Sechrest, 1966). Cross-culturally, this controversy is paralleled by the recent presentation of two diverging points of view concerning the culture-free versus culture-bound nature of therapy experience. On the one hand, Torrey (1972), in a recent, uncommonly readable and almost seductively persuasive book, has minced no words in upholding the view that the fundamental techniques of psychotherapy are recognizably similar, and often identical, whether practiced in Metropolitan New York or rural Ethiopia. To quote the words of his own opening statement (Torrey, 1972: 1):

> Witchdoctors and psychiatrists perform essentially the same function in their respective cultures. They are both therapists; both treat patients using similar techniques; and both get similar results. Recognition of this should not downgrade psychiatrists; rather it should upgrade witchdoctors.

What are these similar techniques? In Torrey's view and very entertainingly described by him, the first and foremost is the existence of a shared world view which enables the therapist to supply the name or the explanation of the client's disorder in a way that would make sense to the client and fit in with his general knowledge of the world and himself. This phenomenon Torrey whimsically calls the Rumpelstiltskin effect. Other cross-cultural commonalities in the therapists' modes of operation include providing genuineness, warmth, and empathy, a quality shared by an American campus-based Rogerian with an Eskimo healer or a Mexican-American curandero and also, to proceed in Torrey's tongue-in-cheek style, with a terry cloth covered computer. There is also the matter of patient's expectation of being helped and cured, a hope enhanced by the imposing paraphenalia and artifacts displayed by the therapist. With a side-glance at the plush psychotherapists' offices of Beverly Hills and New York's Park Avenue, Torrey labels this the edifice complex. Finally, significance is accorded to the similarity of specific interventions, in the form of catharsis, confrontation, interpretation, reflection, and many others, as they are employed by the therapists throughout the world. According to Torrey (1972: 56):

> There is no technique used in Western therapy that is not also found in other cultures. There *are* techniques, however, used in other cultures that are only rarely used by Western psychotherapists. Cultures, as we will see, often favor certain types of therapy or particular techniques, but the difference is one of quantity—how often they are used. These differences in the quantitative use of techniques are directly related to particular values of each culture. Overall the similarities in the techniques used by witchdoctors and psychiatrists far outweigh the differences.

To extend Torrey's argument, modern "scientific" psychotherapists are the inheritors of a rich historical tradition of which they are typically not aware. Contemporary psychotherapy in this country and elsewhere is but the up-to-date garb of emotionally arousing traditional avenues of therapeutic intervention. Another implication of Torrey's position is that modern psychotherapy cannot claim to be an advance over the traditional treatments; it has added nothing new and created nothing better.

The opposing side of the argument is presented by Pande (1968), who places emphasis upon the culture-bound elements of psychotherapy as it is currently practiced in the West. According to Pande, the experience of psychotherapy is crucially tied up with Western notions of individuality, time, space, and rationality. To expand, psychotherapy is a means of recapturing love, preparing for and examining crucial decisions of one's lifetime, fitting childhood recollections into the matrix of one's experiences, critically reviewing one's life-style, and overcoming feelings of alienation and isolation. In short, therapy is viewed as a reintegrating experience for a fractionated and compartmentalized man, a product of contemporary Western civilization. Doi (1969), a Japanese psychoanalyst with a Japanese clientele, similarly articulates the cultural difficulty that has to be overcome if integration is to be achieved between the tenets of psychoanalysis and of biographical experience as a lifelong participant in the Japanese culture.

As with so many other arguments, part of the issue is semantic. It is evident that Torrey's concept of psychotherapy is more inclusive than Doi's or Pande's. Moreover, the analogies and parallels among psychotherapeutic practices are most impressive when they are considered at a specific point in time; within this frame of reference, therapists in very different cultures say ard do the same things. Implicitly, Pande and Doi seem to take the longer view as they consider therapy rationale and process. It is these experiences traversing several stages and culminating in termination that have proved difficult to export across culture lines.

In any case, psychotherapy, in relation to its alleged core that immutably exists in all psychotherapeutic interventions, is an issue that cannot be decided on the basis of naturalistic, descriptive accounts of psychotherapists in action. Indispensable as these eye-witness reports are, they constitute but the first stage of needed documentation, roughly comparable to the case studies that have played so important a role in the historic development of modern psychotherapies. In reviewing much of this descriptive literature, I have been struck by the near-absence of descriptions of failure of any of the traditional therapies. The conclusion is easily suggested that various traditional practitioners are superior to our own psychotherapists and that they have unlocked the secret of failure-proof psychotherapy. More skeptically, three possible sources of selection and bias come to mind which might have affected not the veracity of any discrete account, but the total picture that results from their accumulation. First of these is the practitioners' bias. Western observers of non-Western psychotherapy are typically at the mercy of the goodwill of the practitioners whom they are studying. Exposed to such cross-cultured scrutiny, it is certainly not beyond the realm of imagination that our colleagues on the African bush or the New Guinea hills would be as protective of their reputations as Western psychotherapists are. If so, they might preselect and display before their far-away visitors those cases that would show the highest chance of being successfully helped by their techniques. Second, the culturally relativistic orientation, widespread among anthropological observers and other social scientists (e.g., Honigmann, 1969), emphasizes the potentially functional and functioning character of all the practices encountered in a given cultural setting. In its application to psychotherapy, this orientation might result in highlighting the manner in which psychotherapy works on its culture's own terms and might overlook those instances where it fails to accomplish its social and individual ends. Finally, there is the attitude of professional humility on the part of investigators and practitioners of psychotherapy as a result of two or more decades of somewhat inconclusive psychotherapy outcome research. This attitude stimulates psychotherapists to learn from other cultures' therapeutic experience and might conceivably bring about instances of its overevaluation.

In my view, the issue of effectiveness of psychotherapy practiced across culture lines is an open one, both intraculturally and cross-culturally. We do not know what the outcomes of psychotherapy in most other cultures are, and we have not even begun the comparison of process and outcome of psychotherapy in two or more cultures. In cases of extreme cultural contrast, pitting for example, traditional, small-scale, nontechnological societies against those of the modern complex nation states of East or West, it might be difficult to carry out such a comparison meaningfully. Even there, however, it might under favorable circumstances be possible to obtain quantitative data with meaningful, and operationally defined criteria related to therapy outcome. In the case of historically different, yet technologically and educationally comparable societies, such as those of Japan and the United States, more ambitious objectives might be possible of realization. Interest in such a comparison is increased by the fact that a number of therapeutic techniques indigenous to Japan have been developed on the same mixed theoretical and empirical basis that has been prominent in the history of Western psychotherapy. Prominent among these is Morita therapy, a procedure that has been extensively described by foreign observers and Japanese experts (Cerny, 1967; Kora, 1965; Miura and Usa, 1970). Without duplicating the details of these accounts, Morita therapy achieves its ends by a route that is strikingly different from those employed in Western psychotherapy; its techniques are directive, repressive, and ritualized. The client is repeatedly admonished to "forget his symptoms," and these exhortations are embedded in a highly specific, multistage treatment program under the direction of an active, authoritarian, and decisive therapist. Yet, outcome data quite akin in extent and quality to traditional Western psychiatric therapy outcome documentation are available on Morita therapy (Miura and Usa, 1970). From this base, three lines of investigation could be pursued. First and relatively easiest to implement would be the comparison, with maximally specific and objective criteria, of Morita therapy with the several Western therapeutic approaches represented in Japan: Freudian psychoanalysis, Rogerian client-centered psychotherapy, and others. The conclusiveness of such a study would, of course, hinge on the comparability of client populations treated with these therapy techniques, a thorny and complex but not insurmountable problem.

The second line of proposed investigation is more ambitious and therefore more speculative. It is related to the proposal made several years ago by the German psychologist, Wendt (1967), for the inauguration of one or several Morita clinics in Europe and America which would serve as sites of intensive investigation into the mechanisms of such culturally transplanted therapy. Moreover, the implementation of this proposal, which, as far as I know, has not yet taken place, would counteract the ethnocentrism implicit in the assumption that Western therapies are cross-culturally exportable unless proven otherwise, while therapy approaches developed in non-Western countries are, at best, objects of fascination and curiosity outside of their cultural setting. To expand on this asymmetry, Shoma Morita and Sigmund Freud were almost contemporaries; yet while Freud's contributions have spread worldwide, the impact of Morita's work has, until recently, been confined to Japan. Conceivably, both of these therapies are specific to their cultures, or both, or either, may be interculturally applicable. Proceeding from Wendt's proposal, a simultaneous comparison of Morita therapy and psychoanalysis—or other modes of Western therapy—in Japan and in one or several Western countries could resolve this issue. The third direction of study might inquire into the characteristics of Japanese clients who seek, and differentially profit from, different modes of psychotherapy of Western and Japanese derivation. Do they differ in sociological characteristics, values, symptoms, and more broadly, in the overall balance of traditionally Japanese and Westernized life-styles? Answers to some of these questions may already be available in the ramified and voluminous Japanese psychiatric literature, but, if so, this information has not yet penetrated the language barrier. In any case, the model of the triple approach should be applicable in other cultural settings as well.

On the practical plane, the problem of intercultural commonality of therapeutic experience comes up in relation to the practical issue of program planning. In many developing countries, should traditional psychotherapeutic practices be integrated into programs of intervention? Lambo (1962) in Nigeria has forcefully argued for such a course of action for both practical and theoretical reasons. The shortage of mental health personnel acts as a stimulant for improvisation and innovation. The cultural incompatibility of models of intervention imported from abroad provides another reason for trying out the locally available resources. The experience of blending of local healing practitioners with standard Western interventions has been, on the whole, positive, not only in Nigeria (Lambo, 1962), but in Guyana (Singer et al., 1967) and Senegal (Collomb, 1967) as well. The contrast appears to be telling between these venturesome programs and the custodially oriented Western-type psychiatric hospitals set up in a culturally alien milieus, as described by Berne (1956), Dawson (1964), Singer et al., (1967), and Wulff (1967). Yet, this avenue of community mental health practiced across culture lines is not without its critics. Notably, Margetts (1960) had been outspoken in his rejection of the principle of mental health programs built around the services of local healers, with their magical orientation. Drawing a sharp line between the naturalistic scientific-medical tradition of Western psychiatry and the supernatural ethos of many of the local interventions, he sees no more justification for active cooperation with such practitioners in psychiatry than he would in internal medicine and surgery. Again, the resolution of this clash would seem to depend on empirical data. To this end, data more systematic than those now available are needed. A research design involving either presence or absence of traditional interventions, over and above the baseline of generally available "scientific" services, or the comparison of their different proportions or weights within an interculturally blended program would be an appropriate means for resolving this issue.

In this manner, a clearer delineation of the pancultural universals of therapy experience becomes possible. But what about its culture-specific particulars? Torrey (1972), it will be recalled, maintained that they were subsidiary to those aspects of therapy that are identical in all cultures. Nonetheless, even he allowed for quantitative differences in the distribution of several components of therapy around the world and recognized the complementarity between cultural characteristics and the prevailing therapeutic techniques. Let us therefore reserve the remainder of this chapter for the brief enumeration of some of the cultural dimensions that conceivably might shape approaches and practices to therapy. Prince (1969) has proposed a generalization to the effect that cultures that foster the development of internal controls in their members also favor the practice of insight-oriented, reconstructive, and open-ended psychotherapy, while cultures that rely upon external controls are partial to the application of authoritarian, directive techniques focused upon specific and concrete outcomes. Going beyond Prince's formulation, the nature of psychotherapy practiced would also seem to depend upon the structure of the culture in which it occurs and, especially, on the "degrees of freedom" that are open to most of its members. To the extent that an individual's place in his social world is predetermined by tradition, political control, economic opportunity, or other influences, therapeutic change would be basically autoplastic and specifically and directively aimed at reeducating the individual for fitting into the social slot he must occupy. Such a state of affairs would also obtain where a given culture is regarded by its members as being the only truly human and practically possible one.

Related to the foregoing are the intercultural differences concerning shared beliefs on environmental and human changeability. On the former point, typologies from Benedict's (1934) Appolonian versus Faustian to Diaz-Guerrero's (1967) passive versus active syndromes refer to the socially shared attitudes on the immutability and changeability of the external milieu as something ultimately given in one case or as something to be molded and reshaped in the other. On the latter point, there has been less conceptual and empirical effort expanded. Yet, it would seem that societies differ in holding how changeable people are, or in their implicit theories of nature versus nurture. In the extreme and limiting case where neither man nor environment are thought to be changeable, the raison d'etre for psychotherapy disappears. I do not know of any social group that would exemplify this hypothetical state of affairs. Yet, I am willing to venture a tentative generalization that psychotherapy thrives in particular in those settings where social change and social mobility coexist with an environmentalist attitude toward human nature. Beyond the sheer prominence of psychotherapy, constancy of social structure, accompanied by believed human changeability, would favor psychotherapy geared toward individual adaptation; social flux would favor psychotherapy of individuation and liberation.

So far it has been assumed that these social tenets are culturally constant and stable. In a recent historic and philosophical analysis, the Israeli psychologist, Rotenberg (1972), has detected a number of implicit contraditions in Western European and American attitudes toward the "people-changing enterprise" expressed through psychotherapy. Currents of Western thought, going back to Calvin's doctrine of predestination, bring about ambivalence and confusion on the subject of changing people; while some people are thought to be capable of experiencing continuous growth toward perfection, others are damned to realize their negative potentialities and cannot be changed for the good. Calvin's theological precepts have little current impact, but, so Rotenberg contends, they survive in such rigid dichotomizations as psychotic versus neurotic, preoccupation with good versus bad prognosis, and reification of social acts into characteristics and categories of people who have committed them. It would be interesting to ascertain whether other societies also harbor internal contradictions of their own in relation to the assumptions on which the practice of psychotherapy is based.

Finally, culture shapes the characteristics of its therapists. In the United States, two types of therapist personality have been identified (Chartier, 1971;

Razin, 1971; Whitehorn and Betz, 1960) that are differentially effective with neurotics and psychotics, respectively; the former preferring an uncovering, interpretive mode of intervention and the latter, an emotional sharing. The respresentation of these two types, roughly corresponding to "expert" and "helper," respectively, is a potential source of cross-cultural variation and a possible principle for more economically organizing the manifold cultural characteristics of the therapist's role.

No doubt more axes of potential contrast could be added, but there is little point in indefinitely extending this list, in the absence of data that would empirically anchor these dimensions. Instead, let us look back at the findings and problems of the field which has been rather rapidly reviewed. One safe conclusion is that, at this point, problems predominate over findings. A lot of raw information has been collected, a number of articulate positions have been formulated, but the data that would be decisive in favor of one or another of these stands are not extant. What is known is that psychotherapeutic change and expertise are no monopoly of any one culture and are close to being worldwide in their scope. But what are the personal and interpersonal conditions that panculturally produce such change? Adding to Torrey's four universals, I would propose that psychotherapy is a "special" experience discontinuous in a limited sense from the daily flow of events, more intense, concentrated, emotionally charged. Different cues across cultures produce such a state, but a differentiated, trustful relationship with the therapist is one prerequisite for it. The opportunity to behave, think, and feel differently from one's day-to-day experience is another common denominator of many very different therapeutic procedures. Conspicuously absent, however, from any such list of cultural universals are permissiveness and insight, neither of which seems to be necessary for personality change, although both or either episodically occur in a great many places around the world. So viewed, psychotherapy is an affectively charged avenue of social influence, a conclusion that is consonant with Strupp's (1970) recent formulation on the basic and general components of psychotherapy which transcend their very different trappings across schools and across cultures.

REFERENCES

BENEDICT, R. (1934) Patterns of Culture. Boston: Houghton Mifflin.
BENOIT, G. (1968) "A propos d'une recherche en matiere de psychiatrie transculturelle." Paper presented at the Second International Congress of Social Psychiatry, London.
BERENSON, B. G. and R. R. CARKHUFF (1967) "Emerging directions: a synthesis," in B. G. Berenson and R. R. Carkhuff (eds.) Sources of Gain in Counseling and Psychotherapy. New York: Holt, Rinehart & Winston.
BERNE, E. (1956) "Comparative psychiatry and tropical psychiatry." American Journal of Psychiatry 113: 193-200.

ČERNÝ, J. (1967) "Zu den psychopathologischen und philosophischen Fragen der japanischen Neurosen-Psychotherapie nach der Morita-Konzeption (System Zen)." Aktuelle Fragen der Psychiatrie und Neurologie 6: 66-81.

CHARTIER, G. M. (1971) "A-B therapist variable: real or imagined?" Psychological Bulletin 75: 22-33.

COLLOMB, H. (1967) "Aspectes de la psychiatrie dans l'Ouest africain (Senegal)." Aktuelle Fragen der Psychiatrie und Neurologie 5: 229-253.

DAWSON, J. (1964) "Urbanization and mental health in a West African community," in A. Kiev (ed.) Magic, Faith, and Healing: Studies in Primitive Psychiatry Today. New York: Free Press.

DIAZ-GUERRERO, R. (1967) "The active and the passive syndromes." Revista Interamericana de Psicologia 1: 263-272.

DOI, L. T. (1969) "Japanese psychology, dependency needs, and mental health," in W. Caudill and T. Lin (eds.) Mental Health Research in Asia and the Pacific. Honolulu: East-West Center Press.

DOOB, L. W. (1970) Resolving Conflict in Africa: The Fameda Workshop. New Haven, Conn.: Yale University Press.

DRAGUNS, J. G. (1973) "Comparisons of psychopathology across cultures: Issues, findings, directions." Journal of Cross-Cultural Psychology, 4: 9-47.

——— and L. PHILLIPS (1971) Psychiatric Classification and Diagnosis: An Overview and Critique. Morristown, N.J.: General Learning Press.

——— (1972) Culture and Psychopathology: The Quest for a Relationship. Morristown, N.J.: General Learning Press.

———, I. K. BROVERMAN, W. CAUDILL, and S. NISHIMAE (1971) "Symptomatology of hospitalized psychiatric patients in Japan and in the United States: a study of cultural differences." Journal of Nervous and Mental Disease 152: 3-16.

FRANK, J. D. (1961) Persuasion and Healing: A Comparative Study of Psychotherapy. Baltimore: Johns Hopkins University Press.

FRANKL, V. E. (1959) Man's Search for Meaning. Boston: Beacon.

FREUD, S. and J. BREUER (1959) Studies in Hysteria. New York: Basic Books.

FUNDIA, T. A. DE, J. G. DRAGUNS and L. PHILLIPS (1971) "Culture and psychiatric symptomatology: a comparison of Argentine and United States patients." Social Psychiatry 6: 11-20.

GENDLIN, E. T. (1962) Experiencing and the Creation of Meaning. New York: Free Press.

GOLDSTEIN, A. P., K. HELLER and L. B. SECHREST (1966) Psychotherapy and the Psychology of Behavior Change. New York: John Wiley.

HONIGMANN, J. J. (1969) "Middle class values and cross-cultural understanding," in J. C. Finney (ed.) Culture Change, Mental Health, and Poverty. Lexington: University of Kentucky Press.

KIEV, A. [ed.] (1964) Magic, Faith and Healing: Studies in Primitive Psychiatry Today. New York: Free Press.

KIMURA, B. (1965) "Vergleichende Untersuchungen uber depressive Erkrankungen in Japan und in Deutschland." Fortschritte der Neurologie und Psychiatrie 33: 202-215.

KIMURA, B. (1967) "Phanomenologie des Schulderlebnisses in einer vergleichenden psychiatrischen Sicht." Aktuelle Fragen der Psychiatrie und Neurologie 6: 54-65.

KORA, T. (1965) "Morita therapy." International Journal of Psychiatry 1: 611-619.

LAMBO, T. (1962) "The importance of cultural factors in psychiatric treatment." Acta Psychiatrica Scandinavica 38: 176-179.

LEIGHTON, A. H. (1969) "Cultural relativity and the identification of psychiatric disorders," in W. Caudill and T. Lin (eds.) Mental Health in Asia and the Pacific. Honolulu: East-West Center Press.

MARGETTS, E. L. (1960) "The future of psychiatry in East Africa." East African Medical Journal 37: 448-456.

MARSELLA, A. J., E. BARKER and F. JOHNSON (1973) "The relationship between depression and self-concept discrepancy in female college students of Caucasian and Japanese ancestry." International Journal of Social Psychiatry 19: 77-82.

MIURA, M. and S. USA (1970) "A psychotherapy of neuroses: Morita therapy." Psychologia 13: 18-34.

MOWRER, O. H. (1960) "Some constructive features of the concept of sin." Journal of Counseling Psychology 1: 185-188.

MURPHY, H. B. M. [ed.] (1955) Flight and Resettlement. Paris: UNESCO.

OPLER, M. E. (1936) "Some points of comparison and contrast between the treatment of functional disorders by Apache Shamans and modern psychiatric practice." American Journal of Psychiatry 92: 1371-1387.

PANDE, S. K. (1968) "The mystique of Western psychotherapy: an Eastern interpretation." Journal of Nervous and Mental Disease 146: 425-432.

PARIN, P. (1967) "Zur Bedeutung von Mythus, Ritual und Brauch fur die vergleichende Psychiatrie," Aktuelle Fragen der Psychiatric und Neurologie 6: 179-196.

———, F. MORGENTHALER and G. PARIN-MATTHEY (1963) Die Weissen denken zuviel. Zurich: Atlantis-Verlag.

PFEIFFER, W. (1970) Transkulturelle Psychiatrie: Ergebnisse und Probleme. Stuttgart: Thieme.

PHILLIPS, L. (1968) Human Adaptation and its Failures. New York: Academic Press.

PRICE, R. H. (1972) Abnormal Behavior: Perspectives in Conflict. New York: Holt, Rinehart & Winston.

PRICE-WILLIAMS, D. (1970) "Introduction," in D. Price-Williams (ed.) Cross-Cultural Studies. Baltimore: Penguin.

PRINCE, R. (1969) "Psychotherapy and the chronically poor," in J. C. Finney (ed.) Culture Change, Mental Health, and Poverty. Lexington: University of Kentucky Press.

RAZIN, A. M. (1971) "A-B variable in psychotherapy: a critical review." Psychological Bulletin 75: 22-33.

ROTENBERG, M. (1972) "The Protestant ethic versus the people changing sciences." Paper presented at Symposium on the Protestant Ethic and Abnormal Psychology, Convention of the American Psychological Association, Honolulu (September).

SACHS, W. (1947) Black Anger. Boston: Little, Brown.

SANUA, V. D. (1966) "Sociocultural aspects of psychotherapy and treatment: a review of the literature," pp. 151-190 in L. Abt and B. Riess (eds.) Progress in Clinical Psychology. New York: Grune & Stratton.

SEWARD, G. H. (1956) Psychotherapy and Culture Conflict. New York: Ronald Press.

SINGER, P., L. AARONS and E. ARONETTA (1967) "Integration of indigenous practices of the Kali cult and Western psychiatric modalities in British Guiana." Revista Interamericanade Psychologia 1: 103-114.

STRUPP, H. H. (1970) "Specific or nonspecific factors in psychotherapy and the problem of control." Archives of General Psychiatry 23: 393-401.

TEJA, J. S., R. L. NARANG and A. K. AGGARWAL (1971) "Depression across cultures." British Journal of Psychiatry 119: 253-260.

TORREY, E. F. (1972) The Mind Game: Witchdoctors and Psychiatrists. New York: Emerson Hall.

TRIANDIS, H. C., V. VASSILIOU, G. VASSILIOU, Y. TANAKA and A. SHANMUGAM [eds.] (1972) The analysis of Subjective Culture. New York: John Wiley.

TSENG, W. S. and J. HSU (1969) "Chinese culture, personality formation, and mental illness." International Journal of Social Psychiatry 16: 5-14.

VEXLIARD, A. (1967) "Autoplastie et alloplastie." Psychologia 10: 56-68.

——— (1968) "Tempérament et modalités d'adaptation." Bulletin de Psychologie 21: 1-15.

WENDT, I. Y. (1967) "Eine japanische zen-Klinik im Western." Schweizerische Zeitschrift fur Psychologie und Ihre Anwendungen 24: 366-370.

WHITEHORN, J. C. and B. J. BETZ (1960) "Further studies of the doctor as a crucial variable in the outcome of treatment with schizophrenic patients." American Journal of Psychiatry 117: 215-223.

WITTKOWER, E. D. (1969) "Cultural psychiatric research," in W. Caudill and T. Lin (eds.) Mental Health Research in Asia and the Pacific. Honolulu: East-West Center Press.

WORCHEL, P. and D. BYRNE [eds.] (1964) Personality Change. New York: John Wiley.

WULFF, E. (1967) "Ein psychiatrischer Bericht aus Vietnam." Aktuelle Fragen der Psychiatrie und Neurologie 5: 1-84.

——— and H. RIN (1965) "Transcultural psychiatry." Archives of General Psychiatry 13: 387-394.

Chapter 12

PRIMITIVE MENTALITY–CIVILIZED STYLE

DOUGLASS PRICE-WILLIAMS

University of California, Los Angeles

> *Walking down Telegraph Avenue, Berkeley, California, I noted a Japanese tourist taking a snapshot of a Hare Krishna chanter. I did not take a photo of this as a colleague wanted me to, but if I had done so, the photograph would have been taken by an Englishman of a Japanese who in turn was taking a picture of an American trying to behave like an Indian. [Personal encounter, 1970. This is the perspective of this chapter.]*

> *"Are you prepared to leave the world as you know it and live in a mountain retreat on a very basic diet?" I signified that I was. "You see," he nodded his head regretfully, "you still feel that to find knowledge you must seek a solitary life away from impure things. This is a primitive attitude and one satisfactory for savages." [Quotation from an encounter of a young European with a Sufi teacher, LeFort 1966: 105. This is the theme of this chapter.]*

Cross-cultural psychology has become accustomed to the application of Western scientific categories to non-Western styles of thought. At the same time other researches have paid attention to indigenous modes of classification which may or may not be congruent with the Western mode. Previously I have compared these two approaches and commented upon the problems associated with each (Price-Williams, 1972). In this paper, however, I am going to do something different; namely, to invert the first approach by selecting a domain within our own culture now courted by some psychologists, indicate the relatively primitive state of our thinking about it, and then turn to other cultures to find out what we may learn from their handling of it.

The domain in question is what has come to be called "altered states of consciousness." This area of study now has attracted at least three journals, and

Author's Note: My thanks are due to the following people who read over a previous draft and gave me helpful advice: Professors Richard Brislin, Michael Diamond, Juris Draguns, John Kennedy, and Mr. Jim Turner. The work was supported in part by Research Grant No. HD 04612, NICHD, Mental Retardation Research Center, University of California, Los Angeles; by the California Department of Mental Hygiene and the University of California.

[291]

many prominent books and articles,[1] most of which are at least on the saner side of the lunatic fringe. While this paper will deal more with the cognitive side of this subject, it cannot escape attention that the movement associated with the study of altered states of consciousness (ASC) has deep sociological implications, and it will be an integral part of this paper not to divorce the two.

I will tackle the subject in three sections. The first comments on the scientific and social attention presently given to ASC, attempting to view it in a context wider than just a curious incursion into the mystical and mysterious. The second section focuses upon the classifications and analyses made by contemporary investigators of ASC. The third section then delves into the contributions made by other cultures to this same area.

EXTENT OF INTEREST IN ASC WITHIN OUR OWN CULTURE

The phenomena of ASC, which used to lie even in the history of our own culture within the confines of an introverted religious framework, had now be better interpreted as a focus on a pretty wide spectrum that embraces the desire to enhance the ordinary sensory world. The context within which ASC is better regarded would have to include the variety of psychotherapeutic techniques of muscular relaxation, imagery production, sensitivity sessions, encounter groups, and perhaps even those psychosexual methods employed for increased gratification of patient and partner. At the other end of the spectrum we have the psychedelic groups and the various group or individual efforts in what is thought to be Eastern meditation and contemplation. The social movement associated with all of these techniques pervades not only the psychiatrist's couch or psychologist's clinic but also the lay world. For this reason alone it deserves the attention of the cultural psychologist who might be thought to interpret the phenomenon in a wider framework than just the American or English scene. There is another reason for including this subject in the present context of cultural learning, and that is on account of the fact that the movement appears to constitute a massive attempt at *un*learning—unlearning traditional thought patterns, unlearning basic habits of activity, unlearning conditioned responses. It would be more accurate to say that there are two stages involved. The first stage is this unlearning of one's standard cultural response. The second stage is the learning of another cultural style. In the West it is difficult to determine exactly what this second stage is, as the various adoptions do not integrate with the larger society, so that in one sense they become deviant; also the philosophies adopted are often muddled versions of the original article. In any case, "unlearning" can be recognized as a preliminary step to a reorganization of experience which thus constitutes a new learning, involving both cognitive and affective elements. Anthony Wallace (1966) makes a significant contribution to the subject in his treatment of the ritual learning process when he points out that the ritual reorganization of experience is a kind of learning, though not of the sort usually treated by experimental psychology. He calls it the Law of Dissociation, which incorporates five steps, labeled: prelearning, separation, suggestion, execution, and maintenance. In a larger perspective I suggest that what may well be happening is an imminent breakdown of metaphysical categories that have influenced our culture for centuries.

How the kaleidoscope will eventually settle is a question I do not seek to answer; I wish only to point out, however, that the phenomenon does not seem to be a simple matter of culture contact, that is, a borrowing from another culture. There *does* appear to be borrowing, but it is completely eclectic. The Western movement takes this from Sufi tradition, that from Patanjali, and something else from Western Africa. At the same time the tendency is thoroughly mixed with scientific paraphernalia, as in biofeedback methods, and theologically ranges from pure pantheism to Christomorphic sects. Even the usual conservative Catholicism is not untouched as witnessed by the pentacostal movement within it. Given this potpourri of influences, therefore, I prefer to view it as an unlearning phenomenon, as there does not seem any obvious goal to which the term learning would apply. Our age has been called many things. A further label that might fit is to call it the Age of Redefinition, for many of our most steadfast categories are now in question: "life" becomes redefined when experimental biology is on the threshold of creating it artificially; "death" has already become a problem for the medico-legal world. Possibly Reich (1970) is correct in seeing all of this as a revolution, though he neglects the cognitive aspect I am emphasizing. An index of the latter can be noted in the lexicon generated with marijuana usage (*Journal of Psychedelic Drugs,* 1971) indicating the need of terms for different modes of experience.

Another way of expressing this movement is to state that what used to be traditionally sacred now lies in the secular region and thus is at one piece with our myths which have long since become profane, to use Durkheimian language.

SCIENTIFIC APPROACH TO ASC

What now has the psychologist to say of this subject? From the point of view of the attitude of this chapter, it is significant that the psychologist has felt the need to revert back to a predominantly nineteenth-century and theoretically rejected term as the key concept—I mean the term "consciousness." *States* of consciousness reveals a further archaic way of speaking, and together the full phrase "states of consciousness" (altered or otherwise) regresses to a mode of psychological interpretation that was discarded for very good reasons fifty years or so ago. As it *is* the current term, I shall go on using it here for purposes of exposition; and in criticizing its formulation, I am not implying that I wish to place myself in the oppositional camp, that is, behaviorism. The critique is not aimed at its present users, only to illustrate the inadequacy of our psychological metaphysics that compels us into crude choices. We need more refined distinctions than are available to us with the blanket term "consciousness" and its opposite "unconsciousness," such as that given in Zen, for example (Suzuki 1958: 145).

At this point we will claim that our understanding of ASC and related matters is "primitive" with comparison to the understanding of some other cultural groups. We will need, however, to express the manner in which the term "primitive" is used.

The study of psychology is necessarily reactive; that is to say, it is responsive to what there is in fact there for analysis. If our own condition of ASC is underdeveloped, then our analysis of it is likewise so. One is reminded of Levi-Strauss's reference to what he called the archaic illusion (1969). By this he meant the resemblances we see between primitive and child thought. His argument turns on the point that the child is a "polymorphous socialite," meaning that the child has not yet been socialized in a single strand of social behavior. And when we look at another set of customs other than our own, into which we have not been socialized, then it seems to us puerile and reminds us of our own childish state of presocialized behavior. In the same way, I suggest, what we designate in the domain of ASC appears primitive to us, just because we have not socialized or cultured it. Hence the need to turn to those societies that have, to a certain extent, done this. With notable early exceptions such as William James (1935), Bucke (1901), and Underhill (1911), our scientific treatment of ASC up to very recently was to relegate it to the field of psychopathology. When the discipline of psychology approached the subject more exhaustively and less judgmentally, it became quite clear that severe problems of classification and analysis arose. Concerning attempts to classify ASC, let us take two contemporary examples. The first is that of Ludwig (1966) which has been described as "one of the most comprehensive overviews available." He makes a fivefold classification based on the use of certain variables or combination of variables which elicit the production of ASC. Ludwig agrees that there is much overlap here and that his scheme is artificial, and he goes on later to specify some of the characteristics of ASC which can be thought of as dependent variables. Really there is no attempt at an overall phenomenology, and what he gives us is a list depending on the reduction or increase of stimulation and increased alertness. We find little differentiation or precision in the scheme, and if we found this in some African tribe we would tend to say that it was highly concrete and situational. When we turn to a scheme more experimental in character, as with that of Masters and Houston in their book *The Varieties of Psychedelic Experience* (1966), we fare little better. Their scheme is concerned only with the effects of LSD, but the full range of ASC is encountered. The Masters and Houston scheme is not unlike the dependent variable collection of Ludwig. We find ASC characterized in like descriptions of altered body image and time distortion. It is only when they begin to ponder what they term the "recollection-analytic" level that Masters and Houston get their teeth into the difficult terminological problem, and it is at this point that the authors rely heavily on symbol interpretation and religious analogues. It is doubtful whether their incursions here are any advance on those of James and Underhill before them. A third example can be given, which is the very recent attempt at categorizing different kinds of thinking associated with ASC, which the author labels "straight versus stoned" thinking (Weil, 1972). Here we confront an avowed failure of traditional language by slipping into slang or "pop" jargon.

The truly epistemological difficulties that face us in this realm are beautifully represented in the discussion of Carlos Castenada (1968: 130) with his mentor Don Juan, when the former tries to pin down from his teacher whether he had actually flown as a crow when he partook of the *Datura* plants, or had only imagined that he had.

> ". . . I mean, did my body fly? Did I take off like a bird?" "You always ask me questions I cannot answer. You flew. That is what the second portion of the devil's weed is for. . . . What you want to know makes no sense. Birds fly like birds and a man who has taken the devil's weed flies as such." "As birds do?" "No, he flies as a man who has taken the weed."

Clearly the teacher and his pupil do not share the same universe of discourse, as Castenada has always recognized. And I contend that in the world of ASC we professionals meet the same problem; we attain the same level in it as a Bush African does with the Stanford-Binet. It is significant that other investigators, once they have entered into this brave new world of ASC, have realized that quite radical and fundamental postulates about the physical and biological world have to be encountered. Simplistic models of the mind, whether Cartesian or those stemming from the spirit of logical positivism, have to be rejected. It is here, at this logical point of analysis, that analysts tend to flounder around, groping for appropriate frameworks. When a framework is found, it is highly speculative and revolutionary. Lilly (1967), for instance, has felt the need to postulate a complicated "metaprogramming" model of the organism in order to cover the ground. Puharich (1973), taking off from the experiences of the Yogin and the Shaman, has put forward a "psi plasma" theory which requires drastic revisions in our knowledge of biology and physics. Clark (1972) is impelled to adopt a logical map of "inner space" that involves a highly complicated network for the purpose of understanding the experiences reported by the mystics.

Be they elementary or sophisticated, schemes put forward to explain ASC all share the belief that the invading investigator can account for the phenomena without surrendering the scientists' customary armory of conceptual analysis and methodological criteria. Particularly there is kept the belief that investigation into this realm can go forward without losing an objective perspective, that the scientist can keep apart from his subject matter. By the same token there is the assumption that the inherent approach which proved so successful with the physical world, of abstracting attributes of the domain inspected and analyzing them independently, will be equally appropriate with ASC. It is here that we encounter the widest chasm between our own culture's approach to this subject and that of those that have grappled with it for some time. Ornstein (1972: 96) has well pin-pointed it when he states: "Scientific knowledge is perhaps the highest development of the linear mode, but the linear mode is only *one* mode possible for us. We find that another major mode of consciousness manifests itself culturally, personally, and physiologically. . . . Such a mode is difficult to encompass within the lineal, verbal terms so dominant in our culture, but it is this mode of knowing which is cultivated in the esoteric traditions." It is in relation to this alternative mode of knowing that the title of this chapter refers. In other words, our analysis of ASC may be brilliant in terms of sophisticated methodology and even of explanatory models based on our customary scientific mode of thought. What bedevils us and where we are least developed is the realization that the proper understanding of this domain requires an alternative mode of knowing.

INDICATIONS FROM OTHER CULTURES CONCERNING ASC

At the outset we face a monumental difficulty in attempting to evaluate indications from other cultures on this topic, a difficulty that few Western commentators have acknowledged. The difficulty is that, if in fact an alternative, nonlineal mode of knowledge is being transmitted, whether it be by oral tradition or put down in documents, then we are faced with a task of translation not just that from one language to another but from one mode of interpretation to another. When we encounter processes in other cultures which we have sometimes labeled "primitive mentality," "animalistic thinking," and "primary process thinking," we may have to recognize that this is not really what we consider as "thinking" in our own culture. Or at least it is not our customary lineal thinking. Treating straightforward or even annotated translations from, say, Tantric or Zen schemes as codified explanations of ASC material will not serve us well in attempting to understand what they are all about. Especially we will flounder if we try to squeeze the context of Western experience into them. As Watts had put it (1959: 36): "The difficulty with our translations is that 'mind' is too intellectual, too cortical, and that 'heart' . . . is too emotional—even sentimental."

Therefore we had better adopt an oblique approach and explore social, attitudinal, as well as cognitive, indicators of these cultures in order to extract the different mode suggested. I will propose five such indicators.

(1) In this book Draguns (Chapter 11) has drawn attention to the fact that in cultures other than our own psychotherapy is marked by a unity of the medical, the psychological, and the spiritual. He also noted that this unity disintegrated a

long time ago in the West. A similar impression strikes one in seeing how ASC is approached in other cultures, being intimately woven into the structure of society on the one hand and into the ordering of the external universe on the other hand. As Firth has remarked in talking about spirit mediumship in Africa: "What stands out in so much of the material is that spirit mediumship and, in many cases, spirit possession also, is not an isolated individual phenomenon but a cult. It is part of a complex series of ideas and practices of a relatively integrated kind, oriented to the recognition of extra-human powers" (1969). Even when ASC is restricted to a single individual in a culture, such as the shaman, he is given an honored status and is perceived as the psychopomp of the group (Eliade 1964). There is also an attempt at coordinating the ordering of ASC with that of the universe. This was perfectly familiar in Western history from the time of Origen at least in the third century, up to the seventeenth-century Fludd, in the theory of macrocosm and microcosm. As is well known, the advent of modern science eroded the isomorphism. The relationship is implicit in the thinking of Aztec and Babylonian mythologies as has been noted by Danzel (1960): "In such insights we find confirmed what has been taken as the basic trait of mythical thinking, namely that a perception which to us splits into a psychological or subjective component on the one hand and an objective component on the other, presents itself to the mythological thinking man, as a single unit. . . . Cosmology is at the same time psychology, and cosmic phenomena becomes the correspondence of psychological life." In contemporary societies we find identity of form in cosmology and psychology in widely separate communities such as the ordering of the physical house in the Atori of Indonesian Timor (1972), and temporal-spatial referents in the Chamulas of Chiapas, Mexico (1972). Such representations have been unsupported in our own world view as, empirically—as a matter of fact—the physical universe and the psychological universe do *not* appear to have any similarities. Here, I think, we need to distinguish models *of* reality and models *for* reality as Geertz has done (1972). We tend to regard "consciousness" as a *thing, a ding an sich* to be detected and inspected. This is a legacy of the attitude that stands man apart from his universe. What seems to be indicated by the so-called primitive people's conception of consciousness is that it is an energy that pervades through man and not just "in" him and thus extends to nonhuman things as the doctrine that we think of as animism suggests. While we tend to think of this as a kind of magical extrapolation, it may be no more than a nominalistic way of expressing unity: "consciousness," then, not being a "thing," that is, not substantive, but a relation.

(2) If there is one point upon which most cultures agree in this field, it is that "unusual" states of consciousness do not come ready-made without discipline, training, and initiation of some kind. Precourt (Chapter 9) has stressed the educational aspect of initiation ceremonies and secret ceremonies, particularly with respect to what he calls the "hidden curriculum" side of these. In the

present chapter it is argued that in similar societies the attainment of ASC is learned in much the same way as, for example, visual perception is in our own culture. That is to say the mores and norms of the culture lay down limits of categorization so that we learn to perceive phenomena in a certain manner. Training concerning ASC may be more explicit in these other cultures: the point made here is that the mode of knowing needs to be educated. Put more figuratively, it has to be forged, fashioned, and crystallized. One could see how the symbolism of alchemy could so easily arise (Eliade, 1971). The state of the infant's perceptual world described by James as a "blooming, buzzing confusion" applies equally to the potential state of the mode of perception incipient in ASC. There is a practical lesson to be drawn from this: investigation of ASC in human beings needs to take into consideration that it constitutes a process in exactly the same manner as Kragh and Smith (1970) interpret our ordinary perception, and that in some people it is undeveloped and in others highly developed. This is less severe for the discipline of psychology than at first sight might appear. During the nineteenth century when the study of introspection was in vogue, it became necessary for workers in Europe and America to train their subjects in the art. Even in contemporary mathematical psychology, those operating in the field of subjective probability have found it necessary to train their subjects in reporting probabilities. Psychologists studying extrasensory perception have selected subjects who have trained themselves in some way. However the training associated with ASC does extend into a region that makes it somewhat different from merely learning a skill, which is the ethical domain. If, for instance, we were to take seriously Swami Akhilananda's precept, expressed in his book *Hindu Psychology* (1946), that the teacher of "Higher Psychology" must have his mind "fully illumined—first, through ethical practices and next, through practices of concentration, meditation, and other disciplinary practices," it would seem to go beyond our purely scientific considerations. And yet the scientist has his ethics: the honesty implicit in the relationship of theory to fact, the commitment to public report, the basic faith in order. Nevertheless this is a delicate matter for the Western scientist, who is still imbued with G. E. Moore's Naturalistic Fallacy, of the mistake of confusing "is" and "ought."

(3) Already it is being insinuated that the study of ASC in other cultures is not approached in the same way as we would, for instance, investigate the mating habits of Arachnida. Models of experience do exist, for example, the Tantric psychophysiological scheme of *chakras,* yet it is doubtful with this scheme, as with others that have principally arisen from an oral tradition, if they are presented as an explanatory model in the sense that we are accustomed. They appear to be more in the nature of a chart or map through which people, following them, are able to share experiences. This has been well apreciated by Metzner in his little monograph entitled *Maps of Consciousness* (1972). There is an added sophistication in these "maps," for they are not static charts, but

provide symbolic notation that imply flux and polymorphic referents. Aberle has remarked in his study on Peyote symbolism among the Navaho that "the more numerous the meanings, the richer the ritual for the participants, so a point-for-point exegesis of the meaning of ritual objects or rituals is not expected . . ." (1966: 174).

What is being inculcated is a mode of awareness continuously creative, indicating a fluid activity that avoids the tendency to select any one thing from a constant generation of images. Here again we note the tendency to regard consciousness less as an entity and more as a process. Our term "set" might apply if we could look upon this as multivalued. At any rate the notion of looking at the contents of the mind as some kind of mental furniture to be inventoried is as inappropriate in these cultural psychologies as it was for postintrospection psychology.

(4) We come now to the relationship of knower to known, or of observer to observed. It has appeared to many of those who have been involved in ASC that the phenomenon is better described by the passive mood of verbal description than the active mood. This is true from the most rudimentary states of possession of Voodoo spirit entities which "mount" or "enter the head" of its *cheval* (the person possessed), to Mahayana Buddhism in the tradition of which Ashvaghosa can say "One should think: there is walking, there is stopping, there is realizing; not, I am walking, I am doing this . . ." (Huxley 1966: 332). Jung once made the remark that "the primitive does not think; the thought comes to him," (1958: 161) which is misleading if one interprets it as the "primitive" always thinks passively. I believe, though, that Jung's insight is better relegated to the domain we are considering, not to thinking as a whole. The problem of identity that is produced by this way of speaking is seen in one of those seemingly idiotic exchanges that take place between teacher and pupil in Zen (Suzuki 1958: 92):

Kuan (Master): "As long as there is 'I and thou,' this complicates the situation and there is no seeing Tao."

Monk: "When there is neither 'I' nor 'thou,' is it seen?"

Kuan: "When there is neither 'I' nor 'thou,' who is here to see it?"

This kind of talk is not at all conducive to our Indo-European emphasis on subject-object relationship,[2] and if there is any truth at all in the proposition that this is what we have to accept in ASC, then the usual conception of personal identity needs to be altered in turn. We require a more complex psychology of identity than that given by the elementary terms "ego," "self," and other synonyms for the first person pronoun. As a matter of fact, psychoanalysis went some way in this, especially in the early formulations of

Groddeck (1923), but what may be needed is a formula in which the "I" is placed in a total cybernetic or ecosystem as Bateson suggests, in which a part to whole relationship is assumed. Certainly this is a murky area for the psychology of self, but one which I suggest is central for the proper understanding of ASC.

(5) A last point concerns thresholds. The concept of ASC implies a deviation from some status quo. We just do not know if we can apply a homogenous norm of "ordinary" consciousness for all peoples, so that it makes sense to talk about its being altered equally for all. What may be a "giant leap" for us Western people may only resemble a minimal increment for an aborigine. We do not have a psychophysics for ASC. There are some indications in other cultures that the continuum is differently paced for them. Stanner's (1972) account of the process called "The Dreaming" among the Australian aborigines reveals that these people can switch easily from metaphysical and poetic thought to the most prosaic and rational thinking in mundane activity. Stewart's (1969) description of the attitude of the Senoi of Malay toward dream-life suggests little differentiation between waking and sleeping life as far as decision making and adjustment are concerned. I myself noticed, in witnessing the Bori "trance" activity in Zaria, Nigeria, that the participants would suddenly come out of what seemed to be the deepest dissociated condition to talking to their neighbors about (I was told) mundane affairs of the village, and then just as suddenly plunge back into the same dissociated state. Kiev (1961), too, in describing spirit possession in Haiti, notes that "most hungans (i.e., Voodoo priests) preserve an amazingly keen awareness and consciousness of the ongoing situation and their role into it," and further mentions "the characteristic feature of the hungan's possession is the facility and ease of transition to such a state." This kind of behavior is just as difficult to analyze as the phenomenon of role behavior in hypnosis. All we can safely say is that there are big differences in thresholds of ASC in different cultures.

CONCLUSIONS

The picture we have drawn from a discussion of these five points is of a mode of knowing which is not markedly aberrant from ordinary existence; relates the knower to his social and physical universe; and provides the participant with a scheme to organize certain experiences, which often can best be described as happening to him. The approach appears to be least concerned with a coherent and consistent body of knowledge about the nature of man or the universe; indeed, it is almost antagonistic to a purely intellectual presentation. Ornstein has well realized this in the conclusion of his book (1972: 229) when he says: "It would be the height of absurdity if we were to settle, now, for a strictly intellectual understanding of the existence of a second mode of consciousness."

The big difficulty for the Western investigator of this so-called second mode of consciousness is that he can only represent it in the mode of his ordinary consciousness, and express it in the customary mold of his logical mentation and linguistic categories. The interesting and perhaps really revolutionary thing that is occurring in our own culture is that many people are trying out modes of experiencing which for them are quite novel. These methods extend beyond a purely intellectual approach and seem to carry with them their own inherent sense of validity. The question as to whether a more than merely personal validity can be assigned to them is a philosophical and social problem. Philosophers, after all, have forever found some difficulty in finding validity for our usual sense experience. In the last analysis the validity may be found in social consensus.

The thrust of my viewpoint focuses on this second mode of consciousness. I have indicated that our culture is relatively underdeveloped on this, although it is obvious that it is developing. I have suggested that an examination of those other cultures that have apparently had more experience with it is salutary for us, provided that we do not try to put the new wine into old bottles, trying to fit these conceptions into our own mold of thought. I have further suggested that the revolutionary issue in all this is not so much that of uncovering a new content of knowledge as assimilating a different approach to the theory of knowledge. The discipline of psychology raised in the traditional canons of scientific investigation has no recourse other than to bring to bear on the subject all the logic and methodology that it has found so trustworthy in other domains of inquiry. Yet there is slowly dawning on some writers that there is a more fundamental note to be struck. Ornstein (1972), Rogers (1968: 55), and Maslow (1969: 45) have all appreciated that there is a truly epistemological frontier to be crossed. By all means let us continue our incursions into ASC. Let us appreciate, however, that not only may we find we have a tiger by the tail; let us appreciate it may not be, in fact, a tiger.

N O T E S

1. The journals are: *Psychedelic Review, Journal for the Study of Consciousness,* and *Journal of Transpersonal Psychology.* The literature is voluminous, and well documented in C. Tart (ed.), *Altered States of Consciousness* (New York: John Wiley, 1969); B. Aaronson and H. Osmond (eds.), *Psychedelics* (New York: Doubleday, Anchor Books, 1970). For an indication of the social coverage within the United States, see Nat Freeland, *The Occult Explosion* (New York: Berkeley Medallion Books, 1972).

2. When this passage was read at the original conference, Professor Y. Tanaka informed me that it had made clear sense to him. The meaning of the passage is that the person must look into himself for an answer to his question. The last statement of the Zen master is aimed at arresting the pupil in his ordinary train of thought, so that he is constrained to examine his thinking. Professor Tanaka exemplified the quotation as a kind of "loop-logic," analogous to computer programming, where the program comes to a halt and is reverted back to the executive unit for fresh instructions.

REFERENCES

ABERLE, D. F. (1966) The Peyote Religion Among the Navaho. Chicago: Aldine.

AKHILANANDA, S. (1946) Hindu Psychology. New York: Harper and Brothers.

BATESON, G. (1972) Steps to an Ecology of Mind. New York: Ballantine Books.

BUCKE, R. M. (1901) Cosmic Consciousness. Rev. ed. New York: Dutton.

CASTENADA, C. (1968) The Teachings of Don Juan: A Yaqui Way of Knowledge. Berkeley: University of California Press.

CLARK, J. H. (1972) "A map of inner space," in R. Ruddock (ed.) Six Approaches to the Person. London: Routledge & Kegan Paul.

CUNNINGHAM, C. E. (1972) "Order in the Atoni House," in W. E. Lessa and E. Z. Vogt (eds.) Reader in Comparative Religion. 3d ed. New York: Harper & Row.

DANZEL, T. W. (1960) "The psychology of ancient Mexican symbolism," in Spiritual Disciplines: Papers from the Eranos Yearbooks, New York: Pantheon Books.

ELIADE, M. (1964) Shamanism: Archaic Techniques of Ecstasy. Princeton: Princeton University Press.

――― (1971) The Forge and the Crucible: The Origins and Structures of Alchemy. New York: Harper & Row.

FIRTH, R. (1969) "Foreword," in J. Beattie and J. Middleton (eds.) Spirit Mediumship and Society in Africa. New York: Africana Publishing.

GEERTZ, C. (1972) "Religion as a Cultural System," in W. E. Lessa and E. Z. Vogt (eds.) Reader in Comparative Religion. 3d ed. New York: Harper & Row.

GOSSEN, G. H. (1972) "Temporal and spatial equivalents in Chamula ritual symbolism," in W. E. Lessa and E. Z. Vogt (eds.) Reader in Comparative Religion. 3d ed. New York: Harper & Row.

GRODDECK, G. (1923) Das Buch von Es. Leipzig: Internationaler Psychoanalytischer Verlag.

HUXLEY, A. (1966) The Perennial Philosophy. London: Chatto & Windus.

JAMES, W. (1935) The Varieties of Religious Experience. New York: Longmans. (Originally published in 1902.)

Journal of Psychedelic Drugs (1971) "Glossary of drug-related terms." 4, 2: 205-210.

JUNG, C. G. (1958) Psychology and Religion. Collected Works, Vol. 11. London: Routledge & Kegan Paul.

KIEV, A. (1961) "Spirit possession in Haiti." American Journal of Psychiatry 118: 133-138.

KRAGH, U. and G. SMITH [eds.] (1970) Percept-Genetic Analysis. Lund: Gleerups.

LEFORT, R. (1966) The Teachers of Gurdjieff. London: Gollancz.

LEVI-STRAUSS, C. (1969) The Elementary Structures of Kinship. Boston: Beacon Press.

LILLY, J. C. (1967) Programming and Metaprogramming in the Human Biocomputer. Menlo Park, Calif.: Whole Earth Catalog.

LUDWIG, A. M. (1966) "Altered states of consciousness." Archives of General Psychiatry 15: 225-234.

MASLOW, A. H. (1969) The Psychology of Science: A Reconnaissance. Chicago: Henry Regnery.

MASTERS, R. E. L. and J. HOUSTON (1966) The Varieties of Psychedelic Experience, New York: Holt, Rinehart & Winston.

METZNER, R. (1972) Maps of Consciousness. New York: Collier Books.

ORNSTEIN, R. E. (1972) The Psychology of Consciousness. New York: Viking Press.

PRICE-WILLIAMS, D. R. (1972) "Cross-cultural psychology and the problem of categorial determination." Paper presented at Brock University, St. Catharine's, Ontario, Canada (May).

PUHARICH, A. (1973) Beyond Telepathy. New York: Doubleday.

REICH, C. (1970) The Greening of America. New York: Random House.

ROGERS, C. R. (1968) "Some thoughts regarding the current pre-suppositions of the behavioral sciences," pp. 55-72 in W. R. Coulson and C. R. Rogers (eds.) Man and the Science of Man. Columbus, Ohio: Charles E. Merrill.

STANNER, W. E. H. (1972) "The dreaming," in W. E. Lessa and E. Z. Vogt (eds.) Reader in Comparative Religion. 3d ed. New York: Harper & Row.

STEWART, K. (1969) "Dream theory in Malaya," in C. Tart (ed.) Altered States of Consciousness. New York: John Wiley.

SUZUKI, D. T. (1958) The Zen Doctrine of No-Mind. London: Rider.

UNDERHILL, E. (1911) Mysticism. London: Methuen.

WALLACE, A. F. C. (1966) Religion, An Anthropological View. New York: Random House.

WATTS, A. (1959) The Way of Zen. New York: Mentor Books.

WEIL, A. (1972) The Natural Mind: A New Way of Looking at Drugs and the Higher Consciousness. Boston: Houghton Mifflin.

Chapter 13

AN ANALYSIS OF THE PREPUBLICATION EVALUATION OF CROSS-CULTURAL MANUSCRIPTS: IMPLICATIONS FOR FUTURE RESEARCH

W A L T E R   J.   L O N N E R

Western Washington State College

Despite the many advances in the understanding of human behavior which cross-cultural psychology has given to psychological science in general, the field has been pockmarked by numerous and legendary methodological difficulties. From the early work on perception by Rivers (1901, 1905), which many psychologists view as the "seedling" cross-cultural studies, to the present, the years have been littered with countless published cross-cultural studies. The past decade in particular has been one of positive acceleration in the area. While many of these studies have been robust enough to merit applause from even the skeptics, too many have appeared which have led some to conclude that the field is faddish and replete with opaque half-truths, seldom if ever contributing eternal verities which any science cherishes. Within most academic departments of psychology, those faculty members who consider themselves to be cross-culturalists have often been on the defensive about "what they do." Some may even feel as if they represent a one-man lunatic fringe amid an otherwise staid and cloistered group who are dutifully pursuing what they were taught to pursue in graduate school. Currently, this characterization may be a trifle harsh, but not too long ago this was indeed the case. Those who have had the opportunity to talk with some of the pioneers in cross-cultural psychology are told how off-beat they once appeared.

Most, if not all, psychologists now agree that the cross-cultural method in psychology is a worthy one. But, unfortunately, somewhat less than full status is usually accorded cross-cultural data. Researchers say that cross-cultural evidence "should be considered in due course," but they tend to gloss over such evidence by asserting that at present it is generally too "rough," "fragmented," "diffuse," or "uninterpretable," at the same time often invoking the "critical" findings— from cross-cultural research—needed to give their parochial research more complete credibility. On the other hand, many researchers who identify with the cross-cultural method are unwittingly helping to sustain such partially accurate characterizations by conducting cross-cultural research without properly attending to the inherent, but solvable, problems of method that are always present. The longer the avoidable errors are sustained, the more time will it take for all cross-cultural data in psychology to be accepted fully for the immense potential that they have.

This chapter attempts to pinpoint some of the more pervasive and recurring methodological errors that are made in cross-cultural psychology, and perhaps in cross-cultural research in other areas as well. Before presenting the rationale and method employed, however, it may be helpful to place the current status of the method in brief historical context.

THREE ERAS IN CROSS-CULTURAL PSYCHOLOGY

Since the turn of the century, it can be said that cross-cultural psychology has gone through two "eras," and has recently entered a third. The first can be called the "era of the unfortunate protostereotype" and covered the first 30 years of the century. Most studies during this period were typically done in a hurried manner by a psychologist-turned-temporary-anthropologist, who found himself in an exotic culture, gave a few tests or tasks to "primitive" people, and then made sweeping and often erroneous and possibly demeaning generalizations about the "savage mind" and its "peculiarities." Clearly, the "findings" must have made good fodder for an academic travelogue. Those who made such treks had their chance to explain how "they" (the "natives") thought and behaved and lived. While such researchers may have had noble intentions, their unabashed psychological ethnocentrism went basically unchecked. Moreover, there were no attempts to develop in any systematic way a planned and integrated research program of the type that years later, for psychology in general, was to be called the "nomological network" (Cronbach and Meehl, 1955). Not until sufficient numbers of methodologists pointed to possible serious errors did these psychological sorties decline.

The second era, generally spanning the 30 years from 1930 to 1960, is when the "workhorse model" appeared. Augmented by attempts of universalists and cultural relativists alike to develop "culture fair" intelligence and personality tests, researchers quite unsuccessfully tried to settle issues like "nativist versus empiricist" and "nature versus nurture." The typical design involved taking samples of children from two different cultures who took a test loaded with "g," or with personality tests whose items cut across national boundaries. The resultant test scores were used to refute or support certain theoretical positions, and interpretations of data could shift with equal ease between polarities in theory. Rhetoric far outweighed any stable findings. This period is now viewed retrospectively as one in which researchers were implicitly asking two questions: (1) How well can they do on our tricks? and (2) Is, as I believe, my trick better than yours? This era was by no means devoid of significant gains, however. Several pioneering techniques developed during the period led to many respectable current instruments and perspectives. And the biggest value of the period may have been that it purged forever the notion that one "other" culture, one researcher, and one instrument can result in anything meaningful, or at least stable.

The third era has only recently emerged. Here the better studies either (1) employ multimethods which are coordinated by multiresearchers in multicultures, or (2) systematically and longitudinally study human behavior by carefully selecting cultures and ecologies after appropriate and purposeful rationales have been decided upon. Problems of equivalence of stimuli are settled, translation problems are minimized, and clear theoretical and anthropological rationale for conducting the study are determined at the outset. Finally, interpretations of data are synchronized within the context of both theory and cultures—never one without the other.

The third era is co-evolving with increasing refinement in methodology. The Campbell and Fiske (1959) exhortation to use a multitrait and multimethod matrix is a good example of the thoughtful appraisal that marked the start of a recent outpouring of methodological statements. A few of these were the Frijda and Jahoda (1966) article, and Berry's (1969) now-familiar call for an emic-etic analysis. Shortly thereafter came Berrien's "super-ego" paper in which he said (1970: 33-34):

> The best cross-cultural research is that which (1) engages the collaborative efforts of two or more investigators of different countries, each of whom is (2) strongly supported by institutions in their respected countries, to (3) address researchable problems of a common concern not only to the science of psychology but (4) relevant to the social problems of our time. Such collaborative enterprises would begin with (5) the joint definition of the problems, (6) employ comparable methods, (7) pool data that would be 'owned' by the collaborators jointly who are free to (8) report their own interpretations to their own constituents but (9) are obligated to strive for interpretations acceptable to a world community of scholars.

Several books on method have appeared only recently. They include two books written by anthropologists (Naroll and Cohen, 1970; and Pelto, 1969, and two written by psychologists (Triandis et al., 1972; and Brislin, Lonner, and Thorndike, 1973). These and other books often address methodological issues in general, and for the most part do not get terribly specific about the precise nature and scope of methodological flaws. Thus, the justification to write yet another treatise on methodology is that one of the method's leading publication outlets, the *Journal of Cross-Cultural Psychology*, is in a unique position, through its manuscript reviewing procedures, to point to specific, recurring flaws as well as strengths in both published and unpublished cross-cultural research.

JCCP AS AN IMPORTANT SOURCE OF INFORMATION

Since late in 1969 there has been a growing repository of manuscripts submitted for publication in JCCP, one of the two major journals explicitly devoted to the publication of cross-cultural research in psychology.[1] Collectively, these manuscripts, whether published or not, constitute one of the largest files concerning the current tenor of research in cross-cultural psychology. In addition to the immediate value that the published papers may offer, all these manuscripts and the correspondence concerning them can be useful in other ways. One use to which they can be put is that of serving as a guideline for research quality control, and this is the focus that the remainder of this chapter takes.

WHY EDITORIAL CONSULTANTS' OPINIONS ARE
VALUABLE FOR ARCHIVAL PURPOSES

When an appropriate manuscript is submitted to JCCP, it is usually sent to two of some forty cross-cultural researchers who are on the Editorial Advisory Board. These "referees" vote for or against acceptance, and with few exceptions give specific reasons for their judgments. Thus, the correspondence for hundreds of manuscripts—over time and across diverse topics—represents a file that is rich in critical analysis of substance and method. An analysis of these critiques can give insights about both accepted (those which are eventually published) and rejected papers, and can lead to better research.

Critiques of the type presented here, for published research, may be considered redundant, because the reader himself can critique and judge the research; however, most journals in psychology boast a high rejection rate, and we are thus seeing the "good" papers, seldom knowing what specific factors led to the rejection of the unsuccessful publication attempts. In other words, the "good" are published and the "bad" are filed away. It can be argued that while many researchers emulate designs, strategies, presentations, and the like given in published research, equally valuable benefits can be derived from an analysis of unsuccessful publication attempts. We explain to entire classes of students the rationale for failing grades; so too should we explain to researchers the specific reasons why so many manuscripts are not accepted for publication. I would like to see the American Psychological Association, for example, require their journal editors to engage in periodic analyses similar to this one in a further effort to guide psychological research.

METHOD OF CONTENT ANALYSIS

The folders for all manuscripts which by about November 15, 1972,[2] had been acted upon (some 30 were still in various stages of review or revision) were sorted into one of two categories: (1) rejected, or (2) accepted for publication. Next, non-cross-cultural papers (automatically rejected) and those that were reviews or which dealt with theoretical issues were identified and excluded. This left 272 (of 326) cross-cultural manuscripts which handled researchable topics in an empirical manner. Of these, 156 had been rejected and 116 had been published or were awaiting publication. Finally, the manuscripts were sorted into three separate piles corresponding to the first three years of publication, late 1969-1970, 1971, and 1972. These data are summarized in Table 1. The most noteworthy item given in Table 1 is that the rejection percentage has shown a consistent annual increase, from 52.5% in 1969-70 to 65.2% in 1972, and these percentages include only the 272 papers that were cross-cultural and empirical.

Table 2 gives further data for the 272 manuscripts, again for the three years and for the rejected and accepted categories. The average number of authors per paper has been increasing annually. This average is consistently higher and is increasing more rapidly for accepted papers.[3] Table 2 also shows that papers of the experimental type (the planned and systematic manipulation of variables) consistently have a much better chance of survival than the correlational type (where data, not treatment conditions, are manipulated). This trend is increasing dramatically. Overall, 11% of the rejected manuscripts reported on experimental data, while 28% of the accepted papers did so.

Not presented in Table 2 are some pertinent data concerning single versus

TABLE 1

NUMBER OF REJECTED AND ACCEPTED MANUSCRIPTS
SUBMITTED TO *JCCP*, AND REJECTION PERCENTAGES,
DURING A THREE-YEAR PERIOD

Year	Number Submitted[a]	Review Articles	Rejected Cross-Cultural	Non-C-C	Total[b]	Accepted	Rejection Percentage (b/a)
1969-70	141	11	67	7	74	56	52.5
1971	90	7	39	12	51	32	56.6
1972	95	5	50	12	62	28	65.2
Totals	326	23	156	31	187	116	57.3

NOTE: These data are based on cumulative figures from September, 1969 through November 15, 1972.

multiple authorship of the accepted papers. Paralleling the increase in multiple authorship is the *decrease* in solo authorship (52%, 47%, and 32% for the three consective years). The overall percentage of solo authors for the three years was 45.7%. This figure is in almost perfect accord with the 45.4% rate of single-author publications found for a recent sample of 6,925 articles published in 17 journals representing a cross-section of North American publications in psychology (Over and Smallman, 1973). The rate of single-author publications in psychology, it was noted, falls between what have been called "data disciplines" (chemistry, 17%; biology, 30%; physics, 33%) and "word disciplines" (education, 80%; mathematics, 85%; philosophy, 95%). Moreover, cross-cultural psychology, represented by the *Journal of Cross-Cultural Psychology*, has a rate of single-author publication similar to such publications as *Journal of Educational Psychology*, *Journal of Consulting Psychology*, *Journal of Personality*, and *Journal of Social Psychology*. Over and Smallman noted that at present "journals specializing in specific data areas such as clinical, social, applied, and traditional experimental psychology cannot be differentiated in terms of relative frequency of single-author publication" (1973: 162).

It remains to be seen whether or not single-author publication in cross-cultural psychology will continue to decrease to the point where multiple authorship in this area of psychology matches the very high rate of multiple authorship found in such data disciplines as biology and physics. The trend seems to be in that direction, but the rate of single-author publication may stabilize at about 45%. This would reflect the heavy "social and personality" nature of cross-cultural psychology. A continued increase in multiple authorship should, of course, reflect the success of any continued efforts to encourage needed collaboration.

TABLE 2

MEAN NUMBER OF AUTHORS PER MANUSCRIPT AND PERCENTAGES OF CORRELATIONAL AND EXPERIMENTAL APPROACHES FOR 272 REJECTED AND ACCEPTED "EMPIRICALLY-ORIENTED" MANUSCRIPTS SUBMITTED TO *JCCP* DURING A THREE-YEAR PERIOD

	Rejected			Accepted		
Year	Authors (Mean N)	Correlational Percentage	Experimental Percentage	Authors (Mean N)	Correlational Percentage	Experimental Percentage
1969-70	1.4	65 (97%)	2 (3%)	1.7	45 (80%)	11 (20%)
1971	1.5	34 (87%)	5 (13%)	1.9	24 (75%)	8 (25%)
1972	1.6	42 (84%)	8 (16%)	2.2	15 (54%)	13 (46%)
Totals	1.5	141 (89%)	15 (11%)	1.9	84 (72%)	32 (28%)

Carrying these descriptive analyses further, the topics of the manuscripts, again by acceptance and rejection categories, were pinpointed and listed. Following that, all correspondence from referees for each paper was reviewed. As mentioned previously, the referees vote for or against acceptance, and with very few exceptions give specific reasons for their judgments. Thus an analysis of these reviews—over time, over diverse topics, and involving the insights and critiques of some 40 cross-cultural researchers—has led to this quantification of strengths and weaknesses. Some unintentional unreliability is quite likely to occur when only one person reviews some 550 separate pieces of correspondence ranging from "O.K., accept" to a seven-page review, which itself should have been published instead of the article it criticized. Nevertheless, an analysis of these judgments is distilled in Tables 3 and 4.

Table 3 concerns the accepted papers. The primary and secondary strengths are tabulated. And, since no paper in its original form was judged to be flawless, the primary weaknesses are also tabulated. Paralleling Table 3, Table 4 lists the tabulated primary and secondary weaknesses of rejected papers. Because none of these papers is without some redeeming value, the single major strength of each is identified, and these are summed and listed.

The methods used in cross-cultural psychology differ from typical and traditional psychological methodology in only a few major ways. The three most important of these differences are: (1) sampling, (2) establishing equivalence conceptually (constructs across cultures) and linguistically (translation), and (3) synchronizing anthropological material with psychological precedents as rationale for research. Deficiencies in any one or more of these could easily lead to one or more alternative explanations, commonly known as the plausible rival hypothesis analysis.

Clearly, Table 4 (concerning the rejected manuscripts) documents that the aborted attempts to communicate cultural information were generously targeted as deficient in one or more of the above areas. What is more important, those papers that did or will see the light of print, and hence communicated data about people in other cultures, had many of the same judged weaknesses as the rejected papers, although the magnitude of the weaknesses among them is not as marked and were obviously also more than offset by their strengths.

The top five strengths as well as the top five weaknesses of both accepted and rejected papers are given in Table 5, for emphasis. One may use the various strengths to characterize the hypothetical "perfect" manuscript. First, the methods used must be clearly stated. Next, an established frame of reference (Piaget, perception, or acculturation, for example) must serve as the syntax of the paper, and instruments with proven reliability and validity must be used. Then, a clear combination of psychological and anthropological rationale should be used. The question "How does psychological theory coincide with the context of relevant cultural variables" captures the essence of this strength. Large samples, plus some degree of "cuteness" (which may be synonymous with

TABLE 3

TOPICS, STRENGTHS, AND WEAKNESSES TABULATED FOR 116 ACCEPTED MANUSCRIPTS 1969-1972

Topics	N	Strengths — Primary	N	Secondary	N	Weaknesses	N
Socialization, acculturation, ethnic identification	22	Clear methodology	23	Clear methodology	19	Samples, including "matching"	31
Personality (general)	22	Use of established frame of reference	12	Use of established instrument	17	Plausible rival hypothesis(es)	13
Intelligence, ability	17	Original, innovative	10	Use of established frame of reference	12	Clarity of design	10
Attitudes, attitude change, stereotypes	12	Direct implications to education	9	Use of previous research	8	Excessive length	10
Norming of personality tests	9	Excellent sample	9	Cultural/psychological rationale	7	Concepts weak	8
Perception, illusions	7	Clearly written	8	Major problem analyzed	6	Post hoc analysis, speculation	7
Linguistics, bilingualism, communication	4	Scarce material	8	Direct implications to education	5	Weak literature review	5
Values	4	Cultural/psychological rationale	7	Multicultural	5	Translation problems	5
Competition-Cooperation	4	Data from little-studied culture	5	Literature review	5	Limited generalizeability	4
Mental health, psychiatric disorders	3	Use of established instruments	5	Original, innovative	4	Poor writing	4
Need achievement	3	Norming of viable cross-cultural test	4	High interest value	4	Faulty use of statistics	4
Methodological innovation	1	Literature review	4	Statistical treatment	4	Poor or unknown instruments	4
Physiological processes, translation, time perspectives, population, 2 each	8	"Cute"	3	Clearly written	3	No comparison groups, non-equivalence of methods for groups	4
		Multiresearcher	3	Part of large project	3	Not enough descriptive data	3
		Refutation of prior findings, multimethod, use of ethnographies, timely topic— 2 each		Large Ns	3	Low on theory-relatedness	3
				Multimethod	3	Proliferation of data from same study	1
				Replicability, infrequently studied problem, careful sample selection— 2 each	6		
				Ethographic material, good translation— 1 each	2		

NOTE: There is no continuity between rows or columns; the listings by categories (columns) are rank-orderings from most to least mentions. Ns in each column sum to 116.

TABLE 4
TOPICS, WEAKNESSES, AND STRENGTHS TABULATED FOR 156 REJECTED MANUSCRIPTS, 1969-1972

Topics	N	Weaknesses				Strengths	N
		Primary	N	Secondary	N		
Personality (general)	46	Samples, including "matching"	36	Samples, including "matching"	32	"Important" topic	20
Attitudes, attitude change, stereotypes	30	Too unicultural or U.S. subcultural	15	Too long, including post hoc analyses, speculation	19	"Cute"	18
Socialization, acculturation, ethnic identification	23	No new data	15	Poor or unknown instrument	17	Large N	16
Norming of personality tests	9	Too long, including post hoc analysis, speculation	14	Translation problems	13	Educational problem	14
Educational problems	8	Faulty research design	11	No cultural/psychological rationale	11	Followed precedent	12
Values	8	No cultural/psychological rationale	9	Faulty statistics	9	Statistical treatment	12
Mental health, psychiatric disorders	8	Faulty statistics	8	Plausible rival hypothesis(es)	8	Attempt to find cause-effect in difficult data	11
Linguistics, bilingualism, communication	7	Nonequivalence of measures for groups	8	Concepts not defined	8	Attempt to understand "universals"	6
Intelligence, ability	3	Concepts not defined	8	Selectivity in reporting data	6	Use of established instruments	6
Modernism	3	Poor or unknown instruments	7	Poor research design	5	Timely	6
Managerial behavior	2	Poorly written	3	Nonequivalence of data between groups	4	Replication attempt	5
Perception, illusions	2	No attempt to explain findings	3	No clear purposes	4	Well written	4
Delinquency, sexual behavior, time perspectives, "love magic," political association, spiritual counseling, experimenter effects—1 each	7	No references, or weak literature review	3	No contribution	4	Theory relatedness	4
		Faulty interpretation	2	Simplistic	3	Literature review	4
		Translation problems	2	Poor writing	3	Well designed	3
		Data juggling	2	No references, or weak literature review	2	Data from little-studied culture	3
		Interview data, dittoed, educational value, non-replicable, too sociological, proliferation of data from same study, and plausible rival hypothesis—1 each	7	Unbelievable results	2	Multimethod	3
				Old data, no external validity, irrelevant, non-empirical, proliferation of data from same study—1 each	5	Ethnographic analysis	2
						Attempt to correlate instruments	2
						Uncommon topic	2
						Individual testing, data interpretation, multi-cultural—1 each	3

NOTE: There is no continuity between rows or columns; the listings by categories (columns) are rank-orderings from most to least mentions. Ns in each column sum to 156.

[313]

creativity or ingenuity of design) would be the capstone. Finally, but not less important, the study should have direct educational implications. All these strengths imply that the better studies will contribute to the "nomological net" mentioned earlier (Cronbach and Meehl, 1955). In the context of cross-cultural psychology, the nomological net can be pictured as a grid. In each square of the grid there will be a union of method, theory, and culture so that genuine piecemeal approximation leading to a final and comprehensive network of interrelationships can be made. A good example of this is the work of Berry (1966, 1971a, 1971b, and Chapter 8 in this volume), who is studying the relationships between culture, ecology, and behavior. Further examples include several chapters in this book, notably the work by Cole (Chapter 6).

The five most important weaknesses given in Table 5 can be used to characterize the type of study that would surely be doomed. Such a hypothetical manuscript may report the use of "casual," "convenient," or "accidental" samples, making reasonable generalizations about an entire culture impossible. The concepts or constructs would fall short of agreed-upon meaning, there would be little or no rationale linking psychological processes and anthropological or ecological factors; the study, in Berry's (1969) words, would thus be "a mere anecdote." Moreover, poorly translated instruments with little or no

TABLE 5

THE TOP FIVE STRENGTHS AND WEAKNESSES (PRIMARY AND SECONDARY, COMBINED FROM TABLES 3 and 4) FOR BOTH ACCEPTED AND REJECTED MANUSCRIPTS

Strengths	
Accepted Manuscripts	Rejected Manuscripts
1. Clear methodology	1. "Important" topic
2. Use of established frame of reference	2. "Cute"
3. Use of established instrument	3. Large N
4. Direct implications to education	4. Educational problem
5. Cultural/psychological rationale	5. Followed precedent

Weaknesses	
1. Samples	1. Samples
2. Plausible rival hypothesis(es)	2. Too long, including post hoc analyses
3. Clarity of design	3. No cultural/psychological rationale
4. Excessive length	4. Poor or unknown instrument
5. Concepts weak	5. Translation problems

proven validity or reliability may be used with wild abandon. Next, any number of plausible rival hypotheses may be invoked to account for the findings. Finally, extended discussions of the "findings" would be replete with ad hoc anthropological musings about why an expected relationship was not found or how the results relate to any number of previous findings.

A more complete account of the many factors which may "doom" a cross-cultural paper submitted for publication is given in Brislin and Lonner (1974). A summary of these "guidelines for having research ignored" is as follows (the cynical has been separated from the serious by using a dash, so as to avoid confusion):

(1)   Admit that a certain technique was chosen for convenience so that long, individual data gathering sessions would not be necessary. —This has been an issue with group-administered projective tests, as Spain (1972) points out. He suggests that only hard work will solve certain methodological faults.

(2)   Use instruments for which the overwhelming body of evidence indicates no reliability or validity. Do not even be concerned with these two concepts. Or, alternately, develop your own measurement device because other candidates "do not quite fill your needs." Then confidently use this instrument as if it were around since the days of Archimedes.

(3)   For subjects, use school children in areas where school attendance is rare. Then generalize from these to the whole population, including school nonattenders. —This, of course, is one aspect of the sampling problem. The articles by Brislin and Baumgardner (1971) and Heider (1972) may be helpful in suggesting approaches to choosing and obtaining data from subjects when random sampling plans are unfeasible.

(4)   When using factor analysis, use samples too small to obtain reliable results. Compare samples of 100 college students with a large random sample of a country, and then suggest that it is the latter that was wrong. —With regard to the use of factor analysis, Thorndike (Brislin, Lonner, and Thorndike, 1973) makes the strong statement that the number of subjects should be determined by this formula: square the number of variables and add 50. Thus for 20 variables the number of required subjects would be 450.

(5)   Use only one method to measure one variable so that all the faults of the method and the vagueness of the variable confound data interpretation. —Campbell and Fiske (1959) is still the best presentation of the problem, and they suggest a solution.

(6)   To obtain a "control group," match each member of an experi-

mental group to a person of the same age, amount of schooling, socioeconomic status, and so forth. Analyze the results as if the groups were equivalent. —This procedure ignores the powerful data contaminant, "regression artifacts." The book by Campbell and Stanley (1966) gives a good exposition of this problem and how matching causes it. A more difficult and longer exposition can be found as Appendix D in Hovland, Lumsdaine, and Sheffield (1949). In its simplest form this means that when people from population B are matched to individuals in population A, the people selected from B are not representative of B's as a whole (because they were chosen on the basis of the A's). In addition, some of the A's will not be used because no matching B can be found. Thus, the resulting A group will not be representative of *all* A's.

(7)   When comparisons across variables result in significance tests that approach, or even go beyond, statistical significance, use them as a license to make any interpretation you wish. When data are in line with expectations, gloat, and close the case; when data are not in line with expectations, explain them away with armchair speculation. In really tough spots, select those writings from cultural anthropologists which you know will sound convincing. —This problem involves the so-called significance test controversy that abounds in the behavioral sciences. A book of readings by that title is a valuable aid in preventing overinterpretation or even underinterpretation (see Morrison and Henkel, 1970).

(8)   Choose a research topic or a specific hypothesis, not because of its importance, but because there is a convenient technique or instrument available to test it.

(9)   Choose topics that will yield a large number of publications rather than in a contribution to an understanding of human behavior.

(10) Do one study, for instance on French-English bilinguals in Canada, and then generalize to the world's bilinguals. —In contrast to such pretentiousness, the collection of papers by Chomsky (1972) is an excellent example of a modest, tempered presentation of a theoretical position.

(11) Do not bother translating because of the hard work necessary to obtain equivalence of measures. Instead, use as subjects people who speak a language of convenience, even though such people are unrepresentative of the entire population.

(12) When a number of small studies are done to investigate one hypothesis, publish each of the small studies in a separate place. When asked a question about what data are in what article, be unable to answer.

(13) Do not bother doing a literature review. Do not be concerned with the work of others so that there might be a link made between one set of data and another.

(14) Resist any temptation to admit that other theories or rival hypotheses may explain your data.

(15) Make sure that the report is as long as possible, and that complex tables and fancy figures will exonerate you of any misinterpretation you have unknowingly made. Early in the report, be sure to tell the reader that this is perhaps the best and most important study ever done.

(16) As soon as differences across cultures are found, immediately make conclusions about underlying competence. —This common procedure ignores a host of plausible rival hypotheses (understanding of instructions, sample differences, differential motivation to do task, and so forth). One of the contributions of the Cole, Gay, Glick, and Sharp (1971) research was to show how group differences should only be a *starting point* for a series of further experiments that might determine the "why" of the original differences. Cole expands on this idea in this volume (see Chapter 6).

The problem of ad hoc analyses (point 7, above) is worthy of further comment. The social, personality, and clinical areas in psychology are, for the most part, suffering from a mild malady of diffuseness and endless partial truths (or, more generously, countless successive approximations to truth). Everything works, and nothing works. Anything can be explained, if one is nimble with words. On the other hand, many contend that the "experimental" wing of psychology is too rigid, too sterile, and too artificial. It is true, for example, that conclusions and summary sections of articles published in personality and social psychology journals have significantly more qualifying adjectives ("hedging") such as "however," "nevertheless," "but," "on the other hand," "may," "perhaps," and "possibly" than do corresponding sections of articles published in journals devoted to the more "hard-headed" quarters of psychological research (Lonner and Monson, 1972). These adjectives tend to perpetuate an aura of endless tentativeness in the "softer" circles of psychology, and they are related to the methodological paradox in hypothesis testing about which Meehl (1967) and others have written.

A RECAPITULATION

Little in this chapter is new to those who have been in the cross-cultural business for several years or more. The basic reason that I did this content analysis is to document for graduate students and neophytes what probably will have to be done (or avoided) to get their research published in the future. Every academic psychologist with instinct for survival wants to publish, and publication of cross-cultural research in the past has been relatively easy. But things must change and they are changing. Journals that publish cross-cultural research should no longer be considered outlets for research that would not pass muster in the more "sanctified" journals.

There is a powerful residual reason more care must be used in planning, conducting, and reporting cross-cultural research, and publications in this area of psychology must be wary of what is published. This reason concerns the dual problem of what should be printed for public consumption about other cultures and to what degree such research should be considered to be "truthful" (in the way truthful is used publicly). Cross-cultural researchers are becoming increasingly sensitive about what is communicated about "other cultures" in the name of psychological science. Because the layman may tend to believe anything "scientific," and because "startling" or "cute" findings will likely be seized upon by the popular media, researchers studying other cultural systems and their inhabitants had better be more careful than ever before about publishing material that may give only a very blurred view of people whom the readers of the media may never experience firsthand. Hundreds of cross-cultural researchers are already seeing the door to other cultures or subcultures slammed in their faces. That they have been "studied to death" is a major factor here, of course, but distorted images, unwittingly presented in journals and books, is certainly a strong reason also.

SUMMARY AND CONCLUSIONS

The archival data presented in this chapter pointed to major strengths and weaknesses present in published and unpublished cross-cultural data-oriented manuscripts. The source of the data were some 550 separate evaluations of 272 manuscripts (approximately two evaluations per manuscript) which were submitted to the *Journal of Cross-Cultural Psychology* during a two and one-half year period. The evaluations were made by some forty researchers who are immersed in various cross-cultural areas, and thus stability of judgments is no doubt present.

To put the analysis of the evaluations in proper context, a preliminary historical scanning of cross-cultural research resulted in characterizing the method as having gone through two eras, and as recently entering a third. Researchers in this present era can profitably make use of the tabulated strengths and weaknesses of material submitted for publication. The tables in this chapter can serve as a checklist to be used, along with other and more comprehensive data, in planning and conducting cross-cultural research. The point was made that seasoned cross-cultural researchers carry variations of these checklists around in their heads. Thus, those who may benefit most are those just getting started in this exciting field.

Of course, the general, overriding intent of this exercise was to help point the way toward a systematic linking of each study with its most recent predecessor so that a solid network of findings will emerge as a logical and complete picture. Having done this, anecdotal studies will be on the wane. The beneficiaries will be the cross-cultural method as a developing area, as well as behavioral science in general. An important residual gain will be the increasing assurance that the media, when they do popularize scientific findings about "other cultures," are not perpetuating possible demeaning and will-o-the-wisp characteristics about them.

NOTES

1. The other being the *International Journal of Psychology*. Other journals, of course, publish cross-cultural psychological research, but not regularly as a part of specific publication policy.

2. This analysis could have included more than 100 additional manuscripts that were acted upon by the time the final draft of this paper was written; however, the number of papers on which this chapter's data are based is sufficiently large to capture the basic trends.

3. This trend does not hold for the papers published in the first 27 issues of the *International Journal of Psychology* during the period 1966-1972. There was an average of 1.7 authors for the 159 articles published in that journal during that seven-year period. This tally, however, is for *all* IJP articles, and not just the empirical ones, which are the focus of this chapter.

REFERENCES

BERRIEN, F. K. (1970) "A super-ego for cross-cultural research." International Journal of Psychology 5: 33-39.

BERRY, J. W. (1966) "Temne and Eskimo perceptual skills." International Journal of Psychology 1: 207-229.

––– (1969) "On cross-cultural comparability." International Journal of Psychology 4: 119-128.

––– (1971a) "Ecological and cultural factors in spatial perceptual development." Canadian Journal of Behavioral Science 3: 324-336.

––– (1971b) "Psychological research in the North." Anthropologica 8: 143-157.

BRISLIN, R. W. and S. BAUMGARDNER (1971) "Non-random sampling of individuals in cross-cultural research." Journal of Cross-Cultural Psychology 2: 397-400.

––– and W. J. LONNER (1974) "Methodological approaches to cross-cultural research." Seminar presentation at the inaugural meeting of the International Association for Cross-Cultural Psychology, Hong Kong. (In J. L. M. Dawson and W. J. Lonner [eds.] Readings in Cross-Cultural Psychology: Proceedings of the First International Conference of the International Association for Cross-Cultural Psychology. Hong Kong: University of Hong Kong Press, 1972.)

––– and R. M. THORNDIKE (1973) Cross-Cultural Research Methods. New York: Wiley-Interscience.

CAMPBELL, D. T. and D. W. FISKE (1959) "Convergent and discriminant validity by the multitrait-multimethod matrix." Psychological Bulletin 56: 81-105.
––– and J. C. STANLEY (1966) "Experimental and quasi-experimental designs for research." Chicago: Rand McNally.
CHOMSKY, N. (1972) Language and Mind. Enlarged ed. New York: Harcourt Brace Jovanovich.
COLE, M., J. GAY, J. GLICK and D. SHARP (1971) The Cultural Context of Learning and Thinking. New York: Basic Books.
CRONBACH, L. J. and P. E. MEEHL (1955) "Construct validity in psychological tests." Psychological Bulletin 53: 281-302.
FRIJDA, N. and G. JAHODA (1966) "On the scope and methods of cross-cultural research." International Journal of Psychology 1: 109-127.
HEIDER, E. (1972) "Probabilities, sampling, and ethnographic method: the case of Dani color names." MAN 7: 448-466.
HOVLAND, C., A. LUMSDAINE and F. SHEFFIELD (1949) Experiments in Mass Communication. New York: John Wiley.
LONNER, W. J. and S. K. MONSON (1972) " 'Hedging' in 'soft' psychology journals: support for Meehl's Paradox?" Unpublished manuscript. Bellingham, Wash.: Western Washington State College.
MEEHL, P. (1967) "Theory-testing in psychology and physics: a methodological paradox." Philosophy of Science 34: 103-115.
MORRISON, D. and R. HENKEL (1970) The Significance Test Controversy. Chicago: Aldine.
NAROLL, R. and R. COHEN [eds.] (1970) A Handbook of Method in Cultural Anthropology. New York: Natural History Press.
OVER, R. and S. SMALLMAN (1973) Maintenance of individual visibility in publication of collaborative research by psychologists. American Psychologist 28: 161-166.
PELTO, P. J. (1970) Anthropological Research. New York: Harper & Row.
RIVERS, W. H. R. (1901) "Primitive colour vision." Popular Science Monthly 59: 44-58.
––– (1905) "Observations on the senses of the Todas." British Journal of Psychology 1: 321-396.
SPAIN, D. (1972) "On the use of projective techniques for research in psychological anthropology," in F. L. K. Hsu (ed.) Psychological Anthropology. New ed. Cambridge, Mass.: Schenkman.
TRIANDIS, H. C., V. VASSILIOU, G. VASSILIOU, Y. TANAKA and A. V. SHANMUGAM (1972) The Analysis of Subjective Culture. New York: Wiley-Interscience.

ABOUT THE CONTRIBUTORS

JOHN W. BERRY is an Associate Professor of Psychology at Queen's University, Kingston, Canada. He received his Ph.D. from the University of Edinburgh in 1966. He has contributed to various shcolarly journals and books, and has co-authored and co-edited several books. For the past ten years, his research has focused on mapping ecological, cultural, and behavioral interactions.

STEPHEN BOCHNER is Senior Lecturer of Psychology at the University of New South Wales. He has taught at Rutgers University, and has conducted research at the East-West Center in Honolulu under the Center's fellowship program. He has written several articles on culture contact, and he is the co-editor of *Overseas Students in Australia,* the first comprehensive treatment of Australian involvement in international education.

RICHARD BRISLIN is a Research Associate at the Culture Learning Institute, East-West Center in Honolulu, specializing in social and cross-cultural psychology. His publications include a co-authored book, *Cross-Cultural Research Methods.* He is currently conducting research on how best to implement the anthropological and psychological findings of cross-cultural research to benefit the particular cultures.

LEONARD W. DOOB is Professor of Psychology and Chairman of the Council on African Studies at Yale University. He has also served as research associate and visiting professor at several African universities, including Makerere, Natal, Tanzania, and Legon. His publications include numerous contributions to scholarly journals and books, as well as several authored and edited books, most recently *Resolving Conflict in Africa* (1970) and *Patterning of Time* (1971).

MICHAEL COLE is Associate Professor of Ethnographic Psychology and Experimental Anthropology at The Rockefeller University. He is co-author of several books, including *Culture and Thought* (1974).

ANDREW R. DAVIDSON is a Research Scientist at Battelle Human Affairs Research Centers, Seattle. He received his Ph.D. in Social Psychology from the University of Illinois where he was a National Science Foundation Predoctoral

Fellow. His empirical work has focused on testing the generality of current attitude-behavior theories in both field and cross-cultural contexts. He is currently conducting cross-cultural research on the prediction of fertility and contraceptive choice behaviors from attitudinal and normative variables.

JURIS G. DRAGUNS is Professor of Psychology at Pennsylvania State University. He received his Ph.D. in clinical psychology from the University of Rochester. Previously he served in research and clinical capacities at Rochester State Hospital and Worcester State Hospital. His research interests include the relationship between culture and psychopathology, conceptual models of abnormal behavior, personality assessment, and the interface between perception and personality.

GEORGE M. GUTHRIE is Professor of Psychology at Pennsylvania State University. He completed his graduate study in clinical psychology at Minnesota. His interest in the social determinants of behavior and psychopathology took him to the Philippines in 1959-60 on a Fulbright appointment. Since then he has returned to that country on several occasions to study the impact of Philippine culture patterns on Americans as well as Filipinos.

WALTER J. LONNER is Professor of Psychology at Western Washington State College. He is editor of the *Journal of Cross-Cultural Psychology*, and co-editor of the new Sage Publications series, "Cross-Cultural Research and Methodology." His publications include a co-authored book, *Cross-Cultural Research Methods* (1973).

WALTER E. PRECOURT is an Assistant Professor of Anthropoloty at the State University of New York at Buffalo, specializing in anthropology and education. Currently he is conducting anthropological fieldwork in an Appalachian community in Eastern Kentucky, investigating a general cross-cultural theory of education being developed by the Project in Ethnography and Education at SUNY.

DOUGLAS PRICE-WILLIAMS is Professor of Psychiatry and Anthropology at the University of California at Los Angeles. A graduate of the University of London, he has taught at the London School of Economics, Kansas University, and Rice University. He has been associated with cross-cultural psychology since 1959, working with both the Tiv and the Hausa in Nigeria, in rural communities in Guatemala and Mexico, and with Black and Chicano children in the United States. Currently he is conducting research with Hawaiian children.

RONALD P. ROHNER is Associate Professor of Anthropology and Human Development at the University of Connecticut. He is a member of the Executive

Council of the Society for Cross-Cultural Research, and of the Executive Committee of the Human Development Studies Group at the University of Connecticut. He is a contributor to numerous journals and books, and is the author of *The People of Guilford* and *The Ethnography of Franz Boaz* and co-author of *The Kwakiutl*. He has conducted anthropological field research among the Kwakiutl of British Columbia, and in Morocco and Turkey.

ELEANOR ROSCH is Assistant Professor of Psychology at the University of California at Berkeley. She received her Ph.D. from Harvard University in 1969. She has contributed numerous articles to journals and books, and she has conducted field research among the Dani people of West Irian (Indonesian New Guinea).

HARRY C. TRIANDIS is Professor of Psychology at the University of Illinois at Urbana. He is on the editorial board of several journals, including *Sociometry, Journal of Applied Psychology, Journal of Applied Social Psychology,* and *Journal of Cross-Cultural Psychology.* His publications include *Attitude and Attitude Change* (1971) and *The Analysis of Subjective Culture* (1972), as well as numerous journal articles and book contributions on intergroup attitudes, attitude measurement, cross-cultural comparisons, and interpersonal communication.

S. M. HAFEEZ ZAIDI is Professor of Psychology and Dean of the Faculty of Arts and Letters at the University of Karachi, Pakistan. He received his Ph.D. in psychology from the University of London in 1955. He has served as a Visiting Scholar at the Institute of Advanced Projects at the East-West Center in Honolulu, and has been a Visiting Professor at Northwestern University and at the University of Wisconsin at Green Bay. He has contributed to scholarly journals both in his own country and abroad. He is the author of *The Village Culture in Transition* (1970), and the editor of *Pakistan Journal of Psychology.*

AUTHOR INDEX

Aarons, L., 284, 288
Aaronson, B., 301
Abrahams, D., 7, 36
Aiken, L., 199, 203
Ajzen, I., 18, 34
Akhilananda, S., 298, 302
Albert, E., 161, 174
Allen, M., 234, 235, 248
Allen, V., 46, 76
Alnot, W., 249
Altman, I., 48, 73
Amir, Y., 62, 73, 139, 152
Anderson, N., 55, 56, 57, 73
Angell, R., 117, 129
Anthony, A., 234, 250
Argyris, C., 7, 34
Arnoult M., 199, 203
Aronetta, E., 284, 288
Aronson, V., 7, 36
Arrgarwal, A., 279, 288
Asch, S., 216, 226
Astrachan, B., 152
Attneave, R., 182, 199, 200, 203
Austin, G., 173, 174
Azrin, N., 108, 111, 114
Back, K., 44, 73, 146, 152
Bacon, M., 29, 34, 209, 211, 224, 226, 260, 266
Bailey, S., 131, 152
Bakan, D., 28, 34
Baldwin, S., 256, 266
Bandura, A., 46, 74, 264, 266
Barker, E., 279, 288
Barker, R., 54, 74
Barry, H., 29, 34, 209, 211, 224, 226, 260, 266
Bartlett, F., 203
Baruch, D., 256, 268
Bateson, G., 165, 174
Battig, W., 187, 194, 203
Baumgardner, S., 315, 319
Becker, W., 256, 261, 266
Behrman, B., 199, 203
Beller, E., 266
Beller, H., 189, 203
Bellman, B., 162, 174
Bender, L., 256, 267
Benedict, R., 285, 286

Bennet, J., 117, 129
Bennett, W., 245, 248
Benoit, G., 277, 286
Berenson, B., 280, 286
Berger, S., 46, 74
Berkowitz, L., 47
Berlin, B., 183, 184, 195, 198, 202, 203
Berne, E., 284, 286
Bernstein, B., 160, 174
Berrien, F., 10, 11, 34, 307, 319
Berry, J., 12, 24-26, 29, 34, 61, 74, 169, 175, 207-212, 215-219, 221, 223, 226-228, 307, 314, 319
Berscheid, E., 7, 36
Bettelheim, B., 234, 248
Betz, B., 286, 289
Bevan, W., 196, 206
Blackman, S., 81, 91, 93
Bloomfield, L., 138, 152
Blumberg, L., 66, 74
Bochner, S., 3, 10, 12, 14, 17, 18, 23, 30, 34, 35
Bolles, R., 46, 52, 74
Bottenberg, E., 62, 74
Boulding, K., 137, 139, 152
Bourne, L., 179, 203
Bowlby, J., 256, 267
Bransford, J., 202, 204
Brayfield, A., 97, 114
Breedlove, D., 195, 198, 203
Breese, F., 266
Brein, M., 97, 114
Breuer, J., 274, 287
Bright, J., 195, 203
Bright, W., 195, 203
Brislin, R., 3, 15, 23, 26, 34, 97, 114, 307, 315, 319
Bridy, G., 261, 267
Broverman, I., 279, 287
Brown, D., 199, 203, 204
Brown, J., 234, 248
Brown, R., 177, 178, 183, 203
Bruner, J., 163, 164, 169-170, 173-175, 186, 203
Brunswick, E., 198, 203
Bucke, R., 294, 302
Bulmer, R., 198, 203, 204
Bunker, D., 149, 152

Bunker, S., 44, 73
Burton, J., 151, 152
Burton, R., 234, 248
Byrne, D., 46, 74, 274, 289
Byrnes, F., 128, 129
Campbell, D., 19, 29, 34, 35, 40, 45, 54, 75,
   117, 129, 130, 169, 175, 213, 217, 265,
   267, 307, 315, 316, 320
Canon, L., 46, 76
Caplan, J., 249
Carkhuff, R., 280, 286
Carroll, J., 178, 204
Castenada, C., 295, 302
Catlin, J., 194, 205
Caudill, W., 279, 287
Cawte, J., 217, 227
Cermak, G., 195, 205
Cerny, J., 282, 287
Chambers, J., 256, 267
Chapanis, A., 18, 34
Chapanis, N., 18, 34
Chapnick, B., 47, 75
Chapnick, J., 47, 75
Chartier, G., 285, 287
Chemers, M., 64, 75
Child, I., 29, 34, 209, 211, 224, 226, 266
Childs, C., 172-173, 175
Chomsky, N., 316, 320
Christie, R., 54, 74
Clark, J., 295, 302
Clignet, R., 9, 34
Cohen, R., 26, 35, 249, 265, 268, 307, 320
Cohen, Y., 234, 237, 248
Cole, L., 256, 267
Cole, M., 22, 23, 25, 30, 101, 102, 114, 158
   162, 165, 169, 174-175, 314, 317, 320
Collins, B., 131, 152
Collomb, H., 284, 287
Conrad, K., 63, 74
Cook, Captain, 25
Cook, J., 68, 76
Coopersmith, S., 261, 267
Cornelison, A., 268
Coser, L., 134, 152
Crockett, W., 63, 74, 97, 114
Cronbach, L., 7, 34, 306, 314, 320
Damas, D., 209, 227
D'Andrade, R., 241, 249
Danzel, T., 297, 302
Dasen, P., 169-171, 174, 223, 227
David, K., 23, 35, 71-72, 74, 97, 112, 114

Davidson, A., 17, 18, 79, 92
Davis, E., 71, 75, 77
Dawson, J., 61, 74, 207, 209, 227, 260,
   267, 284, 287
DeLamater, J., 9, 34
Denenberg, V., 253, 267
Deutsch, K., 139, 152
Deutsch, M., 46, 74, 131, 153, 158, 174
De Valois, R., 185, 204
DeVore, I., 253, 267
Dewalt, B., 27, 35
Dewey, J., 147, 152
Diaz-Guerrero, R., 285, 287
Diamond, J., 198, 204
Diamond, S., 250
Dickinson, T., 63, 74
Dodwell, P., 35
Doi, L., 277, 281, 287
Donaldson, M., 172, 175
Donaldson, W., 180, 206
Doob, L., 8, 21, 117, 129, 138, 146, 151,
   152, 164, 175, 274, 287
Dossett, D., 70, 76
Doster, J., 256, 267
Draguns, J., 29, 30, 34, 131, 140, 141, 151,
   152, 273, 278-279, 287, 296
Driver, M., 62, 63, 76
Drucker, P., 215, 227
Druckman, D., 131, 140, 141, 151, 152
Dubos, R., 209, 227
Dulany, D., 46, 51, 75
Dunnagnan, C., 45, 73
Durkheim, E., 235
Dyk, R., 61, 77, 209, 227
Eide, I., 20, 34
Eisen, M., 52, 75
Ekman, P., 186, 204
Eliade, M., 233, 248, 297, 298, 302
Elkin, A., 25, 34
Eurich, A., 150-152
Evan, M., 131, 153
Evan, W., 139, 152
Evans-Pritchard, E., 161-162, 175
Farina, A., 47, 75, 256, 267
Faterson, H., 61, 77
Feldman, J., 71, 77, 79, 92
Feshbach, S., 261, 267
Festinger, L., 46, 75, 125, 129
Fiedler, F., 39, 63, 68, 70, 75, 76, 79, 81,
   92
Finney, J., 261, 267

Firth, R., 297, 302
Fishbein, M., 18, 34, 46, 48, 51, 52, 75
Fiske, D., 29, 34, 265, 267, 307, 315, 320
Flavell, J., 172, 175
Fleck, S., 268
Foa, E., 59, 77
Foa, U., 46, 59, 64, 75, 77
Fodor, J., 190, 204
Foltz, W., 151, 152
Forsat, R., 128, 129
Forsyth, G., 204
Fortes, M., 237, 248
Frank, J., 278, 287
Frank, J.J. 202, 204
Frankl, V., 276, 287
Freeland, N., 301
Freud, S., 4, 234, 248, 274, 287
Friendly, M., 80, 82, 84, 92
Frijda, N., 307, 320
Fromkin, H., 63, 68, 76
Fundia, T., 279, 287
Galanter, E., 46, 76
Galton, F., 27
Galtung, J., 135, 152
Garner, W., 180, 196, 197, 199, 204
Garnett, A., 20
Gay, J., 102, 114, 158, 162, 165, 169,
    174-175, 317, 320
Gearing, F., 231, 248, 249, 250
Geertz, C., 297, 302
Geis, F., 54, 74
Gendlin, E., 276, 287
Gibson, E., 54, 55, 69, 70, 73, 75
Gilbert, R., 104, 114
Gladwin, T., 30, 34, 172, 175
Glaser, E., 10, 34
Glick, J., 102, 114, 162, 165, 169, 174, 317,
    320
Glucksberg, S., 80, 82, 84, 92
Goldfarb, W., 256, 267
Goldsmith, R., 182, 205
Goldstein, A., 249, 280, 287
Goldstein, M., 71, 75
Goodenough, D., 61, 77
Goodenough, W., 249
Goodnow, J., 173-174
Goody, J., 164, 175
Gordon, W., 171, 175
Gough, H., 217, 227
Green, P., 80. 92
Greenfield, P., 164, 169-173, 174, 175

Grinspoon, L., 147, 152
Groddeck, G., 300, 302
Gruenfield, L., 61, 75
Guetzkow, H., 131, 152
Gumperz, J., 172, 175
Gunderson, W., 100-101, 114
Guthrie, G., 19, 20, 26, 27, 35, 97, 101,
    102, 105, 106, 114
Haag, R., 110, 114
Hake, D., 108, 111, 114
Hall, E., 101, 114
Hallowell, A., 215, 216, 221, 227
Handel, S., 196, 199, 204
Hansen, J., 249
Harlow, H., 253, 267
Harrington, C., 233, 249
Harrington, R., 8, 35
Harris, J., 104, 114
Hartup, W., 256, 267
Hattwick, B., 261, 167
Harvey, O., 40, 62, 76
Haythorn, W., 48, 73
Heathers, G., 266, 267
Heckethorn, C., 233, 249
Hefner, R., 9, 34
Heider, E., 177, 183, 204, 315, 320
    (see also Rosch, E.)
Heider, F., 46, 75
Heilbrun, A., 256, 267
Heller, P., 280, 287
Hellmer, L., 266
Henkel, R. 316, 320
Henley, N., 192, 204
Henry, J., 236, 237, 249
Hering, E., 185, 204
Heron, A., 170, 175
Herskovits, M., 169, 175
Herzog, J., 231, 234, 237, 249
Holmes, T., 100, 114
Holsti, K., 134, 152
Homans, G., 46, 75
Honigmann, J., 211, 215, 216, 221, 227,
    282, 287
Hood, W., 40, 75
Houston, J., 294, 302
Hovland, C., 316, 320
Hovland, E., 197, 205
Howard, A., 268
Hsu, J., 277, 278, 289
Huang, I., 196, 204
Hull, C., 4

Hurley, J., 256, 267
Hutchinson, R., 108, 111, 114
Huxley, A., 299, 302
Hymes, D., 172, 175
Imai, S., 196, 199, 204
Inayatullah, 117, 130
Ingram, E., 164, 175
Inhelder, B., 181, 204
Inkeles, A., 9
Irwin, F., 46, 75
Jacobs, G., 185, 204
Jahoda, G., 260, 267, 307, 320
James, W., 294, 302
Janis, I., 147, 152
Jenkins, H., 197, 205
Jensen, A., 35
Johnson, F., 278, 288
Johnson-Laird, P., 174-175
Jones, E., 42, 71, 75
Jones, P., 224, 227
Jorgenson, C., 23, 35
Jourard, S., 216, 227
Jung, C., 299, 302
Kahneman, D., 194, 204
Kalhorn, J., 266
Kanner, L., 256, 267
Karp, S., 61, 77
Katz, D., 135, 153
Katz, H., 256, 267
Katz, J., 180. 190, 204
Katz, L., 265, 268
Kay, P., 181, 183, 184, 202, 203
Kearney, G., 22, 35
Keele, S., 202, 205
Keesing, F., 9, 35
Keesing, R., 9, 35
Kelly, G., 62, 75
Kelly, H., 46, 76, 131, 153
Kelman, H., 7, 35, 79, 92, 131, 139, 153
Kidder, L., 128, 130
Kiev, A., 275, 278, 287, 300, 302
Kimura, B., 279, 287
Kinstler, D., 256, 267
Klein, E., 152
Klein, H., 8, 9
Kleinjans, E., 33
Klineberg, O., 55, 75
Kluckhohn, C., 3
Kluckhohn, R., 234, 250
Koebben, A., 244, 249
Kohn, M., 62, 75

Kora, T., 282, 287
Kragh, U., 298, 302
Krauss, R., 160, 175
Kroeber, A., 162, 175
Kruskal, J., 86, 92
Kuhn, T., 45, 46, 75
Labov, W., 161, 175
Lakoff, G., 191, 205
Lambert, Wm., 46, 74
Lambo, T., 283-284, 287
Leach, E., 178, 205
LeFort, R., 291, 302
Leighton, A., 276, 287
Leiss, A., 138, 152
Lenneberg, E., 177, 183, 203, 205
Levin, H., 268
LeVine, R., 19, 35, 40, 75
Levi-Strauss, C., 59, 73, 75, 294, 302
Levy, D., 256, 267
Lewin, K., 12, 46, 75
Lidz, T., 256, 268
Lieberman, M., 68, 75, 136, 153
Lilly, J., 295, 302
Linton, H., 216, 227
Lippman, H., 256, 268
Locke, E., 46, 75
Loftus, E., 189, 205
Lomax, A., 64-66, 75
Lonner, W., 3, 15, 26, 31, 32, 34, 307, 315, 317, 319, 320
Lowie, R., 233, 249
Lowry, L., 256, 268
Ludwig, A., 294, 302
Lumsdaine, A., 316, 320
Luria, Z., 266
Lynch, F., 97, 104, 114
Maccoby, E., 261, 268
Mann, J., 217, 227
Maretzki, T., 97, 104, 114
Margetts, E., 284, 288
Marsella, A., 279, 288
Maslow, A., 301, 302
Masters, J., 261, 268
Masters, R., 294, 302
Maxant, J., 249
McClaran-Stefflre, M., 190, 205
McClelland, D., 23, 35, 141, 150, 153
McCord, J., 256, 261, 268
McCord, W., 256, 261, 268
McDaniel, C., 195, 205
McElwain, D., 22, 35

McGuiness, E., 46, 75
McGuire, W., 7, 35
McHugh, P., 172, 175
Medvene, A., 256, 268
Metxner, R., 298-299, 302
Meehl, P., 15, 35, 79, 92, 306, 314, 317, 320
Meredith, G., 10, 35
Merritt, R., 139, 152
Mervis, C., 194, 205
Middleton, R., 211, 227
Miles, M., 68, 75
Millenson, J., 107, 114
Miller, A., 63, 75
Miller, G., 46, 76
Miller, H., 256, 268
Miller, J., 152
Miller, N., 234, 249
Minsky, M., 180, 205
Mischel, W., 113, 114
Mishler, A., 150, 153
Misiti, R., 47, 75
Mitchell, R., 189, 205
Mitchell, T., 39, 68, 70, 75, 76, 81, 92
Miura, M., 282-283, 288
Monson, K., 317, 320
Montague, W., 187, 194, 203
Moore, F., 240, 249
Morgenthaler, F., 277, 288
Morris, R., 20, 35
Morris, T., 80, 92
Morrison, D., 316, 320
Mowrer, W., 274, 288
Murdock, G., 212, 227, 241, 245, 249
Murphy, H., 275, 288
Mussen, P., 262, 268
Narang, R., 279, 288
Naroll, R., 26, 28, 35, 234, 240-242, 249,
    265, 268, 307, 320
Nassiakou, M., 48, 53, 56, 60, 77, 200, 205
Neisser, U., 200, 205
Nelson, C., 81, 92
Ness, R., 27, 35
Nimkoff, M., 211, 217
Nisbett, R., 42, 71, 75
Nishimae, S., 279, 287
Mordlinger, E., 150, 153
Nuttin, J., 46, 76
Oberg, K., 97, 114
Oldfield, R., 182, 205
Olver, R., 169, 175
Opler, M., 276, 288

O'Reilly, J., 110, 114
Orne, M., 172, 175
Ornstein, R., 296, 300-301, 302
Osgood, C., 84, 92, 147, 153
Osmond, H., 301
Over, R., 310, 320
Owen, D., 199-203
Panagides, S., 138, 153
Pande, S., 281, 288
Parin, P., 277, 288
Parin-Matthey, G., 277, 278
Peabody, D., 84, 85, 92
Peak, H., 52, 76
Pelto, P., 211, 215, 228, 307, 320
Perls, F., 145, 153
Peterson, D., 266
Pfeiffer, W., 278, 279, 288
Phillips, L., 273, 278-279, 287, 288
Piaget, J., 160, 175, 181, 204
Pike, K., 91, 92
Pool, T., 150, 153
Porteus, S., 22, 23, 35
Posner, M., 182, 189, 202, 205
Pospisil, L., 245, 249
Postal, P., 180, 204
Precourt, W., 20, 26, 28, 29, 273, 297
Pribham, K., 46, 76
Preusser, D., 196, 204
Price, R., 273, 288
Price-Williams, D., 29, 30, 31, 171, 175, 273,
    288, 291, 302
Prince, R., 284, 288
Pryor, K., 110, 114
Pugh, W., 100-101, 114
Puharich, A., 295, 303
Quay, H., 266
Radcliffe-Brown, A., 234, 249
Rahe, R., 100-101, 114
Ramirez, M., 171, 175
Ranson, R., 100-101, 114
Rappaport, R., 209, 228
Rausch, H., 35
Raven, P., 195, 198, 203
Razin, A., 286, 288
Reed, S., 202, 205
Reich, C., 293, 303
Reich, P., 190, 205
Reik, T., 234, 249
Riegel, O., 128, 130
Riessman, D., 158, 175
Rin, H., 278, 289

Ring, K., 18, 35
Rips, L., 189, 192, 193, 205
Rivers, W., 305, 320
Rogers, C., 301, 303
Rohner, R., 26, 27, 29, 35, 256, 260, 265, 268
Rosch, E., 12, 24, 25, 184, 187, 188, 190, 194, 205
    (see also Heider, E.)
Rosenberg, M., 52, 76
Rosenberg, S., 81, 82, 84, 92
Rotblat, J., 151, 153
Rotenberg, M., 285, 288
Rotter, G., 160, 175
Rotter, J., 156, 167
Rouman, J., 256, 268
Rubin, R., 100-101, 114
Russell, J., 23, 35
Rutherford, E., 262, 268
Ryan, T., 46, 76
Sachs, W., 277, 288
Salmon, P., 256, 268
Sanua, V., 275, 278, 288
Sarbin, T., 46, 76
Schachter, S., 110, 112, 114
Schaefer, J., 241, 149
Scheerer, M., 46, 76
Scheff, R., 189, 205
Schmidt, N., 249
Schonfeld, W., 256, 268
Schroder, H., 62, 63, 76, 81, 91, 93
Schwartz, R., 129, 130
Scott, W., 62, 63, 76, 80, 92
Sears, R., 256, 261, 268
Sechrest, L., 129, 130, 280, 287
Segall, M., 169, 175
Seligman, M., 47, 76
Sells, S., 25, 35
Serpell, R , 196, 205
Service, R., 236, 250
Seward, G., 275, 288
Shanmugam, A., 39, 44, 48, 57, 60, 77, 278, 289, 320
Sharp, D., 102, 114, 162, 165, 169, 174, 317, 320
Sheffield, F., 316, 320
Shepard, R., 180, 195, 197, 205
Sherif, C., 21, 35, 40, 75
Sherif, M., 21, 35, 40, 76
Shoben, E., 189, 205
Shoemaker, D., 266
Shulman, H., 256, 268

Siegelman, M., 256, 261, 268
Simmelhag, V., 109, 114
Singer, J., 110, 112, 114
Singer, M., 256, 268
Singer, P., 284, 288
Skinner, B., 46, 76, 109, 114
Slack, B., 68, 76
Smallman, S., 310, 320
Smith, E., 189, 205
Smith, G., 298, 302
Sommerlad, E., 217, 228
Spain, D., 315, 320
Spencer, R., 101, 106, 114
Staddon, J., 109, 114
Stagner, R., 256, 261, 268
Stanley, J., 316, 320
Stanner, W., 300, 303
Stefflre, V., 190, 205
Steiner, I., 53, 76
Stephan, C., 64, 76
Stephan, W., 64, 76
Stewart, K., 300, 303
Stotland, E., 46, 76
Streufert, S., 62, 63, 68, 76
Strickland, B., 256, 267
Strodtbeck, F., 4, 35
Strupp, H., 286, 288
Suchman, R., 196, 205
Suci, G., 84, 92
Suzuki, D., 293, 299, 303
Symonds, P., 256, 268
Szanton, D., 98, 100, 115
Tagiuri, R., 186, 203
Tagumpay-Castillo, G., 9, 10, 35
Tanaka, Y., 39, 44, 48, 57, 60, 77, 278, 289, 320
Tannenbaum, P., 84, 92
Tart, C., 301
Taylor, S., 10, 34
Teja, J., 279, 288
Thibaut, J., 46, 76, 131, 153
Thorndike, R., 15, 26, 34, 307, 315, 319
Tiger, L., 233, 250
Rinkelpaugh, O., 109, 115
Tolman, E., 46, 76
Torgerson, W., 86, 93
Torrey, E., 275, 278, 280-281, 284, 286, 288
Trabasso, T., 196, 205
Triandis, H., 8, 17-19, 21, 39, 44, 48, 53, 54, 56, 57, 59, 60, 67, 68, 70, 71, 75-77, 79, 81, 91, 92, 260, 269, 278, 289, 307, 320

Trifonovitch, G., 34, 36
Tseng, W., 277, 278, 289
Tucker, G., 152
Tucker, L., 58, 77
Tulving, E., 180, 206
Turnbull, C., 96, 115
Turner, J., 59, 77
Tversky, A., 194, 204
Tyler, M., 188, 204
Tyler, S., 177, 181, 206
Underhill, E., 294, 303
Usa, S., 282-283, 288
Useem, J., 117, 129, 130
Useem, R., 117, 129, 130
Van Buren, H., 12
Van Gennep, A., 232, 235, 238, 245, 250
Vassiliou, G., 39, 42, 43, 44, 48, 57, 60, 77,
    278, 289, 320
Vassiliou, V., 42, 43, 48, 53, 56, 60, 67, 77,
    278, 289, 320
Vayda, A., 209, 228
Vexliard, A., 275, 289
Vivehananthan, P., 81, 92
Wallace, A., 292, 302
Walster, E., 7, 36
Walters, R., 46, 74, 264, 266
Warr, P., 81, 91, 93
Wason, P., 174-175
Watt, I., 164, 175
Watts, A., 296, 303
Wax, M., 250
Webb, E., 129, 130
Webster, H., 238, 250
Webster, N., 238, 250
Wedge, B., 151, 153
Weil, A., 295, 303

Weldon, D., 71, 77
Welton, K., 182, 205
Wendt, I., 283, 289
Werner, H., 60, 62, 73, 77
White, B., 40, 76
Whitehorn, J., 286, 289
Whiting, J., 233, 234, 248, 250
Whorf, B., 178, 206
Wicker, A., 54, 77
Wight, A., 79, 93
Wilkins, A., 189, 206
Willems, E., 35
Winch, R., 66, 74
Wing, H., 196, 206
Winter, D., 141, 150, 153
Witkin, H., 61, 62, 77, 207-209, 212, 216,
    225-228
Wittkower, E., 278, 279, 289
Wober, M., 225, 228
Wohlwill, J., 172, 175
Wolberg, L., 256, 261, 269
Worchel, P., 274, 289
Wright, Q., 131, 153
Wulff, E., 284, 289
Wynne, L., 256, 268
Yalem, R., 138, 153
Yalom, I., 68, 75, 136, 153
Yarrow, L., 256, 269
Yonas, A., 256, 267
Young, F., 86, 93
Young, F.W., 231, 233, 234, 235, 250
Zaidi, H., 20, 21
Zajonc, R., 46, 50, 77, 127, 130
Zektick, I., 105, 114
Zimbardo, P., 110, 111, 115
Zingg, R., 245, 248

SUBJECT INDEX

Acculturation, 164, 207, 215, 218, 224-225; see also socialization

Acculturative stress, 207, 211, 212, 217, 225-226, 275

Adaptive cultural characteristics, 218, 273, 285

Adjustment to overseas experiences; see sojourns in other cultures

Affect, 51-58, 68, 211, 216

Aggression, 39, 47, 108-109, 127, 255

Altered states of consciousness, 30-31, 291-301

Amae, 277

Antecedents of events, 57, 69, 157, 209, 225, 278

Attitudes, 97, 110, 217, 222, 293

Attributes, correlations of in categorization, 196, 201
  generic object in, 200-201
  "integral", 199
  orthogonality of, 196-200
  "separable", 199
  universality in, 196-200

Attribution in causes of behavior, 17, 21, 41, 68, 96; see also isomorphic attributions

Behavior setting, 54

Behavioral intentions, 47, 49-60

Behavioristic approach, 17, 19, 46, 69, 71-71-72, 95, 115

Canonical correlation, 89

Categories, in learning and concept formation, 24, 179-196

Categorization, analog functions, 179, 181-196
  digital model in, 178-179, 182
  of colors, 180
  orthogonal attributes and, 196-200
  prototypes in, 179, 181-196

Chiefdom societies, 232-248

Classification in human perception; see categorization

Clustering in free recall, 157, 165-167

Codability, linguistically of color, 183

Coding procedures, in hologeistic research, 240-241, 246, 248

Cognition, 80, 157, 175, 179, 196, 207-226, 292-293, 296

Cognitive ability
  assessment of in "other" cultures, 22-24
  difference vs. deficit, 22-24, 30-31

Cognitive complexity, 44, 60-68, 72, 73, 80-81

Cognitive differentiation, 79-83

Cognitive vs. behavioral learning, 18-19

Color categories, 180

Color space, categorization of, 183, 185

Comparability, cross-cultural, 212; see also methodology, cross-cultural

Componential analysis, 181

Concept formation, 180

Conflict intervention; see social conflict intervention

Conformity, 212, 217; see also independence of judgment

Consciousness, 293, 297, 300; see also altered states of consciousness

Consequences of events, 49, 57, 69

Conservation performance, 157, 170-171

Content analysis of cross-cultural manuscripts; see *Journal of Cross-Cultural Psychology*

Content of intercultural difficulties, 44

Contractual arrangements, 51, 52

Correlated attributes in prototype formation, 194, 196-201

Creative behavior, 110

Cross-cultural psychology
  as meta-method, 4-7, 31
  correlational vs. experimental research in, 309
  "guidelines for having research ignored", 315-317
  identity crisis, 3-4
  media and, 318
  "super-ego" in, 307

Cross-cultural research
  criteria of rigor, 14-16
  culture as independent variable, 13-14, 19
  equal status collaboration, 10-13
  ethical guidelines, 10-13
  ethical issues, 7-13
  gaining entry into reserach setting, 8-10
  national differences of practitioners, 11-13
  pure vs. applied, "mixed", 12-13, 24-25
  systematic dependent variables, 14, 25

Cross-cultural survey method; see hologeistic method

Cultural differences, 39, 95, 102, 174, 218, 220-222, 280, 284, 296

Cultural diffusion; see Galton's Problem
Cultural ecology, 25, 209; see also ecology
Cultural group; definition, 39
Culture, definition and anthropological study
   of, 39, 65-67, 70; see also ethnographies,
   use of
Culture assimilators, 45, 70-72, 81, 91
Culture contact, 164, 225-226, 275, 293; see
   also acculturative stress
Culture fatigue, 97, 106
Culture learning, 17-31, 95, 97, 103, 111-
   113, 117, 207, 292
Culture shock, 97
Culture training, 70-72, 73, 79-93, 97, 98,
   277; see also culture learning
Data Quality Control, 28, 241-242; see also
   hologeistic method
Dependence, 256, 257, 261-266
Depression, 279
Desentization, 112
Deviant case analysis, 244-245
Differentiation, 45, 60-68, 69, 73, 80, 91,
   207-226
Disadvantaged child, concept of, 158
Dissonance, 18, 20, 122, 125
Dreams, 300
Ecology, 171, 207-226, 285
Education, effects of, 158, 164, 215,
   219-220
Egocentric speech, 160, 164
Emic-etic distinction, 91, 215
Emotion, 110, 112-113, 211, 216, 220, 222,
   286, 196
Ethics, 7-13, 274, 298
Ethnographic Atlas, 241, 244
Ethnographies, use of, 26-29, 157-174, 209,
   214, 215-216, 220
Expectations about social situations, 52-54,
   124-126, 280
Experiences, discontinuous, 97, 98, 102-104,
   113, 120, 273, 278, 292; see also accul-
   turative stress
Experiments, 157-158, 162-165, 169, 172-
   173, 224, 292
External factors, 39, 40, 42
Extinction produced aggression, 108-109
Facial expressions
   as natural categories, 186
   emotional prototypes and, 186
Facilitating conditions, 49, 56, 57
Factor analysis, 48, 58, 59

Parental acceptance and rejection; 27, 251-
   269
Peace Corps experiences, 19-20, 96-101,
   104-106
Perceived consequences, 49, 51, 52, 56, 58
Perceptual processes, 54, 55, 70-71, 72-73,
   207-226, 297-298
Perceptual style, see differentiation
Performance in other cultures, 97, 99,
   104-105
Personality variables, 43, 54, 71, 97, 102,
   110, 113, 274-276, 286; see also situa-
   tional variables; self-concept
Philotimos, 43
Piagetian research, 157, 160, 170-171, 223
Plant taxonomies, lexical systems for, 195;
   see also Linnaean system
Plural society, 226, 279
Prejudice, 71
Primary Socializing Agent (PSA), 265; see
   also socialization
Primitive-civilized, concept of, 167, 291-
   301
Prototypes, as biological "givens" 182; see
   also categorization
Psychic unity, 162, 164-165
Psychological differentiation, see
   differentiation
Psychopathology, 273-274, 279, 292, 294
Psychotherapy, 29-30, 292, 296
   definition, 276
   non-Western approaches, 273-286,
   296-297
   help-seekers, 274
Publication criteria, 31-32
Quality Control Sample, 240; see also
   Hologeistic method
Reinforcement paradigm, 46, 69, 73, 106-
   113; see also behavioristic approach
Rejection-Acceptance Project, 252, 254,
   265; see also parental acceptance and
   rejection
Reserve, 216, 220, 222, 226
Rites of passage, 232, 242, 245
Roles, 17, 45, 46, 51, 57, 69, 276, 286
Safari-research, 8
Salience of colors, see focal points
Sanza, 161
Schema, in categorization research, 181,
   182, 192
Schemas, and kinship terminology, 237

Failure to perform, interpretation, 163-168
Family, 208, 211, 214; see also socialization; parental acceptance and rejection
Field dependence/independence, see differentiation
Focal colors, see focal points
Focal points
    in color term clusters, 183-196
    salience of, 183-196
Food accumulation, 209, 213, 214, 215, 220
Foreign student adjustment, see sojourns in other cultures
Free sorting tasks, in categorization research, 195, 196-201
Galton's Problem, 27, 241; see also hologeistic method
Gestalt therapy, 145
Habit, 49, 50, 56, 97
"Hedging" in research reports, 317
Hidden curriculum, 29, 231-248, 297
Hologeistic method, 26-29, 239-242, 252-253, 260, 262, 265, 266
Human Relation Area Files, 26-29, 65, 212, 240
Identity, see self-concept
Images about other groups, 124-125
Independence of judgment, 212, 216, 220, 222
Indigenous modeso

Indigenous modes of thought, 157-174, 291
Inferential processes, 167-168
Information, 59-60, 64-65, 73, 97, 173
Initiation ceremonies, 20, 231-248, 273, 297
Integration, 66, 208; see also differentiation
Intelligence, 157, 168-169, 295-296
Intentions, see behavioral intentions
Intercultural relations, 39, 42, 44, 67-68, 95, 122, 127, 211, 217, 222, 274, 295
Internal factors, 40
International Journal of Psychology, 319
Interpersonal communication, 39, 42, 44, 53, 66, 101-102, 122, 123, 159-169, 211, 276, 278, 295
Interpersonal relations, 39, 41, 42, 44, 45, 53, 66, 69, 95, 122-127, 211, 277
Interveners in social conflicts, 134-140

Intervention, 283-284; see also social conflicts
Intracultural community studies, 252, 254, 265
Isomorphic attributions, 41, 42-43, 45, 68, 69
Journal of Cross-Cultural Psychology, 307-314
    single vs. multiple authorship in, 309-310
    strengths and weaknesses of manuscripts, 3 311-314
Kruskal's stress measure, 86
Language learning, 97, 100-101, 103, 122-123
Learning, experimental studies, 157-174
Learning, in social conflict workshops, 131-153
Linguistic determinism, 177
Linguistics, in color naming, see codability
Linked pair test, see Galton's Problem
Linnaean classification system, 198; see also plant taxonomies
Local healers, 280-281, 284
Love, 59-60, 64, 65, 73, 281
Machiavellianism, 54
Matching, 315-316
Methodology, cross-cultural, 169-171, 212, 213, 215, 223-224, 277, 282-283, 291, 299
Militancy-nonmilitancy, as scaled belief dimension, 89-91
Mind-body dualism, concept of, 276, 291-301
Mnemonic skills, 165-167
Model testing, 212, 223-226
Morita therapy, 282-283
Multidimensional scaling, 80, 82, 86, 91; see also TORSCA; factor analysis; dimensionality in, 86; see also Kruskal's stress measure
    disassociation measure in, 82, 84
Multimethod research, 251-253, 265, 307
Munsell chips, in color coding, 183, 199
Mystical, concept of, 291-301
Nomological network, 306, 314
Noncontinuity of performance, see experiences, discontinuous
Nonreactive measures, 104, 129
Norms, 44-46, 51, 57, 68, 69
ORDMAT computer program, 241

Secret ceremonies, 297
Self-concept, 46, 51, 52, 58, 69, 99, 216, 258, 263, 264, 299-300
Self-disclosure, 216
Semantic categories, 187-196; see also categorization
hedges in, 191
mental representations in, 189
pedacity in, 192
substitutability in, 190-191
Semantic differential, 84, 85
Sensory deprivation, 98
Situational factors, 97, 102, 109-111, 166, 169, 171-174
"Slick dude-jive" as belief dimension, 89
Social conflicts, 8, 17-18, 21, 131-153
Social conflicts, interveners
assumptions of, 138-139
attributes of, 136-137
ethics of, 135-136
goals of, 137-138
motives of, 134-135
Social conflicts, intervention
characteristics of interveners in, 134-140
methods used in, 144-147
participant attributes and selection, 140-143
procedures in, 143-147
re-entry from, 147-148
results of, 148-151
sites and duration of, 143-144
Social conflict intervention workshops
brainstorming in, 147
Belfast, 132
Bethel, 134
controlled communication, 132, 146
Fermeda, 132, 151
friends, 132
intercession, 132
NTL, 134, 137
Pugwash, 132-134
summary characteristics of, 132-134
T-groups, 134-145
Tavistock, 134, 137, 145, 146
Social determinants, 51, 56, 106, 113-114
Social factors, 173, 211, 216, 220-221, 273, 285; see also situational factors
Social learning, 46, 49, 71-72, 107, 110,

112-113, 273; see also reinforcement paradigm
Socialization practices, 62, 170, 208-212, 215, 265, 273-275, 294
Societal organization, 235-239
differentiation of, 238, 239, 242-244
egalitarianism, 236
incipient stratification, 236, 237
mechanical solidarity, 235-236
organic solidarity, 235-236
stratification, 236
Sojourners in other cultures, 19-21, 96, 106, 110, 117-129, 275
Somatic illness, 100-101
Standard Ethnographic Sample, 242; see also Data Quality Control
Status, 59-60, 64-65, 67, 73
Structure of intercultural difficulties, 44; see also intercultural relations
Study abroad, 117-129; see also sojourners in other cultures
Subjective culture, 17-18, 21, 39, 44, 45, 278
Subsistence economy, 224
Superordinate goals, 21, 40
Superstitious behavior, 109
Thinking, 286, 291, 296; see also cognition
Third world, definition, 129
Time, adjustment as function of, 78, 107, 127-128
TORSCA, 86; see also multidimensional scaling
Trait inferences, 84
Trait sorting task, in multidimensional scaling, 81-82
Tribal societies, 232-248
Uncertainty, 55, 100
Universals, in human categorization, 177-207
Universalist approach, 251-252, 265; see also Rejection-Acceptance Project
Values of consequences of act, 51-53, 57-58
Workshops, see also Social conflict intervention workshops
Fermeda, 132-151
Pugwash, 132, 146, 151
Tavistock, 134, 137, 145, 146

NOTES

NOTES

NOTES

NOTES

NOTES

NOTES